nd Surveys

Series DS No. 11

The health of
our children

Decennial Supplement

**The Registrar General's decennial supplement
for England and Wales**

Edited by Beverley Botting

London: HMSO

© Crown copyright 1995
First published 1995
Second impression 1996

ISBN 0 11 691643 5

The views expressed in this report are not necessarily those
of the Office of Population Censuses and Surveys.

Printed in the United Kingdom for HMSO
Dd 302443 4/96 C5 G3397 10170

Foreword

Infant mortality has traditionally been a major measure of the health of a nation. In developed countries, however, mortality levels are at an all-time low. It is therefore time to consider levels of morbidity in childhood, their causes (if known) and the social and health costs of children with disability of various degrees. Therefore, this volume brings together from a wide range of contributors an overview of the health of our children, concentrating on the 1970s and 1980s.

Against a background of improvements in mortality, inequalities of health outcomes have persisted between social groups. There has been an increasing recognition of children in recent years (for example The Children's Act 1989 which came into force on 14 October 1991) and their need for special health services and continued surveillance. These different perspectives on the health of children are brought together in this volume.

There has recently been much interest in the relationship between childhood morbidity and adult ill-health. Other work has suggested that adverse influences acting around the time of birth can be risk factors for cardiovascular disease in adults. It has also been claimed that social class inequalities in adult health are at least in part caused by childhood conditions. It is therefore timely to investigate childhood mortality and morbidity patterns in recent years, in advance of the OPCS volume currently being prepared on the health of adults.

This volume is the result of several years work. Since the chapters were written a number of relevant reports have been published. It was not possible to include material from these at such a late stage. The reports include *Morbidity Statistics from General Practice* (MSGP4), *fourth national survey 1991-92, National Diet and Nutrition Survey: children aged $1^{1}/_{2}$ to $4^{1}/_{2}$ years,* and *Sexual Behaviour in Britain: the national survey of sexual behaviour and lifestyles.*

Main contributors

Dr Ross Anderson
Department of Public Health Sciences
St George's Hospital Medical School
Cranmer Terrace
London SW17 0RE

Tel: 0181 725 5424 Fax: 0181 725 3584

Mrs Beverley Botting
Office of Population Censuses and Surveys
St Catherines House
10 Kingsway
London WC2B 6JP

Tel: 0171 396 2221 Fax: 0171 404 1186

Dr Angela Dale
Census Microdata Unit
Faculty of Economic and Social Studies
The University of Manchester
Oxford Road
Manchester M13 9PL

Tel: 0161 275 4721 Fax: 0161 275 4722

Dr Gerald Draper
Department of Paediatrics
University of Oxford
Childhood Cancer Research Group
57 Woodstock Road
Oxford OX2 6HJ

Tel: 01865 310030 Fax: 01865 514254

Dr Susan Hall
Floor C
Stevenson Building
Children's Hospital
Western Bank
Sheffield
South Yorkshire
S6 6CY

Tel: 0114 271 7344 Fax: 0114 275 5364

Professor Stephen Jarvis
Community Child Health
Aidan House
Sunderland Road
Gateshead NE8 3EP

Tel: 0191 477 6000 Fax: 0191 477 0370

Dr Barbara Maughan
Medical Research Council Child Psychiatry Unit
Institute of Psychiatry
De Crespigny Park
London SE5 8AF

Tel: 0171 919 3480 Fax: 0171 708 5800

Dr Berry Mayall
Social Science Research Unit
Institute of Education
University of London
18 Woburn Square
London WC1H 0NS

Tel: 0171 612 6392 Fax: 0171 612 6400

Dr Anna McCormick
Office of Population Censuses and Surveys
St Catherines House
10 Kingsway
London WC2B 6JP

Tel: 0171 396 2493 Fax: 0171 404 1186

Dr Chris Power
Institute of Child Health
University of London
30 Guildford Street
London WC1N 1EH

Tel: 0171 242 9789 Fax: 0171 813 8233

Dr Veena Soni Raleigh
Institute of Public Health
Chancellor Court
20 Priestley Road
The Surrey Research Park
Guildford
Surrey GU2 5YL

Tel: 01483 450540 Fax: 01483 450351

Acknowledgements

I am very grateful to the many colleagues who have helped in the production of this volume. In particular I would like to thank Nigel Physick, Damian Braganza, David Evans, Gita Ladva and David Fitzgerald who produced data for tables and charts for many authors and who proofread the entire volume. I would also like to thank Peter Pharoah, Leslie Davidson, Susan Cole, Hugh Markowe and other colleagues at the Department of Health who refereed an earlier version of the volume.

Beverley Botting
OPCS

Contents

Foreword iii
Main contributors iv
Introduction vii

1   Longer-term perspectives
        Beverley Botting
1.1   Changes in the size of the population of
        children   1
1.2   The impact of changes in fertility and
        mortality   1
1.3   Improved survival of children born since
        1950   5

**2   The changing context of childhood:
        demographic and economic changes**
        Angela Dale
2.1   Demographic and economic changes   9
2.2   Changes in the family circumstances of
        children   14
2.3   Changes in the social climate for young
        people   17
2.4   Conclusions   19

**3   The changing context of childhood:
        children's perspectives on health care
        resources including services**
        Berry Mayall
3.1   Background   21
3.2   The increasing visibility of children   22
3.3   The social contexts of children's knowledge   22
3.4   Health services and resources for children   23
3.5   Children's access to resources and services   23
3.6   Children's experience of services   23
3.7   Children's assessment of resources and
        services   24
3.8   Conclusions   25

4   Children's physical development
        Chris Power
4.1   Birthweight   28
4.2   Height and growth   34
4.3   Weight-for-height   37
4.4   Conclusions   39

5   Health related behaviour
        Chris Power
5.1   Diet   42
5.2   Physical activity   45
5.3   Smoking   48

5.4   Alcohol consumption   51
5.5   Volatile substance abuse   53
5.6   Teenage sexual behaviour   54
5.7   Discussion and conclusions   57

**6   Trends and patterns in childhood
        mortality and morbidity**
        Beverley Botting and Rachel Crawley
6.1   Trends in mortality   62
6.2   Trends in morbidity   65
6.3   Impact of birthweight and multiple births
        on mortality and morbidity   71
6.4   Specific conditions   72
6.5   International comparisons   77
6.6   Conclusions   81

**7   The health of infants and children among
        ethnic minorities**
        Veena Soni Raleigh and R Balarajan
7.1   Methodological issues   82
7.2   Population size   83
7.3   Mortality   85
7.4   Morbidity   90
7.5   Uptake of health care   91
7.6   Conclusions   92

8   Accidents
        Stephen Jarvis, Elizabeth Towner and Sean Walsh
8.1   The scale of the problem   95
8.2   Trends in mortality rates   95
8.3   The injury 'iceberg'   99
8.4   Non-fatal injuries   99
8.5   Causes of unintentional injuries to children   104
8.6   The Newcastle studies   107
8.7   Conclusion   110

**9   Respiratory disease and Sudden Infant Death
        Syndrome**
        *Ross Anderson, John Britton, Aneez Esmail,
        Jen Hollowell and David Strachan*
9.1   Trends and patterns of respiratory disease   113
9.2   Lower respiratory infections (pneumonia
        and bronchitis)   120
9.3   Asthma   123
9.4   Hay fever   125
9.5   Cystic fibrosis   127
9.6   Sudden Infant Death Syndrome   130
9.7   Summary and conclusions   131

10   Cancer
Gerald Draper
10.1   Incidence of childhood cancer in Britain   135
10.2   Variations in incidence and possible
       aetiological factors   137
10.3   Mortality   141
10.4   Survival rates   143
10.5   Conclusions   146

11   Congenital anomalies
Beverley Botting
11.1   Background   148
11.2   National congenital malformation
       monitoring system   148
11.3   Comparisons with other sources of
       malformation information   149
11.4   Trends in notification rates   149
11.5   Mortality due to malformations   149
11.6   Abortion after prenatal diagnosis of
       abnormality   149
11.7   Geographical variation in notified
       malformations   153
11.8   Effect of occupation on anomalies   153
11.9   Role of diet, drugs and other teratogens
       in the epidemiology of malformations   155
11.10 Impact of maternal age on congenital
       malformations   155
11.11 Ethnic differences in malformation rates   156

11.12 International comparisons   156
11.13 Conclusions   157

12   Mental health
Barbara Maughan
12.1   Background   159
12.2   Epidemiological and other community
       studies   160
12.3   Trends over time   162
12.4   Conclusions   166

13   Infectious diseases in childhood
Anna McCormick and Susan Hall
13.1   Sources of data   168
13.2   Reasons for changing incidence   169
13.3   Diseases of declining incidence   170
13.4   Diseases with varying incidence   174
13.5   New or increasing infections   174
13.6   Conclusions   176

Appendix 1 Sources of data for monitoring
           child health   178

List of tables and figures   183

Index   187

Introduction

Eva Alberman

The major demographic, social, behavioural and medical developments which have occurred over this century have been reflected in the changes which have occurred in the health of the childhood population. Although family size has fallen there have been sharp increases in the number of children in the population, and marked improvements in health and risk of infant and childhood death. Perhaps the most dramatic change has been the rapid fall in deaths and morbidity due to acute infections, but chapters in this book also document an increased rate of growth, improvements in dental health, and reduced mortality from genetic diseases such as cystic fibrosis and childhood cancers. The health of new immigrants, initially poorer than that of UK - born children, show some encouraging signs of improving over time.

Nevertheless, there is abundant evidence that the quality of children's health is threatened by a multitude of new problems of many different types, the pervasive effects of adverse demographic, economic, cultural developments and changes in priorities.

The early chapters in this book stress the importance to child health of factors outside the health area. Changes in female fertility, maternal age, marriage, employment and regional patterns can all have profound effects on child-care provision and housing, and through these on childhood morbidity, educational achievement, behaviour and growth. Major changes have included the sharp increase of births outside marriage, and the break-up, and often reconstitution of families, all of which can have adverse effects on the children. The changes in family structure have contributed to the numbers of children living in relative or absolute poverty, and reduced the numbers of supporting adults in the family.

There has been an overall increase in childhood adverse health behaviour (Chapter 5), with high levels of tobacco, alcohol, drug and volatile substance misuse, and early sexual activity and evidence of poor diets, falls in physical activity and increases in obesity. New studies on the mental health of children have revealed high levels of disabling behaviour and psychiatric problems (Chapter 10).

There has been no detectable reduction in the use made for, or by, children of the health services (Chapters 1 and 3), and increases in the prevalence of diseases related to allergy, in particular asthma (Chapter 9). Congenital conditions, such as cerebral palsy, where birth prevalence has remained constant but case fatality has fallen, are more prevalent, and remain severely disabling (Chapter 6). For some conditions, such as cystic fibrosis there is disturbing evidence of variable survival, possibly related to inequalities of medical care. Still with us are the historical problems of infanticide, of child abuse and of racial tensions. Areas of particular interest, because of the potential for prevention action, are ethnic differences in health (Chapter 7), which are largely secondary to socioeconomic disadvantage and cultural variations, and the high level of accidental injuries and deaths (Chapter 8). Epidemiological patterns for the latter show that often accidents are predictable, and related to poor design of housing, roads and vehicles, and a lack of appreciation of children's perceptual abilities.

On the positive side, Chapter 3 draws attention to welcome and important changes occurring in our recognition of the child's rights and perspectives. The acceptance of the importance of these should lead to important initiatives which could affect children's health and educational possibilities, leading to modifications of health and social services for children, and an increasing respect for and realisation of the importance of their own views.

Finally, chapters in this book remind us of the areas which remain of more basic scientific concern. We still have little knowledge of the many causes of congenital malformations, of children's cancers and the apparent rise in allergic diseases. Although it is clear that, above all, children with disabilities need a good and loving home, there is still an urgent need for research into improving their quality of life by finding technical aids to help them overcome their disabilities. Moreover, there is increasing interest in the fetal and childhood origins of adult disease which is directing more attention to the biology of early development.

In conclusion, childhood remains a time of great vulnerability, as well as great promise. Any readers of this volume will want to reflect on the importance of the effects of our current social and behavioural standards and practices on our children, and will appreciate the need to rethink these in terms of their rights, the health of the adults they will become, and of the health of future generations. There remains a need for scientific advances in the more resistant diseases in childhood, but above all children need to be loved, to live under good conditions, and receive the benefits of a good education. Together these will act to continue the reduction in mortality and morbidity in childhood of which we have rightly been proud.

1 Longer-term perspectives

Beverley Botting

Key points

* The size of the population of children aged under 20 almost doubled between 1841 and 1911 from 7.3 million in 1841 to 14.4 million in 1911. In 1991 this population numbered 13.0 million.

* In 1991 children aged under 20 comprised 27 per cent of the population of males and 24 per cent of the population of females, compared with 47 per cent and 45 per cent respectively in 1841.

* Whilst boys' survival to age 20 is lower than that of girls, the gap between them is reducing.

This introductory chapter gives an overview of changes in the population of children in England and Wales in the past 150 years. This places in perspective the demographic, economic and health changes affecting children during the 1970s and 1980s.

1.1 Changes in the size of the population of children

An important demographic change of the last 150 years in England and Wales has been the three-fold increase in the total population from almost 16 million in 1841 to 51 million in 1991 (Table 1.1). Much of this increase has been due to rising life expectancy from 41.2 years in 1841 to 73.4 years in 1991 for males and from 43.3 years to 78.9 years respectively for females. As a result of this ageing of the population, the proportion of the total population who were aged under 20 fell from 47 per cent for males and 45 per cent for females in 1841 to 27 per cent and 24 per cent respectively in 1991. This fall was not uniform over this period, however. Between 1841 and 1891 children comprised between 44 per cent and 50 per cent of the total population. This proportion then fell until 1951, increasing slightly until 1971 before falling again. These figures reflect both changes in fertility patterns and falling mortality rates at all ages.

Despite children comprising a smaller proportion of the total population, their absolute number has increased, as shown in Table 1.1. The size of the population of children aged under 20 almost doubled between 1841 and 1911 from 7.3 million in 1841 to 14.4 million in 1911. In 1991 this population numbered 13.0 million. Between 1851 and 1871, and since 1921 except 1941 the size of the population of boys aged under 20 has been larger than that of girls. The population of boys aged 10–14 years has been larger than that of girls in every census since 1841 except 1891 and 1911. The population of

boys aged 15–19 years, however, has only been larger than that of girls in 1931 and then since 1961. This is a result of the higher mortality rates for boys aged 15-19, compared with girls of the same ages, particularly during the nineteenth century. The increase in the population aged under 20 over time has varied between the different five-year age groups. Figure 1.1 shows population pyramids of the number of children aged under 20 by sex for selected census years since 1841. These show the increase in the population of children between 1841 and 1911, since when there has been little change. The size of the population aged under 20 increased continually between successive censuses from 1841 for both sexes, reaching a maximum in 1911 for those aged 9 and under and in 1921 for older children. Between 1911 and 1921 the number of children aged under five fell by 13 per cent for boys and 15 per cent for girls, reflecting the lower fertility rates during World War I.

1.2 Impact of changes in fertility and mortality

Two Acts of Parliament passed in 1836 established the basic registration system which is still operating today. These were *An Act for Marriages in England* and *An Act for Registering Births, Deaths and Marriages in England.* As a result of two further Acts, a registration system was set up in Scotland in 1855 and in Ireland nine years later. The civil registration of births was not compulsory in England until 1874, and stillbirths did not have to be registered until 1927 in England, 1939 in Scotland and 1961 in Northern Ireland.

Figure 1.2 shows that fertility increased between the 1830s and the 1880s, then fell continually until 1940 except for a temporary increase after World War I. A similar increase after World War II was more sustained reaching a peak in the mid 1960s. The decline in the number of births was of great concern in the 1930s. As

Table 1.1 Population of children aged under 20 and life expectancy by sex: 1841–1991, England and Wales

Year	Age group					Total (all ages)	Population under 20 (%)	Life expectancy (years)
	0-4	5-9	10-14	15-19	Total under 20			
Males								
1841	1,048,400	953,200	880,400	781,600	3,663,600	7,777,600	47.1	41.2
1851	1,176,753	1,050,228	963,995	873,236	4,064,212	8,781,225	46.3	39.2
1861	1,354,907	1,172,960	1,059,889	957,930	4,545,686	9,776,259	46.5	39.8
1871	1,536,464	1,350,819	1,220,770	1,084,713	5,192,766	11,058,934	47.0	40.2
1881	1,757,657	1,568,579	1,402,230	1,268,269	5,996,735	12,639,902	47.4	42.1
1891	1,775,062	1,693,372	1,610,858	1,465,175	6,544,467	14,060,401	46.5	43.7
1901	1,855,361	1,738,993	1,670,970	1,607,522	6,872,846	15,728,613	43.7	45.3
1911	1,969,000	1,848,000	1,739,000	1,646,000	7,202,000	17,476,000	41.2	50.6
1921	1,704,000	1,767,000	1,837,000	1,728,000	7,036,000	18,098,000	38.9	56.1
1931	1,518,400	1,675,800	1,623,500	1,722,200	6,539,900	19,160,000	34.1	58.0
1941	1,449,000	1,399,000	1,482,000	1,444,000	5,774,000	17,228,000	33.5	59.4
1951	1,910,000	1,642,000	1,422,000	1,333,000	6,307,000	21,044,000	30.0	65.8
1961	1,877,900	1,672,400	1,886,800	1,647,200	7,084,300	22,448,700	31.6	68.0
1971	2,003,500	2,079,000	1,874,000	1,716,100	7,672,600	23,815,100	32.2	69.3
1981	1,542,100	1,642,000	1,996,600	2,114,400	7,295,100	24,160,100	30.2	71.1
1991	1,760,600	1,657,000	1,573,600	1,685,000	6,676,200	24,995,100	26.7	73.4
Females								
1841	1,057,900	951,700	851,700	805,200	3,666,500	8,136,500	45.1	43.3
1851	1,171,354	1,042,131	949,362	883,953	4,046,800	9,146,384	44.2	41.2
1861	1,345,875	1,171,106	1,045,287	974,712	4,536,980	10,289,965	44.1	42.2
1871	1,534,812	1,355,707	1,203,469	1,095,699	5,189,687	11,653,332	44.5	43.2
1881	1,763,207	1,578,817	1,398,101	1,278,963	6,019,088	13,334,537	45.1	45.3
1891	1,778,428	1,701,806	1,612,709	1,485,690	6,578,633	14,942,124	44.0	47.2
1901	1,861,347	1,748,298	1,670,770	1,638,621	6,919,036	16,799,230	41.2	49.2
1911	1,956,000	1,850,000	1,753,000	1,683,000	7,242,000	18,660,000	38.8	54.2
1921	1,663,000	1,752,000	1,823,000	1,775,000	7,013,000	19,834,000	35.4	60.0
1931	1,486,200	1,642,800	1,590,800	1,713,700	6,433,500	20,828,000	30.9	62.0
1941	1,393,000	1,358,000	1,461,000	1,617,000	5,829,000	21,515,000	27.1	64.5
1951	1,819,000	1,568,000	1,377,000	1,370,000	6,134,000	22,771,000	26.9	70.7
1961	1,778,200	1,592,100	1,799,000	1,602,800	6,772,100	23,850,300	28.4	73.9
1971	1,901,900	1,974,000	1,771,100	1,621,200	7,268,200	25,118,800	28.9	75.5
1981	1,463,500	1,554,300	1,892,100	2,015,400	6,925,300	25,474,200	27.2	77.1
1991	1,669,900	1,565,600	1,484,700	1,586,500	6,306,700	26,104,400	24.2	78.9

Sources: *Registrar General's Statistical Reviews 1841-1971*
OPCS, Population Estimates 1981,1991
Government Actuary's Department

Figure 1.1
Population pyramids of population aged under 20 by sex: 1841-1991 (selected years), England and Wales

0-4 years

5-9 years

10-14 years

15-19 years

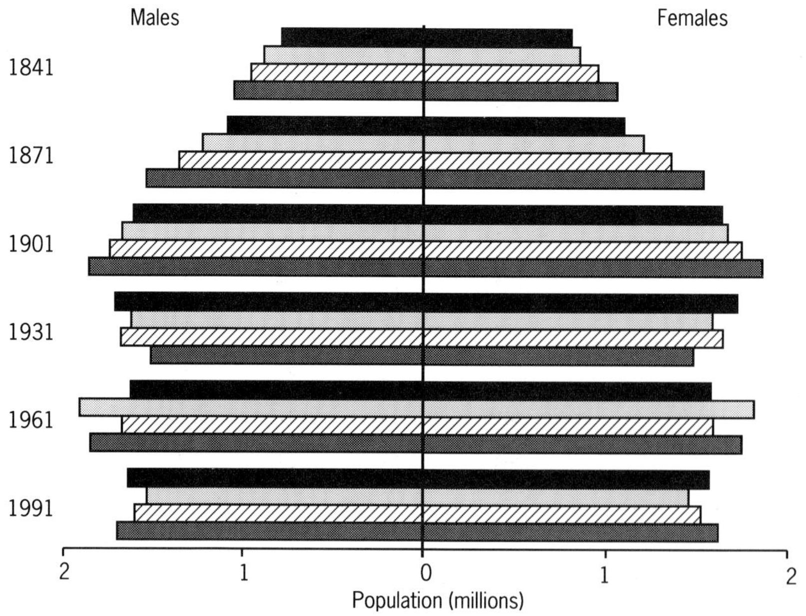

Sources: Registrar General's
Statistical Reviews 1841-1961
OPCS Population Estimates 1991

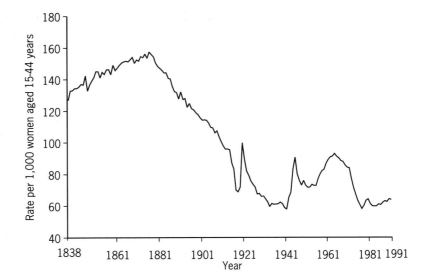

**Figure 1.2
Fertility rates: 1838-1991,
England and Wales**

Sources:
Registrar General's
Statistical Reviews 1838-1973
OPCS Birth Statistics. 1973-91

a result, the *Population (Statistics) Act* of 1938 was passed to allow more detailed information about these births to be collected on a confidential basis. This included the mother's age, and parity for births inside marriage.

Mortality rates among children aged 1–19 years fell almost continuously between 1838 and 1939, apart from an increase during the 1918 influenza epidemic (Table 1.2, Figures 1.3 and 1.4). The same decrease was seen, between 1838 and the outbreak of World War I, in deaths among adults under 45. Infant mortality, on the other hand, stayed at about the same level from 1838 to 1900 with a small downward trend in the 1870s and 1880s followed by an increase in the 1890s. Since 1900, the infant mortality rate has continued to fall, apart from a brief increase at the beginning of World War II.

During the nineteenth century some births were not registered. This is important in the interpretation of trends in infant mortality. The numbers which were not registered were estimated after each census by cross-checking enumerated populations with numbers of registrations of births and deaths. The deficit in birth registration became smaller between 1840 and 1870. It is likely that some infant deaths were also not registered even after death registration became compulsory in 1874. This would mean that the infant mortality rates for the 1840s and 1850s could have been higher than registration data implied. Therefore, had registration been complete throughout the nineteenth century, a decline would have been also observed in these rates. More recent falls in the mortality rates are discussed in Chapter 6.

Table 1.2 Mortality rates* by age and sex: 1841–1991, England and Wales

Year	Males				Females			
	0–4	5–9	10–14	15–19	0–4	5–9	10–14	15–19
1841	7526	1122	583	783	6494	1105	621	869
1851	7697	933	487	1614	6642	923	566	1713
1861	7571	726	475	703	6554	729	475	757
1871	7562	887	475	691	6597	806	481	711
1881	5657	581	325	455	4807	569	325	472
1891	6862	503	284	533	5745	510	308	462
1901	5900	403	229	345	4948	408	239	323
1911	4665	347	206	306	3947	338	207	273
1921	3186	281	176	284	2546	271	182	269
1931	2235	229	146	260	1742	199	147	240
1941	1824	225	150	294	1455	186	124	228
1946	1342	97	86	152	1034	75	67	117
1951	735	65	57	89	568	45	37	64
1956	649	46	41	79	498	33	27	36
1961	614	48	39	92	480	32	25	39
1966	515	44	42	106	395	29	25	41
1971	454	44	37	90	349	29	24	39
1976	347	34	31	88	258	24	21	35
1981	309	27	29	82	234	19	19	32
1986	263	21	23	71	199	17	17	29
1991	201	21	23	69	157	16	15	28

* Rate per 100,000 population.

Sources: *Registrar General's Statistical Reviews* 1841-1971
OPCS, *Mortality Statistics - general* 1976-91

Figure 1.3 Mortality rates for boys by age: 1841-1991, England and Wales

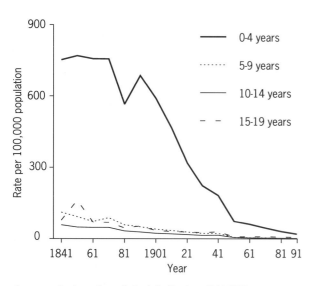

Sources: Registrar General's Statistical Reviews 1841-1973
           OPCS Mortality Statistics - general 1974-91

Figure 1.4 Mortality rates for girls by age: 1841-1991, England and Wales

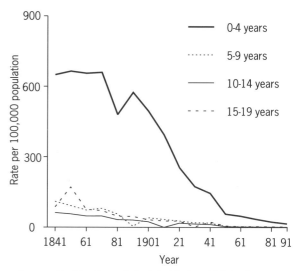

Sources: Registrar General's Statistical Reviews 1841-1973
           OPCS Mortality Statistics - general 1974-91

Table 1.3 Stillbirth and infant mortality rates: 1931– 91, England and Wales

Year	Stillbirths**	Early neonatal*	Late neonatal*	Neonatal*	Postneonatal*	Infant*	Number of live births
1931	40.9	22.1	9.5	31.6	34.8	66.4	632,081
1936	39.7	21.9	8.3	30.2	28.4	58.5	605,292
1941	34.8	20.6	8.3	28.9	30.7	59.7	579,091
1946	27.2	17.6	6.6	24.2	16.7	40.9	820,719
1951	23.0	15.5	3.4	18.9	11.0	29.8	677,529
1956	22.9	14.2	2.6	16.8	6.8	23.6	700,335
1961	19.0	13.3	2.1	15.3	6.1	21.4	811,281
1966	15.3	11.1	1.7	12.9	6.1	19.0	849,823
1971	12.5	9.9	1.7	11.6	5.9	17.5	783,155
1976	9.7	8.2	1.5	9.7	4.6	14.3	584,270
1981	6.6	5.3	1.4	6.7	4.4	11.1	634,492
1986	5.3	4.3	0.7	5.3	4.3	9.6	661,018
1991	4.6	3.4	0.6	4.4	3.0	7.4	699,217

*   Rate per 1,000 live births.
**   Rate per 1,000 live and stillbirths.

Sources: *Registrar General's Statistical Reviews* 1931-1971
         OPCS, *Mortality Statistics -childhood* 1976-1991

Figure 1.5
Stillbirth and infant mortality rates:
1931-91, England and Wales

- - - -   Stillbirth*

————   Neonatal

·······   Postneonatal

━━━━   Infant

*stillbirth rates per 1,000 live + stillbirths

Sources:
Registrar General's Statistical Reviews 1931-73
OPCS Mortality Statistics - childhood 1974-91

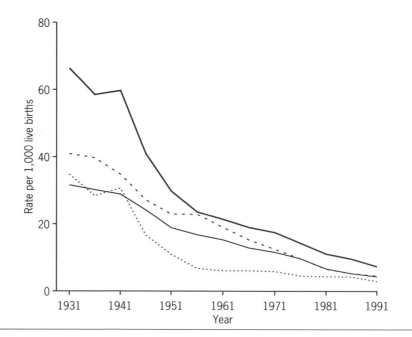

Table 1.3 and Figure 1.5 present data since 1931 for stillbirths and the components of infant mortality. All the rates have declined steadily during this period. The postneonatal mortality rate (deaths at ages 7 days and older but less than one year per 1,000 live births) showed a rapid fall during the years of World War II. The rate then fell steadily until the late 1950s.

1.3 Improved survival of children born since 1950

In recent years the size of the population of children has changed little despite the large fall in fertility rates between the mid-1960s and the mid-1970s. This is a direct result of falling mortality rates for children. Tables 1.4 and 1.5 and Figures 1.6 and 1.7 show the improved survival of children born since 1950. For males born in 1950, 96.6 per cent survived to age 1 year compared with 99.1 per cent of those born in 1990. The comparative figures for females were 97.4 per cent and 99.3 per cent respectively. Similar improvements can be seen for

children at ages 5, 15 and 20 as shown in Figures 1.6 and 1.7. By age 20, 97.1 per cent of those born in 1971 had survived compared with 95.2 per cent of those born in 1950. For females the comparative figures were 97.9 per cent and 96.5 per cent respectively. From Figures 1.6 and 1.7 it can be seen that there are smaller differentials between the proportions surviving at different ages for females than for males. This is particularly pronounced for teenage boys who have raised mortality compared with teenage girls. This is discussed in more detail in Chapter 6. Nevertheless the gap between the proportion of boys surviving to age 20 and that for girls is narrowing. For boys born in 1950 their survival to age 20 was 98.7 per cent that of girls. This figure had improved for boys born in 1971 to a survival rate of 99.2 per cent that of girls.

The improved survival during childhood makes it important to widen our view from mortality, to include morbidity during childhood and its social and health consequences. This is the aim of the remainder of this volume.

Figure 1.6 Percentage survival to 1991 of boys born since 1950, England and Wales

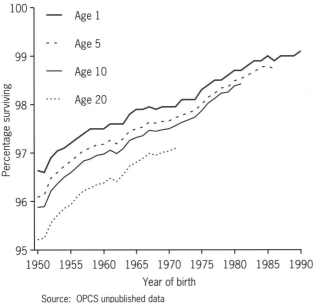

Source: OPCS unpublished data

Figure 1.7 Percentage survival to 1991 of girls born since 1950, England and Wales

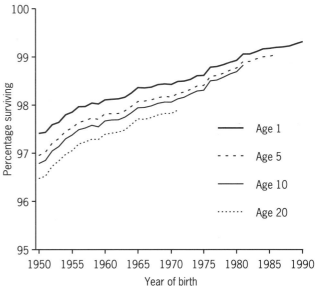

Source: OPCS unpublished data

Table 1.4 Percentage survival to 1991 of boys born since 1950, England and Wales

Year of birth	Live births	Age (years) 1	2	3	4	5	6	7	8	9	10	11	12	13	14	15	16	17	18	19	20
1950	358,715	96.6	96.4	96.3	96.2	96.1	96.0	96.0	96.0	95.9	95.9	95.8	95.8	95.8	95.7	95.7	95.6	95.5	95.4	95.3	95.2
1951	348,604	96.6	96.4	96.3	96.2	96.1	96.1	96.0	96.0	95.9	95.9	95.9	95.8	95.8	95.7	95.7	95.6	95.6	95.5	95.3	95.2
1952	345,878	96.9	96.7	96.6	96.5	96.5	96.4	96.4	96.3	96.3	96.2	96.2	96.2	96.1	96.1	96.0	96.0	95.9	95.8	95.7	95.6
1953	352,037	97.0	96.9	96.7	96.7	96.6	96.5	96.5	96.4	96.4	96.4	96.3	96.3	96.3	96.2	96.2	96.1	96.0	95.9	95.8	95.7
1954	346,455	97.1	97.0	96.9	96.8	96.7	96.7	96.6	96.6	96.5	96.5	96.5	96.4	96.4	96.4	96.3	96.2	96.2	96.1	96.0	95.9
1955	343,673	97.2	97.0	97.0	96.9	96.8	96.8	96.7	96.7	96.6	96.6	96.6	96.5	96.5	96.4	96.4	96.3	96.3	96.2	96.0	95.9
1956	359,881	97.3	97.2	97.1	97.0	96.9	96.8	96.8	96.7	96.7	96.7	96.7	96.7	96.6	96.6	96.6	96.5	96.4	96.3	96.2	96.1
1957	372,298	97.4	97.3	97.2	97.1	97.1	97.0	97.0	96.9	96.9	96.8	96.8	96.8	96.7	96.7	96.7	96.6	96.5	96.4	96.3	96.2
1958	380,944	97.5	97.3	97.2	97.2	97.1	97.1	97.0	97.0	96.9	96.9	96.8	96.8	96.8	96.7	96.7	96.7	96.6	96.5	96.4	96.3
1959	385,689	97.5	97.4	97.3	97.2	97.2	97.1	97.1	97.0	97.0	97.0	96.9	96.9	96.9	96.8	96.8	96.7	96.7	96.6	96.5	96.3
1960	404,150	97.5	97.4	97.3	97.2	97.2	97.1	97.1	97.0	97.0	97.0	96.9	96.9	96.9	96.8	96.8	96.8	96.7	96.6	96.5	96.4
1961	417,768	97.6	97.5	97.4	97.3	97.3	97.2	97.2	97.1	97.1	97.1	97.0	97.0	97.0	96.9	96.9	96.9	96.8	96.7	96.6	96.5
1962	431,663	97.6	97.4	97.3	97.2	97.2	97.1	97.1	97.1	97.0	97.0	97.0	96.9	96.9	96.9	96.8	96.8	96.7	96.6	96.5	96.4
1963	438,476	97.6	97.5	97.4	97.3	97.3	97.2	97.2	97.2	97.1	97.1	97.1	97.0	97.0	97.0	96.9	96.9	96.8	96.7	96.6	96.6
1964	451,072	97.8	97.7	97.6	97.5	97.5	97.4	97.4	97.4	97.3	97.3	97.2	97.2	97.2	97.1	97.1	97.0	97.0	96.9	96.9	96.7
1965	443,190	97.9	97.7	97.6	97.6	97.5	97.5	97.4	97.4	97.3	97.3	97.3	97.3	97.2	97.2	97.2	97.1	97.1	97.0	96.9	96.8
1966	437,262	97.9	97.7	97.6	97.6	97.5	97.5	97.4	97.4	97.4	97.4	97.3	97.3	97.3	97.3	97.2	97.2	97.1	97.0	97.0	96.9
1967	427,901	98.0	97.8	97.8	97.7	97.6	97.6	97.6	97.5	97.5	97.5	97.4	97.4	97.4	97.4	97.3	97.3	97.2	97.2	97.1	97.0
1968	421,130	97.9	97.8	97.7	97.7	97.6	97.5	97.5	97.5	97.5	97.4	97.4	97.4	97.4	97.3	97.3	97.3	97.2	97.1	97.0	97.0
1969	410,052	98.0	97.8	97.8	97.7	97.7	97.6	97.6	97.5	97.5	97.5	97.5	97.4	97.4	97.4	97.3	97.3	97.3	97.2	97.1	97.0
1970	403,371	98.0	97.8	97.8	97.7	97.7	97.6	97.6	97.6	97.5	97.5	97.5	97.5	97.4	97.4	97.4	97.3	97.3	97.2	97.1	97.0
1971	403,223	98.0	97.9	97.8	97.8	97.7	97.7	97.7	97.6	97.6	97.6	97.5	97.5	97.5	97.5	97.4	97.4	97.3	97.3	97.2	97.1
1972	373,982	98.1	98.0	97.9	97.8	97.8	97.7	97.7	97.7	97.7	97.6	97.6	97.6	97.6	97.5	97.5	97.5	97.4	97.3	97.2	
1973	348,678	98.1	98.0	97.9	97.9	97.8	97.8	97.8	97.7	97.7	97.7	97.7	97.6	97.6	97.6	97.6	97.5	97.5	97.4		
1974	329,459	98.1	98.0	98.0	97.9	97.9	97.8	97.8	97.8	97.8	97.7	97.7	97.7	97.7	97.6	97.6	97.6	97.5			
1975	310,751	98.3	98.1	98.1	98.0	98.0	98.0	97.9	97.9	97.9	97.9	97.8	97.8	97.8	97.8	97.7	97.7				
1976	300,313	98.4	98.3	98.2	98.2	98.1	98.1	98.1	98.1	98.0	98.0	98.0	98.0	98.0	97.9	97.9					
1977	292,957	98.5	98.4	98.3	98.3	98.2	98.2	98.2	98.2	98.1	98.1	98.1	98.1	98.1	98.0						
1978	307,088	98.5	98.5	98.4	98.4	98.3	98.3	98.3	98.3	98.2	98.2	98.2	98.2	98.2							
1979	328,308	98.6	98.5	98.4	98.4	98.4	98.3	98.3	98.3	98.3	98.3	98.2	98.2								
1980	335,954	98.7	98.6	98.5	98.5	98.5	98.5	98.4	98.4	98.4	98.4	98.4									
1981	325,711	98.7	98.6	98.6	98.6	98.5	98.5	98.5	98.5	98.4	98.4										
1982	321,352	98.8	98.7	98.7	98.6	98.6	98.6	98.6	98.5	98.5											
1983	323,192	98.9	98.8	98.7	98.7	98.7	98.6	98.6	98.6												
1984	326,039	98.9	98.9	98.8	98.8	98.8	98.7	98.7													
1985	336,835	99.0	98.9	98.8	98.8	98.8	98.8														
1986	338,852	98.9	98.8	98.8	98.8	98.7															
1987	349,624	99.0	98.9	98.8	98.8																
1988	354,954	99.0	98.9	98.8																	
1989	352,381	99.0	99.0																		
1990	361,412	99.1																			
1991	358,407																				

Source: OPCS unpublished data

Table 1.5 Percentage survival to 1991 of girls born since 1950, England and Wales

Year of birth	Live births	Age (years)																			
		1	2	3	4	5	6	7	8	9	10	11	12	13	14	15	16	17	18	19	20
1950	338,312	97.4	97.2	97.1	97.0	97.0	96.9	96.9	96.8	96.8	96.8	96.8	96.7	96.7	96.7	96.7	96.6	96.6	96.6	96.5	96.5
1951	328,925	97.4	97.3	97.1	97.1	97.0	97.0	96.9	96.9	96.9	96.9	96.8	96.8	96.8	96.8	96.7	96.7	96.6	96.6	96.6	96.5
1952	327,857	97.6	97.4	97.3	97.3	97.2	97.1	97.1	97.1	97.1	97.0	97.0	97.0	97.0	97.0	96.9	96.9	96.9	96.8	96.8	96.7
1953	332,335	97.6	97.5	97.4	97.4	97.3	97.3	97.2	97.2	97.2	97.1	97.1	97.1	97.1	97.0	97.0	97.0	97.0	96.9	96.9	96.8
1954	327,196	97.8	97.6	97.6	97.5	97.5	97.4	97.4	97.3	97.3	97.3	97.3	97.2	97.2	97.2	97.2	97.1	97.1	97.1	97.0	97.0
1955	324,138	97.9	97.7	97.6	97.6	97.5	97.5	97.5	97.5	97.4	97.4	97.4	97.3	97.3	97.3	97.2	97.2	97.2	97.1	97.1	97.1
1956	340,454	98.0	97.8	97.7	97.7	97.6	97.6	97.6	97.5	97.5	97.5	97.5	97.4	97.4	97.4	97.4	97.3	97.3	97.3	97.2	97.2
1957	351,083	98.0	97.8	97.7	97.7	97.7	97.6	97.6	97.6	97.5	97.5	97.5	97.5	97.5	97.4	97.4	97.4	97.3	97.3	97.3	97.2
1958	359,771	98.0	97.9	97.8	97.8	97.7	97.7	97.7	97.6	97.6	97.6	97.6	97.5	97.5	97.5	97.5	97.4	97.4	97.4	97.3	97.3
1959	362,812	98.0	97.9	97.8	97.8	97.7	97.7	97.6	97.6	97.6	97.5	97.5	97.5	97.5	97.5	97.5	97.4	97.4	97.4	97.3	97.3
1960	380,855	98.1	98.0	97.9	97.9	97.8	97.8	97.7	97.7	97.7	97.7	97.6	97.6	97.6	97.6	97.6	97.5	97.5	97.5	97.4	97.4
1961	393,515	98.1	98.0	97.9	97.9	97.8	97.8	97.8	97.7	97.7	97.7	97.7	97.6	97.6	97.6	97.6	97.6	97.5	97.5	97.4	97.4
1962	407,103	98.1	98.0	97.9	97.9	97.8	97.8	97.8	97.7	97.7	97.7	97.7	97.7	97.6	97.6	97.6	97.6	97.5	97.5	97.5	97.4
1963	415,579	98.2	98.0	98.0	97.9	97.9	97.8	97.8	97.8	97.8	97.8	97.7	97.7	97.7	97.7	97.6	97.6	97.6	97.6	97.5	97.5
1964	424,900	98.3	98.1	98.1	98.0	98.0	97.9	97.9	97.9	97.9	97.8	97.8	97.8	97.8	97.8	97.7	97.7	97.7	97.7	97.6	97.6
1965	419,535	98.4	98.2	98.2	98.1	98.1	98.0	98.0	98.0	98.0	97.9	97.9	97.9	97.9	97.9	97.9	97.8	97.8	97.8	97.7	97.7
1966	412,561	98.4	98.3	98.2	98.1	98.1	98.0	98.0	98.0	98.0	98.0	98.0	97.9	97.9	97.9	97.9	97.9	97.8	97.8	97.7	97.7
1967	404,263	98.4	98.3	98.2	98.2	98.1	98.1	98.0	98.0	98.0	98.0	98.0	97.9	97.9	97.9	97.9	97.9	97.8	97.8	97.8	97.7
1968	398,142	98.4	98.3	98.2	98.2	98.2	98.1	98.1	98.1	98.0	98.0	98.0	98.0	98.0	98.0	97.9	97.9	97.9	97.9	97.8	97.8
1969	387,486	98.4	98.3	98.3	98.2	98.2	98.1	98.1	98.1	98.1	98.1	98.0	98.0	98.0	98.0	98.0	97.9	97.9	97.9	97.9	97.8
1970	381,115	98.4	98.3	98.2	98.2	98.2	98.1	98.1	98.1	98.1	98.1	98.0	98.0	98.0	98.0	98.0	97.9	97.9	97.9	97.9	97.8
1971	379,932	98.5	98.4	98.3	98.3	98.2	98.2	98.2	98.2	98.1	98.1	98.1	98.1	98.1	98.1	98.0	98.0	98.0	98.0	97.9	97.9
1972	351,458	98.5	98.4	98.4	98.3	98.3	98.2	98.2	98.2	98.2	98.2	98.1	98.1	98.1	98.1	98.1	98.0	98.0	98.0	98.0	
1973	327,275	98.5	98.5	98.5	98.4	98.3	98.3	98.3	98.3	98.3	98.2	98.2	98.2	98.2	98.2	98.1	98.1	98.1	98.0		
1974	310,426	98.6	98.5	98.5	98.4	98.4	98.4	98.4	98.3	98.3	98.3	98.3	98.3	98.3	98.2	98.2	98.2	98.2			
1975	292,694	98.6	98.5	98.5	98.4	98.4	98.4	98.4	98.3	98.3	98.3	98.3	98.3	98.5	98.4	98.4	98.2				
1976	283,957	98.8	98.7	98.7	98.6	98.6	98.6	98.6	98.5	98.5	98.5	98.5	98.5	98.5	98.5	98.4					
1977	276,302	98.8	98.7	98.7	98.6	98.6	98.6	98.6	98.6	98.5	98.5	98.5	98.5	98.5	98.5						
1978	289,330	98.8	98.8	98.7	98.7	98.7	98.7	98.7	98.6	98.6	98.6	98.6	98.6	98.5							
1979	309,720	98.9	98.8	98.8	98.7	98.7	98.7	98.7	98.7	98.7	98.6	98.6	98.6								
1980	320,280	98.9	98.9	98.8	98.8	98.8	98.8	98.7	98.7	98.7	98.7	98.7									
1981	308,781	99.1	99.0	99.0	98.9	98.9	98.9	98.9	98.9	98.8	98.8										
1982	304,579	99.1	99.0	99.0	98.9	98.9	98.9	98.9	98.9	98.8											
1983	305,942	99.1	99.0	99.0	99.0	99.0	98.9	98.9	98.9												
1984	310,779	99.2	99.1	99.1	99.0	99.0	99.0	99.0													
1985	319,582	99.2	99.1	99.1	99.0	99.0	99.0														
1986	322,166	99.2	99.1	99.1	99.1	99.0															
1987	331,887	99.2	99.1	99.1	99.1																
1988	338,623	99.2	99.2	99.1																	
1989	335,344	99.3	99.2																		
1990	344,728	99.3																			
1991	340,810																				

Source: OPCS unpublished data

2 The changing context of childhood: demographic and economic changes

Angela Dale

Key points

* During the 1980s, fertility rates remained low due to women having fewer children rather than more women remaining childless.

* Since 1970 there has been a marked increase in the proportion of all births born to women aged 30 and over.

* The proportion of births in England and Wales which take place outside marriage rose to 31 per cent in 1992. Of these it is estimated that half were born to cohabiting couples.

* The number of dependent children living in a lone parent family in Britain doubled since 1971, from 1.0 million in 1971 to 2.2 million in 1991, representing almost one in five of all dependent children living in families.

* Divorce rates in England and Wales rose from 2 per 1000 couples in 1956–60 to 12 in 1980 and 13 in 1991.

* There has been a steady increase in remarriage rates, reaching 36 per cent of all marriages in 1990.

* It is estimated that one half of all children in Britain can expect to spend their entire childhood living with their married natural parents.

* Children were more likely to have a working mother in 1991 than in 1971.

* In 1989, 23 per cent (2.9 million) of all children in the UK were living in families with no full-time wage-earner.

* The number of children in families receiving supplementary benefit because of unemployment rose from 339,000 in 1979 to 1,087,000 in 1986.

* The number of households accepted as homeless rose from 53,000 in 1978 to 145,800 in 1990. Over 80 per cent of these households (about 117,000 households in 1990) either had dependent children or a household member who was pregnant.

* In 1990 it was estimated that 52 per cent of 16-year-olds were in full-time education, 23 per cent on Youth Training Schemes and under 25 per cent in paid employment.

This chapter provides a context for understanding the changes in child health that have occurred during the 1970s and 1980s. The health of children is related both directly and indirectly to a wide range of demographic and socio-economic factors. This chapter attempts to highlight those changes that have been most significant since 1970.

The chapter is divided into three sections. The first section is concerned with changes which affect how many children are born, when they are born and the circumstances into which they are born. It is therefore mainly concerned with mothers and their decisions over family size, birth timing, employment, marriage and divorce. The second section focuses on the circumstances of the family in which children live, and is mainly concerned with describing social security policies which affect the family, and changes in the economic well-being of families with children, including homelessness and unemployment. The third section takes the child as the unit of analysis and examines, not just the economic changes that impinge upon children and young people directly, but also the changes in attitudes towards them and expectations of them. This includes the lengthening of economic dependency caused by an extended period of education and high youth unemployment, which has paralleled an increase in awareness of children's rights as individuals, and greater sexual freedom for young people.

2.1 Demographic and economic changes

2.1.1 The changing role of women: fertility, marriage and employment

A fundamental change, which can be dated from the 1950s, has been the rise in women's participation in the labour market, particularly amongst women with children. As discussed later in this chapter, by comparison with 20 years ago, children are now much more likely to be growing up in a home where their mother is in paid work. Whilst women's income forms a very important addition to that of their partner, however, there has been little fundamental change in women's economic dependency. The effects of this will be discussed later. During the 1970s and 1980s there has also been a considerable change in the timing and spacing of births and change in women's marital status at childbearing.

2.1.2 Changes in fertility

During the twentieth century total period fertility rates (TPFRs)* have fluctuated considerably, from very low levels of around 1.7 in the 1930s to a recent high of 2.94 in 1964 and back to a low point of 1.68 in 1977. Since

---

* The total period fertility rates (TPFR) is defined as the average number of children who would be born per woman if women experienced the age-specific fertility rates of the period in question throughout their childbearing life span. The TPFR is sensitive to short-term changes in the timing of births and should, therefore, be interpreted with caution.

1980 the TPFR has remained fairly stable at about 1.8, as shown in Figure 2.1. Throughout the period 1971–91, the fertility rates of overseas-born women living in Britain continued to fall. In 1991 rates for Caribbean-born women were 1.5, by comparison with 3.3 in 1971, whilst those for Pakistani- and Bangladeshi-born women were 4.6 compared with 8.8 in 1971.[1,2]

In many other European Union (EU) countries the fall in TPFR has been much greater, with 1991 figures showing former West Germany, Italy, Greece and Spain having particularly low rates of 1.5 and less. Amongst EU countries in 1991, only Ireland had a TPFR greater than 2, whilst the UK and France, both about 1.8, were higher than all other EU countries. Perhaps surprisingly, Sweden (not then in the EU) also had a TPFR greater than 2.

The reasons for this widespread fall in levels of fertility are complex. With the arrival of the contraceptive pill in the late 1960s many women gained greater control over their fertility. In Britain the improved ratio of female to male pay in the late 1970s, brought about by the 1970 Equal Pay Act, increased the cost to women of taking time out of employment for childbearing – although earnings differentials have fluctuated since then. It is noteworthy that Sweden, with very narrow male–female earnings differentials, has high rates of fertility so that one cannot infer a simple relationship between the levels of women's earnings and their fertility. Favourable Swedish arrangements for combining paid work with having children, however, results in a lower cost from taking time out of employment for childbearing compared with that calculated for women in Britain.

Fertility rates were also related to the rise in real house prices during the 1970s and mid-1980s. It was calculated that a 14 per cent increase in women's earnings in relation to men's, and a 60 per cent rise in real house prices, both reduce average family size by about 12 per cent.[3]

Figure 2.1
Total period fertility rate: 1961-91, England and Wales

Sources:
Registrar General's Statistical Reviews 1961-73
Birth Statistics 1974-91

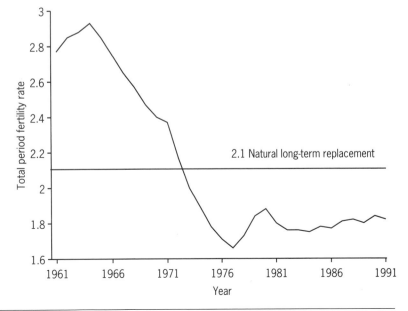

Generation size also affects childbearing: women from larger generations appear to be less likely to begin childbearing in their 20s and more likely to have smaller families. Other factors which are likely to reduce family size include an increased risk of divorce, increased female education and changes in attitude towards women working outside the home.

2.1.3 Impact of family size on child health

The low levels of fertility are primarily due to women having fewer children rather than an increased proportion remaining childless. The size of family into which a child is born and the birth order of the child have both direct and indirect consequences. Given a fixed pool of resources (which include time and money) within the family, more resources are available per child if family size is smaller. There is a large literature on the effect of family size; for example, children from large families are less likely to stay on at school beyond the statutory leaving age, have lower educational attainment and are smaller in physical size.[4-6] The differences are substantial; after allowing for social class, region and sex, at age 7 children from large families (five or more children) were, on average, 12 months behind children from small families (one or two children) in reading scores. By age 11 this difference was even larger and did not vary with the position of the child in the family. The effect of family size on mathematical attainment, however, was much less.[4]

2.1.4 Age at first birth

Although women's average age at first birth fell between the 1960s and 1970s, it rose steadily during the 1980s and represents women's decisions to delay having children. In England and Wales the mean age for all births was 27.5 years in 1991 – the highest since 1961.[2] This is a trend which is echoed in most industrialised countries of Europe and is likely to reflect the increased educational attainment of women, the prevailing economic conditions, and the ability of women to determine the timing of their first birth. Results from the 1989 General Household Survey[7] show that women with qualifications start their families later and have fewer children by age 25 than women with no qualifications.

Since the mid-1970s there has been a marked increase in the proportion of all births to women aged 30 and over. This is shown in Figure 2.2. Whilst in the 1940s births to women aged 30 or more were at a high level (39 per cent in 1941), by 1971 this had fallen to 21 per cent. By 1991, it had risen again to nearly 32 per cent,[2] reflecting the increase in the proportion of women who delay childbearing whilst establishing their career. Recent figures from OPCS *Birth Statistics* had suggested signs of increased levels of childlessness. The most recent figures, however, indicate that younger cohorts of women may be reversing this trend.[2]

The rise in the mean age of mothers is due to more children being born to older mothers, despite a rise in births amongst teenagers.

2.1.5 Change in cohabitation rates and childbirth outside marriage

An increase in the mean age at marriage since the 1970s has been accompanied by a marked increase in cohabitation rates. As with married couples, there is an age difference of a couple of years between cohabiting men and women. The peak age group for cohabitation amongst women is 20–24; rates for this group rose from 6 per cent in 1981 to 16 per cent in 1990.[8]

Related to this dramatic change in cohabitation rates has been an increase in the proportion of births in England and Wales which take place outside marriage, from 7 per cent in 1964[6] to 31 per cent in 1991.[2] International comparisons show that the UK is similar to France and the USA in the proportion of births outside marriage,

Figure 2.2
Age-specific fertility rates: 1961-91, England and Wales

Sources:
Registrar General's Statistical Reviews 1961-73
Birth Statistics 1974-91

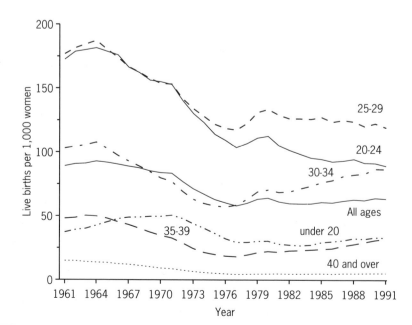

and has considerably lower rates than Sweden or Denmark, although higher rates than those of most other EU countries.[9] In 1991 nearly three-quarters of births outside marriage in England and Wales were jointly registered by both parents; of these, a further three-quarters gave a common address, suggesting that about 50 per cent of all children born outside marriage were born to cohabiting parents.[2] Birth outside marriage, therefore, does not necessarily imply lone motherhood; in fact, the increase in registration of births by only one parent has been much less dramatic. Nonetheless, the proportion of families with dependent children which are headed by only one parent has risen from 8 per cent in 1971 to 19 per cent in 1991.[10]

This increase in the proportion of families headed by only one parent is not due solely to the increased incidence of births outside marriage, but also to the greater frequency of divorce. Between 1971 and 1986 there was a steady increase in the numbers of both single and divorced lone mothers. Since the mid-1980s, however, the number of single mothers has increased much more rapidly and is now set to overtake numbers of divorced lone mothers (Figure 2.3). In 1991, 36 per cent of lone mothers were divorced, compared with 37 per cent who were single; 22 per cent were separated and 6 per cent widowed.[63] In contrast, in 1971 the proportion of lone mothers who were divorced and widowed was similar – 24 per cent of each; 34 per cent were separated and only 18 per cent single.[11] The proportion of one-parent families headed by a lone father fell from 12 per cent in 1971 to 10 per cent in 1986 and remained at this level until 1991. Lone fathers represented about 2 per cent of all families with dependent children in 1991.[11,12]

As a result of these changes in fertility levels and divorce rates, the number of dependent children living in a lone parent family in Britain doubled from 1.0 million in 1971 to 2.2 million in 1991.[12] In 1991 this represented almost 18 per cent of all dependent children living in families.[12]

There are substantial differences in family composition between ethnic groups. For West Indian women, about 50 per cent of all births have been outside marriage since 1976[1] with about 44 per cent of families with dependent children headed by a lone mother. This represents cultural differences whereby common law family households are quite usual and undergoing a legally recognised marriage is more likely amongst the better-off and more religious members of the community.[13] In contrast, amongst women from Pakistan and Bangladesh and from India, the proportion of births outside marriage are consistently low – 0.1 per cent for the former and 2 per cent for the latter, in 1991.[2] In both these communities only about 6 per cent of families with dependent children are headed by a lone mother.[11]

Since 1970 there has been a considerable change in the factors responsible for lone motherhood. The age of the children varies with the reasons for lone motherhood; for example, in 1989–91 63 per cent of single lone mothers had a youngest child aged under five by comparison with 5 per cent of widowed mothers and 15 per cent of divorced mothers.[12] The reason for lone parenthood, as well as the age of the children, will affect the level of resources available to the family and the likely impact of the situation on the child's well-being.

The 1987 Family Law Reform Act finally removed the remaining differences in the legal rights of children born inside and outside marriage and the term 'illegitimate' was removed from legal use.

2.1.6 Divorce, family dissolution and reconstitution

The 1970s and 1980s saw a greatly increased rate of dissolution and reconstitution of families. The 1969 Divorce Reform Act came into force in 1971 and brought with it a sharp rise in the number of divorces. Whilst some of these divorces represented a 'backlog', carried over from the period before the Act, nonetheless, the divorce rate in England and Wales rose from 2 per 1,000 couples in 1956–60 to 12 per 1,000 in 1980. Although in 1985 the Matrimonial and Family Proceedings Act reduced from three years to one the length of time after marriage before divorce was possible, divorce rates have only increased slightly in more recent years, in 1991 reaching 13.5 per 1,000 existing marriages.[14] This is comparable to Denmark but higher than other EU countries. Divorce rates vary considerably between the countries of the UK, however: in 1991 the rate was 10.6 per 1,000 married couples in Scotland, and 3.4 per 1,000 in Northern Ireland.

It has been calculated that 32 per cent of marriages contracted in England and Wales in 1987 will end in divorce within 20 years of marriage and nearly 40 per cent within 33 years.[15] There is, however, a marked class

Figure 2.3   Marital status of lone mothers: 1971 and 1991, Great Britain

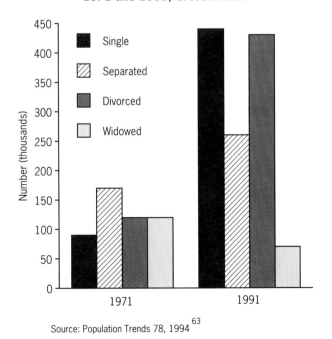

Source: Population Trends 78, 1994[63]

differential in the likelihood of divorce. The standardised divorce rate is highest amongst unskilled men, the unemployed and those in the armed forces. It is lowest amongst those in the professional and intermediate classes (I and II).

An important consequence of divorce is the associated reduction in income of the female lone parent. Longitudinal evidence from the Panel Survey of Income Dynamics shows that for women in the USA who divorce and remain unmarried, relative income drops sharply on divorce and remains at a lower level for at least five years after divorce.[16] For women who remarry, income level five years after divorce resembles that of intact couples; these record a steady rise in relative income over a five-year period. There are not yet any longitudinal data in the UK which provide comparable information. The British Household Panel Survey,[17] however, which started data collection in 1991, will follow the same individuals and their households over eight years. Data are collected each year and income forms an important part of the questionnaire schedule. This will provide precise information on the income consequences of divorce and remarriage.

Whilst family dissolution and lone parenthood have increased, so has family 'reconstitution'. There is a steady increase in remarriage rates, reaching 36 per cent of all marriages in 1990. The mean duration of lone parenthood has been estimated at five years, although there are systematic differences in the likelihood of lone mothers to marry or remarry. Using event history data from the 1980 Women and Employment Survey, it was estimated that never-married lone mothers were likely to marry more quickly than those who had been previously married.[18] It was calculated that 50 per cent of never-married women married within 34 months of becoming mothers, compared with previously married women where 50 per cent remarry within five years. Amongst those previously married women, there were further differences

in the likelihood of remarriage. Older women, those with large families, and those in paid work, are less likely to remarry.[18] In contrast, it was estimated from the General Household Survey (GHS) that duration rates of lone parenthood were similar for single and divorced lone mothers.[11] The GHS does not record completed spells of cohabitation by lone mothers so it may, therefore, overestimate the length of time spent in lone parenthood for never-married mothers.

2.1.7 Relationship between family formation and dissolution, fertility and labour market participation

The proportion of women in full-time work has changed little during the twentieth century.[19] The major change has been in the growth of part-time work, from five per cent of all women aged 15–59 in 1955 to 29 per cent in 1991 (Figure 2.4). This increase in the proportion of women in paid work has been almost entirely amongst married women with dependent children who have been returning to paid work between and after childbearing. Male employment shows no such relationship to family formation. The reasons for women's high levels of part-time working and low levels of continuity in the British labour market during family formation are complex. Social policies on child care and the availability of maternity leave have a direct impact and are discussed in the next section.

2.1.8 Child care in Britain

Section 2.1.7 showed that children were much more likely to have a working mother in 1991 than they were in 1971, but they were only slightly more likely to experience non-family child care. In this respect Britain differs from many other European countries, for example France, Sweden and Denmark, where high levels of labour market participation are associated with extensive child care provision. Britain has little formal child care for the under fives. In 1986, fewer than 6 per cent of children aged under five had places in day nurseries and

Figure 2.4
Economic activity rates for women aged under 60: 1951-91, Great Britain

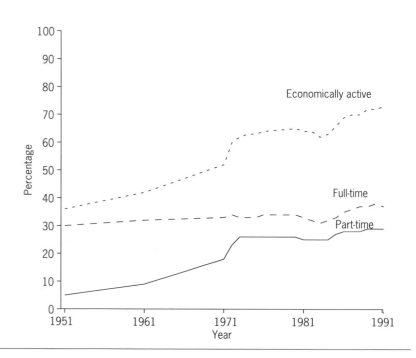

Sources:
Joshi H E. Changing Roles of Women in the British Labour Market and Family, Birkbeck College (London 1988).
General Household Survey 1971-1991

about 4 per cent were cared for by child-minders.[20] These are the only formal child care facilities available, apart from nannies and au pairs, which are only used by a very small proportion of mothers. Although the number of places in private day nurseries has increased since 1986, the extra numbers represent places only for a further 2–3 per cent of children aged under five. There has been no increase in the number of places in local authority day nurseries.[21] In 1990, fewer than 10 per cent of working mothers used any kind of day nursery.[22] Only 2 per cent of children in the UK aged under three have a publicly funded nursery place; this compares with 20 per cent in France and Belgium and 48 per cent in Denmark.[23] In March 1991 there were only about 400 work-place nurseries in the UK despite this being the only form of child care to receive some tax concessions.

The EU Draft Directive on Parental Leave and Leave for Family Circumstances included provision for a statutory minimum of three months' 'parental leave' to cover a child's illness. Britain was the only EU country to oppose this and it has not, therefore, been adopted. Sweden provides a marked contrast with Britain in terms of provision for child care. In addition to parental leave, employed parents have, since 1990, been able to take up to 120 days per year per child under 12 for child illness.[24]

2.1.9 Maternity rights legislation

Maternity rights legislation for Britain was introduced with the 1975 Employment Protection Act, which gave a woman 18 weeks' Statutory Maternity Pay (SMP) (paid by the employer) and also the right to return to her job within 29 weeks after childbirth. These rights are linked to working hours and the length of continuous service with an employer. An amendment in 1980 removed from small employers (fewer than six employees) the obligation to reinstate. In 1988, about 60 per cent of pregnant women qualified for higher rate SMP and the right to reinstatement.[25]

It is interesting to compare this provision with that of Sweden which allows parental leave of 450 week days following the birth of a child; 60 of these can be used before birth. The remainder of the leave can be taken by either parent at any time until the child is 8 years old. Income compensation up to 90 per cent of the usual wage, to a maximum level, is given for the first 360 days and at a lower rate for the remainder.[24]

Britain is one of the few countries in western Europe where it is still customary for women to leave the labour market at childbearing and where part-time working provides the only way in which most women manage to combine child care and paid work. A recent British survey on women's return to work after first childbirth[25] found that, since 1979, there had been a clear increase in the proportion of women who returned to full-time work within nine months of child-birth: from 5 per cent in 1979 to 15 per cent in 1988. A further 30 per cent had returned to work part-time, compared with 18 per cent in 1979. These proportions are likely to be lower for second and subsequent births. Also, because of the lack of child care arrangements, many women do not manage to remain at work: thus, in 1991 only 13 per cent of women with a child aged under five were in full-time work.[10] Nonetheless, this represents a small but significant increase in the proportion of mothers with preschool age children who are working full-time as shown in Figure 2.5.

2.1.10 Employment consequences of childbearing

The effect of absence from the labour market and, particularly, a return to part-time work, often leads to downward occupational mobility.[26–28] Work in both Britain[29] and the USA[30] shows that a break from employment followed by part-time working leads to a fall in income that is not recovered in later life, even if a return to full-time work is subsequently made.

Figure 2.5
Economic activity of women of working age with youngest child aged under five years: 1973-91, Great Britain

Full-time

Part-time

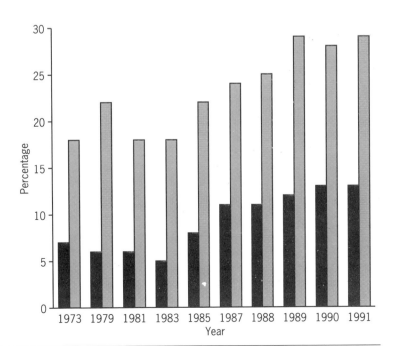

Source: General Household Survey 1973-1991

It has been estimated that a woman who breaks her employment for 8 years whilst having two children, and then works part-time for 12 years before returning to full-time work, loses about 50 per cent of what she would have earned over ages 25–59 had she not had children.[29] The earnings foregone are approximately equally divided between the earnings loss, due to the break in employment, the shorter hours and the lower rates of pay.

It is important to note that differences in economic activity exist between ethnic groups for women with children. For example, West Indian women have economic activity rates considerably higher than white women[30,31] and do not show the same relationship between family formation and employment.[32] West Indian women are more likely to remain in employment, particularly full-time working, while they have dependent children.

2.2 Changes in the family circumstances of children

As described earlier, one of the most significant changes of the last twenty years has been the increased levels of dissolution and reconstitution of families; estimates have suggested that only about one half of all children in Britain can expect to spend their entire childhood living with their married, natural parents.[33] Parental separation and divorce bring disruption into the lives of a large proportion of children and often lead to a marked fall in the disposable income of lone female-headed families.

2.2.1 Impact of divorce and remarriage on children

Research in Britain and America has shown that, amongst the children of parents who subsequently divorce, behavioural difficulties are evident long before the parental separation.[34] While children are usually emotionally upset by the separation and divorce of their parents, it had been assumed that, after an initial period of crisis, most children adapted and adjusted to their new circumstances. Research now suggests, however, that there are long-term effects that continue to disadvantage these children into adulthood.[35] Children whose parents remarry following divorce are more likely to show damaging effects than those whose parents stay single. The National Child Development Study[36] showed that stepchildren were more likely than those living with a divorced mother, to leave school at 16, to leave home due to friction, and to marry by the age of 20. Nevertheless these events were more likely for both stepchildren and those living with a divorced mother than for children in an intact family.

2.2.2 Family dissolution and family poverty

Lone mothers are particularly likely to need financial support – 68 per cent received social security benefits in 1990–1.[37] Fewer lone than married mothers are employed: 43 per cent compared with 62 per cent, according to the General Household Survey for 1989–91. Full-time working amongst lone mothers was higher than amongst married mothers until the late 1980s (when the latter group overtook the former). Although similar proportions of lone and married mothers work full-time, the proportion of lone mothers working part-time is much lower. The benefit system does not make part-time work a viable option for most lone parents; benefits (Family Credit, formerly Family Income Support) are available to low earning parents who are in full-time work – defined as 24 hours a week or more – but are not available to those in part-time work (the definition of full-time was reduced to 16 hours in April 1992). If child care is not available at an affordable price, however, full-time work is not an option, which perhaps explains why only 18 per cent of lone mothers were in full-time work in 1989–91.*

The rise in the level of divorce since the 1960s and the consequent rise in the number of female-headed lone parent families, has increased dramatically the number of children who are dependent upon state benefits. Dependency upon state benefits has also increased for two-parent families. Since the 1960s and early 1970s when the labour market was buoyant, there have been prolonged periods of high unemployment with the result that the experience of claiming unemployment benefit and other state benefits has become much more familiar in the lives of families with children. The following paragraphs discuss these changes in more detail.

2.2.3 Family poverty: the effects of unemployment

By comparison with both earlier and later times, the post-war years saw an unprecedentedly high level of employment. During the 1960s real income rose and Macmillan's claim that 'Most of our people have never had it so good' rang true in the ears of many, if not all. By the mid-1970s, however, youth unemployment was starting to rise, to be followed in 1979 by the collapse of the manufacturing industry and massive unemployment. UK unemployment rose from 1.5 per cent in 1965 to 12 per cent in 1986[38,39] (Figure 2.6).

One feature of the 1980s recession was the marked regional differences. Male unemployment stood at 22 per cent in the North, 18 per cent in the North West and 22 per cent in Northern Ireland in January 1986.[39] Areas associated with manufacturing had the highest levels of unemployment; in some wards and on some housing estates it was much higher than the regional average, for example in the ship-building areas of the North East, parts of Cornwall, and in particular, Northern Ireland. The impact of the recession on the manufacturing industries also meant that it was those in the manual working classes who were hardest hit. By contrast, in the South East male unemployment was 12 per cent in January 1986.

---

* From October 1994 a child care allowance up to £28 per week was payable to families receiving Family Credit. It operates as an earnings disregard; those on the lowest income get no help with child care costs.

Figure 2.6
Male and female employment:
1959-91, UK unadjusted

Source:
Employment Gazette, June 1992,
Historical Supplement No.3

Unemployment fell during the late 1980s but the UK began a further period of recession in 1990. Although official levels of unemployment (9.2 per cent for men and women in the UK in January 1992) were lower than in 1986, these figures are not comparable because the definition of unemployment had changed. Using a similar definition to that used by Government in the beginning of the 1980s, the Unemployment Unit calculated that the UK unemployment rate was 12.7 per cent in January 1992.[41] The count had risen for 22 successive months from March 1990. In contrast to the recession of the early 1980s, however, unemployment rose fastest in the South East, East Anglia, the South West and the East and West Midlands. This led to a regional convergence in levels of unemployment reducing some of the regional inequalities that had been heightened in the previous decade.

Therefore a substantial proportion of children experienced unemployment in their family during the 1980s, some for relatively short periods of time and others, particularly in Northern Ireland and parts of the North East and North West, for many years. In 1988–9, 23 per cent (or 2.9 million) of all children in the UK were living in families with no full-time earner; 12 per cent (1.5 million) of children living with both parents had no full-time earner in the family.[42]

2.2.4 Family poverty
Unemployment, particularly long-term, usually brings sharply declining levels of income. Although unemployment benefit is based upon National Insurance contributions, it can only be claimed for a year, after which families move to means-tested basic assistance benefit, now called Income Support and formerly Supplementary Benefit (SB). During the early 1980s, levels of long-term unemployment rose dramatically. The number of children in families receiving supplementary benefit because of unemployment rose approximately three-fold between 1979 and 1986: from 339,000 to 1,087,000.[43]

Whilst the 1960s and 1970s had seen relatively full employment and rising levels of state benefit, from 1979 there was a sharp increase in the number of families at or below SB level. This was mainly due to the increased levels of unemployment. The increased number of lone parent families, mostly female-headed, also contributed to this rise, as did the rise in the real value of SB over this time period. Whilst levels of SB increased relative to inflation (by 5.8 per cent between 1979 and 1985), nevertheless the level of benefit relative to average male earnings fell by 8.1 per cent over the same time period.[43] This was due to a change in the index-linking of supplementary benefits to the rate of inflation, rather than the rate of earnings. Between 1979 and 1988 the SB scale rate for a couple with one child aged 5–10, as a proportion of mean normal weekly disposable income, fell from 32 per cent to 25 per cent.[43] Therefore, whilst the purchasing power of the unemployed was not eroded, inequalities between those families in paid work and those drawing benefit, widened significantly.

During the 1980s there was a more general increase in income inequality. As well as a widening of the gap between those in paid work and those on benefits there was also an increase in the gap between high and low earners. Government figures showed that the gap in both original income and final income between the highest and lowest quintile groups increased between 1979 and 1987.[43] There was also a polarisation between those households with two or more earners and those with no earners. In 1968, the traditional arrangement of one male breadwinner was the most common one amongst couples aged under 65; by 1977 the position of one- and two-earner couples had reversed, with dual earners being the most frequent, whilst by 1986 there was a growing proportion of couples where neither was in paid work.[44] This reflects unexpectedly low employment rates among the wives of unemployed men, thought to be caused by a combination of financial disincentives due to the benefit system as well as traditional barriers to wives adopting the 'breadwinner' role. The proportion of families with children with no adult in paid work increased from 5 per cent in 1968 to 17 per cent in 1986.[44] It is therefore no surprise to find that, over the same period, the proportion of families with children (including lone parents) falling into the lowest quintile of the earnings distribution, increased from 12 per cent to 17 per cent of all families with children.

Without the increase in women's employment, a much greater proportion of families with children would be at the bottom of the income distribution. The role of women in keeping families out of poverty has been well documented. As long ago as 1970 it was estimated that three times more families would be in poverty if it were not for wives' employment.[45] More recently it was estimated that in 1986 women were even more effective at keeping families out of poverty; 23 per cent of the income of all couples was earned by the wife, and one-earner couples were eight times more likely to be at the lower end of the income distribution than two-earner couples.[44]

In summary, having two earners in the family is becoming increasingly important in maintaining income levels. Those families with only one or with no earner are more likely than in previous years to be at risk of poverty. This risk is considerably higher when the single earner is female.

2.2.5 Housing and living conditions
Generally, housing conditions improved greatly during the 1970s and 1980s. The post-war years saw a massive slum clearance programme that was largely completed by the 1970s. During the 1970s there was a prevailing view that there was no longer a housing shortage and that emphasis could now be shifted to particular areas where improvements to existing housing were needed. Census data show that between 1971 and 1981 the proportion of the population of England and Wales living in households without sole access to an inside bath or shower and WC fell from 14 per cent to just over 3 per cent.[46] The proportion of individuals living in households at a density of more than one person per room similarly fell from 15 per cent in 1971 to 7 per cent in 1981.

There have also been marked increases in the levels of possession of a large range of household amenities. Between 1972 and 1991, households with central heating increased from 37 per cent to 82 per cent; access to a telephone from 42 per cent to 88 per cent and possession of a washing machine from 66 per cent to 87 per cent. By contrast, the availability of a car has increased more slowly, from 52 per cent in 1972 to 67 per cent in 1991. In fact, the percentage of households with access to only one car has remained constant at 43 per cent across this time period; it is only the proportion with two or more cars that has risen, from 9 per cent in 1972 to 23 per cent in 1991. The level of all these amenities tends to be higher amongst households with children than those without.[47]

Against this general picture of improvement over time, it is important to recognise the extent of inequality in housing conditions and access to amenities. This is most clearly identified through the rise in homelessness since the 1970s and the increasing use of temporary accommodation and bed and breakfast hostels to house homeless families with children. This will be discussed later in the chapter.

2.2.6 Change in level of home ownership
The 1970s and 1980s saw a steady increase in home ownership to the point where, in 1991, 67 per cent of households were in owner-occupation; this compared with 49 per cent in 1971.[10] This trend was given an increased thrust by the introduction of the 'right to buy' legislation in the 1980 Housing Act. There was, therefore, a much higher probability of a child being born into an owner-occupied household in 1991, than 20 or 40 years previously. Whilst there are very marked health inequalities associated with tenure (and these remain even after controlling for social class),[48] it is also important to recognise the diversity within each tenure type which, within owner-occupied accommodation, increased considerably during the 1970s and 1980s. It is not possible therefore, to make sweeping assumptions based upon owner-occupation *per se*. By contrast, the diversity of public sector housing decreased during the 1980s, as it was left with the residual role of housing those families who were unable to buy their own home, and managing that housing stock for which no purchasers could be found.

A drop in the availability of local authority rented accommodation and the ready availability of mortgages, led to a rapid growth in home-ownership and a period of record house prices in the late 1980s. Mortgage interest rates rose to a record level of 15 per cent in early 1990, causing great difficulty to many who had borrowed heavily a year or two earlier. A survey of 29 mortgage lenders showed that in 1989, 14 per cent of first time buyers had loans in excess of three times their salaries, compared with only 4 per cent in 1985, 36 per cent had 100 per cent loans.[49,50]

This, together with the growth in unemployment from mid-1990, meant that the resources of large number of new owner-occupiers were stretched to the limit to meet mortgage commitments. During 1990 and 1991 repossessions for non-payment ran at record levels, with about 80,000 families losing their homes in 1991. By March 1991, 783,900 mortgages were in arrears – 8.3 per cent of all home loans, compared with 5.8 per cent the previous year. In the year to March 1991, repossessions totalled 47,940, more than double the figure for the preceding year.[49] Therefore, although owner-occupation is typically seen as providing security and a valuable capital asset, for some families it proved more insecure than local authority accommodation.

2.2.7 Homelessness
Levels of homelessness began to rise well before the 1990 recession. In the early 1970s there was a view that

homelessness could become a thing of the past. During the 1980s, in particular, however, there was a rise in homelessness to levels which were unprecedented in recent times. The 1977 Housing (Homeless Persons) Act obliged local authorities to house those who, within the meaning of the Act, were accepted as homeless. Families with children were one of the priority groups listed in the legislation, provided they were not deemed to have made themselves intentionally homeless, for example by leaving accommodation shared with parents.

Department of the Environment statistics show a huge rise in the numbers of households accepted as homeless, from 53,000 in 1978 to 145,800 in 1990. Over 80 per cent of these households (about 117,000 households in 1990) either had dependent children or a household member who was pregnant. Numbers of households in temporary accommodation in England rose from 4,500 in December 1980 to 39,900 in December 1989 and 59,800 in December 1991. Statutory homelessness as a result of a court order following mortgage default or rent arrears was two and a half times as common in 1990 than in 1981.[1]

In 1990, there were 12,000 homeless households living in bed and breakfast accommodation. The effect of this experience on the well-being and future development of children is yet to be assessed. There can be little doubt that the overcrowding and lack of facilities in bed and breakfast accommodation can have a detrimental effect on the well-being and development of children. Children living in this accommodation are more likely to miss immunisations, whilst overcrowded conditions and poor sanitation encourage infections.[51] Limited cooking facilities shared with many other families not only makes it difficult to eat a healthy diet, but also leads to accidents. The economics of using bed and breakfast accommodation is highlighted by a Department of the Environment estimate that, in 1987–8, the average cost of keeping a family in bed and breakfast for a year in London was £15,440, compared with the annual cost of £8,200 to provide a new council dwelling.[52]

2.3 Changes in the social climate for young people

This section explicitly takes the perspective of children and young people and examines the changing environment in which they have grown up over the last twenty years. During this time, children have found themselves in a world of increasing consumerism, of sophisticated marketing for equally sophisticated products in which they are powerful actors. Associated with this has been a considerable increase in the freedom available to young people, for example in making sexual relationships and in taking decisions. There is also a much greater recognition of the child as an individual and of his or her rights and expectations. At the same time labour market and educational changes have, for many, delayed entry into the adult world of a regular weekly wage packet and the independence that comes

with it. This delay has also been enshrined in social policy changes that have removed the right of 16–18-year-olds to independent benefits and has reduced the level of benefit available to those aged under 25. The full implications of these contradictions are yet to become clear.

2.3.1 Education and employment

Changes in the educational system during the 1970s ended selection at age 11 in most areas, and introduced comprehensive education. In 1973 the school leaving age was raised to 16 and subsequent years saw the first increase in youth unemployment, a problem that has remained throughout the 1980s and into the 1990s. Whilst the rate of unemployment in Britain increased gradually during the 1970s, that for young people rose consistently faster than for the labour force as a whole. In 1982 it was 13.5 per cent overall and 28 per cent amongst 16–19-year-olds.[53] One important reason was the 20 per cent increase in the number of young people between 1974 and 1984. Young people were particularly badly affected by the 1979–81 recession with the result that, despite the larger number of 16–18-year-olds in the population, there were 500,000 fewer young people employed in 1984 than there had been in 1974.[54] Associated with the decline in manufacturing was a collapse of the apprenticeship system which, in the early 1970s, absorbed over a quarter of 16-year-old males but which took only 8 per cent in 1984. Additional factors underlying the high rates of youth unemployment were the widespread policy of 'last in first out' when firms faced job losses, and the increasing number of married women seeking a return to the labour market in a part-time capacity.

Growing levels of unemployment amongst young people led to government fears that these young people would not become socialised into the world of work, would not conform to the norms of society and, as a result, levels of crime and social unrest would rise.[55] At the same time, there were concerns that young people were receiving inadequate training for employment; the education system came under attack for producing school leavers who were barely literate and numerate and, in comparison with other western industrialised nations, the amount of job training given to young people in Britain was low. It was in response to these demands and problems that the Youth Opportunities Programme (YOP) was introduced in 1978 with courses designed to 'prepare young people for work and different kinds of work experience'.[55] The major part of YOP provision was work experience provided by employers.

Until the late 1970s it was still generally accepted that the majority of young people left school at 16 and moved into a full-time job. Indeed, in 1974 slightly over 60 per cent of 16-year-old boys and just under 60 per cent of 16-year-old girls went from school directly into employment; most of the remainder either stayed on at school or went into further education.[56] Since the late 1970s, however, government training schemes have become increasingly important as a means of reducing high youth unemployment whilst also aiming to socialise young people into stable work habits and provide some training for the needs of industry. The relative importance of the aims of social control and training is difficult to assess; it is probable that, for the young person, which of these seems more dominant will depend upon whether the scheme leads to a permanent full-time job or whether it leads back to unemployment. This, in turn, seems to depend largely upon the job opportunities in the local labour market.[57,58]

The Youth Training Scheme (YTS) succeeded the YOP in 1983, and was intended as 'a permanent bridge between school and work'.[59] By 1986, 27 per cent of all young people aged 16 were on YTS schemes and, in recognition of the difficulty which young people experienced in moving from YTS into paid work, the scheme was extended to cover two years rather than one. In contrast to the period 10 years earlier, the most significant change has been the replacement of YTS rather than full-time work as the major activity of 16-year-old school leavers. In 1974, about 60 per cent of young people aged 16 went into paid work and only 3 per cent were unemployed. By 1990, government figures no longer distinguished unemployed 16-year-olds because they were unable to claim benefit (except in some exceptional circumstances). Nevertheless, 52 per cent were estimated to be in full-time education, 23 per cent on YTS schemes and under 25 per cent in paid employment.[60]

As the proportion of 16-year-olds entering paid employment has fallen sharply, so the proportion remaining in full-time education has risen. In 1974, only 35 per cent remained in full-time education beyond school leaving age; this rose to 49 per cent in 1983 – a peak period of unemployment. It fell again during the improved labour conditions of the late 1980s, but in 1990 was the highest ever, at 52 per cent. Despite this increase, the proportion of 16–18-year-olds in full-time education is still substantially below that for many other western countries. In 1986, 31 per cent of British 16–18-year-olds were in full-time education in comparison with 79 per cent in the USA, 76 per cent in Sweden, 47 per cent in Germany, 66 per cent in France and 77 per cent in Japan.[61] Figure 2.7 shows the education and labour market status of young people over the years 1974–90.

2.3.2 Social policies towards children and young people
During the 1970s and 1980s there has been increased recognition of the rights of children, for example through the activities of the Children's Legal Centre. Social work practice has placed greater emphasis on the needs of the child rather than the parents and the 1989 Children Act has been represented as a major advance in giving children greater self-determination, for example, in allowing them to apply for a court order to determine with whom they should live.[43]

Over the same period there has been a marked change in the sexual behaviour of young people. This is discussed more fully in Chapter 5 and is reflected in the increased levels of cohabitation presented earlier in this chapter. The greater sexual freedom of the 1980s is probably related to the greater availability of the contraceptive pill and its reliability. In 1991, 16 per cent of women aged 16–17, and 46 per cent aged 18–19 used the pill as a usual method of contraception.[10] Amongst single women at 'risk' of pregnancy (i.e. sexually active, not sterilised and not pregnant), use of the pill rose to 74 per cent of those aged 16–19.

Income support policies have delayed the age at which young people are able to become financially independent. From September 1988 unemployment benefit has not been available to anyone below the age of 18 and the age of claiming Income Support was raised to 18. This policy was explicitly designed to place the responsibility for young people of this age with their parents and to discourage those under 18 from leaving home.[37] All those aged under 18 without a job were guaranteed a YTS place. For those with no parental home or for whom

Figure 2.7
Education and labour force market status of young people aged 16: 1974-90, Great Britain

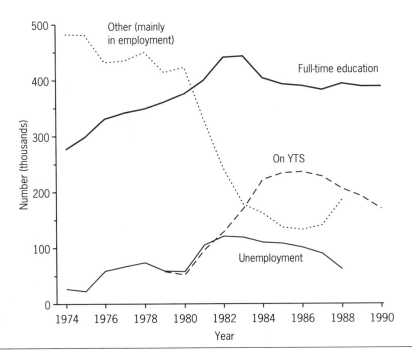

Sources:
Employment Gazette, December 1987;
December 1990; December 1991.

living at home posed a serious threat, Income Support and Housing Benefit could be claimed, although both are paid at a 'junior' rate, making independent living very difficult. Those aged 18 and over are eligible to claim benefits but receive a reduced benefit until the age of 25, again increasing dependency upon parents and making independent living almost impossible.

This policy has undoubtedly contributed to the large increase in homelessness amongst young people. The number of young people, from 16 or 17 upwards, who are sleeping rough has risen to a scale unprecedented in recent years. In part this may also be related to the recession of the late 1980s, and to the problems of unemployment that has affected young people, to a greater or lesser extent, from the mid-1970s onwards. Shelter have estimated that around 15,000 16–19-year-olds experience homelessness each year.

A survey commissioned by the Department of Social Security into young people claiming the discretionary 'Severe Hardship' element of Income Support revealed the extent to which those interviewed were facing financial hardship and homelessness – some through pregnancy, some having been in care, many sexually or physically abused. A coalition of charities concerned about the welfare of young people concluded that: 'The real problems for young people are the unavailability of affordable housing, appropriate training and employment, and the low level of benefit payment'.[62]

2.4 Conclusion

By comparison with earlier decades, children are now much more likely to be born into a family where their mother is in employment (often part-time). They are also more likely to experience living with only one biological parent at some time. Nonetheless, most young children are still cared for by their mother and the use of day nurseries and other forms of child care have not increased in proportion to women's paid employment.

The increase in both lone motherhood and unemployment have had severe consequences for family poverty with a resultant increase in income inequalities between those families with two parents in employment and those families dependent upon state benefits. Whilst housing conditions have improved markedly over recent decades, and there has been a steady increase in home ownership, for some families the recession of the early 1990s and the high interest rates of that period brought mortgage arrears and repossession orders.

For young people, the assumption of a smooth transition from school to work disappeared during the 1970s, with rising youth unemployment. By 1990, the rates of entering post-compulsory education had risen considerably whilst the proportion of school leavers entering Youth Training Schemes was about the same as those taking paid employment. As the economic dependency of young people has increased, sexual freedom and expectations of independence have also increased. The inequality between those young people with educational

qualifications and a paid job and those with few or no qualifications who cannot obtain paid work is, perhaps, one of the most disturbing aspects of the 1970s and 1980s.

References

1. Central Statistical Office *Social Trends*, **23** HMSO (London 1992).
2. *1991 Birth Statistics England and Wales*, Series FM1, No. 20. HMSO (London 1993).
3. Ermisch J F. Women's economic activity and fertility in the United Kingdom. In *Study on the Relationship between Female Activity and Fertility*, Volume 2, National Reports, Eurostat (Brussels 1991).
4. Fogelman K. Developmental correlates of family size. *British Journal of Social Work*, **5** (1), 1975; 43-57.
5. Fogelman K and Goldstein H. Social factors associated with changes in educational attainment between 7 and 11 years of age. *Educational Studies*, **2** (2), 1976; 95-109.
6. Essen J and Wedge P. *Continuities in Childhood Disadvantage*. Heinemann Educational Books (London 1982).
7. Breeze E, Trevor G and Wilmot A. *1989 General Household Survey*. OPCS, HMSO (London 1991).
8. Smyth M and Browne F. *1990 General Household Survey*. HMSO (London 1992).
9. Family Policy Studies Centre. *The Family Today: Fact Sheet 1* (London 1991).
10. Bridgwood A and Savage D. *1991 General Household Survey*. HMSO (London 1993).
11. Haskey J. Estimated numbers and demographic characteristics of one-parent families in Great Britain *Population Trends*, **65**, 1991.
12. Haskey J. Trends in the numbers of one-parent families in Great Britain. *Population Trends*, **71**, 1993.
13. Barrow J. West Indian families: an insider's perspective. In Rapport RN, Fogarty MP and Rapoport R (eds). *Families in Britain*. Routledge and Kegan Paul (London 1982).
14. Central Statistical Office. *Annual Abstract of Statistics*. HMSO (London 1994).
15. Haskey J. One-parent families and their children in Great Britain: numbers and characteristics. *Population Trends*, **55**, 1989.
16. Duncan G J and Hoffman S D. Economic consequences of marital instability. In Smeeding T and David M (eds). *Horizontal Equity, Uncertainty and Well-being*, National Bureau of Economic Research, Income and Wealth Conference. Chicago. University of Chicago Press, (1985) 429-70.
17. Rose D *et al*. Micro-social change in Britain: an outline of the role and objectives of the British Household Panel Study. *Working Papers of the ESRC Research Centre on Micro-social Change*, Paper 1, University of Essex (Colchester 1991).
18. Ermish J F and Wright R E. *The Duration of Lone Parenthood in Britain*. Centre for Economic Policy Research, Discussion Paper Series No. 303 (1989).
19. Joshi H. Motherhood and employment. In *Measuring Socio-Demographic Change*. Occasional Paper No. 34, OPCS (London 1985).
20. OPCS. *General Household Survey 1986*. HMSO (London 1989).

21. Central Statistical Office. *Social Trends*, **21**, HMSO (London 1991).

22. Witherspoon S and Prior G. Working mothers: free to choose? In Jowell R, Brook L and Taylor B (eds). *British Social Attitudes*, 8th Report. Dartmouth (London 1991).

23. Labour Research Department. *Bargaining Report*, No. 111. LRD (London 1991).

24. Leira A. Combining work and the family. British Social Association Annual Conference, Canterbury, April 1992.

25. McRae S and Daniel W W. *Maternity Rights: the Experience of Women and Employers*. Policy Studies Institute (London 1991).

26. Martin J and Roberts C. *Women and Employment*: a *Lifetime Perspective*. HMSO (London 1984).

27. Dex S. *Women's Occupational Mobility*. Macmillan (Basingstoke 1987).

28. Joshi H and Newell M-L. Job downgrading after childbearing. In Uncles MD (ed). *London Papers in Regional Science 18*. Pion (London 1987).

29. Joshi H E. The cash opportunity cost of childbearing: an approach to estimation using British evidence. *Population Studies*, **44** (March), 1990, 41-60.

30. Corcoran M, Duncan G J and Ponza M. A longitudinal analysis of white women's wages. *The Journal of Human Resources*, **XVIII** (4), 1983, 497-520.

31. OPCS. *Labour Force Survey 1990 and 1991*. HMSO (London 1992).

32. Ward C and Dale A. Geographical variation in women's labour market participation: an application of multilevel modelling. *Regional Studies* **2b** (3), 1992, 243-256.

33. Clarke L. Children's family circumstances: recent trends in Great Britain. *European Journal of Population* **8**, 1992, 309-340.

34. Kiernan K E and Chase-Lonsdale P L. Children and marital breakdown: short and long term consequences. *Proceedings of the European Demographic Conference,* Paris, **2**, 1991.

35. Kuh D and Maclean M. Women's childhood experience of parental separation and their subsequent health and socioeconomic status in adulthood. *Journal of Biosocial Science,* **22,** 1990, 121-135.

36. Kiernan K E. The impact of family disruption in childhood on transitions made in young adult life. *Population Studies*, **46,** 1992.

37. Roll J. *Young People: Growing up in the Welfare State*. Occasional Paper No.10. Family Policy Studies Centre (London 1990).

38. Department of Employment. *Employment Gazette Historical Supplement*, 1984.

39. Department of Employment. *Employment Gazette*, 1987.

40. Department of Employment. *Employment Gazette*, **97** (6), 1989 521-3.

41. Unemployment Unit and Youth Aid. *Working Brief*, (March) 1992.

42. Department of Social Security. *Households Below Average Income: A Statistical Analysis, 1979-1988/89*. HMSO (London 1992).

43. Bradshaw J. *Child Poverty and Deprivation in the UK*. National Children's Bureau (London 1991).

44. Joshi H E and Davis H. Gender and income inequality in the UK: the feminization of earning or of poverty? Conference of the European Society for Population Economics, Istanbul, June 1990.

45. Land H. Women: supporters of supported? In Barker D L and Allen S (eds). *Sexual Divisions and Society: Process and Change*. Tavistock (London 1976).

46. Williams M and Dale A. *Measuring Housing Deprivation using the OPCS Longitudinal Study*. LS Working Paper No.72. SSRU, City University (London 1991).

47. Dale A. The effects of the life-cycle on three dimensions of stratification. In Bryman A *et al* (eds). *Rethinking the Life Cycle*. Macmillan, Basingstoke (1987), 170-91.

48. Fox A J and Goldblatt P O. *Socio-demographic Mortality Differentials 1971-75*. LS Working Paper No. 1. HMSO (London 1982).

49. Ford J. Mortgage misery deepens. *Roof* (The magazine of Shelter), July and August, 1991, 9.

50. Ford J. *Mortgage Arrears*. Institute of Employment Research, University of Warwick (1991).

51. Lowry S. *Housing and Health*. British Medical Journal (London 1991).

52. Committee of Public Accounts. *Homelessness*. Session 1990-91, 22nd Report House of Commons (London 1991).

53. Roberts K. *School Leavers and their Prospects: Youth and the Labour Market in the 1980s*. Open University Press (Milton Keynes 1984).

54. Equal Opportunities Commission. *Men and Women in Britain: a Statistical Profile*. HMSO (London 1986).

55. Finn D. *Training Without Jobs: New Deals and Broken Promises*. Macmillan (Basingstoke 1987).

56. Department of Education and Science. *Statistical Bulletins* 5/86, February, 1985.

57. Roberts K, Dench S and Richardson D. *The Changing Structure of the Youth Labour Market*. Department of Employment Research Paper No. 59. Department of Employment (London 1987).

58. Ashton D and Maguire M. *Young Adults in the Labour Market*. Department of Employment Research Paper No. 55. Department of Employment (London 1986).

59. Cockburn C. *Two Track Training: Sex Inequalities and the YTS*. Macmillan (Basingstoke 1987).

60. Department of Employment. *Employment Gazette*, December, 1991, 666.

61. Robinson P. *Education and Training for Young People in the 1990s*. Campaign for Work Research Report, **4** (3), 1992.

62. COYPSS. *Young People and Severe Hardship: A COYPSS response to MORI/DSS Survey of 16- and 17-year-olds*. Coalition On Young People and Social Security (London 1992).

63. Haskey J. Estimated number of one-parent families and their prevalence in Great Britain. *Population Trends*, **78,** 1994.

3 The changing context of childhood: children's perspectives on health care resources including services

Berry Mayall

Key points

- There is a growing awareness of the value in treating children as participants in health care in their own right.

- Children's own access to help from services on health-related issues is limited.

- More research is needed on children's health beliefs and views on services.

- Research has shown that when children understand their medical conditions they are more willing to co-operate with treatment, endure painful treatment more patiently and recover better.

It is significant that this report has a chapter on children's perspectives on health care. It reflects developing concern that children should be conceptualised as people: as subjects rather than objects, as people with rights, and as contributing members of society, rather than as presocial projects for adults to work on. This new concern, however, must be seen in the context of long-established and still powerful concepts surrounding childhood in the UK.

3.1 Background

Social policies for children's health, education and welfare tend to place reliance on parental and state responsibilities, with the complementary assumptions about children's vulnerability and incompetence. A recent report noted that in developing law, policy and practice, there is a tendency to rely too heavily on presumptions of children's biological or psychological vulnerability and too little on their competence and on their rights.[1] Recent government statements on education, for example, stress parental rather than children's rights; for instance: 'You have the right to a proper education for your child...'.[2] Media coverage in the 1990s of changes to state education (national curriculum, and testing), has also focused on parents' interests rather than children's. The conceptualisation of the child as inseparable from the family received political reinforcement in the late 1980s through the removal of 16- and 17-year-olds' right to state financial benefits. As described in Chapter 2, the amount of benefit payable to those aged under 25 has been reduced (on the assumption that parents are responsible for their children), so that people are now newly conceptualised as dependent children up to that age!

Health care professionals have long assumed that children's interests are at one with those of parents. In the 1970s it was argued that people are themselves health-care workers, rather than consumers of others' labour.[3] This argument applies to children as well as adults. Yet a recent discussion of child health surveillance (up to age 16) demonstrated the still common sociological misconception, noting that it 'has to be sensitive to the views of the consumer. Parents expect to be consulted about decisions that involve their children'.[4]

The idea of childhood and children as the object of health and education professionals' interest receives powerful theoretical support from child development theories. These propose that children are presocial beings who move through a series of stages towards the goal of mature adulthood. The legitimacy of interventions to modify childhood is based on the premise that children's present time matters much less than their future; and that they are incompetent thinkers. Adults speak for children on the basis of Piagetian theories of children's in-built incompetence to think 'like adults' until they reach certain developmental stages. The popularity and power of such psychological theories probably derives, partly at least, from their positivist and quantitative framing; including their claim to describe facts about the world in general. For the medical and nursing professions, reared in the same traditions, they provide a firm theoretical framework for thinking, policy and practice.

Indeed, the idea of the child as the object of surveillance and control by a range of professionals may be seen as a critical element in the development in Western industrial societies of public control over citizens;[5,6] such surveillance and control assumes rights over people's psyche as well as over their behaviour. Examples include state intervention (through the child health services) in maternal child-rearing beliefs and practices;[7] and the requirement that schoolchildren not only learn what is taught in the formal curriculum but conform to the social and moral norms of their schools.[8]

3.2 The increasing visibility of children

The 1970s and 1980s saw a developing international interest in promoting the interests of children and their rights to be listened and attended to.[9] Specific measures included the International Year of the Child in 1979, and the UN Convention on the Rights of the Child in 1989, which was ratified by the UK in 1991. An important move in the UK was the Children Act 1989, which lays on courts the duty to have regard to the ascertainable wishes and feelings of the child when determining the upbringing of the child.[10] All these developments reflect and promote the view that children are capable of giving a view and have a right for their views to be taken into account on issues concerning their present and future.

These developments have been paralleled and strengthened by establishing organisations such as the Children's Legal Centre. There has also been a change of focus towards children's perspectives by existing pressure groups, such as Save the Children, and Action for Sick Children (formerly National Association for the Welfare of Children in Hospital); and by professional organisations such as the Health Visitors' Association and the British Paediatric Association.

Academic interest in 'childhood' is also currently and newly fashionable among sociologists and anthropologists, in recognition that the study of childhood must be included within more general concern for the cultural inequalities universally applied within societies according to age.[11] Increasingly it is thought essential to consider the part played by children, their experiences and the constraints and opportunities they encounter according to their age, social class and gender.[12] Study of children's participation helps to promote adequate and comprehensive understanding of social and power structures, within the family, the school and health services (surgeries, clinics and hospitals).

A recent overview and update of research on the utilisation of child health services noted an increase in studies which include both parental and child reporting as a source of information. The authors also noted, however, the paucity of research studies on services for school-age children and adolescents.[13]

3.3 The social contexts of children's knowledge

Attending to the voice of children has acquired a certain respectability in the last few years. It is a slower process, however, to obtain research evidence to increase our knowledge of children's perspectives on the social institutions in which they live and play their part in constructing.

We are beginning to learn from research what children think about health and illness.[14-17] We know little about their views on resources and services for health care and about whether and how children's voices are heard in meetings with health professionals. We know almost nothing about gender and ethnicity as influences on children's experiences and assessments. Our ignorance complements the traditional assumption by researchers and funders that it is adults' views that are worth exploring, rather than children's. Again this reflects the view not only that children are incompetent witnesses to their own experience, but that children's interests are co-terminous with and enclosed within the family.

Most research relating to children's health care (by themselves, by parents or by other adults including professionals) has collected data from mothers. Most of the work focusing directly on children and young people concerns those with serious health problems and handicaps. Studies of, with and about these children and young people, however, provide indications of issues that may relate to young people in general.

Children's principal and most influential resource for knowledge about health and health care is probably the experience of living in and around their homes, as they interact with and learn from their parents, their immediate family, their social networks, and the media (especially the television). When they are old enough to go to preschools and schools they meet other sets of social norms of health behaviour: this is the way we do things here (we wash our hands before eating; we wrap up warm when we go out to play; we don't bring sweets, crisps and fizzy drinks to school, do we?). These norms are powerfully enforced through the authority of the adults in these institutions.

Set against the richness and power of these continuing experiences and normative prescriptions, the efforts of the formal education curriculum to affect children's health-care behaviour look pallid. School health education clearly reveals our contradictory views of children and of how health education works. Children are construed as being part of the family, with its profoundly influential beliefs and behaviours; yet within the education system, they are identified as individuals, who, armed with a little knowledge, should take responsibility for good health behaviour. The ideology of personal responsibility for health promoted by government since the late 1970s has included suggestions that children too should take some responsibility for their own health-related behaviour. The task of attempting to teach children what they should think and do, however, has suggested that children bring to the classroom knowledge they acquire more informally in their social lives. For example, it was found that girls had far more knowledge, and realistic knowledge at that, about motherhood than the health education curriculum and their teachers gave them credit for.[18] We are also beginning to understand what fills the gaps between people's formal knowledge and behaviour, that is how their socioeconomic circumstances influence their behaviour.[19] Recent detailed work on the development and continuation of smoking habits, particularly among girls and young women, has indicated the importance of families' culture of smoking,[20] how the social culture of the school negates narrowly defined health education[21] and how smoking enables people to cope with stressful circumstances.[22,23]

Thus, children can be seen to develop from an early age a complex of understandings about health and health care, derived from their experiences within a range of social institutions. These understandings inform their use of health-care resources, including services.

3.4 Health services and resources for children

Before considering children's access to and experience of services and resources, it might be thought appropriate to list the services and resources available. This apparently simple task is fraught with difficulty, however. Thus, one question is whether the services are for children, or for parents as responsible adults or for health professionals as agents of the overseeing state. There is also the problem, which in part reflects children's low social status, that there is no readily available reference list of health services and resources for children. Finally, depending what we include under health, services provided with other main aims (such as educational psychology) may be regarded as helping children with their health concerns.

Preschool and school health services were established to monitor the development and health of all children until they leave school. These services provide a social and moral framework in which the concerns of adults predominate. Neither preschool, primary or secondary school children are asked if they wish to be examined. At least we do not know that they are: children's consent to surveillance has not been researched. It has been noted, however, that the preventive services provided in schools do constitute a uniquely accessible resource and that the school nurse can be a valued adviser and advocate for children.[24]

There is little information about when, whether and why children perceive GP and hospital services have been provided for them. A recent study indicated that both 5- and 8-year-olds understood certain events (visiting a doctor, dentist, hospital; not feeling well; having an operation) as an ordered sequence of events, just as an adult would order such events.[25] Thus, these events had meaning for the children for participants. As is indicated below, children's experiences have mainly been considered for children with frequent, chronic or serious conditions.

Like adults, children probably use a wide range of resources to acquire health knowledge and for advice. These will be mainly family, friends and teachers. Secondary schools and, in recent initiatives, some primary schools, provide counselling services, linked to personal and social education curricula. These are open to the criticism that they may be used by adults to reinforce school social norms, rather than to respond to pupils' concerns, including their health problems,[26] but again there is little research evidence on pupils' perspectives. It is not until children become problematic in the eyes of policy-makers, as adolescents, that services are provided directly for them in the community, in the shape of youth advisory and family planning services. Their usefulness is suggested by their high usage. We need to know more about users' opinions, especially since services are increasingly required to demonstrate their usefulness to customers.

3.5 Children's access to resources and services

Children have limited access to health-care services if seeking information and help in their own right. The restrictions are both moral and physical. Firstly, their access is circumscribed by their dependent positioning within families; both parents and professionals assume that children will be accompanied by a parent. Indeed an important discussion document on child-health services collapses children and their accompanying parents into the category 'patients'.[27] Secondly, children have restricted physical autonomy and mobility, resulting from parental sense of responsibility, traffic dangers, adult protectiveness and personal poverty.

In complement to children's low status, few services are designed to be friendly to children, and services which allow children access as people in their own right, such as the school health service and youth advisory services, tend to be particularly vulnerable to cuts. Yet children value opportunities to consult a knowledgeable person in confidence with concerns they may not wish to share with teachers and parents, for example fears about serious conditions such as cancer and AIDS, gynaecological and sexual matters, their body shape, spots and rashes.[28] A recent study in a primary school found evidence that the school nurse was a useful resource for some children, although her work-load restricted the hours spent in the school.[29] Access to GPs is more difficult for children and there are few data. In a recent survey of 649 15-year-olds, 26 per cent reported making their own appointment to see the GP.[30]

Such evidence as there is of children's access to confidential information, advice and comfort, as regards serious personal problems[31] and events such as child abuse[32] and divorce,[33] suggests that we have a long way to go in recognising children's needs for help on serious matters, let alone as regards more everyday concerns.

3.6 Children's experience of services

People's experience of illness is powerfully affected by their ability to acquire useful knowledge, and by how far they are respected and listened to. So it is important to consider children as people first and children only second. How children experience health services and how they use such services and other resources, suggests important practical reasons for improving children's experiences. The research evidence is mainly based on children in hospital and with severe conditions.

Research has shown that when children acquire knowledge about their condition, treatment, likely pain and prognosis, they are more willing to co-operate with treatment, they understand better when and why to take drugs, they endure painful treatments more patiently and recover better.[34] It has also been shown that young children have views about whether they wish to give consent to treatment or delegate that responsibility to their parents. Many children can propose an age when they think it appropriate to decide for themselves.[35]

Yet old habits and old power structures die hard. The asymmetric power relations between doctor and patient give patients of whatever age a muted voice and little power. Where the child patient is represented by a parent the child is pushed even further out of centre. Studies of consultations regarding children with conditions requiring many meetings with doctors (cleft palate, Down's syndrome, diabetes) have indicated how, in triangular meetings between doctor, parent and child/young person, the latter is often excluded from discussion, and is granted only limited autonomy.[36] It is not easy for a doctor to negotiate with parents and children together, or with children on their own, their wishes about decision-making. It requires constant reappraisal and sensitivity to the child's wishes.

Research has explored how children dying of leukaemia acquire the knowledge of their impending deaths that adults wish to hide from them.[37] The children's resources included their observation of what happened to other children on the ward, their reading of social arrangements – for instance, that dying children were segregated; their conversations with adults and children; their reading of their parents' behaviour and conversation. Children wanted to make sense of what was happening to them at various stages in their illness. Making sense of their experience was essential so that they could know how and why to bear the treatments and the stages of their illness, how to behave appropriately in the social and medical contexts they encountered, how to help their parents bear the pain of sorrow and bereavement, and so that they could order their affairs before dying.

Where children are very young or severely handicapped, the issues of parental responsibility versus attention to the child's wishes and feelings are thrown into sharp relief. A study of handicapped children and young people shows how even the most handicapped indicate their wishes and feelings, and how parents watch for such signs in order to make informed decisions on their children's behalf.[38] The author calls for greater sensitivity by health care professionals, and greater respect for handicapped young people, as people, for instance in recognising and giving space to their grief over the death of a parent.[39]

At a general level, the data derived from these very painful situations are useful in helping us develop understanding of children's experiences as patients, and understanding how services can best provide for children. The evidence suggests the importance of providers giving children as much information as they ask for, and of recognising that they are people first, rather than members of an inferior social and moral class. Critically, all the research cited here indicates the value parents and professionals should give to ascribing moral status as people to children, not only as a principle, but in order to promote the best health outcome for the child.

It may be proposed that children's experiences of seeking and using health help are critical for the development and maintenance of their self-esteem. In a study of children in hospital, it was argued that control over one's body and control over one's life are central issues in the formation of children's sense of self-esteem.[40] These are put at risk during medical encounters for everyone, but for children the damage to their developing self-esteem may have long-term effects. Therefore, children's views, their feelings and requests for knowledge should be particularly carefully attended to in the interests of their short-term and long-term well-being, as well as in accordance with respect for their rights.

3.7 Children's assessment of resources and services

In general, only adult views have been sought to consider how far health services and other care provisions meet with people's approval. The mothers' view is usually considered the most useful on the service offered to babies and toddlers.[41] Service providers, however, may gain much from even the youngest children's behavioural signs about their feelings.[30] The baby who screams while waiting in a long queue to be seen by the doctor is registering dissatisfaction with waiting times. Two studies of children (aged 3 to 9, and 3 to 14 years respectively) in hospital showed how careful observation of children's behaviour, comments and activities can provide lessons to help provide the most appropriate services for them.[37,40]

Providing health services that people welcome and find usable can be seen as not only a matter of good principle for state services, but also as necessary for the maintenance and restoration of good health in the population. To the extent that services are provided for users rather than for health professionals, it seems that they are provided for adults. Children are here conceptually subsumed within 'parents and children'. It is of interest here to consider service provision for those referred to as older children, teenagers, adolescents or young people. Studies have been made of children and young people attending out-patient clinics, where a topic continuously under negotiation is the child's own part in the consultation, in decision-making and in management of conditions such as diabetes.[36] This negotiation reflects the gradual emergence of the adult individual responsible for their own health care, and how doctor and parent may best identify where the child is at and give recognition to the child's wishes as regards taking some part or some control over health care. Children's health problems require parents and professionals to negotiate and temporise as to who is the responsible patient, but the service offered is essentially based on the idea of the autonomous individual.

A further important point emerges from consideration of children in out-patient clinics: a point raised by Mrs Gillick in respect of contraceptive advice to under-sixteens. She argued that parental rights should take precedence over the value of conceptualising the child as a patient in her own right. The ability of children to give a legally valid consent to medical treatment has been controversial since it was addressed in the 1969 Family Law Reform Act. This legislation stated that a child could consent to medical or surgical treatment on attaining the age of 16 years, but said nothing about whether younger children had the ability to consent. Mrs Gillick lost her case since the Law Lords ruled that certain children aged under 16 can make legally valid, informed, competent decisions. Court of appeal cases in 1991–92 have questioned this ruling, which is still under review. One possible service implication of conceptualising children as patients in their own right would be for them to be seen on their own. Indeed where services treat children, rather than discuss them, parents are sometimes excluded, as in hospitals and at dental services. Perhaps this exclusion relates to professional fear of parental distress and intervention.

Older children and young people are commonly reported as finding health services impersonal or irrelevant. Long experience of being accompanied to health services, or of being talked about, may render the transition to going on their own difficult, as is discussed in a study of 649 15-year-olds in London.[30] A general point is made from another study of extreme cases which noted how young people (aged 18 to 25 years) with physical handicaps were unused to speaking for themselves, or to being treated as the person responsible for their own health care.[42] Young people's health problems may also seem to them, and to doctors, to fall outside medical remits.[28] The problems of surviving the complexities of growing up, combined with socioeconomic problems, may take priority over consulting with minor conditions that some adults would deem worthy of medical attention. There are no adequate data for young people on the incidence of perceived ill-health, and of rates of consultation with a range of advice sources, including social networks, as well as, or instead of, doctors.

Young people are likely to value confidentiality and a sympathetic hearing. Overwhelmingly, the sample of 15-year-olds in London[30] mentioned above thought they should be able to see the GP confidentially (91 per cent), but only 37 per cent felt confident that their GP could be relied on to be understanding.

In general it is probable that providing user-friendly, confidential sources of information, help and comfort leads to high usage, which in turn gives one indication of the kind of service children want. For example, the Childline telephone line received 91,000 calls in its first three and a half years. A Bullying Line set up for three months in 1990 logged 7,600 calls and a Boarding School Line set up for seven months in 1991 after allegations of child abuse at a school led to 10,315 calls.[43] Advisory centres are popular with young people. Each year the Brook Advisory Centre reports visits from over 17,000 people under the age of 20.[44] There is no concerted focus, however, on what help children and young people want, where they go for help, and what gaps there are in formal and informal provision.

3.8 Conclusion

Currently traditional assumptions that responsibility for child health care rests with parents and professionals are being modified by a developing conceptualisation of children as participants in their own right as health-care workers. Nevertheless the interests of parents and the elaborate structure of services for the professional surveillance and care of children remain powerful. Points of overlap and conflict are inherent in the meetings of these three sets of interests and children, parents and professionals must continuously negotiate as satisfactory a compromise at each point as can be reached. Conceptualising the person involved in health care not as a patient (a medical concept emphasising the passive sufferer), but instead as a health-care worker is important. It is important as a principle to inform the provision of services.

Research is teaching adults what children know and think about health and health care, though we have little data so far on their experiences and evaluations of services. Research evidence also points to the practical efficacy of involving people, including children, in their own health care, in terms of their health-status prospects. This applies both as regards ill children and as regards the maintenance and promotion of good health. A recent WHO paper has suggested that it may be productive to involve young people in the planning and management of primary health services, and in provision too, for instance as discussants and counsellors.[45] The same points may be made regarding school health services. A study on accident prevention has pointed to the usefulness to policy-makers of taking account of the views of children, teenagers and adults on the causes of accidents in their area and on ways of preventing them.[46]

This chapter has noted that in general children's access to health care services and resources is limited, and the school health service has an important part to play, potentially, since it is more readily accessible. Data on children's experiences of health services mainly relate to hospital stays and severe conditions. Health services are not always either appropriate for people at different points in their lives (children, young people, adults) or responsive to individual need. This raises the question whether children are best served by services whose sensitive responsiveness allows for adequate provision for all-comers, or by services designed for different groups. In the United States, for instance, there is a long tradition of services provided for specific age/stage groups: such as children and adolescents. The parent (if wealthy or with appropriate health insurance cover) takes the child first to a paediatrician and later to an expert in adolescent medicine (interestingly the philologists have not yet proposed a name for this expert). This move is complemented by medical identification of particular conditions, storms and stresses seen as intrinsic to adolescence.[47] The division of services according to age may be seen as medical empire-building or as important for the provision of expert and appropriate care.

Whether one provides universalist, all inclusive services, or separate services by age and condition, there are likely to be both positive and negative outcomes. Grouping people according to predetermined categories can be one means of controlling them but can be effective in locating and treating conditions. Not dividing them can lead to insensitivity and inappropriate services, but can allow for flexibility, continuity of care and patient satisfaction in being treated as a whole person. It is critical here to understand children's experiences and evaluations of services and resources. These understandings should lead to provision of appropriate services and resources which respond to the concerns of children and young people for their social and psychological, as well as physical health, so that children can benefit maximally from them. In this regard the usefulness of the Children Act 1989 has been a focus for debate. Widely welcomed initially as a basis for increasing the participation of children in decisions that materially affect their lives, more recently it has been criticised as offering more in the way of responsibilities for parents than rights for children.[48]

References

1. Children's Rights Development Unit. *UK Agenda for Children.* CRDU (London 1994).
2. Department of Education and Science. *The Parents' Charter: You and Your Child's Education.* DES (London 1991).
3. Stacey M. The health service consumer: a sociological misconception. In M. Stacey (ed.). *The Sociology of the NHS.* Sociological Review Monograph 22, University of Keele, Staffordshire (1976).
4. Hall DMB (ed.). *Health for All Children.* 2nd ed. Oxford University Press (1991).
5. Foucault M. *The Birth of the Clinic.* Tavistock Publications, (London 1976; first published in France, 1963).
6. Armstrong D. *The Political Anatomy of the Body.* Cambridge University Press (1983).
7. Mayall B and Foster M-C. *Child Health Care: Living with Children, Working for Children.* Heinemann (Oxford 1989).
8. Newson J, Newson E and Barnes P. *Perspectives on School at Seven Years Old.* Allen and Unwin (London 1977).
9. Rosenbaum M and Newell P. *Taking Children Seriously: A Proposal for a Children's Rights Commissioner.* Calouste Gulbenkian Foundation (1991).
10. *Children Act 1989.* HMSO (London 1989).
11. La Fontaine JS. Introduction. In La Fontaine JS (ed.). *Sex and Age as Principles of Social Differentiation.* ASA Monograph 17. Academic Press (London 1978).
12. James A and Prout A (eds). *Constructing and Reconstructing Childhood: Contemporary Issues in the Sociological Study of Childhood.* Falmer Press (London 1990).
13. Roche S and Stacey M. *Overview of Research and the Provision of Utilisation of Child Health and Services in the Community. Update V.* Department of Sociology, University of Warwick (1993).
14. Backett K and Alexander H. Talking to young children about health: methods and findings. *Health Education Journal,* **50** (1), 1991, 34-8.
15. Mayall B. Keeping healthy at home and school: it's my body so it's my job. *Sociology of Health and Illness,* **15** (4), 1993, 464-87.
16. Williams T, Wetton N and Moon A. *A Picture of Health: what do you do that makes you healthy and keeps you healthy.* Health Education Authority (1989).
17. Wilkinson SR. *The Child's World of Illness: The Development of Health and Illness Behaviour.* Cambridge University Press (1988).
18. Prendergast S and Prout A. Some reflections on pupil knowledge as a resource in parenthood and family life education. In: *Childhood.* Open University Press (Course PE631) (Milton Keynes 1985).
19. Harding G. Adolescence and health: A literature review. In: Smith M and Harding G. *Health Education and Young People.* Thomas Coram Research Unit Occasional Paper No.9, TCRU (London 1989).
20. Michell L. *Growing Up in Smoke.* Pluto Press (London 1990).
21. Lees S. *Losing out.* Hutchinson (London 1986).
22. Daykin N. Young women and smoking: sociological perspectives explored. Paper given at BSA Conference, 1991.
23. Graham H. Women's smoking and family health. *Social Science and Medicine,* **25** (1), 1987, 37-56.
24. Nash W, Thruston M and Baly M. *Health at School: Caring for the Whole Child.* Heinemann Medical Books (London 1985).
25. Eiser C, Eiser JR and Lang J. Scripts in children's reports of medical events. *European Journal of Psychology of Education.* **IV** (3), 1989, 377-84.
26. Best R, Ribbins P and Jarvis C with Oddy D. *Education and Care: The Study of a School and its Pastoral Organisation.* Heinemann Educational Books (London 1983).
27. Royal College of General Practitioners. *Healthier children - Thinking Prevention.* RCGPs (London 1982).

28. Bewley BR, Higgs RH and Jones A. Adolescent patients in an inner London practice: their attitudes to illness and health care. *Journal of the Royal College of General Practitioners,* **34**, 1984, 267,543-6.

29. Mayall B. *Negotiating Health: Children at Home and Primary School.* Cassell (London 1994).

30. Brannen B, Dodd K, Oakley A and Storey P. *Young People, Health and the Family.* Open University Press (Milton Keynes 1994).

31. Woods R. Somewhere to turn. *Nursing Times.* November 1987, 40-2.

32. Kitzinger J. Who are you kidding? Children, power and the struggle against sexual abuse. In: James A and Prout A (eds). *Constructing and Reconstructing Childhood.* Falmer Press (Basingstoke 1990).

33. Mitchell A. *Children in the Middle.* Tavistock (London 1985).

34. Alderson P. *Choosing for Children: Parents' Consent to Surgery.* Oxford University Press (1990).

35. Alderson P. *Children's Consent to Surgery.* Open University Press (Milton Keynes 1993).

36. Silverman D. *Communication and Medical Practice.* Sage (London 1987).

37. Bluebond-Langner M. *The Private Worlds of Dying Children.* Princeton University Press (1978).

38. Oswin M. *Holes in the Welfare Net.* Bedford Square Press (London 1978).

39. Oswin M. *Am I Allowed to Cry? A study of bereavement amongst people who have learning difficulties.* Souvenir Press (London 1991).

40. Beuf AH. *Biting off the Bracelet: A study of children in hospitals.* University of Pennsylvania Press (1979).

41. Mayall B. *Keeping Children Healthy.* Allen and Unwin (London 1986).

42. Bax M. Young disabled adults: their needs. *Children and Society,* **4** (1), 1990, 64-9.

43. La Fontaine JS. *Bullying: The Child's View.* Calouste Gulbenkian Foundation (London 1991).

44. Brook Advisory Centre. *Annual Reports for 1989, 1990, 1991.* Education and Publications Unit, Brook Advisory Centre (Birmingham 1989, 1990, 1991).

45. WHO. *Young People's Health: A Challenge for Society.* Technical Reports Series 731. WHO (Geneva 1986).

46. Roberts H. Accident prevention - a community approach. *Health Visitor Journal,* **64** (7), 1991, 219-20.

47. Gallagher JR. *Medical Care of the Adolescent.* 2nd ed. Appleton-Century-Crofts (New York 1966).

48. Hendrick H. *Child Welfare: England 1872–1989.* Routledge (London and New York 1994).

4 Children's physical development

Chris Power

Key points

- The proportion of all babies born live in England and Wales weighing less than 1,500 grams (g) increased from 0.84 per cent of all live births in 1983 to 0.93 per cent in 1991.

- The proportion of all births weighing 3,500 g and over also increased during the 1980s.

- Increases in mean birthweight are evident in all social classes.

- The average height of British children increased throughout the period 1972–90.

- Among English and Scottish school children, weight-for-height increased between 1972 and 1990 except in English boys.

- The prevalence of overweight British young adults also increased.

Interest in the physical development of children comes from a wide range of disciplines. Epidemiologists, nutritionists and other health professionals use physical measures as indicators of health and nutritional status. Physical measurements are particularly attractive to these investigators because they are relatively easy to obtain, while other indicators of child health are, in general, more problematic. As a result, physical measurements are also used by economists, demographers and historians to investigate long-term changes in social, economic and demographic structures of the population.

This diversity of interest has ensured that the physical development of British children has been reasonably well documented. Height and growth have been studied most extensively. More recently, information on birthweight and weight-for-height has been gathered since these are regarded as of increasing importance. While a more detailed overview would include other measures of physical development, such as puberty, this chapter focuses on the birthweight, height and growth, and weight-for-height of British children. Although this is necessarily brief, it highlights interrelationships between important influences.

4.1 Birthweight

Birthweight is a marker of growth *in utero* and is associated with subsequent growth and adult height (as described in section 4.2). As discussed later in Chapter 6, birthweight is also the most powerful predictor of infant survival and is strongly related to morbidity.[1] Consequently it can be regarded as one of the most valuable indicators of the nation's health currently available. It is therefore important to monitor changes in birthweight and to examine associated influences.

In Britain, the first large national studies to record birthweight were birth surveys conducted in 1946,[2] 1958,[3] and 1970.[4] Information on low birthweight live births in England began to be collected by the Department of Health in 1953, and for stillbirths in 1955. It was not until 1975 that birthweight information for all live births was routinely collected in England, Wales and Scotland. Levels of birthweight recording in England and Wales rose steadily until 1983, when data were available for over 99 per cent of livebirths.

The strong relationship between birthweight and infant mortality is demonstrated in Figure 4.1 for singleton live births in England and Wales in 1989–91. In contrast to a mortality rate of 3 per 1,000 live births in babies weighing between 4,000 and 4,399 g, there were 652 deaths per 1,000 live births in babies weighing 500–799 g. The relationship between birthweight and infant mortality persists when neonatal and postneonatal deaths are examined separately. In 1989–91, 44 per cent of all babies born live in England and Wales weighing under 1,000 g died in the first 28 days of life compared with less than two in every 1,000 live born babies weighing 3,000 g or more.[5]

4.1.1 Trends over time

Trends in birthweight since 1958 are indicated in Table 4.1, using national data from the 1958 and 1970 birth cohort studies and from OPCS statistics for England and Wales in 1986. These data show a small increase in the median, but in 1970 there was a lower mean, 10th and 90th percentile than in 1958 or 1986. While this information is limited it suggests a fluctuating trend in birthweight prior to 1986.

Figure 4.1 Smoothed infant mortality rate and birthweight distribution, singleton livebirths: 1989–91 combined, England and Wales

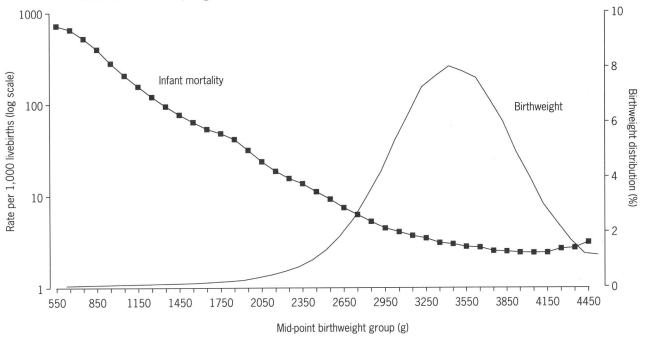

Source: OPCS unpublished data

Table 4.1 Measures of birthweight over time, England and Wales

	Birthweight (g)		
	1958	1970	1986
50th percentile	3,306	3,317	3,347
10th percentile	2,690	2,665	2,684
90th percentile	3,965	3,960	3,975
Mean	3,315	3,302	3,318

Sources: Butler NR, Bonham DG, *Perinatal mortality*[3]
 Chamberlain R et al, *British Births 1970. Vol 1: The First Week of Life*[4]
 Alberman E, *Journal Royal Society Medicine*[7]

A more consistent pattern occurs in the period since 1983 for England and Wales. Figure 4.2 shows that the small proportion of babies of very low birthweight (less than 1,500 g) has increased from 0.84 per cent of all live births in 1983 to 0.93 per cent in 1991. Among other factors, this has been attributed to an increase in the proportion of triplets and higher order multiple births; changes in clinical perception which may have shifted the reported outcomes from non-registrable miscarriages to registered births; and a decrease in the proportion for whom birthweight was not reported which were likely to have been of low weight.[6] Data for Scotland are consistent with those for England and Wales. Indeed they suggest that the proportion of very low weight births has been increasing since 1975.

Of far greater importance numerically are births weighing 3,500 g and over. Figure 4.2 also shows that proportionately this group has shown a steady increase in recent years. In Scotland 34 per cent of births in 1975 weighed 3,500 g or more compared with 41 per cent in 1991. This represents an improvement because birthweights over 3,500 g have the lowest infant mortality rates (Figure 4.1). Increases in mean birthweight are evident in all social classes and there is some suggestion these may be more marked in lower social classes. When examined by country of birth of mother, however, the trend is absent in the Caribbean group.[7]

4.1.2 International comparisons

Trends in birthweight for England and Wales and Scotland have been compared with those for the other countries taking part in the International Collaborative Effort (ICE) on Infant Mortality.[8–10] Birthweight data for singleton live and still births show striking differences between countries: Norway and Sweden have the highest median birthweights, followed by US whites, Bavaria, Scotland, England and Wales, and then Japan and US blacks (Figure 4.3). Within several countries, but particularly in the USA, median birthweight has increased; surprisingly, however, it has fallen consistently in Japan. (These trends may, in part, reflect changes in the definition of a live birth, but not all of the trend is likely to be explained by this.) Hence, with the exception of Japan, the relative position of different countries has remained remarkably stable during the 1970s and 1980s.

International comparisons are hindered by methodological constraints, many of which arise from demographic and ethnic differences in the shape of the birthweight distribution in different populations. It is difficult, therefore, to select an appropriate cut-off in order to compare 'low birthweights'. Furthermore, the data are necessarily limited in that they do not, for example, take account of relevant factors such as gestational age and parity. Even so, only a small number of countries have

Figure 4.2 Proportion of livebirths with very low birthweight (< 1500 g) and heavier birthweight (< 3500 g): 1975-91, England and Wales and Scotland

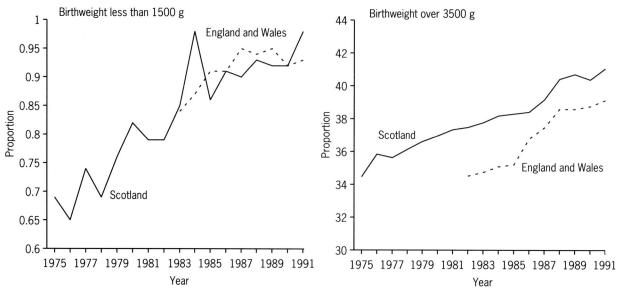

Source: Mortality Statistics - perinatal and infant: social and biological factors 1983-91
Scottish Health Service Common Services Agency.

Figure 4.3

Median birthweight (g) for singletons, live plus stillbirths, for selected countries: 1970-88

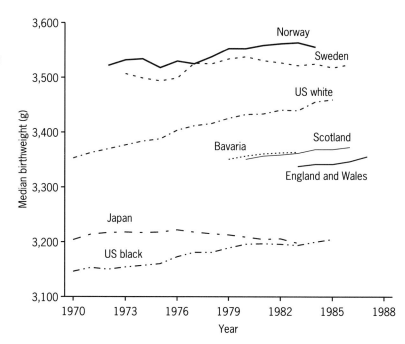

Source:
Alberman E. Journal Royal Society Medicine [7]

the quality of data that allow them to participate in the collaborative effort thus far.

4.1.3 Factors influencing birthweight
Birthweight is influenced by various genetic and environmental factors, many of which are documented in an extensive literature.[11] Figure 4.4 summarises relationships that are well known and others that are suspected but not necessarily proven. Inevitably it is an over-simplification, especially in respect of intergenerational influences, but such an overview is needed, given that the discussion in the text is necessarily limited.

For several factors there are national data which indicate the direction and magnitude of associations. Data for England and Wales on births inside marriage in 1989 demonstrate, for example, that first births are 130 g lighter on average than second or later births, and that births in Social Class V are 100 g lighter than in Class I (Table 4.2). Unfortunately, routinely available data are limited in several respects: for example, country of birth is increasingly becoming a poor indicator of ethnic origin, and data are incomplete in respect of several influences shown in Figure 4.4, particularly data on birth order outside marriage and gestational age for live births.

Table 4.2 Mean birthweight and percentage low birthweight by sociodemographic factors for live births: 1989, England and Wales

	Livebirths		Birthweight less than 2,500 g	
	Mean (g)	Number	%	Number
All groups	**3,319**	**687,725**	**6.5**	**44,978**
Multiplicity				
Singleton	3,340	672,202	5.5	37,034
Multiple	2,389	15,523	51.2	7,944
Maternal age				
Under 18	3,205	15,869	8.5	1,360
18–19	3,223	39,674	8.1	3,231
20–24	3,283	185,239	6.8	12,670
25–29	3,343	242,822	5.9	14,348
30–34	3,357	145,320	6.3	9,089
35–39	3,336	49,465	7.1	3,533
35 and over	3,333	58,801	7.3	4,280
40–44	3,322	8,845	8.1	712
45 and over	3,277	491	7.1	35
Marital status				
within marriage	3,347	501,921	5.9	29,824
outside marriage	3,242	185,804	8.2	15,154
Parity within marriage				
0	3,273	199,766	7.3	14,667
1	3,403	182,111	4.7	8,630
2	3,402	78,056	5.0	3,923
3 and over	3,354	41,988	6.2	2,604
Social class within marriage				
I	3,385	42,650	4.8	2,060
II	3,377	129,480	5.1	6,600
IIIN	3,369	49,850	5.9	2,950
IIIM	3,338	169,720	6.4	10,860
IV	3,306	65,230	6.8	4,430
V	3,285	22,560	7.7	1,730
Country of birth of mother				
UK	3,331	607,228	6.4	38,660
Irish Republic	3,362	6,561	6.1	397
Australia, Canada, New Zealand	3,388	2,772	5.4	150
New Commonwealth and Pakistan	3,152	49,532	9.3	4,604
Bangladesh	3,095	5,085	9.4	480
India	3,066	8,830	11.1	980
East African Commonwealth	3,061	6,742	11.7	787
Rest of Africa	3,259	4,721	8.3	392
Caribbean Commonwealth	3,180	4,032	10.6	427
Mediterranean Commonwealth	3,319	2,511	4.7	117
Remainder New Commonwealth	3,247	5,362	6.1	327
Pakistan	3,164	12,249	8.9	1,094
Remainder of Europe	3,348	9,488	5.6	528

Sources: *Mortality statistics - perinatal and infant: social and biological factors 1989*
OPCS unpublished data.

Figure 4.4 Main factors influencing birthweight: summary of inter-relationships

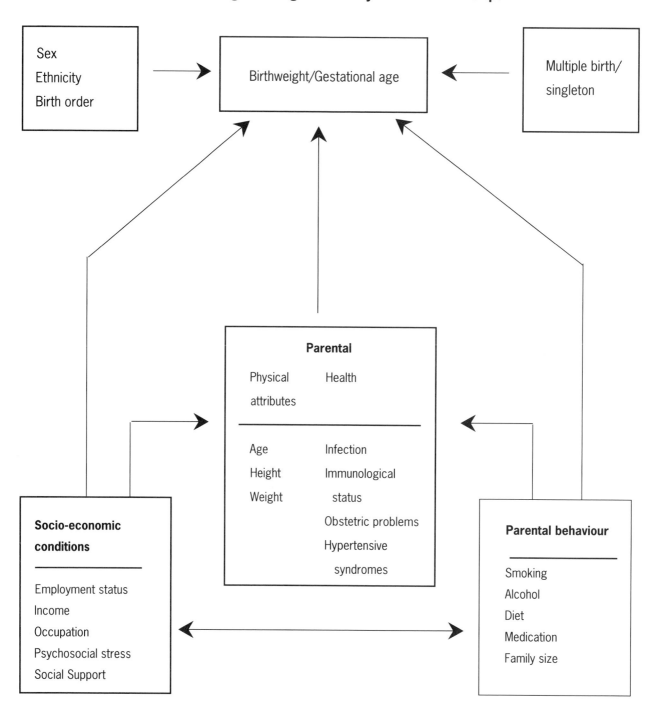

Some information is, however, available from the birth cohort studies, most recently for the 1970 birth cohort. Table 4.3 shows that birthweight increased with gestational age (from 1,404 g on average for births less than 30 weeks gestation to 3,441 g for those 42 weeks or more); with maternal height (from 3,163 g in women under 5 ft 2 in to 3,414 g in those 5 ft 5 in and over), and within non-smoking mothers (3,200 g for current smokers and 3,376 g for those who had never smoked). Birthweight decreased with increasing number of cigarettes smoked: from 3,307 g on average for women smoking less than five cigarettes per day to 3,144 g for smokers of more than 15 a day.[12] These results confirm those reported from the 1958 birth cohort. Although it is now over 20 years since the birth studies were undertaken, the relative importance of different influences remained fairly stable for the period they covered.[13,14]

Table 4.3 Summary of selected factors associated with birthweight* in the 1970 birth cohort

	Mean (g)	Number
Gestation (weeks)		
<30	1,404	80
30-33	1,996	150
34-37	2,828	1,007
38-41	3,369	10,899
42 and over	3,441	1,442
Maternal height		
Under 62 in	3,163	3,089
62–64 in	3,311	5,941
65 in and over	3,414	4,427
Smoking		
Now	3,200	5,478
Never	3,376	5,471

* Restricted to singleton births and mothers who were certain of their last menstrual period date.

Source: Chamberlain R et al, *British Births 1970. Vol 1: The First Week of Life*[4]

Interpretation of the associations presented above is complicated by interrelationships between the different factors. For example, family size is related to socioeconomic group, maternal age and height; ethnicity is also associated with socioeconomic circumstances.

Given this, it is not altogether clear when a particular factor has an important independent effect. Efforts directed at disentangling the evidence, however, lead to some general conclusions. For example, birth order is considered to be quite important in determining the population distribution of birthweight, while maternal age is likely to be less so.

Maternal height has been shown to have an important effect on birthweight. This represents genetic influences to some extent, but, as Figure 4.4 suggests, it also represents the sum of social and environmental influences such as diet during the period in which the mother grew-up. Maternal *in utero* exposure may also have important implications for birthweight in the following generation, as suggested by a study of the effects of the Dutch famine of 1944–5: mothers exposed to famine during their first and second trimester *in utero* had offspring with birthweights lower than mothers not exposed to famine.[15] Some investigators propose a direct intergenerational influence of birthweight, that is between the birthweight of the mother and the birthweight of her children, although others argue that such an effect is small.[16]

Ethnicity-related influences have been difficult to investigate in Britain in the absence of data which would allow its effects to be disentangled from those of other (e.g. socioeconomic) influences. Thus evidence mainly derives from other populations. In the USA, for example, an investigation of racial differences in birthweight showed increasing mean weights across black, mixed and white race babies even after known sociodemographic factors had been taken into account.[17]

In contrast, the effect of maternal smoking on birthweight has been investigated in large population samples in Britain. Since the 1950s when smoking was considered in such studies, its influence has become well-known; increasingly it is recognised as having an independent and important effect on birthweight. One recent study suggests, for example, that smoking during pregnancy accounts for a wide range of other suggested influences on birthweight (after adjustment for sex, maternal height and parity), including relationships with alcohol and caffeine intakes, socioeconomic factors, psychosocial influences and social support.[18]

Such studies argue for an important causative effect of maternal smoking but various questions concerning this remain. First, the diets of smokers are known to differ substantially from those of non-smokers, as demonstrated in large population-based surveys[19] and specifically in studies of pregnant women.[20,21] Mothers who smoke eat fruit much less frequently, meat somewhat less and fish and green vegetables slightly less frequently than mothers who do not smoke. Mothers who smoke also take more drinks (in particular tea), and take much more sugar with drinks.[22] It cannot be discounted therefore that dietary differences could explain part of the association between smoking and birthweight.

Second, even though independent statistical effects of socioeconomic circumstances and psychological factors are not apparent after allowing for smoking habits, this begs the question of which factors precede others in the causal sequence. Abundant evidence exists, particularly for women living in poor socioeconomic circumstances, that smoking behaviour cannot be separated from the circumstances in which women live.[23] Data from a large national survey show differences in maternal behaviour according to whether partners were unemployed or at high risk of being so.[24] Similarly, other psychosocial stresses may promote adverse maternal behaviours and thereby influence birthweight.[25,26] Hence, any assessment of the effects of maternal behaviours such as smoking, should acknowledge (as Figure 4.4 attempts to do) interrelationships with socioeconomic conditions.

The interrelationship between social and biological factors also affects studies of growth during childhood and so will be discussed further in the next section. Such interrelationships lead to controversy, not just in research on determinants of birthweight, but also in the debate concerning the influence of birthweight on adult disease and mortality.[27,28] In order to resolve such issues it will be necessary to have information from a variety of sources monitoring national trends in birthweight and associated factors, which can investigate changes in circumstances and behaviour and their impact on disease and mortality.

4.2 Height and growth

As with birthweight, there is support for using anthropometric measures such as height as markers of child health. It has been stated that 'a child's growth rate reflects, perhaps better than any other single index, his state of health and nutrition; and often indeed his psychological situation also'.[29] Research suggesting that height is predictive of adult mortality raised the prospect of it being an indicator of future health as well as that in childhood.[30,31] Increasingly, therefore, height has been used as an overall index of child health in both developed and developing countries, although recently this practice has been questioned. Meanwhile, there has been considerable interest in monitoring the changes in height among British children.

There has been no routine data collection by government agencies on the height of British children but several large population samples have been studied in recent years. Unfortunately, there were no similar samples of preschool children.

Anthropometric measurements for schoolchildren were first obtained from national samples in the follow-ups of subjects enrolled in the birth surveys of 1946, 1958 and 1970. The data are representative of births in a particular week in those years. The surveys were not initiated specifically for the study of growth but amongst the information collected were height and weight measurements at ages 4, 6, 7, 11 and 14 for the 1946 study;[2] ages 7, 11, 16 for the 1958 (adult heights are also available for each of these cohorts);[32] and ages 5 (height only), 10[33] and 16 for the 1970 study.[34]

In contrast, the National Study of Health and Growth (NSHG) was designed specifically to monitor growth in 5–11 year-old children and it covered a more recent period (1970s and 1980s).[35–42] Areas in England and Scotland were selected according to the level of unemployment, uptake of free school meals and proportion of children who left school by age 15, so that the sample could be weighted towards poorer areas. The social class distribution of the achieved sample, however, resembled that for England and Wales. Measurement of this sample commenced in 1972. A further sample representing the poorest sectors of the community (inner city wards with a high proportion of Afro-Caribbean and Indian born individuals) was included in 1983.

For older schoolchildren, aged 10/11 and 14/15, heights and weights were surveyed in a dietary survey in 1983;[43] while 16–19 year olds were measured in OPCS surveys in 1980[44] and 1986/7.[45] The latter two surveys used comparable methods and they provide details of factors associated with height and weight. Inevitably their usefulness for studying changes over time is limited by the length of the intervening time period.

4.2.1 Trends over time

Evidence on changes in male height among military recruits in their late teens and early twenties is available from the mid-eighteenth century in Britain and Ireland. Although height appears to have increased there have been irregularities and interruptions in this progression.[46] From the turn of the century, however, the trend for adult height has been increasing with little suggestion of sudden changes in rate of progress[47] and it is likely that this would have been reflected in children's heights. Even so, the gradient for adults appears less steep in recent years, particularly for women, with the result that the heights of men and women have tended to diverge since World War II. Adult heights were shorter on average in lower social classes and showed no appreciable improvement relative to higher classes since the turn of the century.

More recent data from the NSHG have been examined to estimate trends in height for schoolchildren aged 5–11 years between 1972, 1979 and 1986.[40] The design of this study facilitates comparison over time. Over the period 1972–9, height increased by 0.5 cm on average for English boys and girls, and 1.1 cm and 0.9 cm respectively for Scottish boys and girls (after adjusting for age) (Table 4.4). The trend in increasing height has continued to 1990.[42]

Data collected in the NSHG allows the investigators to relate these trends to changes in factors associated with height. It was estimated that about 50 per cent of the trends in height observed for 5–11 year olds between 1972–9 were accounted for by decreases in family size, with some contribution from increases in parental height and from birthweight (Table 4.4). Hence, the results are suggestive of a causal effect of family size, but because not all concurrent changes can be monitored in such studies the evidence is not conclusive. The effect of family size is likely to be indirect, possibly acting through its influence on diet.

Changes in the heights of older age groups are apparent from a comparison of OPCS surveys of British adults in 1980 and 1986/7.[45] The average height of young women (aged 16 to 24 years) increased from 161.6 to 163.2 cm over the period, but among young men it remained similar (175.3 and 175.2 cm respectively) (Table 4.5).

Secular increases in height of children and adolescents have been reported for other developed countries such as Canada,[48] Sweden[49] and Norway.[50] In the latter two countries, the increase has been accompanied by changes in the differences between social classes. Also in the USA, differences in height between poor and non-poor white children aged 6–11 decreased between 1971–5 and 1976–80, although no consistent change in height differences emerged for 1–5-year-olds.[51] For British children there is some evidence of a reduction in class differences in recent years, although this has not been of sufficient magnitude to eradicate height differentials.[47,52]

Table 4.4 Mean increase in height from 1972 to 1979 before and after adjusting for social and biological variables

		Mean increase in height (cm) ± standard error adjusted for area and:					
		(a)	(b)	(c)	(d)	(e)	(f)
		Age	(a)+family size	(a)+social class	(b)+social class variables	(a)+biological variables	(d)+biological variables
English	boys	0.51 ± 0.16***	0.24 ± 0.16	0.52 ± 0.16***	0.27 ± 0.16	0.26 ± 0.14	0.06 ± 0.14
	girls	0.52 ± 0.17**	0.28 ± 0.17	0.49 ± 0.17**	0.26 ± 0.17	0.43 ± 0.14**	0.18 ± 0.15
Scottish	boys	1.11 ± 0.36**	0.67 ± 0.37	1.06 ± 0.36**	0.70 ± 0.37	0.95 ± 0.29**	0.67 ± 0.31*
	girls	0.94 ± 0.35**	0.69 ± 0.36	0.74 ± 0.36**	0.69 ± 0.37	0.60 ± 0.31*	0.44 ± 0.32

All estimates based on more than 1000 subjects, so Normal distribution is appropriate for calculation of *P* values and confidence intervals.
*   *P*<0.05   **   *P*<0.01   ***   *P*<0.001

Source: Chinn S et al, *The Secular trend in height of primary school children in England and Scotland 1972-79 and 1979-86*[40]

Table 4.5 Mean height and BMI in British 16–24 year olds

	Height		BMI			
	Number	Mean (cm)	Number	Mean	% overweight (BMI 25–30)	% obese (BMI over 30)
Men						
1980	1,037	175.3	996	22.2	14	3
1986/7	223	175.2	222	22.9	18	3
Women						
1980	1,105	161.6	1,044	22.3	14	3
1986/7	194	163.2	193	22.9	17	6

Sources: Knight I, *The Heights and Weights of Young Adults in Great Britain*[44]
Gregory J et al, *The Dietary and Nutritional Survey of British Adults*[45]

4.2.2 International comparisons

Comparison of heights between children in the UK and other countries is limited because not all nations have representative population data. For many countries, samples are restricted to a particular location, usually a large urban centre. Nevertheless, an analysis of an extensive collection of height data concluded that European populations are fairly homogeneous.[29] Even so, boys and girls of some nationalities are taller in general (Netherlands, Sweden, Norway, Czechoslovakia, Germany); whilst those from urban areas of Paris, Athens, Naples and Bilbao are shorter on average. Mean heights of UK schoolchildren tend to be intermediate between these extremes and possibly towards the shorter end of the range at particular ages.

4.2.3 Factors influencing height

Height during childhood is associated with many factors, as summarised in Figure 4.5 Again the summary over-simplifies the interrelationships and does not convey the relative importance of different factors. Age is obviously of great importance. Parental height is also regarded as an important influence[36,38,53] which extends beyond childhood to the attainment of full adult stature.[54] The variation in children's heights explained by parental height is not constant, however, differing for example

for ethnic groups.[37] Ethnicity appears to be an important factor for children's heights within England. There are large differences in height with Afro-Caribbean children being 3–4 cm taller on average and other ethnic groups between 0.5 and 3 cm shorter than a predominantly Caucasian sample of English children.[37]

Birthweight and family size are also relatively important influences; height increasing with birthweight but diminishing with increasing family size. Young maternal age, smoking during pregnancy, low social class background and indicators of poor socioeconomic circumstances such as parental unemployment and child in receipt of free school meals are all associated with decreases in height. Such factors show lesser effects in statistical models designed to account for variations in height, when compared with parental height, birthweight and family size, but this partly reflects the position of particular influences in the causal sequence. For example, maternal smoking during pregnancy appears to exert an effect on height of offspring primarily through its influence on birthweight, adding little to the explanation of height once birthweight is accounted for.[55] It would, however, be erroneous to conclude that smoking during pregnancy was unimportant, since we have seen from the previous section that smoking during pregnancy is a salient factor for birthweight.

Figure 4.5 Factors influencing height: summary of inter-relationships

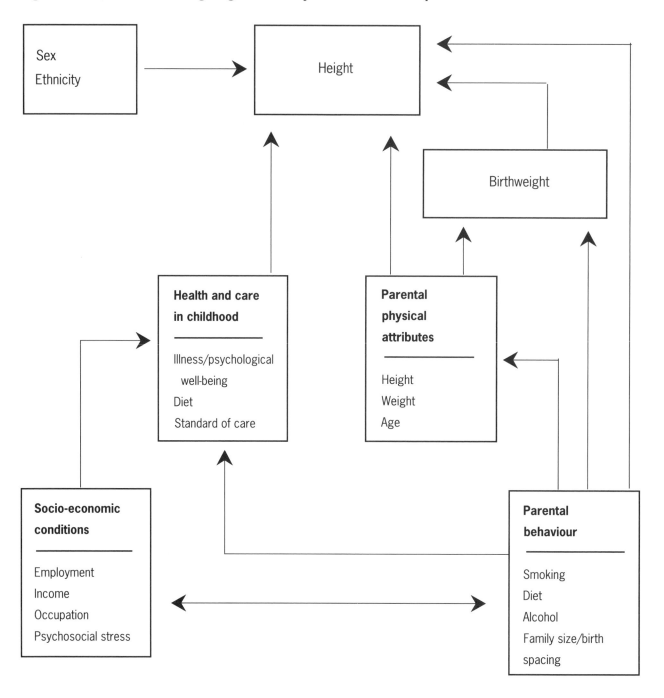

Given this, attempts to apportion the biological and social contributions towards height are problematic and lead inevitably into the genetic versus environment argument. When 'biological' variables (e.g. parental height, length of pregnancy, birthweight and ethnic group) are grouped together they are readily equated with 'genetic', even though such factors as birthweight and parental height result from the combined effect of genes and environment.

While height in childhood is affected by many factors it is also a portent of socioeconomic conditions and health later in life. Young adults of short stature are more likely to be downwardly mobile socially, compared with their taller peers.[56] In British society at least, taller stature appears to be a valued attribute. It is not surprising that parents of short children are choosing to have their children treated, now that it is possible to manipulate

human growth with hormonal therapy. For the majority of short children this may be inappropriate because short childhood stature is not necessarily an efficient predictor of adult shortness.[57] The sensitivity of growth and height as indicators of the range of physical and psychological health in childhood needs to be reappraised. For individual children in developed countries it is not clear that height and health are strongly related except in the case of a few rare illnesses. A child's height reflects, primarily, his parents' height, his birthweight, family size and other socioeconomic circumstances. Even in developing countries, where growth monitoring might be expected to be particularly useful as a screening instrument for malnutrition, infection and risk of mortality, its efficiency is being questioned.[58,59]

Future monitoring of height on a regular and systematic basis should assist in clarifying the influences responsible for the changing size of British children. It may also indicate nutritional status in the population. Overdependence on any single index is likely to be problematic, however, and alternative assessments of child health are needed.

4.3 Weight-for-height

Overweight and obesity have been identified as a public health problem, although it is in later life that the most adverse effects on morbidity and mortality become apparent.[60] Nevertheless, fatness in childhood has attracted considerable interest for a variety of reasons, in particular as a predictor of adulthood obesity in populations and individuals (hence adulthood trends might be detected at an earlier stage), and to identify children at risk of particular (e.g. psychological) detrimental effects in earlier life. These points argue for monitoring weight in British children.

As with height, there has been no routine data collection of childhood weights, although national information is available from the birth cohort studies, NSHG and OPCS/DH surveys in 1980, 1983, and 1986/7. Recently these surveys have been examined to establish whether British children have become fatter over time. While some data are available for skinfold thickness, surveillance of overweight and obesity in large population samples relies, mainly, on an index of weight adjusted for height. A weight-for-height index is commonly used: for adults this is usually the Body Mass Index (BMI) (calculated as wt/ht^2); while for children there are various weight-height indicators depending upon the age studied.[61] Definitions of overweight and obesity rely upon the choice of an arbitrary cut-off, but unfortunately not all studies use the same standard.

4.3.1 Trends over time
We know little about the heights and weights of children in the nineteenth century although it is possible that weight-for-height was lower in the early nineteenth century than a century later.[46] Trends during the 1970s and 1980s have, however, been documented in a recent study.[42] Among English and Scottish school children, weight-for-height and triceps skinfolds increased between 1972 and 1990 (except for weight-for-height in English boys). The increase was more marked from 1982 to 1990 than from 1972 to 1982, and among girls and Scottish children. For English girls the trend is equivalent to an increase in median weight of half a kilogram for a height of 150 cm, less for a shorter girl, while for Scottish girls it varies from 0.5 to 1.7 kg for heights of 110–150 cm. Only a third of the increasing trend appears to be associated with increasing weight of parents and decreases in family size, so most of the increase remains to be explained.

Increases in childhood fatness are evident in other industrialised countries. In Sweden for example, data for urban schoolchildren show an increase in mean BMI (especially for girls) from those born in 1955 to those born in 1967.[62] In the USA, the proportion of white children aged 6–11 years defined as obese, increased by 17 per cent between surveys conducted between 1971–4 and 1976–80.[63]

British data for young adults also suggest recent increases in the prevalence of overweight. Two OPCS studies used standard measurement procedures in 1980[44] and 1986–7.[45] Comparison of these data show a significant increase in mean BMI for men and women, and also an increase in the proportion defined as overweight and obese. Table 4.5 shows that the youngest age group in these surveys was affected by this general trend. Although the proportion of 16 to 24-year-old men with BMI greater than 30 did not appear to increase, a change could be obscured by rounding of small percentage figures. A significant increase in mean BMI was also reported for a study of young adults (mean age approximately 32 years) in England and Scotland 1973–88 for women but not for men.[38] The latter was based on parents of primary school children, however, and may not be entirely representative of the adult population.

Among young male draftees (aged 18–26) in Denmark there appears to have been an increase in obesity (BMI≥ 30 kg/m^2),[64] while data from the USA show a trend towards increasing BMI for women aged 18–24 and 25–34 years between 1960 and 1980, but less pronounced secular changes for men.[65,66]

4.3.2 International comparisons
As with height, there are few national data for weight and weight-for-height which are readily comparable. Hence, attempts to compare data for English children with those from other European countries were limited to studies in particular locations within a country rather than data which are nationally representative. These necessarily crude comparisons do suggest, however, that amongst Europeans the heaviest children are to be found in Athens, Warsaw, and Zagreb; the lightest in Paris (France), Belgium, England, Stockholm (Sweden) and Kormend (Hungary).[29] At 3 years of age English girls are among the lightest for their height; at age 8 English boys are among the lightest for their height.

Even with considerable collaborative commitment, worldwide studies of weight-for-height encounter substantial difficulties. These relate largely to the lack of a standard sampling strategy and differences in measurement techniques. Furthermore, it could be argued that detailed comparison is of limited value when different body shapes and sizes have evolved under particular environmental conditions, such as temperature. Hence comparison of UK children with countries beyond Europe is especially problematic, although countries with populations which are related through common ancestry (e.g. Canada and USA) are exceptions. Unfortunately, one of the most recent comparisons of overweight in Britain and North America uses data for adults.[67] It is noteworthy however, that overweight and obesity were less prevalent in British men compared with US and Canadian men in all ages (20–64 years), while among women overweight and obesity were most prevalent in the British group for age 20–24 years but not in older age groups. Such differences may have developed during childhood but evidence supporting this is lacking.

4.3.3 Factors influencing weight-for-height

A summary of factors suggested as influencing weight adjusted for height is given in Figure 4.6. As with previous summaries it is an over-simplification of numerous interrelationships. It attempts to convey the multifactorial nature of influences since only a limited account can be given here. As with the summaries for birthweight and height (Figures 4.4 and 4.5), environmental factors shown in the figure interact with genetic factors.

One of the main factors associated with children's weight-for-height is their parents' body size. This is illustrated for English and Scottish 5–11 year-olds in the NSHG, especially in the older age children in this age group.[35,42] Observations of parent–child relationships have been used as support for the argument that weight-for-height is mainly inherited. There is continuing controversy surrounding this, and any general statement would seem to be elusive. There are, however, large differences in weight-for-height between ethnic groups. Within Britain, Afro-Caribbean children have similar weight-for-height to Caucasian children but they are thinner than Caucasians in terms of triceps skinfold thickness; whereas Indo-Pakistani children are lighter than other groups.[41]

Figure 4.6 Factors influencing weight-for-height: summary of inter-relationships

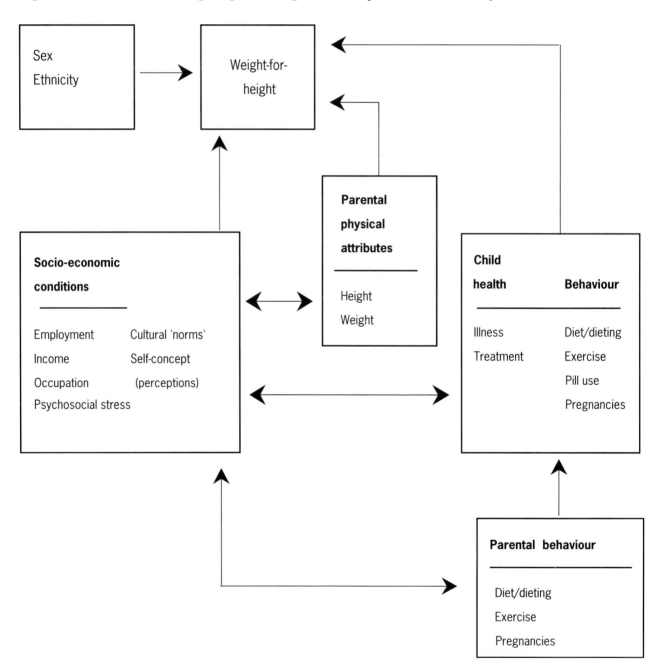

Longitudinal follow-up of British birth cohorts demonstrates the relationship between lower childhood socioeconomic conditions and later life obesity[68,69] but only weak associations are found between such circumstances and weight-for-height in childhood.[35] A possible exception to this is family size: in the NSHG children in larger families were lighter and thinner than children in smaller families.[42] It is interesting that the inverse relationship between social class and obesity in adults reported in Britain and other developed countries is not observed in childhood population samples. This has now been confirmed in several studies: no consistent class differences were shown among school children aged 7 years in the 1958 birth cohort,[69] aged 5–11 years in the NSHG,[35] and ages 10/11 and 14/15 years in a Department of Health survey in 1983.[43] It appears, therefore, that most obesity in lower social classes develops after the ages studied in these samples, but adulthood class differences also reflect the greater persistence of childhood overweight among those with lower class backgrounds.[69]

Table 4.6 shows that heavier weight-for-height among those from manual class backgrounds starts to become apparent by 16–19 years.[44] Generally social class differences in adulthood are more pronounced among women than men. Similar observations in young adults in the USA prompted Flegal and colleagues[65,66] to remark that body weight in young men was less influenced by sociodemographic factors and less subject to social control than was bodyweight in young women. Clearly hypotheses relating social factors to obesity need to accommodate differences in effects for men and women.

Table 4.6 Average BMI by social class for 16–19 year olds

Social class	Men		Women	
	Number	Mean	Number	Mean
I & II	108	21.0	108	21.5
IIIN	60	21.2	59	21.5
IIIM	167	21.9	193	22.1
IV & V	90	21.4	81	22.0

Source: Knight I, *The Heights and Weights of Young Adults in Great Britain*[44]

Many other influences on weight-for-height have been studied. In particular a child's diet influences their weight. Surprisingly, therefore, no consistent correlations between BMI and energy intake were found in the Department of Health survey of 10/11 and 14/15-year-olds.[43] Other research emphasises the social stigma that overweight children experience. In addition, and despite the fact that childhood obesity is a comparatively poor predictor of obesity in later life,[68] overweight children are nevertheless at greater risk of obesity in adulthood. Further understanding of the factors influencing the development of childhood overweight is therefore needed before preventive strategies can be developed.

4.4 Conclusions

Trends in the physical development of British children as represented by birthweight, height and weight-for-height have become apparent in recent years. Recent trends suggest general improvements, on the one hand, in that the proportion of the birthweight distribution associated with lower mortality has been increasing, even though there has been a simultaneous increase in the percentage of very low birthweight babies. Correspondingly, average height has increased throughout the period 1972–90. On the other hand, there appears to be an increasing prevalence of overweight.

International comparisons have been undertaken although these have been less systematic for height and weight than for birthweight. These suggest that while weights of babies born in England, Wales and Scotland are lower than those in selected Scandinavian countries and US whites, they are increasing at a similar rate to those in other countries. Summaries of influences on birthweight, height and weight-for-height serve to illustrate the extent to which similar factors are involved and the interrelationships between these specific measures of physical development. There are some intriguing inconsistencies between birthweight and height; for example, birthweight is higher on average in Scotland than in England and Wales, but average height is shorter in Scotland.

Parental heights and weights appear to be major factors accounting for variation within populations, while other factors such as changes in family size may account for trends over time. Declining family size may affect height through changes in nutrition and care, but possibly also through infection rates. One analysis hypothesised that median age of infection increased with declining family size and that this has been responsible in large part, for the decline in infant mortality since the turn of the century.[70] Clarification of the role of this and other potential influences on physical development is needed.

Each of the physical measures discussed here – birthweight, height and weight adjusted for height – is used as an indicator of child health and, in some instances, as a predictor of health in later life. Further assessment of the extent to which this practice is justified is needed, especially since the implications of these indicators may change over time (for example, the improved survival of low birthweight babies). Over-reliance on any particular measure is likely to be misleading.

References
1. Alberman E. Prematurity: epidemiology, prevalence and outcome. In: Pless I B, (ed.). *The Epidemiology of Childhood Disorders.* OUP (New York 1994).
2. Joint Committee of the Royal College of Obstetricians and Gynaecologists and the Population Investigation Committee. *Maternity in Great Britain.* Oxford University Press (1948).
3. Butler N R, Bonham D G. *Perinatal Mortality.* Livingstone (Edinburgh 1963).

4. Chamberlain R, Chamberlain G, Howlett B and Claireaux A. *British Births 1970. Vol 1: The First Week of Life*. Heinemann Medical (London 1975).

5. OPCS. *Mortality Statistics. Perinatal and Infant: Social and Biological Factors 1991*. Series DH3 no. 25. HMSO (London 1993).

6. Alberman E and Botting B. Trends in prevalence and survival of infants of very low birthweight. *Archives Diseases Childhood*, **66**, 1991, 1304-8.

7. Alberman E. Are our babies becoming bigger? *Journal Royal Society Medicine*, **84**, 1991, 257-60.

8. Alberman E, Bergsjo P, Cole S *et al*. International Collaborative Effort (ICE) on birthweight; plurality; and perinatal and infant mortality. I: Methods of data collection and analysis. *Acta Obstetrica Gynecologica Scandinavica*, **68**, 1989, 5-10.

9. Evans S and Alberman E. International Collaborative Effort (ICE) on birthweight; plurality; and perinatal and infant mortality. II: Comparisons between birthweight distributions of births in member countries from 1970 to 1984. *Acta Obstetrica Gynecologica Scandinavica*, **68**, 1989, 11-7.

10. Centers for Disease Control/National Center for Health Statistics. *Proceedings of the International Collaborative Effort on Perinatal and Infant Mortality*. US Department of Health and Human Services (Hyattsville, Maryland, 1992).

11. Alberman E and Evans S J W. The epidemiology of prematurity: aetiology, prevalence and outcome. *Annales Nestlé*, **47**, 1989, 69-88.

12. Rush D and Cassano P. Relationship of cigarette smoking and social class to birthweight and perinatal mortality among all births in Britain, 5–11 April 1970. *Journal Epidemiology Community Health*, **37**, 1983, 249-55.

13. Peters T J, Golding J, Butler N R, *et al*. Plus ca change: predictors of birthweight in two national studies. *British Journal Obstetrics Gynaecology*, **90**, 1983, 1040-5.

14. Alberman E D. Sociobiologic factors and birthweight in Great Britain. In: Reed D M and Stanley F (eds). *The Epidemiology of Prematurity*. Urban and Schwarzenberg (1977) pp. 145-56.

15. Lumey L H. Decreased birthweights in infants after maternal *in utero* exposure to the Dutch famine of 1944-1945. *Paediatric Perinatal Epidemiology*, **6**, 1992, 240-53.

16. Carr-Hill R, Campbell D M, Hall D M and Meridith A. Is birthweight genetically determined? *British Medical Journal*, **295**, 1987, 687-9.

17. Migone A, Emanuel I, Mueller B, Daling J and Little R E. Gestation duration and birthweight in white, black and mixed race babies. *Paediatric Perinatal Epidemiology*, **5**, 1991, 378-91.

18. Brooke O G, Anderson H R, Bland J M, Peacock J L and Stewart C M. Effects on birthweight of smoking, alcohol, caffeine, socioeconomic factors, and psychosocial stress. *British Medical Journal*, **298**, 1989, 795-801.

19. Whichelow M J, Golding J F and Treasure F P. Comparison of some dietary habits of smokers and non-smokers. *British Journal Addiction*, **83**, 1988 295-304.

20. Haste F M, Brooke O G, Anderson H R, Bland J M and Peacock J L. Social determinants of nutrient intake in smokers and non-smokers during pregnancy. *Journal Epidemiology Community Health*, **44**, 1990, 205-9.

21. Elwood P C, Sweetnam P M, Gray O P, Davies D P and Wood P D P. Growth of children from 0–5 years: with special reference to mother's smoking in pregnancy. *Annals Human Biology*, **14**, 1987, 543-57.

22. Department of Health and Social Security. *Medical Aspects of Food Policy*. Subcommittee on Nutritional Surveillance, 3rd Report. DHSS (London 1987).

23. Graham H. Women's smoking and family health. *Social Science Medicine*, **25**, 1988, 47-56.

24. Golding J, Thomas P and Peters T. Does father's unemployment put the fetus at risk? *British Journal Obstetrics Gynaecology*, **93**, 1986, 704-10.

25. Rutter R D and Quine L. Inequalities in pregnancy outcome: a review of psychosocial and behavioural mediators. *Social Science Medicine*, **30**, 1990, 553-68.

26. Newton R W and Hunt L P. Pyschosocial stress in pregnancy and its relation to low birth weight. *British Medical Journal*, **288**, 1984, 1191-4.

27. Barker D J P and Martyn C N. The maternal and fetal origins of cardiovascular disease. *Journal Epidemiology Community Health*, **46**, 1992, 8-11.

28. Elford J, Whincup P and Shaper A G. Early life experience and adult cardiovascular disease: longitudinal and case-control studies. *International Journal Epidemiology*, **4**, 1991, 833-44.

29. Eveleth P B and Tanner B. *Worldwide Variation in Human Growth*. Cambridge University Press (1990).

30. Marmot M G, Shipley M J and Rose G. Inequalities in death – specific explanations of a general pattern. *Lancet*, **1**, 1984, 1003-6.

31. Waaler HTH. Height, weight and mortality. The Norwegian experience. *Acta Medica Scandinaica*, Supp 679, 1984.

32. Power C. A review of child health in the 1958 birth cohort: National Child Development Study. *Paediatric Perinatal Epidemiology*, **6**, 1992, 81-110.

33. Thomas P W, Peters T J, Golding J and Haslum M N. Weight-for-height in two national cohorts with particular reference to 10-year-old children. *Annals of Human Biology*, **16**, 1989, 109-19.

34. Ekinsmith C, Montgomery S, Bynner J and Shepherd P. The integration of the 1970 birth cohort study and the National Child Development Study. *Intercohort Comparison Working Paper*, 1,1992.

35. Rona R J and Chinn S. National Study of Health and Growth: social and family factors and obesity in primary schoolchildren. *Annals Human Biology*, **9**, 1982, 131-45.

36. Rona R J, Swan A V and Altman D G. Social factors and height of primary schoolchildren in England and Scotland. *Journal Epidemiology Community Health*, **32**, 1978, 147-54.

37. Rona R J and Chinn S. National Study of Health and Growth: social and biological factors associated with height of children from ethnic groups living in England. *Annals Human Biology*, **13**, 1986, 453-71.

38. Guilliford M C, Rona R J and Chinn S. Trends in body mass index in young adults in England and Scotland from 1973 to 1988. *Journal Epidemiology Community Health*, **46**, 1992, 187-90.

39. Chinn S and Rona R J. Secular trend in weight-for-height and tricep skinfold thickness in primary schoolchildren in England and Scotland from 1972 to 1980. *Annals Human Biology*, **14**, 1987, 311-19.

40. Chinn S, Rona R J and Price C E. The secular trend in height of primary school children in England and Scotland 1972–79 and 1979–86. *Annals Human Biology*, **16**, 1989, 387-95.

41. Rona R J and Chinn S. National Study of Health and Growth: social and biological factors associated with weight-for-height and triceps skinfold of children from ethnic groups in England. *Annals Human Biology*, **14**, 1987, 231-48.

42. Chinn S and Rona R J. Trends in weight-for-height and triceps skinfold thickness for English and Scottish children 1972 to 1982 and 1982 to 1990. *Paediatric and Perinatal Epidemiology*, **8**, 1994; 90-106.

43. Department of Health. *The Diets of British Schoolchildren*. RHSS 36. HMSO (London 1989).

44. Knight I. *The Heights and Weights of Young Adults in Great Britain*. HMSO (London 1984).

45. Gregory J, Foster K, Tyler H and Wiseman M. *The Dietary and Nutritional Survey of British Adults*. HMSO (London 1990).

46. Floud R, Wachter K and Gregory A. *Height, Health and History: Nutritional Status in the United Kingdom, 1750–1980*. Cambridge University Press, (1990).

47. Kuh D, Power C and Rodgers B. Secular trends in social class and sex differences in adult height. *International Journal Epidemiology*, **20**, 1991, 1001-9.

48. Shephard R. The Canada Fitness Survey. *Journal of Sports Medicine*, **26**, 1986, 292-300.

49. Lindgren G W and Cernerud L. Physical growth and socioeconomic background of Stockholm schoolchildren born in 1933–63. *Annals Human Biology*, **19**, 1992, 1-16.

50. Brundtland G H, Leistol K and Walloe L. Height, weight and menarcheal age of Oslo schoolchildren during the last 60 years. *Annals Human Biology*, **7**, 1980, 307-22.

51. Jones D Y, Neisham M C and Habicht J-P. Influences on child growth associated with poverty in the 1970s: an examination of HANES1 and HANES11, cross-sectional US national surveys. *American Journal of Clinical Nutrition*, **42**, 1985, 714-24.

52. Rona R J. A surveillance system of growth in Britain. In: Tanner J M (ed). *Auxology '88. Perspectives in the Science of Growth and Development*. Selected papers from the Fifth International Auxology Congress, Exeter UK July, 1988. Smith-Gordon (Nishimura) (London 1989).

53. Goldstein H. Factors influencing the height of seven-year-old children. Results from the National Child Development Study (1958 cohort). *Human Biology*, **43**, 1971, 92-111.

54. Kuh D and Wadsworth M. Parental height: childhood environment and subsequent adult height in a national birth cohort. *International Journal Epidemiology*, **18**, 1989, 663-8.

55. Fogelman K and Manor O. Smoking in pregnancy and development into early adulthood. *British Medical Journal*, **297**, 1988, 1233-6.

56. Power C, Manor O and Fox A J. *Health and Class: the Early Years*. Chapman & Hall (London 1991).

57. Greco L, Power C and Peckham C. Adult outcome of normal children who are short or underweight at age 7 years. *British Medical Journal*, **310**, 1995, 696-700.

58. Van Lerberghe W. Growth, infection and mortality: is growth monitoring an efficient screening instrument? In: Tanner J M (ed). *Auxology '88. Perspectives in the Science of Growth and Development*. Selected papers from the Fifth International Auxology Congress. Exeter, UK. July, 1988. Smith-Gordon (Nishimura) (London 1989).

59. Leung S S F and Davies D P. Anthropometric assessment of nutritional status: a need for caution. In: Tanner J M (ed). *Auxology '88. Perspectives in the Science of Growth and Development*. Selected papers from the Fifth International Auxology Congress. Exeter, UK. July, 1988. Smith-Gordon (Nishimura) (London 1989).

60. Royal College of Physicians. Obesity. *Journal Royal College Physicians*, 1983, 17.

61. Cole T J. Weight/height^p compared to weight/height^2 for assessing adiposity in childhood: influence of age and bone age on p during puberty. *Annals of Human Biology*, **13**, 1986, 433-51.

62. Lindgren G W and Hauspie R C. Heights and weights of Swedish school children born in 1955 and 1967. *Annals Human Biology*, **16**, 1989, 397-406.

63. Gortmaker S L, Dietz W H, Sobol A M and Wehler C A. Increasing pediatric obesity in the United States. *American Journal of Diseases in Childhood*, **141**, 1987, 535-40.

64. Sorenson T I A and Price A. Secular trends in body mass index among Danish young men. *International Journal Obesity*, **14**, 1990, 411-19.

65. Flegal K M, Harlan W R and Landis J R. Secular trends in body mass index and skinfold thickness with socioeconomic factors in young adult women. *American Journal Clinical Nutrition*, **48**, 1988, 535-43.

66. Flegal K M, Harlan W R and Landis J R. Secular trends in body mass index and skinfold thickness with socioeconomic factors in young men. *American Journal Clinical Nutrition*, **48**, 1988, 544-51.

67. Millar W J, Stephens T. The prevalence of overweight and obesity in Britain, Canada and United States. *American Journal Public Health*, **77**, 1987, 38-41.

68. Braddon F E M, Rodgers B, Wadsworth M E J and Davies J M C. Onset of obesity in a 36-year birth cohort study. *British Medical Journal*, **293**, 1986, 299-303.

69. Power C and Moynihan C. Social class and changes in weight-for-height between childhood and early adulthood. *International Journal Obesity*, **12**, 1988, 445-53.

70. Reves R. Declining fertility in England and Wales as a major cause of the twentieth century decline in mortality. *American Journal Epidemiology*, **122**, 1985, 112-26.

5 Health related behaviour

Chris Power

Key points

- Prevalence rates for breast-feeding fall short of current recommendations: only about a quarter of mothers breast-feed four months after birth.

- During childhood, iron deficiencies are common among Asian infants.

- Among adolescents the contribution of fat to energy intake is higher on average than the recommended intake.

- Levels of physical activity decline at around 15 years of age, especially among girls.

- By age 16 to 24 years it is estimated that over a third of men and over half of women do not take regular exercise.

- In 1990, 16 per cent of children in England aged 11–15 were regular or occasional smokers. Comparable figures for Scotland and Wales were 20 and 15 per cent respectively. By late adolescence (age 16–19) 30 per cent of Britain's young people smoke.

- Consumption of alcohol is especially high among young adults: a study in 1989 showed that 26 per cent of 16–17-year-olds and 39 per cent of 18–24 year old men drank more than eight units of alcohol (that is, four pints of beer or the equivalent) on at least one occasion during a one-week period.

- In 1991 there were 9.3 conceptions per 1,000 women in England and Wales aged under 16 and 51 per cent of these ended in abortion.

Many serious diseases in later life are thought to be preventable by improving lifestyles. It is argued that prevention should start in childhood because habits established early on set the pattern, to some extent, of later lifestyles.[1] Some behaviours have more immediate effects in childhood and adolescence. Those that have received particular attention in recent years include diet, physical activity, smoking, alcohol consumption, use of drugs and volatile substances and sexual behaviour. This chapter gives a brief review of current data on these behaviours, in so far as it relates to British children. Drug-taking is also discussed in Chapter 12.

5.1 Diet

5.1.1 Breast-feeding

The importance of diet in early life for child health has been recognised for some time. It is also suspected that early diet may have long-term effects, although less is known about this. Reports of the beneficial effects of breast-feeding have been documented for gastrointestinal and respiratory infections, obesity and mental ability[2-7] although there is some debate about whether the beneficial

effects observed for intellectual development are due to the content of breast milk or, whether physical contact in breast-feeding or other parenting behaviours are responsible.

In 1974 the Panel on Child Nutrition set up a Working Party to review current practices in infant feeding and their effects on infants' well-being. It concluded that mothers should be encouraged to breast-feed their infants preferably for 4–6 months, but at least for the first few weeks of life. It also recommended that the introduction of solid foods before 4 months should be discouraged. These recommendations were repeated in subsequent reports of the Working Party[8] and from the Committee on the Medical Aspects of Food Policy.[9]

5.1.2 Trends over time

Data collected from a series of regional studies in the UK, and shown in Figure 5.1, indicate that the prevalence of breast-feeding at 3 months of age declined from around 50 per cent in 1930 to 10–20 per cent in the early 1970s and then rose rapidly. The resurgence since the early 1970s has occurred in other industrialised countries such as Canada.[10] Surveys of infant feeding have been repeated

Figure 5.1 Breastfeeding at 3 months: 1920-86, England

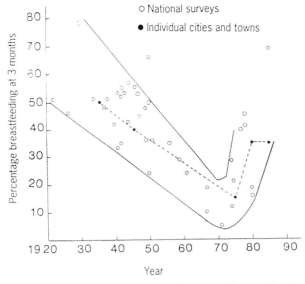

Source: Whitehead et al. Journal of Human Nutrition and Dietetics. 85

in Britain at intervals of five years since 1975: for England and Wales this includes 1975, 1980, 1985 and 1990; for Scotland information is available for each of these years except 1975.

These surveys show an increase in breast-feeding during the late 1970s. For example, 51 per cent of mothers in England and Wales in 1975 breast-fed initially compared with 67 per cent in 1980, but there was no further increase to 1990 when 63 per cent of mothers were breast-feeding their infants.[11] The proportion of mothers breast-feeding declines rapidly in the first few weeks of life: in 1990 the 63 per cent initially feeding declined to 50 per cent at 2 weeks and then to 25 per cent by 4 months. The report suggests that most of the mothers who had given up had done so reluctantly because they had encountered problems.[11]

Feeding of second or later babies mainly reflects the mother's experience with her first baby. Hence, when a decline in breast-feeding among women having their first child was observed in the 1985 survey, it was anticipated that a decline in breast-feeding among women with more than one child would follow in subsequent years.[11] This concern appears to have been substantiated by a local study conducted in Sheffield between 1979 and 1988.[12]

It is also noteworthy that while there was no substantial change in the incidence of breast-feeding for all women surveyed in 1980 and 1985, decreases did occur for particular groups. This was especially notable for women with no partner and for women whose husband's occupation could not be classified.

Factors associated with breast-feeding are mainly social and cultural, with wide disparities occurring by birth order, social class, mother's education, age, region, and smoking behaviour. In 1990, the percentage breast-feeding initially ranged from 69 per cent for first born to 52 per cent for fourth or later born infants; from 86 per cent in Social Class I to 41 per cent in Class V (48 per cent in those with no partner) (Figure 5.2); from 91 per cent in mothers completing their education after age 18 to 50 per cent in those finishing before age 16; from 86 per cent in mothers aged 30 years or more to 39 per cent in those aged less than 20 years; from 74 per cent in London and south eastern England to 50 per cent in Scotland; and from 69 per cent in non-smokers to 46 per cent in those who smoked during their pregnancy.[11]

Trends in the introduction of solid food are also evident from the infant feeding surveys. The proportion of mothers giving solid food before the age of 3 months declined between 1975 and 1980 from 85 per cent to 56 per cent. This trend did not continue; it was 62 per cent in 1985 and 68 per cent in 1990. Most mothers fed their babies with solids, usually cereals or rusks, by 4 months of age and by 9 months babies were given a wide range of foods.

Figure 5.2

Proportion of infants put to the breast at birth and proportions of infants being breast fed at 6 weeks by social class of husband*, Great Britain 1990

■ At birth

▨ At 6 weeks

*As defined by occupation

Source: White A, Freeth S and O'Brien M. Infant feeding 1990.[11]

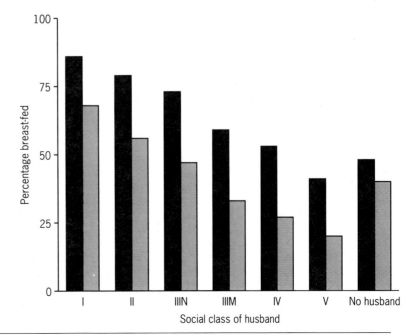

These data alert policy makers to adverse trends in feeding practices for infants. They indicate those groups of mothers whose habits are especially resistant to change and, as shown by the latest survey, some of the obstacles that such women face in starting and maintaining breast-feeding.

5.1.3 Diet after infancy

The importance of diet in early childhood is the subject of some controversy, as, for example, in the possible long-term role of fat intake in early life and over the life course in relation to later cardiovascular disease. Preliminary evidence from Lucas[7] suggests that early diet can affect later rather than current obesity since energy intake at 3 months was not correlated with skinfold thickness at that age but at age 2. Hence the upward trend in obesity, discussed in Chapter 4, might signify early dietary excesses and be associated subsequently with adverse health outcomes. There is a lack of knowledge on the stability of dietary patterns from childhood to adulthood. Consequently the influence of early dietary habits on later life habits cannot be assessed.

Dietary information for individuals is notoriously difficult to obtain. It is not surprising, therefore, that until recently there have been few national surveys attempting to measure diet. The National Food Survey (NFS) monitors the food purchasing habits of private households[13] and because data have been obtained for almost 40 years it provides information on national trends. To some extent the diets of British children are represented by NFS data, although there are large variations at different age groups.

During the 1980s, however, several national dietary surveys were undertaken. At the time of writing these have not included young children between 1 and 10 years of age. Knowledge of dietary habits was particularly scarce for preschool children. (In addition there is the National Diet and Nutrition Survey programme set up in 1992 by the Ministry of Agriculture, Fisheries and Food and the Department of Health. The first survey, carried out in 1992/93, covered children aged 1½ to 4½ in Great Britain. The published results were not available, however, at the time of writing this chapter.)

Information for older children is also limited, although four main surveys establish baseline information from which future trends can be monitored and which indicate current dietary inadequacies. Two of these studies include younger adolescents: first a study of 10-year-olds in 1980, which was part of the second follow-up of the 1970 birth cohort,[14] and second a study on the diets of British school children which included 10/11- and 14/15-year-olds in 1983.[15] The remaining two studies covered older ages, in a study of the dietary habits of 15–25-year-olds in 1982[16] and the nutritional survey of British adults which included those aged 16 and over in 1986–7.[17]

A particularly notable finding of the first two of these surveys was the wide variation in the diets of different social groups. In 1980, 10-year-old children from lower social class backgrounds had poorer diets than those from higher classes in that they reported more frequent consumption of sweets and sweet drinks and less frequent consumption of more healthy foods.[14] This pattern, obtained from a limited food frequency questionnaire, was confirmed by the more detailed dietary recording in the 1983 survey of 10/11- and 14/15-year-olds.[15]

The latter survey revealed that the main sources of energy intake of schoolchildren are bread, chips, milk, biscuits, meat products, cake and puddings.[15] Chips and milk were the two major items of diet that varied most between social groups. Higher median chip consumption was recorded among Social Classes IV and V, children with unemployed fathers, children from families receiving Supplementary Benefit, children taking school meals and those children who ate out of school (for example at cafés). Milk consumption was lower among most of these groups. Hence, children from lower social classes derived a greater proportion of their energy and fat intake from chips.

Apart from showing these differences, the survey suggested that the nutrient and energy intakes of British schoolchildren were adequate, inasmuch as they avoided major deficiency disorders. A potential area of concern was noted, however, in that mean and median iron intakes of girls were below the Recommended Daily Amounts (RDA). Iron deficiency is a matter of concern both in developed and developing countries, although it is in infancy that deficiencies may be particularly problematic. Deficiency has been shown to relate to poor developmental performance[18] which may have long-lasting effects. Local studies suggest that iron deficiency is common among Asian infants in the UK.[19–21]

The surveys of older age groups listed above also suggest that iron intakes are low, particularly among women. In addition it is notable that among the quota sample of 1,015 15–25-year-olds, 43 were 'dieting' and a further 126 were watching their weight.[16] Energy intakes did not reach the RDA but were likely to be generally adequate (the RDAs have a considerable margin of safety and do not represent minimum requirement levels for nutrients) except among a weight conscious group (those perceiving themselves to be overweight, dieters and those 'watching their weight') for whom intakes were low.

In the fourth national survey, the Dietary and Nutritional Survey of British Adults,[17] 3 per cent of men and 12 per cent of women aged 16–24 years, were on a slimming diet. Even so, the report highlighted discrepancies between observed intakes and the COMA recommendation that 35 per cent or less of food energy should be derived from fat. The average for 16–24-year-olds (40.2 per cent for men and 39.8 per cent for women) was similar to that for all ages. Results showed that 16–24-year-olds had the highest average carbohydrate intake but lower vitamin intakes per unit of energy. Data from 7-day weighed records confirmed that iron intakes of young women (median 9.5 mg/day) were low compared with the RDA of 10 mg/day.

Additional information on eating habits in Britain is available from population-based surveys of 11–16 year-olds in Wales[22] and Scotland[23] and 11–18 year-olds in Northern Ireland.[24] It was reported that 65 per cent of the Northern Ireland sample ate fruit and vegetables three or more times a week. The remainder, therefore, ate such foods infrequently. The Scottish survey found that school-age girls in particular were concerned about their weight to the extent that they were either dieting (15 per cent) or thought they needed to diet (30 per cent).[23] International comparisons are difficult to make in the absence of standard methods. However, in a co-ordinated study organised through WHO, Welsh schoolchildren had the lowest proportion of daily fruit consumption and were among the highest daily consumers of chips and snack foods such as crisps and sweets.

In summary, surveys of British children and adolescents suggest that on average they are well nourished, although intake of fruit and vegetables is lower and fat intake higher than is currently recommended. There are wide variations in the diets of British children and a concern remains that some children have deficient diets. It has been argued that British children might benefit from vitamin–mineral supplements, as indicated by performance on intelligence tests. The benefit to children in developing countries is not disputed, but evidence for developed countries is less clear.[25]

5.2 Physical activity

Physical activity and fitness are increasingly recognised as having health benefits. During childhood, it is argued, exercise has positive effects on growth and development, while at older ages protective effects have been documented, particularly for cardiovascular disease, but also in the more effective treatment of diabetes, in protection against osteoporosis and in the reduction of hypertension.[26] Childhood and adolescent exercise habits are of importance because they are associated with habits later in life. This is illustrated in a longitudinal study for a national birth cohort in which physical activity in adolescence was associated with participation in active sports at age 36. Odds of a high level of activity at age 36 were lower for those with below average ability at games during adolescence (0.72) and higher for those with above average ability (1.35) compared with those of average ability.[27] Evidence from a recent National Fitness Survey[28] also suggests that adult participation in sport and recreation is associated with teenage activity levels.

There is little information on children's physical activity and fitness levels from national survey data in Britain. The survey data currently available tend to exclude young children since self-reported activity is obviously not feasible for young children. In order to obtain such information it will be necessary to develop appropriate methods of assessment.

Information on the physical activity of schoolchildren has been collected from population samples in Wales, Scotland, Northern Ireland, and most recently for young people aged 16 and above in England (National Fitness Survey) and Great Britain (General Household Survey).

(a) Wales
The Welsh Health Surveys provide comprehensive information on the physical activity of teenagers. Data on the frequency of physical activity of Welsh 11, 13 and 15-year-olds and similar data for Scotland were found to compare favourably with those for other countries in a WHO health behaviour survey in 1989–90.[29] A less favourable comparison was found for the duration of activity in girls as shown in Figure 5.3. Differences between countries may be due in part, however, to methodological problems inherent in cross country comparisons.[30] The surveys conducted in Wales were repeated and can be used to examine trends in physical activity. Data presented in Figure 5.4 provide support for an increase in frequency of physical activity among teenagers between 1986 and 1988.[22] An increase in vigorous exercise (i.e. four or more hours of activity causing breathlessness or sweating) was also reported for 15/16-year-olds between 1985/6 and 1989/90.[30] It remains to be seen, however, whether these trends can be maintained over a longer period.

Other Welsh survey data for 1985 show the decline of activity with age. Those aged 12–17 were more active than adults although less than half of males and a fifth of females in this age group took vigorous exercise. By age 18–24 more than half of the women were inactive.[31] The most common reasons given by teenagers for not participating in physical activity were work commitments and lack of relevant interesting activities, community facilities, money and personal transport.

(b) Scotland
As mentioned above and shown in Figure 5.3, the physical activity of Scottish schoolchildren has been assessed and included in international comparisons.[23] Another Scottish survey, conducted in 1988, interviewed a sample of 8–18-year-old children.[32] Most children had taken part in sport during the four months preceding interview (96 per cent of boys and 89 per cent of girls) even if walking (2 miles), dancing, and snooker/billiards/ pool were excluded (92 per cent of boys, 85 per cent of girls). Participation among 15–18-year-olds was lower than that of younger children, reflecting the reduction of compulsory physical education at school plus a decline in activity on leaving school.

(c) Northern Ireland
A decline in physical activity with age was also apparent in the Northern Ireland Health and Fitness Survey.[24] This study examined activity patterns in 3,211 children aged 11–18 years. Figure 5.5 shows that boys and girls aged 17–18 years were generally less active than those aged 11–14 years. While 75 per cent of exercise taken was not related to school, physical exercise classes constituted the only exercise taken by one third of pupils. The

Figure 5.3 Percentage of schoolchildren aged 11, 13, and 15 who exercised four or more hours a week outside scho 1989-90, selected countries

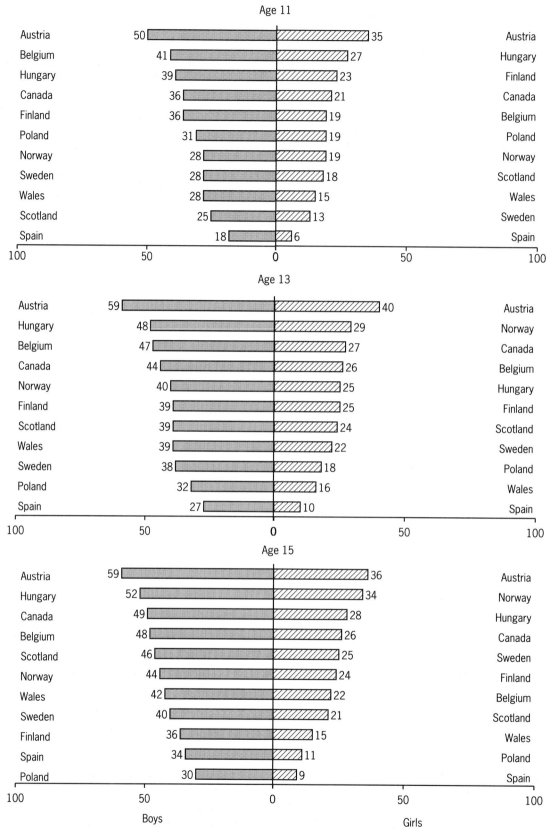

Age 11

	Boys	Girls	
Austria	50	35	Austria
Belgium	41	27	Hungary
Hungary	39	23	Finland
Canada	36	21	Canada
Finland	36	19	Belgium
Poland	31	19	Poland
Norway	28	19	Norway
Sweden	28	18	Scotland
Wales	28	15	Wales
Scotland	25	13	Sweden
Spain	18	6	Spain

100 — 50 — 0 — 50 — 100

Age 13

	Boys	Girls	
Austria	59	40	Austria
Hungary	48	29	Norway
Belgium	47	27	Canada
Canada	44	26	Belgium
Norway	40	25	Hungary
Finland	39	25	Finland
Scotland	39	24	Scotland
Wales	39	22	Sweden
Sweden	38	18	Poland
Poland	32	16	Wales
Spain	27	10	Spain

100 — 50 — 0 — 50 — 100

Age 15

	Boys	Girls	
Austria	59	36	Austria
Hungary	52	34	Norway
Canada	49	28	Hungary
Belgium	48	26	Canada
Scotland	46	25	Sweden
Norway	44	24	Finland
Wales	42	22	Belgium
Sweden	40	21	Scotland
Finland	36	15	Wales
Spain	34	11	Poland
Poland	30	9	Spain

100 — 50 — 0 — 50 — 100

Boys   Girls

Source: From The Health of Canada's Youth, Health Canada, 1992.[29] Reproduced with permission of the Minister of Supply and Services Canada, 1995.

46   *The health of our children*

Figure 5.4 Frequency of participation in games or activities outside school in Welsh school children: 1986-88

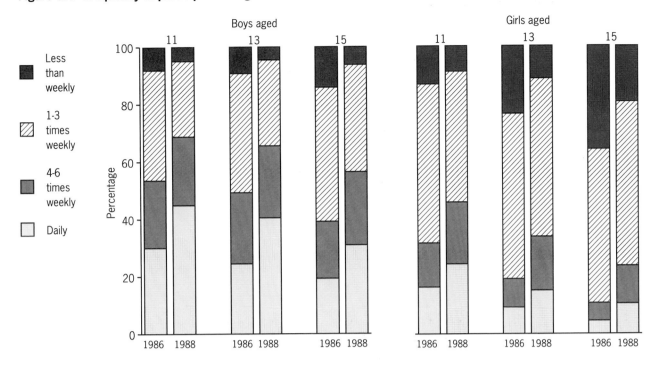

Source: Nutbeam D. Health for all young people in Wales.[29]

**Figure 5.5
Weekly time (minutes) spent
taking exercise: children aged 11-18
by sex and age: Northern Ireland**

········ Boys all exercise

– – Girls all exercise

—— Boys vigorous exercise

—— Girls vigorous exercise

Source: Riddoch C et al. Long term health implications
of fitness and physical activity patterns.[24]

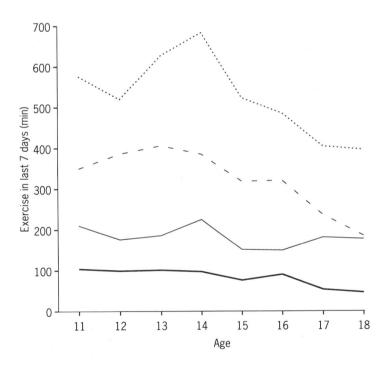

Northern Ireland survey used a battery of tests to assess fitness (flexibility, leg power, trunk/strength/endurance, handgrip strength, and running speed/agility). Fitness of boys, as indicated by these tests, improved appreciably with age but less dramatic changes and in some cases, no improvements were observed for girls. The age trends may be exaggerated, however, by poorer representativeness of the 17- and 18-year-olds in the study compared with that of younger ages.

(d) England
More recently, the National Fitness Survey assessed physical activity and fitness in a random population sample in England during 1990.[28] The sample included young people aged 16–19 years. It was an unusually comprehensive survey in its coverage of physical activity, extending beyond leisure time. Occupational activity, domestic tasks and gardening, brisk walking and cycling were included in addition to sport and recreation. These activities were categorised according to the intensity of effort involved in participation. Intensity ratings were then combined with reports of frequency and duration of activity to identify the five levels of activity given in Table 5.1. Not unexpectedly, the study demonstrated

greater participation in vigorous physical activity in the youngest age group surveyed (16–24-year-olds). Even within this group, however, about a third of men and over half of the women took no regular activity (i.e. an average of three or more occasions a week). Furthermore, only 30 per cent of men and 9 per cent of women aged 16–24 years exercise at a level which is currently regarded as conferring health benefits. Although there is likely to be some inaccuracy in such population estimates of activity (because non-responders may differ from subjects included in the study) the NFS provides the best estimates of activity levels to date for young people in England.

Table 5.1 Activity of 16–24-year-olds in The National Fitness Survey: 1990, England

Activity level (20 min. occasions in past 4 weeks)	Men	Women
	%	%
12+ occasions of vigorous activity	30	9
12+ occasions mixed between moderate and vigorous activity	23	16
12+ occasions of moderate activity	15	22
5–11 occasions mixed between moderate and vigorous activity	14	26
1–4 occasions mixed between moderate and vigorous activity	11	18
None	7	9
Total	100	100

Source: Allied Dunbar, *National Fitness Survey*[28]

(e) Great Britain

Information on physical activity was also recorded in one of the surveys mentioned earlier. Of 1,015 British 15–25 year olds included in a quota sample,[16] 30 per cent reported taking daily exercise, 25 per cent exercised two or three times a week, 15 per cent once a week, 5 per cent less than once a week, 7 per cent once a month and 19 per cent never exercised. The proportion admitting to never taking exercise varied by age and sex. For example, 23 per cent of women and 25 per cent of those aged 22–25 years made this assessment of their activity. Differences by socioeconomic group are also suggested by these data with 10 per cent of the higher (AB) socioeconomic group taking no exercise, compared with 25 in the lowest (DE) group.

All the above surveys focus on physical activity, whereas until recently the General Household Survey (GHS) obtained more general information on participation in leisure activities. These data are available for 16–19 year olds but not for younger children. In the GHS for 1987[33] and 1990[34] there was a change of focus to sports and exercise. This makes the data more pertinent to national physical activity assessment, although only a limited measure is available which differentiates those who were active during a 4-week and 12-month period. The participation in physical activities of 16–19-year-olds appears to be high. Table 5.2 suggests a slight increase

in participation among young women between 1987 and 1990 (the methodological change in 1987 hinders comparison with previous years[33]). Inactivity was more common among women in both years: the majority of men had taken part in at least one sporting activity in the month preceding the interview, while a quarter of women took no activity other than walking. Walking and snooker/billiards/pool were the most common activities (42 per cent and 43 per cent participation in previous month in 1987) followed by darts (22 per cent), cycling (21 per cent), football (21 per cent) and swimming (20 per cent). GHS data show differences in adult participation in sport by social class, with non-manual groups in general having higher rates than manual. It is likely that there are similar social variations among 16–19-year-olds in the sample.

5.2.1 International comparisons

Table 5.2 Participation in sports of 16–19-year-olds: 1987 and 1990, Great Britain

Participation in preceding	Men		Women	
4 weeks				
1987	93	(91)	78	(69)
1990	93	(90)	82	(75)
12 months				
1987	98	(97)	92	(89)
1990	98	(97)	97	(94)

Figures in brackets exclude walking.
Sources: Matheson J, *Participation in Sport. General Household Survey 1987*[33]
General Household Survey 1990[34]

Other countries have attempted national data collection of physical activity and fitness, mostly among teenagers rather than young children. Activity was assessed, for example, in the Canadian Fitness Survey among 10–19-year-olds in 1981;[35] in the US National Children and Youth Fitness Survey of 10–18-year-olds in 1984 (NCYFS I) and of 6–9-year-olds in 1986 (NCYFS II);[36,37] and in the Australian Health and Fitness Survey of 7–15-year-olds in 1985.[38] Methodological differences generally discourage international comparisons in physical activity. An exception is the WHO health behaviour survey in 1989–90 that included data from Wales and Scotland seen in Figure 5.3.

In other countries, as in England, repeat surveys from which time trends can be established have not yet been undertaken. Without these data it is difficult to substantiate claims that children are any less active than they once were. Such data will be necessary for evaluation of public health campaigns which seek to increase physical activity across all age groups.

5.3 Smoking

The health risks of smoking are well recognised. It is now known that adverse effects[33], such as respiratory disorders, are not confined to older ages but are also a concern for young people.[39] Uptake of smoking early in life is particularly problematic because the younger that smokers start the less likely they are to give up. Duration of exposure to the harmful effects of tobacco will thereby increase. This has important consequences, in that risk of lung cancer is related to the length of time of smoking, not just the total exposure: consumption of 20 cigarettes per day for 30 years produces a greater risk than 40 cigarettes per day for 15 years.[40] In addition to the adverse outcomes in adult life, there are more immediate health effects of smoking during childhood. Notable among these are increases in respiratory symptoms and reduced physical fitness.

This section describes childrens' own smoking habits, although it is recognised that adverse health effects are experienced as a result of passive smoking. In contrast to the other health behaviours considered so far, there have been systematic national studies of adolescent smoking. It has been essential to monitor smoking prevalence to identify trends and influences on smoking habits of young people. For younger age groups, data are available for the last decade, while for older adolescents they span a 20-year period. This section will provide only an overview of recent trends and associated influences.

5.3.1 Trends over time

In 1990 the percentage of 11–15-year-olds who reported regular or occasional smoking was 16 per cent in England and 15 per cent in Wales. The prevalence for 12–15-year-olds in Scotland was 20 per cent[41] (regular smoking is defined as usually smoking at least one cigarette a week). Thirty per cent of Britain's 16–19-year-olds were smokers in the same year.[42]

These data derive from separate series of adolescent and adult surveys. Both series indicate time trends although the information is not directly comparable due to differences in methods (e.g. question wording). The OPCS surveys of smoking among secondary school children collected data biennially since 1982.[41,43-46] These data suggest that there was little change in the prevalence of regular smoking between 1982 and 1990 (Figure 5.6). It is encouraging that the percentage of children who tried smoking before the age of 11 decreased from 23 per cent of pupils in England in 1982 to 13 per cent in 1990. Similarly, the Welsh Youth Health Surveys suggest that experimentation with smoking may have decreased between 1986 and 1992, but also show no improvement in the percentage of regular teenage smokers.[47,48]

The adult data series in the GHS,[42] indicates trends in smoking prevalence for 16–19-year-olds since 1972 (data were collected annually to 1976 and thereafter biennially). It is notable that smoking prevalence among this age group declined throughout the period, but less markedly in the 1980s (Figure 5.7). The levels of smoking in women in this age group was no lower in 1990 than in 1980.

Figure 5.6　Regular smoking in children aged 11-15 years: 1982-90, England

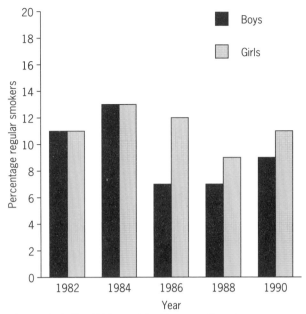

Source: Lader D and Matheson J. Smoking among Secondary School Children in 1990.[41]

Figure 5.7　Cigarette smoking among 16-19 year olds by sex: 1972-90, Great Britain

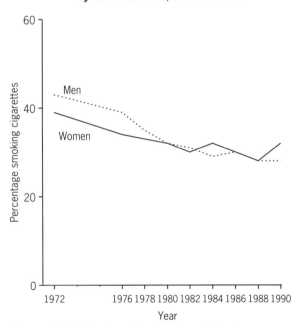

Source: OPCS Monitor General Household Survey: Cigarette Smoking 1972 to 1990.[42]

During the 1970s smoking prevalence was greater among men than women. By the end of the 1980s sex differences in smoking prevalence had disappeared. Although differences were not in general statistically significant in either the 11–15 or 16–19-year-old samples, recent surveys are consistent in showing slightly higher prevalence in young women, the reverse of the pattern observed 20 years ago. Thus, among 16–19-year-olds in 1990, 32 per cent of women smoked compared with 28 per cent of men.[42] Male smokers, however, appear to have heavier consumption levels. For example, in England

11–15-year-old male smokers recorded an average of 37 cigarettes per week compared with 33 recorded by female smokers.[41]

5.3.2 International comparisons

There have been two major WHO collaborative studies of tobacco consumption in children in recent years, mainly including European countries. Scotland and Wales were among those countries providing comparable data for the second cross-national health behaviour survey in 1989–90 referred to earlier.[29] The ages studied were 11, 13 and 15 years. As would be expected, only a minority of 11–year–olds reported smoking at least occasionally (Figure 5.8). As previously reported,[41] prevalence rates for Scotland and Wales were similar. Rates for boys compare favourably with other countries while those for girls are generally less favourable. It is noteworthy that the higher female smoking prevalence mentioned above is also evident in the WHO collaborative study. By age 15, but not at age 11, smoking prevalence was generally higher amongst girls than amongst boys in most of the participating countries. A similar trend has been documented in other industrialised countries, including New Zealand, Australia, USA and the Netherlands.[49]

Figure 5.8 Cross-national comparison of smoking* in school-aged children: 1989-90

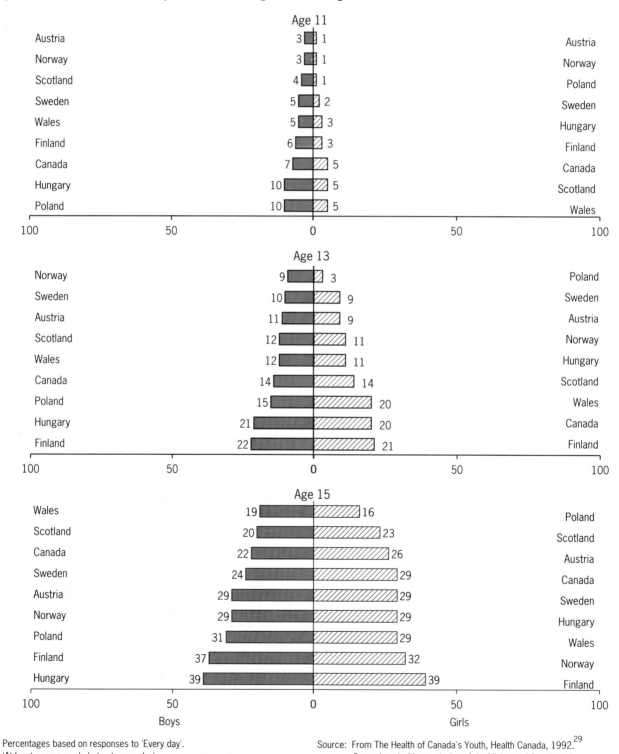

* Percentages based on responses to 'Every day'.
   'At least once a week, but not every day'.
   'Less than once a week'.

Source: From The Health of Canada's Youth, Health Canada, 1992.[29]
Reproduced with permission of the Minister of Supply and Services Canada, 1995.

5.3.3 Factors associated with smoking

Numerous influences on smoking uptake and maintenance have been suggested, ranging from individual characteristics, family, school and peer groups to socioeconomic environment, and availability, price and promotion of tobacco.[39] Age is especially important during childhood, since there are marked increases in prevalence of smoking from ages 11 and 12 when few children smoke (less than 1 per cent and 2 per cent respectively) to age 15 when 25 per cent are regular smokers.[41]

OPCS conducted a longitudinal study of secondary schoolchildren to investigate factors associated with uptake of smoking.[50] The most important factors to be identified were being female, siblings smoking, parents smoking, living in a lone-parent household, low educational aspirations and willingness to identify oneself as a smoker in the future. Negative attitudes towards smoking were also less in evidence among those who became smokers. Other surveys confirm the relevance of such factors to adolescent smoking.[41,42,51] There is also evidence from several surveys that teenagers are more likely to smoke if their best friends do so, although the role of peer group relationships in smoking uptake and maintenance is not clear.[51,52]

A pronounced socioeconomic gradient in smoking is evident among adults, with unskilled manual groups having the highest consumption.[42] Differences in adolescence are less consistent, with some studies suggesting that there are no notable socioeconomic differences in smoking prevalence among schoolchildren.[51] Children from lower social groups, however, appear to smoke more than those in higher classes.[51] By ages 16–19 smoking prevalence is highest among semi-skilled and unskilled manual groups and lowest among professional groups (Figure 5.9) even though the gradient is not as consistent as in older adults. Interpretation of data by socioeconomic groups is, however, particularly problematic for young people because it is based on the occupation of the head of household. Many young people still live at home and are therefore likely to be classified according to another adult's occupation (usually a parent), while others will be the head of their own household.

Price and availability of tobacco also affect consumption levels. It has been shown, for example, that consumption fluctuates with the real price of cigarettes, increasing with a real price decrease and vice versa.[39] The widespread availability of tobacco is demonstrated in the most recent OPCS survey of adolescent smoking.[41] In 1990, 32 per cent of children in England, 45 per cent in Scotland and 37 per cent in Wales, had tried to buy cigarettes in the previous year. Only 15 per cent of those in England had been refused on the last occasion they had attempted a purchase. Comparable data for Wales and Scotland were 14 per cent and 12 per cent respectively.

Advertising targeted on young women may be an important factor in promoting cigarette consumption in

Figure 5.9 Prevalence of cigarette smoking among 16-19 year olds by sex and by socio-economic group of head of household: 1990, Great Britain

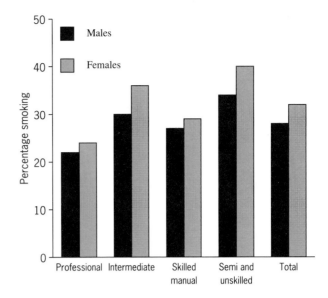

Source: General Household Survey (unpublished data)

this age group. It was estimated that seven million women aged 15–24 were exposed to cigarette advertising even after the introduction in 1986 of voluntary restrictions on advertising in magazines.[53] Young people who are aware of cigarette advertising are at a slightly increased risk of taking up smoking in the future.[50] There is more convincing evidence for imposing tighter restrictions on tobacco promotion. Restrictive legislation in other countries have been shown to reduce consumption.[39]

In 1987 the WHO set a target that a minimum of 80 per cent of Europe's population should be non-smokers by 1995.[54] This reduction in smoking prevalence is now a stated target within England, as detailed in the recent white paper *The Health of the Nation*[55] although the time scale has been extended to the year 2000. The government specifies targets for 11–15-year-olds, among whom it aims to reduce smoking prevalence by at least a third by 1994 (from 8 per cent in 1988 to less than 6 per cent). In Scotland the national policy statement published in 1991 *Health Education for Scotland* has a target for the year 2000 to reduce by 30 per cent, the 12 per cent of smokers aged 12–15 years and 40 per cent of smokers aged 16–19 years. The OPCS survey on why children started to smoke concluded that at least up to the age of 14 or 15 smoking is erratic and probably opportunistic, given that attitudes and behaviour are generally unstable during this period.[50] Therefore, there would appear to be scope for change if there is concerted action to influence tobacco promotion, price and availability of cigarettes to children, as well as health education.

5.4 Alcohol consumption

The basis for concern about alcohol use by adolescents is only in part due to related health consequences. There are other concerns that adolescent drunkenness plays an increasingly important role in social unrest, although this is contested. Whatever the public and political debates surrounding this topic, it is indisputable that alcohol contributes to mortality and morbidity in children and adolescents.

5.4.1 Trends over time

As will be discussed in Chapters 6 and 8, accidents are the major cause of childhood deaths. At the end of the 1970s about a third of accident fatalities in 16–19-year-olds were associated with alcohol. This is likely to be an underestimate of deaths associated with alcohol in this age group because teenagers have more accidents at low blood alcohol levels than adults.[56] Figure 5.10 shows an improvement in alcohol-related mortality between 1980 and 1990 which may in part reflect increased vehicle safety and mandatory seat belt use. It is also possible that there has been a recent decline in drink-driving as suggested by a national survey of drinking behaviour.[57]

Injuries contribute substantially to disability in young people[58] and thereby have lasting health effects. There is only weak evidence, however, that adolescent behaviour will determine later drinking and hence adult health. The period of follow-up has been limited, but overall there appears to be no strong association between adolescent and adult drinking, although heavier and more frequent adolescent drinkers are likely to have heavier drinking levels subsequently.[59,60]

National data from which to establish trends in alcohol consumption in young people are scarce. It was not until 1988 that 16–17-year-olds were included in the GHS; hence trends in these data are limited to young people aged over 18 years.

Adolescent alcohol use was the focus of a separate OPCS survey in 1984[61] and has also been monitored as part of national adolescent smoking surveys.[41,45] Older adolescents are included in adult drinking surveys for England and Wales[57] and in the GHS. It is recognised that these and other survey data underestimate alcohol consumption. At younger ages the problem of deliberate under-reporting is compounded by difficulties of characterising drinking behaviour before patterns have become established.

The prevalence of alcohol use has varied markedly between surveys using different methods. Estimates of drinking were higher in the 1984 adolescent survey, which used a detailed 7-day record, than in the 1990 survey of smoking among secondary school children which relied on more limited data.[41] For example, as shown in Table 5.3, the percentage of 15 year olds who reported that they usually drank alcohol weekly was 41 per cent in the 1984 study and 29 per cent in the 1990 study.

The proportion of young people drinking weekly was shown to increase evenly with age. Less than 10 per cent of 11–12-year-olds reported that they drank alcohol in the survey week, rising to almost 80 per cent of 18–19-year-olds, although the peak occurs around age 20.[57] Table 5.4 shows that at age 16–17 few adolescents were categorised as heavy drinkers. By ages 18–24, however, 20 per cent of men and 5 per cent of women drank at levels which are widely accepted to be detrimental (more than 35 units of alcohol per week for men and more than 25 for women). A further indicator of harmful drinking practice is the amount of alcohol consumed on any one occasion. In 1989, 26 per cent of 16–17–year–old men and 39 per cent of 18–24-year-old men reported drinking more than 8 units of alcohol (4 pints or the equivalent in other drinks) on at least one occasion during the preceding week; among females 18 per cent and 25 per cent of 16–17 and 18–24-year-olds respectively reported drinking more than 6 units[57] Thus there are pronounced differences in drinking patterns between men and women.

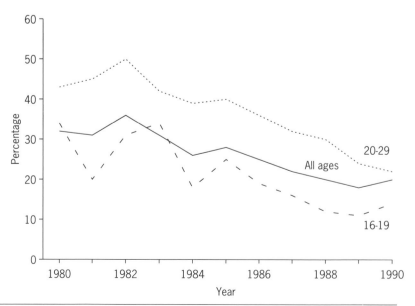

Figure 5.10
Drivers of cars and other motor vehicles: percentage of fatalities in excess of 80mg/100ml blood alcohol level by age: 1980-90, Great Britain

Source: Road Accidents Great Britain 1990[83]

Table 5.3 Reported drinking among 13-15 year olds: comparison of 1984 survey of adolescent drinking in England and Wales and 1990 survey of schoolchildren's smoking in England

	Age					
	13 years		14 years		15 years	
	1984	1990	1984	1990	1984	1990
Proportions usually drinking weekly	15	9	26	19	41	29
Proportions never drinking	24	38	13	20	10	12
Proportions saying their most recent drink was last week	29	18	40	32	56	40
Mean units (SAUs) per drinker last week	6.8	3.4	9.7	5.1	12.9	6.9
Proportions of recent drinkers drinking 15 or more (SAUs)	10	4	17	6	27	11
Bases						
All pupils	*538*	*602*	*638*	*598*	*735*	*660*
*Pupils drinking last week**	*300*	*74*	*415*	*130*	*549*	*183*

* Excluding no answer to amount drunk.

Source: Lader D and Matheson J, *Smoking Among Secondary School Children in 1990*[41]

Table 5.4 Type of drinker among 16-17 and 18-24 year olds by sex: 1987 and 1989 combined, England and Wales

	Age	
	16–17	18–24
	%	%
Men		
Non-drinker	10	6
Drinks sometimes, but not last week	27	10
Recent drinker		
light (1–20 units)	50	51
moderate (21–35 units)	9	13
fairly heavy (36–50 units)	1	10
very heavy (51+ units)	2	10
Base = 100%	*180*	*553*
Women		
Non-drinker	9	7
Drinks sometimes, but not last week	28	19
Recent drinker		
light (1–14 units)	56	57
moderate (15–25 units)	6	10
fairly heavy (26–35 units)	1	2
very heavy (36+ units)	1	3
Base = 100%	*184*	*647*

Source: Goddard E, *Drinking in England and Wales in the late 1980s*[57]

5.4.2 International comparisons

Drinking behaviour of 11, 13 and 15-year-olds in Wales and Scotland was compared with that in other countries as part of the 1989–90 WHO health behaviour survey mentioned earlier.[29] Of the participating countries, shown in Figure 5.8, Wales had the highest proportion of respondents who had tasted alcohol, who drank weekly, and who admitted to being drunk on at least one occasion. In general, rates for Scotland were also comparatively high.

5.4.3 Factors influencing consumption

It is well documented that most adolescent drinking takes place with parents and in the home.[51] In addition, alcohol is generally associated with many adolescent and early adulthood social activities. It is, in part, related to social background, although this is not straightforward: experimentation and regular drinking appear to be more common in adolescents from higher socioeconomic groups than in those from lower socioeconomic backgrounds; whereas the trend reverses for high consumption levels.[51] As with smoking, there is evidence to suggest that alcohol consumption is influenced by price, availability and to some extent advertising.[56]

Employment experiences appear to be relevant in adolescence: unemployment of six months or more was significantly associated with an increased risk of heavier drinking among men in the 1958 birth cohort study.[63] Probably the most important moderating influence on the heavier drinking behaviour of older adolescents and young adults is the formation of stable partnerships and families.[64]

An association between adolescent drinking and smoking behaviour has been demonstrated in national survey data, such that the more frequently children drink, the greater the likelihood that they also smoke regularly.[41,51] In England in 1990, for example, only 8 per cent of regular smokers reported that they never drank at all, compared with 55 per cent of those who had never smoked. Whereas 43 per cent of regular smokers drank once a week or more often, only 5 per cent of those who had never smoked did so.[41]

5.5 Volatile substance abuse

The number of deaths associated with the abuse of volatile substances (VSA) is a continuing cause of concern. A

Figure 5.11
Volatile substances abuse mortality rates for 15–19-year-olds by sex: 1983-91, United Kingdom

■ Males

▨ Females

Reproduced with permission of
St George's Hospital Medical School

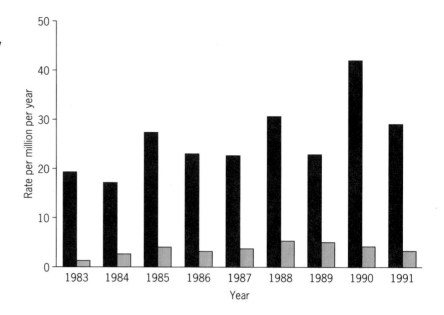

dataset compiled at St Georges Hospital Medical School covers deaths since 1971 associated with the deliberate inhalation of volatile substances.[65] Their information is provided from three main sources: OPCS, HM Coroners, and press clippings agencies. They have collected data in a systematic way since 1983. In the period to the end of 1991, a total of 1,239 deaths had been identified. These deaths comprise an important proportion of all deaths in young people as death from any cause in this group is rare. Seventy three per cent of these VSA deaths were to those aged under 20. Taking into account the population at risk Figure 5.11 shows the mortality rates for the 15–19 age group by sex. In 1990 there was a substantial increase in the mortality rate for males aged 15–19. In 1991 there was a lower rate, although it was still the third highest rate recorded for this age group.

5.6 Teenage sexual behaviour

This section summarises the relevant national data on teenage sexual behaviour, including contraceptive practice, fertility and abortion. Changes in the sexual behaviour of young people have been discussed briefly in Chapter 2. Public and political concern about teenage sexual behaviour has traditionally centred on adolescent pregnancy. The literature cites several associated detrimental effects, such as an increased risk of abortion, low birthweight and behavioural and educational problems in the offspring. It is often assumed, however, that teenage pregnancy is problematic. It has been argued that there is a confusion of concepts particularly between pregnancies to women aged under 20, unplanned pregnancy, unwanted pregnancy and pregnancies to unmarried or unsupported women.[66] There are important correlates of teenage pregnancy, such as lack of prenatal care, poor socioeconomic circumstances and single marital status which may in part account for some of the adverse outcomes generally attributed to bearing a child during the teenage years.[67]

In recent years interest in teenage sexual behaviour has increased with the knowledge that HIV infection can be transmitted heterosexually. Teenagers are thought to be a key factor in the heterosexual epidemic, but not because they are particularly promiscuous or irresponsible about protection.[68] Rather, adolescence is important because it is a period of experimentation and vulnerability in seeking a partner, although it is also recognised as a stage when sexual behaviour can be influenced.[68]

HIV/AIDS and sexual health were identified as main target areas for the government's health strategy for England in *The Health of the Nation*.[55] This document states that the incidence of gonorrhoea (providing an indirect indication of HIV/AIDS trends) should be reduced by at least 20 per cent between 1990 and 1995 and that the rate of conceptions amongst those aged under 16 should be reduced by at least 50 per cent between 1989 and 2000. Hence sexual health, particularly that of teenagers, is likely to retain a high profile in the near future.

There are few sources of data on teenage sexual behaviour which are from representative population samples. Recently, however, several important studies have been conducted. In 1990 there were surveys of teenage sexual behaviour in both Scotland[69] and England.[70] In both countries similar proportions of 15–16-year-olds reported having experienced sexual intercourse: 30 per cent in Scotland and 31 per cent in England. The English survey, covering ages 16–19, showed increasing sexual activity to age 19, when 70 per cent reported having had sexual intercourse.[70] Just under half (47 per cent) of sexually active 16–19-year-old men reported having had sex with one partner over the preceding 12 months, compared with 70 per cent of women; while 17 per cent and 4 per cent respectively reported having had sex with four or more partners over the 12 month period.[70]

The National Survey of Sexual Attitudes and Lifestyles was also undertaken during 1990–1991.[71,72] It covered the UK and included adolescents aged 16–19. Although the main results had not been published when this chapter was written, the feasibility survey suggests that marked generational changes in sexual attitudes and behaviour have occurred. For example, median reported age at first intercourse was four years younger for women aged 16–24 years than for those aged 45–59 years. Data from the National Survey of Sexual Attitudes and Lifestyles will provide a basis against which future changes in behaviour can be measured. Meanwhile evidence for change in some sexual behaviours is indicated by data on contraception and fertility.

5.6.1 Contraception

From the 1960s onwards access to contraceptives increased for all ages, but particularly for young people. It is difficult to establish how teenage contraceptive behaviour was affected by changes in access since early surveys on contraceptive use did not include those aged under 18 years. Initially this was the case when the GHS obtained information on contraception in 1983.[73] Subsequently, however, the 1986 and 1989 GHS covered 16–19-year-old women.[74,75] These data show that about a quarter of 16–17-year-old women and half of 18–19-year-olds were using contraception (Table 5.5). The pill was the most common method of contraception in both age groups, being used by 19 per cent and 39 per cent respectively in 1989, although condom use appeared to be increasing, possibly in response to the first major AIDS prevention publicity campaign, combined with concerns about side effects of the pill. According to the GHS, only a minority of 16–19-year-olds in 1989 (less than 3 per cent) were exposed to an unplanned pregnancy because they were not using contraception, but in the absence of information on whether contraceptive methods were used consistently, this can be regarded as an underestimate. Lack of contraception was found to be a major factor in unintended pregnancies among teenagers in England and Wales.[76]

Table 5.5 Contraception use among 16–19 year-old women: 1983–89, Great Britain

	Age (in years)	1983	1986	1989
			Proportions using method	
Currently using at least one method	16–17	-	27	23
	18–19	50	50	52
Current use – pill	16–17	-	20	19
	18–19	43	42	39
Current use – condoms	16–17	-	6	6
	18–19	5	6	12
Base nos	*16–17*	-	*352*	*307*
	18–19	*328*	*317*	*318*

Source: *General Household Survey 1983, 1986, 1989*[73-75]

5.6.2 Fertility

Conception rates for England and Wales are published annually by OPCS.[77] They derive from birth registrations and abortion notifications (miscarriages are not included due to poor data ascertainment) based on estimated year of conception. Overall there has been a decline in teenage conception rates between 1969 and 1991, but as Figure 5.12 shows, this has not been a steady decline and fluctuations have occurred. After a period of decreasing rates between 1970 and 1976 there was an increase to 1979, at least among 16–19-year-olds. This was followed by another decline and thereafter a rise, mainly among older adolescents. In 1991 the conception rate for under 16-year-olds in England and Wales was 9.3 per 1,000 women aged 14 and 15, and for under 20-year-olds it was 65.1 per 1,000 women aged 15–19.[77] Most teenage conceptions were outside marriage and, as in older women, conceptions outside marriage represent an increasing proportion of all conceptions (Table 5.6).

Table 5.7 shows that teenage fertility varies within the UK (rates are based on birth registrations but do not

**Figure 5.12
Conception rates for teenage women: 1969-91, England and Wales**

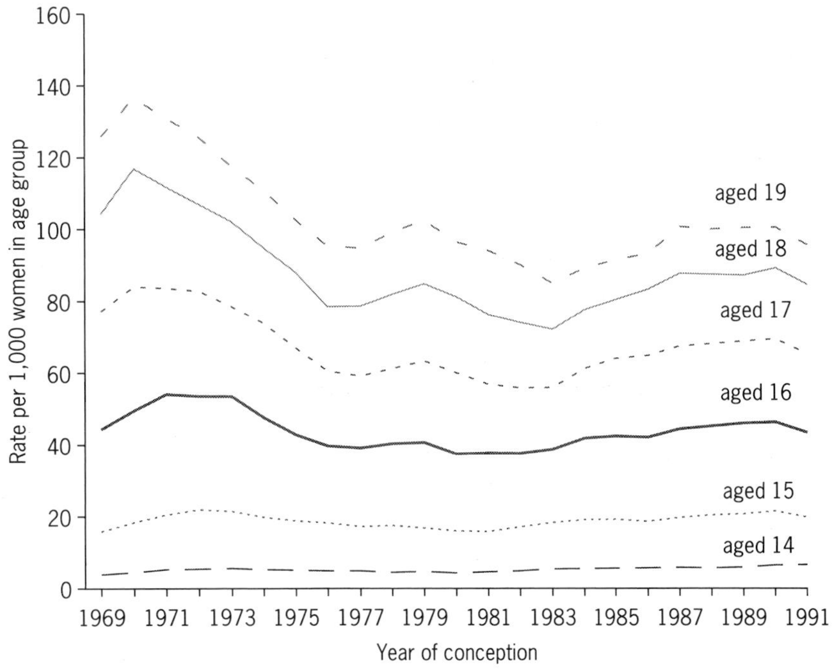

Source: OPCS

Table 5.6 Outcome of conceptions inside and outside marriage by age of women at conception: 1979-91 (selected years), England and Wales

	All ages					Under 20					Under 16				
	1979	1984	1989	1990	1991	1979	1984	1989	1990	1991	1979	1984	1989	1990	1991
All conceptions															
Base number (thousands)	774.1	790.1	864.7	871.5	853.7	120.9	118.2	117.5	115.1	103.3	9.1	9.6	8.4	8.6	7.8
Percentage conceived:															
Inside marriage	74	67	58	57	56	27	17	11	10	10	0	0	0	0	0
Outside marriage	26	33	42	43	44	73	83	89	90	90	100	100	100	100	100
Percentage leading to:															
Maternity	84	83	80	80	81	70	67	64	64	66	45	44	48	49	49
Legal abortion*	16	17	20	20	19	30	33	36	36	34	55	56	52	51	51
Conceptions inside marriage															
Base number (thousands)	570.6	526.8	499.2	494.4	480.2	32.2	20.4	12.4	11.3	9.9	0	0	0	0	0
Percentage leading to:															
Maternity	92	93	92	92	92	96	96	95	95	95	0	0	0	0	0
Legal abortion*	8	7	8	8	8	4	4	5	5	6	0	0	0	0	0
Conceptions outside marriage															
Base number (thousands)	203.5	263.4	365.6	377.1	373.5	88.8	97.9	105.1	103.8	93.4	9.1	9.6	8.3	8.6	7.8
Percentage leading to:															
Maternity outside marriage	37	47	53	55	57	34	46	54	55	57	38	41	47	48	48
Maternity inside marriage	23	16	10	9	9	26	14	7	6	5	7	3	1	1	1
Legal abortion*	40	37	36	36	34	40	40	39	39	38	55	56	52	51	51

* Legal termination under 1967 Abortion Act.

Source: OPCS, *Birth Statistics 1990, 1992*[77]

Table 5.7 Fertility rates per 1,000 women aged under 20[1] for selected countries: 1966-91 (selected years)

Country	1966	1976	1986[2]	1991[3]
United Kingdom	47	33	30	33
England	47	32	30	33
Wales	49	39	36	39
Scotland	46	35	31	33
Northern Ireland	36	33	30	29
France	27	23	12	9
West Germany	34	20	9	13
Italy	26	31	11	9
Spain	11	25	25	11
Irish Republic	14	22	17	17
Denmark	50	23	10	9
Netherlands	22	11	5	6
Belgium	32	27	16	12
Sweden	50	25	11	13
Australia	49	36	22	22
Canada	48	33	24	26
USA	71	54	52	63
Japan[4]	3	4	4	4

1. Rates for women aged under 20 years of age are based upon the population of women aged 15-19.
2. Where 1986 figures are not available, figures for most recent year are given: 1980 for Spain, 1983 for Belgium, 1984 for Italy and Australia, 1985 for France, Japan, West Germany, Canada and USA.
3. Where 1991 figures are not available, figures for the most recent year are given: 1988 for Belgium.
4. For Japan 1965 figures are given in place of 1966 which was an exceptional year.

Sources: EUROSTAT, Luxembourg; Council of Europe, Strasbourg; INED, Paris, national publications for Netherlands, Sweden, Australia, USA and Japan; OPCS; *Population Trends*[78]

include abortions). The overall rate of 33 births per 1,000 teenage women in 1991 is lower than that for the USA in the same year (63 per 1,000) but it is generally higher than that for other industrialised countries, especially Japan (Table 5.7). Most industrialised countries have experienced a decline in teenage fertility. This has been more dramatic in some countries such as Sweden and the Netherlands, than in others.[78]

5.6.3 Abortion

Prior to the Abortion Act in 1967 it was recognised that illegal abortions were performed although it is not known what proportion of teenage pregnancies were affected. Immediately following the introduction of the Act there was a rapid increase in the number of legal terminations performed, which was generally thought to reflect at least in part, a replacement of previously illegal terminations.[79] Since then, the increase in the abortion rate has been less dramatic among the under 16 year olds.[80] The increase among older adolescents (16–19 years) is more marked, resembling that for women in their twenties, and thus it is not unique to the adolescent group. As shown in Table 5.6, over the past decade in England and Wales approximately one half of all conceptions to women aged under 16 ended in a legal termination, while the proportion for those aged under 20 was approximately one third.

There is a wide range in abortion rates for women aged under 20 in different industrialised countries (Table 5.8). In 1987 the rate for Scotland (14 per 1,000 women) was lower than that for England and Wales (20.9) but several other countries, notably Italy, Japan and the Netherlands, had markedly lower rates (6.4, 5.8 and 4.2 per 1,000 respectively).

Table 5.8 Legal abortion rates for women aged under 20 and all women, for countries for which data or estimates are available

Country/year	Rate per 1,000 women	
	Women aged under 20[4]	All ages
Australia (1988)	19.5	16.6
Canada (1987)	15.2	10.2
Czechoslovakia (1987)	22.5	46.7
Denmark (1987)	15.7	18.3
England & Wales (1987)[1]	20.9	14.2
Finland (1987)	15.4	11.7
Hungary (1987)	26.1	38.2
Italy (1987)[1]	6.4	15.3
Japan (1987)[2]	5.8	18.6
Netherlands (1986)	4.2	5.3
New Zealand (1987)	13.2	11.4
Norway (1987)	22.1	16.8
Scotland (1987)[3]	14.0	9.0
Singapore (1987)	16.7	30.1
Sweden (1987)	21.5	19.8
United States (1985)	45.7	28.0

1 Residents only.
2 True rates are higher because many abortions are unreported.
3 Including residents of Scotland who obtained abortions in England and Wales.
4 For women aged under 20, the rate is computed per 1,000 women aged 15-19.

Source: Alan Guttmacher Institute, *Induced abortion: a world review*[84]

Within Britain the increase in the abortion rate coincides with a shift in attitudes among the public and medical profession in favour of legal abortion.[80] Some commentators suggest, however, that younger and vulnerable women are more likely to have late abortions because of the difficulties they experience in finding their way through the system involved in obtaining an abortion.[79]

A reduction in the adverse effects of teenage sexual behaviour, namely unwanted pregnancy and sexually transmitted infection, requires change across many social influences. In a recent report the Royal College of Obstetricians[81] identified four major areas as influencing reproductive behaviour: ethical standards based on culture and religion; attitudes to sexuality in the home during childhood, at school and in the community as a whole; the status of women in their roles as workers and at home; and the availability and effectiveness of methods of controlling fertility. As the numerous recommendations of the report suggest, some of these influences are amenable to change. It is likely that the emergence of AIDS will be an important factor providing the impetus for change. One recent development is that surveys of sexual behaviour have now been conducted in several countries. Results from these studies and the National Survey of Sexual Attitudes and Lifestyles in the UK will provide important new data on teenage sexual behaviour.

5.7 Discussion and conclusions

Recent national data suggest that for a substantial proportion of the population changes in behaviour might result in health benefits. Not all lifestyles influencing health in childhood and beyond have been described in this chapter. There are other harmful behaviours such as drug-taking (see Chapter 12) which are also important. It is most important to recognise, however, that in general, the lifestyles described here reflect those of the adult population. They are, furthermore, not unique to British children and adolescents but are concerns in many industrialised countries.

Most but not all lifestyles examined show marked differences between social groups. That the socioeconomic environment exerts an influence during early life may not be surprising, but its role is no less important because of this, especially since life-time habits and later health may also be affected. Few lifestyle factors are easily measured and many are notoriously difficult to measure with accuracy. This in part accounts for a lack of national data on topics such as preschool diet and physical activity of young children. Not surprisingly, therefore, it is only for a limited number of behaviours that data are available to indicate trends over time. In recent years, however, there have been several attempts to rectify data inadequacies and omissions, for example the major new surveys of physical activity and sexual behaviour (which include older adolescents). In some instances, such as the Welsh Youth Health Surveys, this has been achieved in co-ordination with other countries. While difficulties in cross-national comparisons are somewhat inevitable,[30] further efforts to develop a common approach within Britain should improve information on child adolescent health-related behaviour.

From the available data, this brief review indicates that improvements and deteriorations in childhood and adolescent lifestyles are in evidence. For some factors the long-term consequences are now recognised while for others there is speculation rather than empirical support for long-term effects. Further clarification of relationships is therefore important before preventive strategies can be justified.

This is not to deny that for some behaviours, such as adolescent smoking, the need for preventive measures is beyond dispute and clearly, knowledge of harmful effects should be provided to children through health education. It is not sufficient, however, to rely solely on health education in some instances. The HEA survey of 9–15-year-olds suggests that there is a high awareness of risks of smoking (both active and passive) but that awareness of risk is not always a deterrent against smoking.[51] Recent theories to explain health behaviour recognise that other influences operate in addition to the acquisition of knowledge, although there is no unifying theory.[82] The achievement of change through health education may therefore be limited, and social and political solutions are also required.[39] Many behaviours examined here show marked differences between social groups. Early socioeconomic and cultural forces are likely to extend beyond childhood, contributing to life-time habits and later health.

References

1. Coronary Prevention Group. *Should the Prevention of Coronary Heart Disease Begin in Childhood?* Coronary Prevention Group (London 1989).
2. Howie P W, Stewart-Forsyth J, Ogston S A, Clark A and Florey C D. Protective effect of breast feeding against infection. *British Medical Journal*, **300**, 1990, 11-16.
3. Kramer M S. Do breast feeding and delayed introduction of solid foods protect against subsequent obesity. *Journal Pediatrics*, **98**, 1981, 883-7.
4. Pollock J I. Longterm associations with infant feeding in a clinically advantaged population of babies. *Developmental and Child Neurology* **36**, 5; 1994, 429-440.
5. Rodgers B. Feeding in infancy and later ability and attainment: a longitudinal study. *Developmental Medicine Child Neurology*, **20**, 1978, 421-6.
6. Lucas A, Morley R, Cole T J, Lister G and Leeson-Payne C. Breast milk and subsequent intelligence quotient in children born preterm. *Lancet*; **339**, 1992, 261-4.
7. Lucas A. Programming by early nutrition in man. In: Bock G R and Whelan J (eds). *The Childhood Environment and Adult Disease*. Ciba Foundation Symposium **156**, J Wiley (Chichester 1991) pp. 38-55.
8. Department of Health and Social Security. Present day practice in infant feeding. *Report on Health and Social Subjects,* Number 20. HMSO (London 1980).
9. Committee on Medical Aspects of Food Policy Panel on Child Nutrition Policy. Statement on infant feeding. *Health Visitor*, **60**, 1987, 130.
10. McNally E, Hendricks S and Horowitz I. A look at breast-feeding trends in Canada (1963–1982). *Canadian Journal Public Health*, **76**, 1985, 101-7.
11. White A, Freeth S and O'Brien M. *Infant Feeding 1990*. Office of Population Censuses and Surveys. HMSO (London 1992).
12. Emery J L, Scholey S and Taylor E M. Decline in breast feeding. *Archives Diseases in Childhood,* **65**, 1990, 369-72.
13. Ministry of Agriculture, Fisheries and Food. *Household Food Consumption and Expenditure 1988*. HMSO (London 1989).
14. Golding J, Haslum M and Morris A C. What do our ten-year old children eat? *Health Visitor,* **57**, 1984, 178-9.
15. Department of Health The diets of British schoolchildren. *RHSS, 36,* HMSO (London 1989).
16. Bull N L. Dietary habits of 15–25 year olds. *Human Nutrition: Applied Nutrition*, **39A**, 1985, Supplement 1, 1-68.
17. Gregory J, Foster K, Tyler H and Wiseman M. The *Dietary and Nutritional Survey of British Adults*. HMSO (London 1990).
18. Aukett M A, Parks Y A, Scott P H and Wharton B A. Treatment with iron increases weight gain and psychomotor development. *Archives Diseases in Childhood,* **61**, 1986, 849-57.
19. Duggan M B, Steel G, Elwys G, Harbottle L and Noble C. Iron status, energy intake, and nutritional status of healthy young Asian children. *Archives Diseases in Childhood, 66, 1991, 1386-9*.
20. Ehrhardt P. Iron deficiency in young Bradford children from different ethnic groups. *British Medical Journal*, **292**, 1986, 90-3.
21. Grindulis H, Scott P H, Belton N R, Wharton B A. Combined deficiency of iron and vitamin D in Asian toddlers. *Archives Disease in Childhood,* **61**, 1986, 843-8.
22. Nutbeam D. *Health for All Young People in Wales*. Health Promotion Authority for Wales (Cardiff 1989).
23. Currie C and Todd J. *Health Behaviours of Scottish Schoolchildren. Report 1: National and Regional Patterns*. Health Education Board for Scotland, Research Unit in Health and Behavioural Change (1992).
24. Riddoch C, Savage J M, Murphy N, Cran G W and Boreham C. Long term health implications of fitness and physical activity patterns. *Archives Disease in Childhood,* **66**, 1991, 1426-33.
25. Nelson M. Vitamin and mineral supplementation and academic performance in schoolchildren. *Proceedings of Nutrition Society,* **51**, 1992, 303-13.
26. Fentem P H, Bassey E J and Turnbull N B. *The New Case for Exercise*. The Sports Council and the Health Education Authority (1988).
27. Kuh D J L and Cooper C. Physical activity at 36 years: patterns and childhood predictors in a longitudinal study. *Journal Epidemiology Community Health*, **46**, 1992, 114-9.
28. Allied Dunbar. *National Fitness Survey*. Sports Council and Health Education Authority (London 1992).
29. King A J C and Coles B. *The Health of Canada's Youth*. Minister of Supply and Services (Canada 1992).
30. Smith C, Wold B and Moore L. Health behaviour research with adolescents: a perspective from the WHO cross-national health behaviour in school-aged children study. *Health Promotion Journal Australia,* **2**, 1992, 41-4.
31. Heartbeat Wales. *Technical Report Exercise for Health*. Report No. 17. Health Promotion Authority for Wales (Cardiff 1989).
32. Scottish Sports Council, *School-aged Sport in Scotland. Report no. 6.* (Edinburgh 1989).
33. Matheson J. *Participation in Sport*. GHS 1987. OPCS GHS 17 Supplement B. HMSO (London 1991).
34. OPCS. *General Household Survey 1990*. HMSO (London 1992).
35. Canadian Fitness Survey. *Canadian Youth and Physical Activity*. Canadian Fitness Survey (Ottawa 1983).
36. Ross J G and Pate R R. The National Children and Youth Fitness Study II: A summary of findings. *Journal Physical Education, Recreation and Dance,* **58**, 1987, 51-6.
37. Ross J G and Gilbert G G. The National Children and Youth Fitness Study: A summary of findings. *Journal Physical Education, Recreation and Dance,* **56**, 1985, 45-50.

38. Australian Council for Health. *Australian Health and Fitness Survey, 1985.* ACHPER Publications (Parkside, South Australia 1987).

39. Royal College of Physicians. *Smoking and the Young.* RCP (London 1992).

40. Peto R. Influence of dose and duration of smoking on lung cancer rates. In: Zarridge D G and Peto R (eds). *Tobacco: a Major International Health Hazard.* IARC (Lyon, France 1986) pp. 23-33.

41. Lader D and Matheson J. *Smoking Among Secondary School Children in 1990.* OPCS. HMSO (London 1991).

42. OPCS. *General Household Survey: Cigarette Smoking 1972 to 1990.* OPCS Monitor SS 91/3. OPCS (1991).

43. Dobbs J and Marsh A. *Smoking Among Secondary School Children.* OPCS. HMSO (London 1983).

44. Dobbs J and Marsh A. *Smoking Among Secondary School Children in 1984.* OPCS. HMSO (London 1985).

45. Goddard E. *Smoking Among Secondary School Children in England in 1988.* OPCS. HMSO (London 1989).

46. Goddard E and Ikin C. *Smoking Among Secondary School Children in 1986.* OPCS. HMSO (London 1987).

47. Smith C. Smoking among young people: some recent developments in Wales. *Health Education Journal,* **50**, 1991, 8-11.

48. Smith C, Nutbeam D, Roberts C and Catford J. *Smoking and the Young in Wales, 1986–1992.* Youth for Wales Briefing Report no 3. Health Promotion Authority for Wales (Cardiff 1992).

49. Swan A V, Melia R J W, Fitzsimons B, Breeze E and Murray M. Why do more girls than boys smoke cigarettes? *Health Education Journal,* **48**, 1989, 59-64.

50. Goddard E. *Why Children Start Smoking.* OPCS. HMSO (London 1990).

51. Health Education Authority. *Tomorrow's Young Adults.* HEA (London 1992).

52. Directorate of the Welsh Heart Programme Smoking in Youth. *Preventing Teenage Smoking in Wales.* Heartbeat Report No.8. Welsh Heart Programme (Cardiff 1986).

53. Amos A, Jacobson B and White P. Cigarette advertising policy and coverage of smoking and health in British women's magazines. *Lancet,* **337**, 1991, 93-6.

54. WHO. *A 5-year active plan. Smoke-free Europe.* WHO (Copenhagen 1987).

55. Secretary of State for Health. *The Health of the Nation. A Strategy for Health in England.* HMSO (London 1992).

56. Royal College of Physicians. *A Great and Growing Evil: the Medical Consequences of Alcohol Abuse.* Tavistock (London 1987).

57. Goddard E. *Drinking in England and Wales in the Late 1980s.* OPCS. HMSO (London 1991).

58. Barker M and Power C. Disability in young adults: the role of accidents. *Journal Epidemiology Community Health,* **47**, 1993, 349-54.

59. Plant M A, Peck D F and Samuel E. *Alcohol, Drugs and School-leavers.* Tavistock (London 1985).

60. Ghodsian M and Power C. Alcohol consumption between the ages of 16 and 23 in Britain: a longitudinal study. *British Journal Addiction,* **82**, 1987, 193-8.

61. Marsh A, Dobbs J and White A. *Adolescent Drinking.* OPCS. HMSO (London 1986).

62. OPCS. *General Household Survey 1988.* HMSO (London 1990).

63. Power C and Estaugh V. Employment and drinking in early adulthood: a longitudinal perspective. *British Journal Addiction,* **85**, 1990, 487-94.

64. Power C and Estaugh V. The role of family formation and dissolution in shaping drinking behaviour in early adulthood. OPCS *British Journal Addiction,* **85**, 1990, 521-30.

65 Taylor J C *et al. Trends in deaths associated with abuse of volatile substances 1971-1991.* Report No. 6, St Georges Hospital Medical School (June 1993).

66. Macintyre S and Cunningham-Burley A. Teenage pregnancy as a social problem: a perspective from the UK. *Adolescent Pregnancy Conference,* April 13-16 1989, Stanford University USA 1989.

67. Williams S, Forbes J F, McIlwaine G M and Rosenberg K. Poverty and teenage pregnancy. *British Medical Journal,* **294**, 1987, 20-1.

68. Bury J K. Teenage sexual behaviour and the impact of AIDs. *Health Education Journal,* **50**, 1991, 43-9.

69. Currie C and Todd J. *Health Behaviours of Scottish Schoolchildren: Sex Education, Personal Relationships, Sexual Behaviour and HIV/AIDS Knowledge and Attitudes.* Research Unit in Health and Behavioural Change, Report no 3. (Edinburgh 1992).

70. Health Education Authority. *Young Adults Health and Lifestyle: Sexual Behaviour.* HEA (London 1992).

71. Wellings K, Field J, Wadsworth J, Johnson A M, Anderson R M and Bradshaw S A. Sexual lifestyles under scrutiny. *Nature,* **348**, 1990, 276-8.

72. Wadsworth J and Johnson A M. Measuring sexual behaviour. *Journal Royal Statistical Society A,* **154**, 1991, 367-70.

73. OPCS. *General Household Survey 1983.* HMSO (London 1985).

74. OPCS. *General Household Survey 1986.* HMSO (London 1989).

75. OPCS. *General Household Survey 1989.* HMSO (London 1991).

76. Fleissig A. Unintended pregnancies and the use of contraception: changes from 1984 to 1989. *British Medical Journal,* **302**, 1991, 147.

77. OPCS. *Birth Statistics 1992.* Series FM1 no.21, HMSO (1994).

78. Werner B. Fertility trends in the UK and in thirteen other developed countries, 1966–86. *Population Trends,* **51**, 1988.

79. Munday D, Francome C and Savage W. Twenty one years of legal abortion. *British Medical Journal,* **298**, 1989, 1231-4.

80. Botting B. Trends in abortion. *Population Trends,* **64**, 1991.

81. Royal College of Obstetricians and Gynaecologists. *Report of the RCOG Working Party on Unplanned Pregnancy*. RCOG (London 1991).

82. Nutbeam D, Aar L and Catford J. Understanding childrens' health behaviour: the implications for health promotion for young people. *Social Science and Medicine,* **29**, 1989, 317-25.

83. Department of Transport. *Road Accidents Great Britain 1990: The Casualty Report*. HMSO (London 1991).

84 Alan Guttmacher Institute. *Induced abortion: a world review*. (New York 1990) Table 6.

85 Whitehead R G, Paul A A and Cole T J. Diet and the growth of healthy infants. *Journal of Human Nutrition and Dietetics,* **2,** 1989, 73-84.

6 Trends and patterns in childhood mortality and morbidity

Beverley Botting and Rachel Crawley

Key points

- For both sexes, stillbirth and infant mortality rates halved between 1971 and 1991.

- Babies born weighing under 2,500 g in 1991 accounted for 59 per cent of neonatal deaths.

- During the 1980s the rate of multiple births, particularly triplets and higher order births increased. In 1991, 3 per cent of all multiple birth deliveries were triplets or higher order births.

- The risk of cerebral palsy is estimated to be 0.2 per cent in singletons, 1.3 per cent in twins and 7.6 per cent in triplets.

- At all ages in childhood there is increased risk of mortality with lower social class, most marked at ages 1–4. Boys are consistently at higher risk than girls.

- Injury and poisoning are the major cause of death for boys aged 1 and over and for girls aged 5 and over.

- The large fall in postneonatal mortality between 1988 and 1991, from 4.1 to 3.0 per 1,000 live births, was due almost entirely to a fall in deaths attributed to sudden infant death syndrome.

- Respiratory conditions account for over one half of children's consultations with GPs.

- Notification rates for babies born with central nervous system malformations fell from 19 per 10,000 babies in 1981 to 4.6 per 10,000 in 1991.

- By 1991, 92 per cent of children aged under two had been immunised against measles, mumps, rubella, diphtheria, tetanus, whooping cough and polio.

- Between 1970 and 1985 hospital admissions for cancer in children increased more than fourfold, while mortality rates fell by about half.

- One in five children aged 5–15 were reported as suffering from a long-standing illness, although only about one half of these had a resulting limitation in activities.

- In 1993, more than five times as many children were free from dental caries by the age of 15 (37 per cent) than in 1983 (7 per cent).

This chapter examines the general patterns of morbidity and mortality of children during the 1970s and 1980s, using available, routinely collected data, particularly those produced by OPCS, supplemented by some information from special studies. Later chapters will provide more detailed analyses of specific conditions.

The falls in infant and childhood mortality rates in recent decades mean that more children are surviving infancy and childhood to become adults. Nevertheless, children do still become acutely ill. As discussed in Chapter 4, children today are taller and healthier than children of past generations. Compared with previous decades, fewer children now die in infancy and childhood.

6.1 Trends in mortality

6.1.1 Infant mortality and stillbirths

The 1970s and 1980s saw an overall decline in stillbirth and infant mortality rates in England and Wales (Table 6.1). Between 1971 and 1991, there was a downward trend in these rates for both sexes in all age groups. For both sexes taken together the largest changes were in the stillbirth and neonatal death rates, which fell by 63 and 62 per cent respectively between 1971 and 1991. During the same period, the postnoenatal death rate fell by 49 per cent, and the infant mortality rate fell by 58 per cent. The table shows that throughout the first year of life boys have a higher mortality rate than do girls. This difference continues throughout life. Thus in 1991 boys had a life expectancy at birth of 73 years compared with 79 years for girls.

6.1.2 Mortality at older ages in childhood

As shown in Chapter 1, death rates for children aged 1–14 are at historically low levels. Table 6.2 shows the mortality rates by sex and age between 1971 and 1991 in England and Wales. They are based on small numbers and should be considered with care. Over this period, the rates for boys and for girls aged 1–14 both fell by 45 per cent. Nevertheless, death rates for boys were always higher than those for girls. For the five years 1987–91 combined, the rates for boys aged 1–14 were 30 per cent higher than the rates for girls. During the teenage years the risk of dying for both boys and girls increases rapidly with age, the increase for males beginning at age 12, a

year earlier than for females, and continuing a year after the risk for females has begun to level off.

Mortality and morbidity vary according to a number of demographic and economic factors including social class and place of residence. Ethnicity is also an important contributing factor, and this is considered in more depth in Chapter 7.

6.1.3 Social class and sex differences

Social class differences in infant and childhood mortality were analysed for the years around the 1981 Census (1979–80, 1982–3).[1] At the Census, children are categorised by the social class of the head of their household. At the 1981 Census there were relatively more children from Social Class IIIM (manual) and N (non-manual) households, and correspondingly fewer from the other social classes, compared with all households. At all ages in childhood there was a gradient of risk of increased mortality with increasing social disadvantage (Table 6.3), most marked at ages 1–4. Moreover, boys were consistently at a higher risk than girls.

For every social class except Social Class IIIN stillbirth rates were higher for boys than for girls (Figure 6.1). This excess of male mortality rates is found for all ages and across the social classes. Social class differentials were similar for boys and girls and was most marked for deaths at ages 1–4 and postneonatal deaths.

For deaths at older ages in childhood an irregular increase in death rates across the social classes was seen for every

Table 6.1 Stillbirth and infant mortality rates by sex: 1971-91, England and Wales

Year	Stillbirths*		Neonatal deaths**		Postneonatal deaths**		Infant deaths**	
	Boys	Girls	Boys	Girls	Boys	Girls	Boys	Girls
1971	12.3	12.6	13.4	9.8	6.4	5.3	19.8	15.1
1972	11.7	12.3	12.9	10.1	6.4	4.9	19.3	14.7
1973	11.4	11.8	12.6	9.6	6.3	5.1	18.9	13.9
1974	10.8	11.5	12.5	9.5	6.1	4.5	18.6	13.8
1975	9.9	10.8	11.8	9.6	5.6	4.3	17.5	13.9
1976	9.7	9.6	11.1	8.2	5.2	4.0	16.2	12.2
1977	9.5	9.3	10.4	8.1	5.0	4.0	15.4	12.0
1978	8.5	8.5	9.6	7.7	5.1	3.9	14.7	11.6
1979	8.0	7.9	9.4	7.0	5.0	4.1	14.4	11.1
1980	7.3	7.1	8.5	6.8	4.8	3.9	13.3	10.7
1981	6.7	6.5	7.7	5.6	4.9	3.8	12.6	9.4
1982	6.5	6.0	7.1	5.4	5.1	4.0	12.2	9.4
1983	6.0	5.4	6.5	5.2	4.8	3.7	11.3	8.9
1984	6.0	5.4	6.3	4.8	4.3	3.5	10.6	8.3
1985	5.9	5.2	6.0	4.8	4.5	3.5	10.4	8.2
1986	5.6	5.1	6.0	4.5	5.0	3.5	11.0	8.0
1987	5.3	4.7	5.7	4.4	4.7	3.6	10.4	7.9
1988	5.1	4.6	5.5	4.3	4.7	3.5	10.3	7.7
1989	5.0	4.4	5.4	4.0	4.1	3.2	9.6	7.3
1990	4.8	4.3	5.1	4.0	3.8	2.8	8.9	6.8
1991	4.8	4.5	4.8	3.9	3.5	2.5	8.3	6.4

*   Rates per 1,000 total births.
** Rates per 1,000 live births.

Sources: *Registrar General's Statistical Review 1971-73*
            Mortality Statistics: Childhood 1974-91
            Birth Statistics, 1974-91

Table 6.2 Childhood mortality rates (per 100,000 population) by sex and age: 1971–91, England and Wales

Year	1–4 years		5–9 years		10–14 years		5–14 years		15–19 years	
	Boys	Girls	Boys	Girls	Boys	Girls	Boys	Girls	Boys	Girls
1971	76	63	44	29	37	24	41	26	89	38
1972	77	71	40	29	36	20	38	25	84	40
1973	77	60	39	26	34	21	37	23	85	41
1974	73	58	35	26	32	23	34	25	88	37
1975	68	52	33	24	33	18	34	21	86	36
1976	65	46	34	24	31	21	32	23	88	35
1977	60	51	33	20	28	20	31	20	84	34
1978	61	53	33	23	30	21	31	22	90	37
1979	54	47	33	21	29	20	31	21	85	32
1980	56	46	30	21	27	19	28	20	85	34
1981	53	46	27	19	29	19	28	19	83	33
1982	52	41	25	17	28	19	27	18	79	29
1983	47	40	26	19	27	19	27	19	74	31
1984	47	37	23	18	28	18	26	18	71	29
1985	50	41	22	18	29	19	25	18	68	28
1986	44	40	21	17	23	17	22	17	71	29
1987	44	39	19	16	26	17	23	16	71	28
1988	44	39	23	15	26	15	25	15	67	30
1989	44	36	23	16	22	16	23	16	72	30
1990	43	33	20	14	22	16	21	15	74	28
1991	40	26	21	16	22	15	22	15	72	29

Sources: *Registrar General's Statistical Review 1971-73*
Mortality Statistics: cause 1974-91
Population Estimates 1974-91

**Table 6.3 Mortality of children aged 1–15 years
SMRs (all causes) – by age, sex and social
class: 1979–80, 82–83, England and Wales**

Social class	1–4 years		5–9 years		1–15 years	
	Boys	Girls	Boys	Girls	Boys	Girls
I & II	65	73	72	80	71	77
IIIN	79	82	83	92	77	81
IIIM	101	96	93	96	95	95
IV & V	145	139	130	128	126	121

Source: *Occupational Mortality: Childhood Supplement 1979-80,
82-83*[1]

**Figure 6.1 Mortality (all causes) of children aged 1-15 years - SMRs by age, sex and social class:
1979-80, 1982-3, England and Wales**

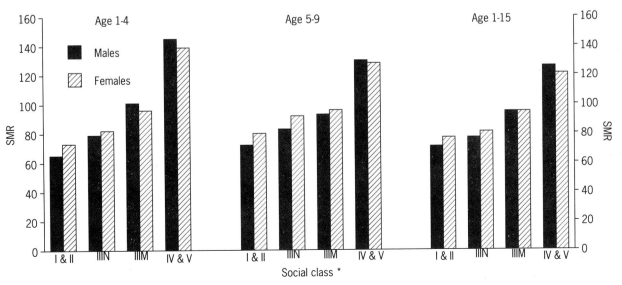

* As defined by occupation
Source: Childhood Supplement 1979-80, 82-83.[1]

age–group and both sexes. Death rates were nearly always higher for males (sometimes markedly so). It is difficult to compare these results with those from the previous two censuses because of different degrees of numerator/denominator bias. It is worth noting, however, that in 1970–2 the ratio of Social Class V mortality rates to those for to Social Class I was largest for 5–9-year-olds, whereas in 1979–83 it was greatest for 1–4-year-olds as seen in Figure 6.1.[1]

Similar analyses by social class (based on the father's occupation) for infant deaths and stillbirths are published each year.[2] Table 6.4 and Figure 6.2 compare infant mortality by social class based on the father's occupation for 1981 and 1991. This confirms the continued existence of the social class gradients. Since 1986 mother's occupation has been recorded at birth registration, albeit on a voluntary basis. An analysis of the first five years' data showed little difference between the rates for Social Classes I to IV, but the rate for Social Class V was 77 per cent higher than that for Social Class I (Table 6.5).[3]

Table 6.4 Infant mortality rates by social class (based on father's occupation): 1981 and 1991, England and Wales

Social class		Rate (per 1,000 live births)	
		1981	1991
All		10.9	7.2
Within marriage	All	10.2	6.3
	I–V	10.0	6.0
	I	7.7	5.1
	II	7.9	5.3
	IIIN	8.5	6.1
	IIIM	10.3	6.2
	IV	12.6	7.1
	V	15.8	8.2
	Other	15.0	11.5
Outside marriage		15.2	9.4

Source: *Mortality Statistics — perinatal and infant: social and biological factors 1981,1991*

Table 6.5 Infant mortality rates by mother's social class (as defined by occupation): 1986–90 combined, England and Wales

Social class	Infant mortality rate (per 1,000 live births)
All stated	6.1
I	6.1
II	5.7
IIIN	5.7
IIIM	7.0
IV	7.0
V	10.8
Armed forces	6.3
Other	10.0
Not stated	9.9

Source: Botting B, Cooper J, *Population Trends* 74[3]

It is not possible to repeat these analyses at older ages in childhood as the population denominators are only available in census years and social class is not routinely coded for these deaths.

6.1.4 Geographic differences

For many years there have been analyses of variations in death rates by area of residence. An analysis of geographic variation in infant mortality for the period 1979–83[4] confirmed the continuation of a regional gradient in mortality from high rates in the North and West to low in the South and East for both males and females. Geographical variations in birthweight specific mortality rates for infants have been examined for 1983–5.[4] The results showed a clear geographical gradient in neonatal mortality rates, with all the regional health authorities (RHAs) in the south of England and only Mersey in the north of England having rates below that for England and Wales as a whole. The rates for Yorkshire, West Midlands and Northern RHAs and for Wales were noticeably above the England and Wales level. For the postneonatal period, rates were higher than average in Yorkshire, North Western, Wessex and South East Thames RHAs. Table 6.6 shows more recent data of differences in mortality rates by Regional Health

Figure 6.2
Infant mortality by social class (for births within marriage): 1981 and 1991, England and Wales

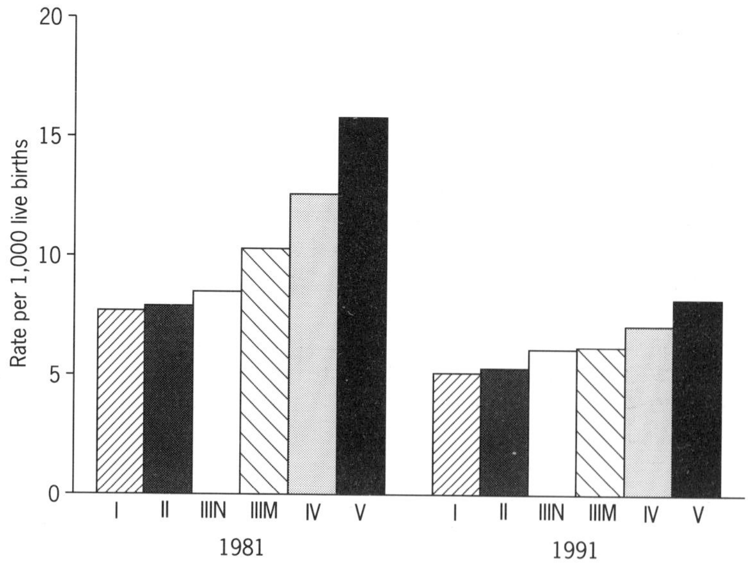

Source: Mortality Statistics: perinatal and infant: social and biological factors 1981, 1991.

Table 6.6 Mortality rates (per 100,000 live births/population) by age and RHA: 1989–91 combined, England and Wales

RHA	Under 1 year	1–4 years	5–9 years	10–14 years	15–19 years
England and Wales	790	38	18	19	52
Northern	830	38	21	19	47
Yorkshire	891	40	19	21	50
Trent	798	37	19	18	56
East Anglian	644	30	12	21	53
North West Thames	710	36	18	18	46
North East Thames	734	36	17	19	48
South East Thames	797	34	16	15	47
South West Thames	668	37	17	16	46
Wessex	738	29	19	16	50
Oxford	748	40	16	14	54
South Western	689	34	17	15	59
West Midlands	950	39	17	20	52
Mersey	729	36	17	24	47
North Western	853	46	19	18	48
Wales	715	42	18	20	52

Source: OPCS unpublished data

Authority for those aged under 20, for 1989–91. Again infant mortality rates are higher in the North and West of England. For older ages in childhood the mortality rates are much lower with smaller differences between RHAs.

6.1.5 Causes of deaths

Table 6.7 compares the proportional distribution of the main causes of death in childhood by sex and age for 1981 and 1991. The 1991 data are presented in Figure 6.3. Neonatal deaths have been excluded from the table and figure because a new neonatal death certificate was introduced in 1986. As a result, cause-specific data for 1981 and 1991 are not comparable for neonatal deaths. There has been little change in the main causes of death over the decade. 'Injury and poisoning' is the commonest cause of death for boys at all ages outside infancy and for girls aged five and over. In 1991 cancer was the cause of 27 per cent of deaths among children aged 5–9 and 19 per cent of those aged 10–14; diseases of the nervous system and sense organs are responsible for approximately 1 in 10 deaths at all ages outside infancy. Congenital malformations account for almost 1 in 5 deaths under the age of five.

As mentioned above, new stillbirth and neonatal death certificates were introduced in England and Wales in 1986. These allow both fetal and maternal conditions leading to the death to be recorded on the death certificate. As a result, however, it has not been possible to derive a single underlying cause of death for stillbirths and neonatal deaths. OPCS convened an expert group including pathologists, paediatricians and obstetricians to agree how the multiple cause of death information could be used most meaningfully. The result was an algorithm which was used to identify the first stage in the development of the fetus or baby when the insult leading to the death first occurred; during the pregnancy, up to the onset of labour, in or shortly after labour, and after delivery. This timing can then be used to provide

a basis for planning preventative action.[5] In the 6-year period from 1986 to 1991, 79 per cent of the neonatal deaths were due to conditions which probably originated in the pregnancy. Of these, 56 per cent were due to conditions related to immaturity, and 43 per cent to congenital defects (Figure 6.4). A further 12 per cent of the neonatal deaths were due to conditions which apparently occurred during or shortly after labour, and 10 per cent to conditions which occurred after delivery.

6.2 Trends in morbidity

6.3.1 Parents' perception of their children's health

OPCS has carried out the General Household Survey (GHS) continuously since 1971.[6] Parents are asked about their children's health and this provides three measures of morbidity; long-standing illness, limitation of activity arising from long-standing illness, and restricted activity arising from illness in the two weeks before the interview. Figure 6.5 shows the proportions of children with different types of reported morbidity from 1981 to 1991.

In contrast to mortality trends, there is no evidence that the health of children, as perceived by their parents, improved during the 1980s. There is some suggestion that rates of long-standing illness among children aged 5–15 increased. In recent years almost 1 in 5 children aged 5–15 were reported as suffering from a long-standing illness although only about 50 per cent had a resulting limitation in activities. While the rates of long-standing illness appear to have increased over the last ten years, illness in the last two weeks was reported for about 1 in 10 children in both age groups consistently during the 1980s. In 1988 the GHS identified the causes of long-standing illness.[6] Among children aged 0–15 respiratory disease was the major illness reported, given by seven per cent of respondents. Ear complaints and skin complaints were each reported in two per cent of children aged 0–15.

Table 6.7 Proportional distribution of main causes of death by sex and age: 1981 and 1991, England and Wales

Cause		Age at death									
		28 days–1 year		1–4 years		5–9 years		10–14 years		15–19 years	
		1981	1991	1981	1991	1981	1991	1981	1991	1981	1991
All causes (001-999)											
	Boys	100	100	100	100	100	100	100	100	100	100
	Girls	100	100	100	100	100	100	100	100	100	100
	All Children	100	100	100	100	100	100	100	100	100	100
Cancer (140-239)											
	Boys	1	1	11	14	19	24	18	18	10	8
	Girls	1	1	13	12	22	31	21	19	15	11
	All children	1	1	12	13	20	27	19	19	11	9
Nervous system and sense organs (320-389)											
	Boys	2	5	8	11	8	9	8	8	5	6
	Girls	3	6	11	14	7	12	7	11	7	6
	All children	2	6	9	12	8	11	7	9	5	6
Disease of respiratory system (460-519)											
	Boys	10	9	15	9	8	3	7	7	4	3
	Girls	9	10	14	8	10	2	9	6	7	4
	All children	10	10	14	8	9	3	8	7	5	3
Disease of digestive system (520-579)											
	Boys	1	1	3	2	2	3	2	2	1	1
	Girls	0	1	4	2	3	1	2	1	2	1
	All children	0	1	3	2	2	2	2	2	1	1
Congenital malformations (740-759)											
	Boys	26	15	19	20	8	13	5	5	2	3
	Girls	29	19	21	20	13	11	10	14	5	4
	All children	27	17	20	20	10	12	7	9	3	3
Perinatal conditions (760-779)											
	Boys	39	10	0	3	0	0	0	0	0	0
	Girls	36	11	0	2	1	0	0	0	0	0
	All children	38	10	0	2	0	0	0	0	0	0
Signs and symptoms (780-799)											
	Boys	15	45	3	4	1	0	0	0	0	0
	Girls	15	37	3	5	0	0	0	0	0	1
	All children	15	42	3	4	0	0	0	0	0	1
Injury and poisoning (800-999)											
	Boys	2	4	25	24	41	34	46	42	71	66
	Girls	3	5	20	19	29	27	30	26	45	53
	All children	2	4	23	22	36	31	40	35	64	62
Other											
	Boys	4	9	16	14	13	14	14	17	8	13
	Girls	5	10	15	19	15	15	21	23	17	19
	All children	4	10	15	16	14	14	19	19	10	15
Total number of deaths											
	Boys	4,119	1,243	651	554	447	341	573	354	1,734	1,208
	Girls	2,902	863	529	439	302	248	368	222	650	462
	All children	7,021	2,106	1,180	993	749	589	941	576	2,384	1,670

Numbers may not add up due to rounding.

Source: *Mortality Statistics: cause 1981, 1991*

Figure 6.3   Main causes of childhood mortality by age and sex: 1991, England and Wales

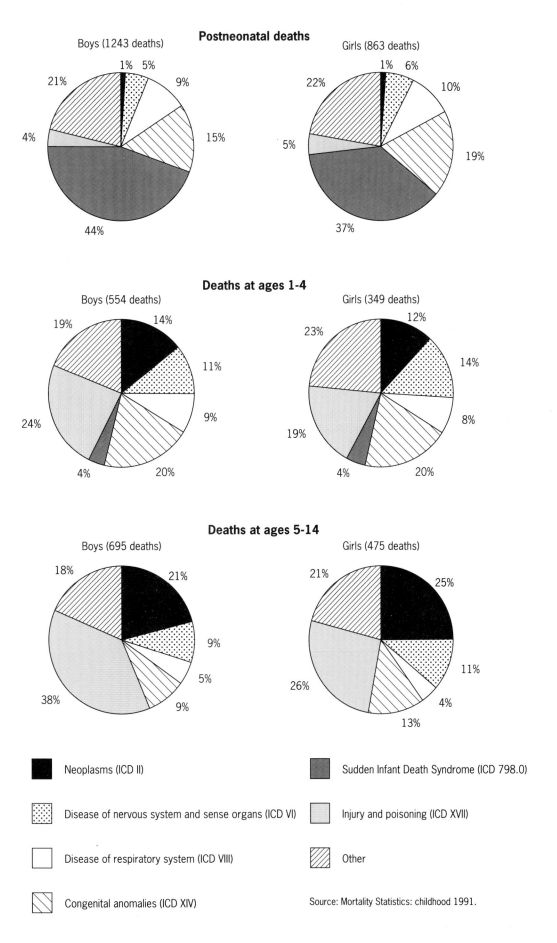

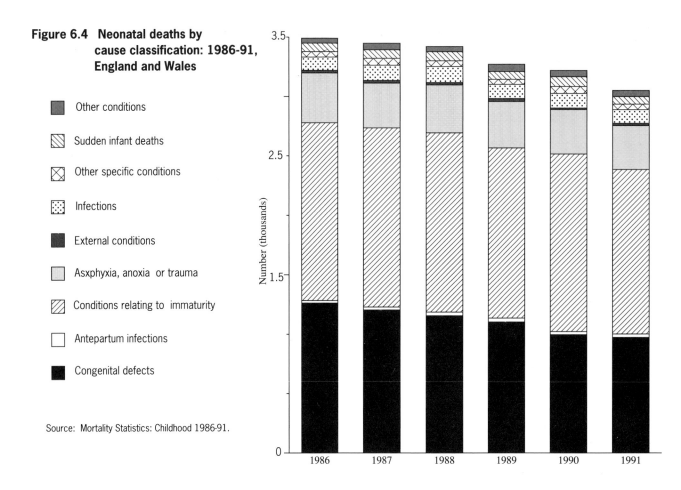

Figure 6.4 Neonatal deaths by cause classification: 1986-91, England and Wales

Other conditions

Sudden infant deaths

Other specific conditions

Infections

External conditions

Asxphyxia, anoxia or trauma

Conditions relating to immaturity

Antepartum infections

Congenital defects

Source: Mortality Statistics: Childhood 1986-91.

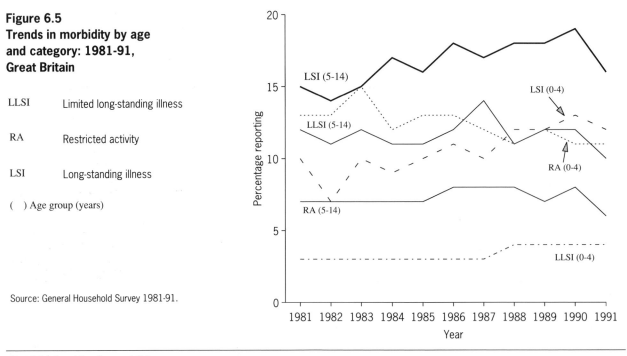

Figure 6.5
Trends in morbidity by age and category: 1981-91, Great Britain

LLSI Limited long-standing illness

RA Restricted activity

LSI Long-standing illness

( ) Age group (years)

Source: General Household Survey 1981-91.

6.2.2 Consultations with GPs and hospital admissions

Other data from the GHS showed that attendances at GPs doubled in the 20 years since the GHS began, but this was not the case for hospital use (Table 6.8). The fourth national study of morbidity in general practice

Table 6.8 Percentages of children using health services by sex and age: 1981, 1991, Great Britain

Service	Age (years)	Boys		Girls	
		1981*	1991	1981*	1991
		Percentage using each service			
GP in last 2 weeks	0–4	21	23	17	21
	5–15	8	10	9	11
In-patient in last year	0–4	-	10	-	8
	5–15	-	6	-	4
Out-patients/casualty in last 3 months	0–4	12	14	9	11
	5–15	11	11	8	8

* 1981 In-patient information not available.

(MSGP4) carried out in 1991/92 was a collaboration between the Royal College of General Practitioners, OPCS and the Department of Health. Between 1 September 1991 and 31 August 1992, 60 general practices in England and Wales recorded details of every face-to-face contact with all patients on their NHS register.[7] Findings from this study for children aged 0–15 consulting their GP by type of condition are given in Table 6.9 and Figure 6.6. Although respiratory diseases account for a small proportion of deaths outside infancy, they account for over one half of consultations with GPs. In contrast, injury and poisoning, which is the major cause of childhood death, accounted for 13 per cent and 19 per cent of consultations by those aged 0–4 and 5–15 respectively. Most of these consultations related to a minor condition. It is likely, however, that children with more serious conditions would have been taken straight to hospital. The other main reasons for GP consultations

Table 6.9 Children consulting (rates per 10,000 person years at risk) by type of condition: 1991/92, England and Wales

Disease group	Age group (years)	
	0–4	5–15
All diseases and conditions	10,221	7,234
Infectious and parasitic diseases	3,648	1,888
Neoplasms	54	88
Endocrine, nutritional and metabolic disease and immunity disorders	60	43
Disease of the blood and blood forming organs	58	56
Mental disorders	228	194
Diseases of the nervous system and sense organs	4,252	1,881
Diseases of the circulatory system	19	26
Diseases of the respiratory system	6,471	3,680
Disease of the digestive system	834	306
Diseases of the genitourinary system	570	453
Complications of pregnancy childbirth and the puerperium	7	5
Diseases of the skin and subcutaneous tissue	2,715	1,418
Disease of the musculoskeletal system and connective tissue	161	489
Congenital anomalies	217	59
Certain conditions originating in the perinatal period	173	0
Symptoms, signs and ill-defined conditions	2,721	1,363
Injury and poisoning	1,293	1,375
Supplementary classification of factors influencing health status and contact with health services	5,313	1,140

Source: *Morbidity Statistics from General Practice 1991/92*[2]

in these age groups were infectious and parasitic diseases, diseases of the nervous system and sense organs, and diseases of the skin and subcutaneous tissue.

Figure 6.7 shows comparable information for children's admissions to hospital derived from the 1985 Hospital In–Patient Enquiry (HIPE).[8] About one fifth of admissions to hospital were for diseases of the respiratory system. This was less than for GP consultations. Injury and poisoning accounted for 1 in 5 admissions for children aged 5–14 and 1 in 10 of those children aged 0–4.

Figure 6.6 Percentage distribution of GP consultations by age and cause: 1991/2, England and Wales

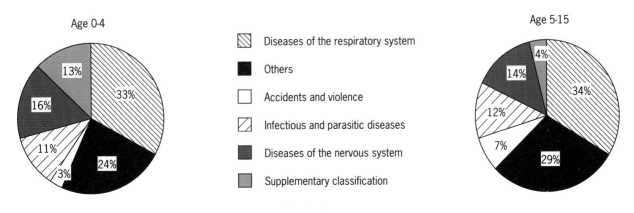

Source: Morbidity Statistics from General Practice 1991/92.[7]

Figure 6.7 Percentage distribution of admissions to hospital by age and cause: 1985, England and Wales

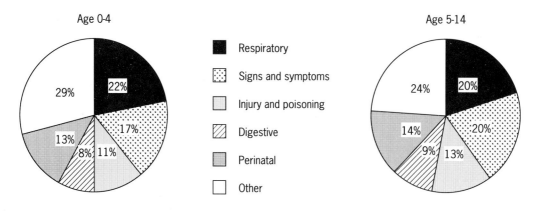

Source: Hospital In-Patient Enquiry 1985 [8]

6.2.3 Disability

There are no routine national data on disability in childhood which could be used to monitor trends in conditions such as cerebral palsy, deafness or blindness. In 1985/86 OPCS carried out a major survey of disability.[9] Its main aim was to estimate the prevalence of disability arising from physical, mental and sensory causes and to classify it by type and severity. Figures 6.8 and 6.9 summarise the findings for children: 3 per cent of children were found to have a high level severity disability. This is slightly lower than the prevalence of limiting long–standing illness recorded in the GHS. This is because the disability survey used a large series of questions and a standard threshold level to determine who should be included in the estimates, whereas the GHS relies on the answer to a single question. Figure 6.8 shows that for each age group boys had a higher prevalence of disability than girls. Prevalence was higher in the 5–9 and 10–15 age groups than in younger children and infants.

In the disability survey[9] children's disabilities were classified into 11 categories: locomotion, reaching, stretching, dexterity, seeing, hearing, personal care, continence, communication, behaviour, and intellectual

Figure 6.8 Prevalence of disability by age and sex: 1985, Great Britain

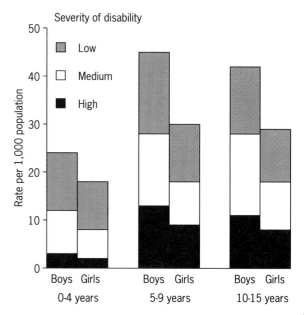

Source: Bone M and Meltzer H: The Prevalence of Disability among Children.[9]

**Figure 6.9
Estimates of prevalence of disability among children: 1985, Great Britain**

Source:
Bone M and Meltzer H: The Prevalence of Disability among Children.[9]

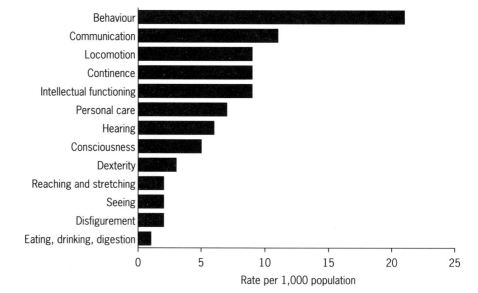

functioning and consciousness. Behavioural disability was the most common, identified in 2 per cent of children; 1 per cent of children were found to have a locomotion disability and the same percentage had continence and intellectual functioning disabilities. The other types of disability were found among fewer than 1 per cent of children. A given disability seldom occurs in isolation. Each child identified as disabled in the survey had an average 2.7 of the 11 categories of disability identified.

6.3 Impact of birthweight and multiple births on mortality and morbidity

As discussed more fully in Chapter 4, during the 1970s and 1980s the proportion of low birthweight babies, born weighing under 2,500 g, remained almost constant at between 6 and 7 per cent. Low birthweight remains a major contributor to perinatal and neonatal mortality, accounting for nearly 60 per cent of neonatal deaths in 1991. Nevertheless, more low birthweight babies are surviving than previously. Multiple births are more likely than singletons to be born prematurely, and of low birthweight. In addition they are more likely to have a slower growth rate and higher mortality than singletons. In England and Wales between 1975–86, twins were three times more likely to die in infancy than singletons, and the death rate among triplets and higher order births were higher than those among twins.[10] The rate of multiple births, particularly triplets and higher order births, has risen since the late 1970s (Figure 6.10), largely as a consequence of the growing use of fertility or ovulation stimulating drugs.[11]

The increased survival (Figure 6.11) of low birthweight babies, whether from a singleton or multiple birth, is due largely to advances in neonatal intensive care. Prematurity and low birthweight are associated with a sharply increased risk of a number of sequelae, however, some acute and some chronic.[12] These are rising in prevalence

as the survival of small babies increases (Figure 6.12). As well as cerebral palsy and defects of sight and hearing, these include an increased risk of hernias, and of undescended testicles. A number of centres which follow the changing outcome of low birthweight births have now shown that the increased survival of these babies has been accompanied by an increase in the prevalence of cerebral palsy.[13] (Figure 6.13) Overall, however, the fall in their mortality has resulted in a net increase of normal survivors.[14]

The risk of some conditions, notably cerebral palsy, is also increased by the fact of having been one of a multiple birth, particularly at normal birthweights. Recent estimates suggest that the risk of cerebral palsy in singletons is 0.2 per cent, in twins is 1.3 per cent, and in triplets 7.6 per cent.[15]

Figure 6.11 Birthweight-specific infant mortality rates: 1982-91, England and Wales

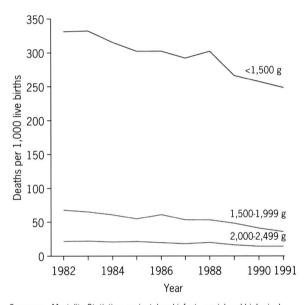

Sources: Mortality Statistics: perinatal and infant - social and biological factors 1986-91. OPCS unpublished data.

Figure 6.10
Proportion of maternities resulting in a triplet or higher order birth: 1938-91, England and Wales

Note: 1981 data are not available

Sources:
Birth Statistics - Historical Series 1837 - 1983
Birth Statistics - 1984 - 91.

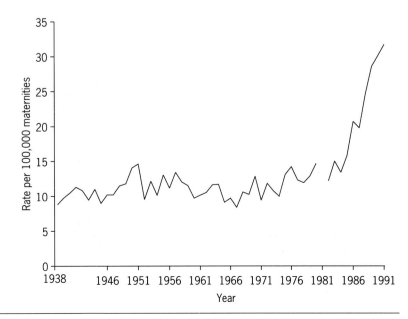

Figure 6.12 Impairment rates in low birthweight survivors: 1979-81 combined, in Mersey, England

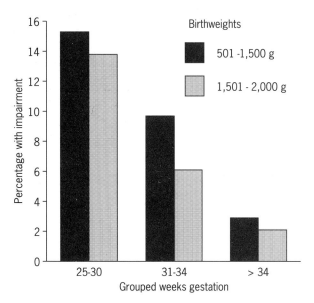

Source: Powell TG, Pharoah POD and Cooke RW. Survival and mortality in a geographically defined population.[12]

Figure 6.13 Neonatal survivors of under 1,501 grams: 1967-83 (three-year moving average) Mersey, England

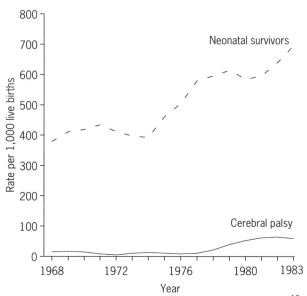

Source: Pharoah POD et al. Birthweight specific trends in cerebral palsy.[13]

6.4 Specific conditions

6.4.1 Respiratory infections and diseases

Respiratory infections and conditions are very common amongst children, especially young children and babies. Respiratory diseases cover a broad range of conditions, from coughs and colds, which are infectious, to asthma, which is a chronic condition. In 1971, child deaths due to diseases of the respiratory system were still a significant cause of mortality, accounting for 16 per cent of boys' and 17 per cent of girls' deaths respectively. In 1991 they accounted for only 8 per cent of boys' deaths and 8 per cent of deaths among girls.

Between 1971 and 1991 the major change in causes of death in childhood has been an increase in the proportion of deaths due to diseases of the nervous system and

sense organs and a fall in those due to respiratory diseases. More dramatic changes occurred, however, in causes of death in the postneonatal period. Figure 6.14 shows that since 1971 the major change has been an apparent transfer from diseases labelled 'respiratory' to those labelled 'Sudden Infant Death Syndrome' (SIDS, ICD9 798.0). This is generally thought to be mainly due to changes in death certification practices. Whilst postneonatal mortality rates for respiratory disease and sudden infant deaths combined remained at a fairly constant level between 1964 and 1988, the rates fell for the other grouped conditions shown in Figure 6.14. The large fall in postneonatal mortality between 1988 and 1991 from 4.1 to 3.0 per 1,000 live births was due almost entirely to a fall in sudden infant death syndrome. There has been much discussion about the cause of this fall, which has been seen in some, but not all other Western countries,

**Figure 6.14
Cumulative postneonatal deaths by selected causes: 1963-91, England and Wales**

Source: OPCS

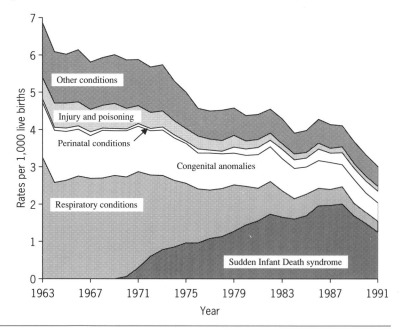

and a possible explanation is the taking up of advice recommending a change in the sleeping position of babies.[16]

Respiratory diseases account for 1 in 5 hospital admissions for children aged 0–4 and 5–14. Children in the 1980s appeared to be more robust than in earlier generations. Following the influenza epidemic of 1989/90, little or no excess mortality occurred amongst children. Respiratory diseases are discussed in more detail in Chapter 9.

6.4.2 Cancer

Cancer is one of the commonest causes of mortality in children, although there has been a marked decrease in case fatality over recent decades. Cancer is one of the few major causes of illness for which we have ongoing incidence data that are reasonably accurate and complete. Over the past twenty years there has been little change in the incidence of childhood cancers. Between 1970 and 1985, however, hospital admissions for cancer in children increased more than fourfold, while mortality rates fell by about half (Figure 6.15). This suggests that children are now admitted more often rather than incidence being higher. As will be discussed in Chapter 10, effective treatment for those with cancer has improved; thus more children now survive for longer and many are cured.

Figure 6.15 Cancer mortality and incidence by sex: 1971-88, England and Wales

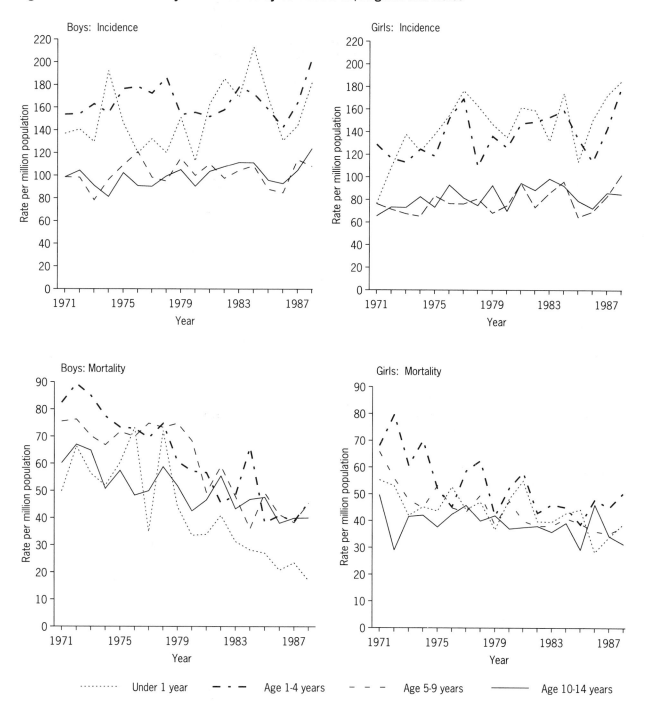

Source: Registrar General's Statistical Review 1971-3
         Mortality Statistics: cause 1974-88
         Cancer Statistics: registrations 1971-88

Figure 6.16
Mortality of children aged 1-15 years from external causes of injury and poisoning (ICD E800-E999): SMRs by social class* and sex: 1979-80, 1982-83, England and Wales

■ Males

▨ Females

* As defined by occupation

Source: Childhood Supplement 1979-80,82-83.[1]

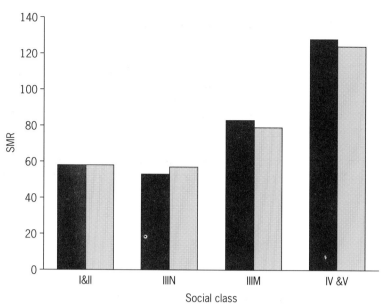

6.4.3 Accidents and violence

Accidents and violence are the major cause of deaths for both boys and girls, accounting for 38 per cent of deaths of boys aged 5–14 in 1991 and for 27 per cent of deaths or girls in the same age group. Although accidents and violence still account for more childhood deaths than any other group of causes, there have been considerable improvements in mortality for this cause during the 1970s and 1980s. Mortality rates for both boys and girls aged 1–4 and 5–9 have generally halved. Those for older children have shown smaller improvements. Children from Social Classes IV and V show higher mortality rates for accidents and violence than those from other classes (Figure 6.16).

Results from the Morbidity Statistics from General Practice 1991–92[7] reveal that accidents (and violence) contribute less than a quarter of all consultations to the GPs. When child hospital admissions in 1985 are studied, however, 11 per cent of admissions for 0–4-year-olds and 20 per cent of admissions for 5–14 year olds were due to accidents and violence.[8] This might be explained by looking at the different uses of health care. A severe injury due to an accident or violence, requires immediate treatment, thus a serious case is likely to be taken directly to the nearest Accident and Emergency Department for treatment, rather than to a GP. Minor accident and violence morbidity is likely to be treated at home or at the GP's surgery or clinic. Therefore, it is likely that hospital data and death data are fairly good measurements of severe injury and poisoning. Since GPs are only likely to be consulted for a proportion of more minor injuries, these data provide an underestimate of childhood morbidity due to accidents and violence. Accidents are discussed in more detail in Chapter 8, and suicide is mentioned in Chapter 12.

6.4.4 Congenital malformations and hereditary disease

Another major cause of infant mortality and morbidity is congenital malformation and hereditary disorders. In 1991 29 per cent of all neonatal deaths (Figure 6.4) were due to congenital malformations. Congenital malformation data are discussed more fully in Chapter 11. As deaths from other causes have fallen, malformations have become an increasingly large proportion of all deaths even though their absolute numbers are also falling. Congenital malformations accounted for 14 per cent and 17 per cent of childhood deaths in 1991 for boys and girls respectively, compared with 11 and 14 per cent respectively in 1971. This is despite the decrease during the 1980s in notifications of many of the major types of malformations. For example, data from the National Congenital Malformation Notification Scheme showed that in 1981, 19 per 10,000 babies were notified as having been born with central nervous system (CNS) malformations. By 1991 the rate had fallen to 4.6 per 10,000. The rates for cleft lip and/or palate were 13.5 in 1981 and 11.2 in 1991, and for Down's syndrome 7.4 in 1981 and 6.3 in 1991. Using information from notifications of abortions we can estimate that only about 30 per cent of the reductions in CNS abnormalities was due to prenatal detection and abortion.

6.4.5 Infectious diseases

It has already been mentioned that infectious diseases are now less likely to cause serious illness and death than at the turn of the century. Even in the last decade there have been improvements. This is because of improvements in health, prevention, and health care. In 1981, 15 children died of measles, whilst in 1991 only one child died of that cause. Measles notifications decreased following the introduction of immunisation in the 1960s, from an average of 403,000 per year in 1960–4 to 170,000 in 1970–4, and 90,000 in 1980–4 (Figure 6.17). In 1988 a combined vaccine for measles, mumps and rubella (MMR) was introduced. The annual number of notifications for measles then decreased to less than 10,000 in 1991. By 1991, in England 92 per cent of children aged under two had been immunised against measles, mumps, rubella, diphtheria, tetanus, whooping cough and polio. Table 6.10 and Figure 6.18 show that during the 1980s the uptake rates for vaccinations to prevent these diseases improved considerably.

As a result the number of notifications for rubella fell from 25,000 in 1989 to 7,000 in 1991 and for mumps from 21,000 to 3,000. These are quite dramatic changes following a mass public health initiative. Whooping cough vaccine has also become more acceptable to parents over recent years. There were only 5,000 notifications in 1991, a reduction of 66 per cent since 1987, although this must be considered with care as there is a cyclical pattern to whooping cough. Notification rates for whooping cough are given in Figure 6.19.

In contrast, the notifications of meningococcal meningitis have been increasing. Between 1977 and 1984 notifications were 400–500 a year. This figure rose to over 1,000 in 1990 and 1991. Food poisoning has also increased generally during the 1980s with rates being highest in children under five years. Infectious diseases are discussed in more detail in Chapter 13.

Figure 6.17 Deaths and notifications of measles: 1971-91, England and Wales

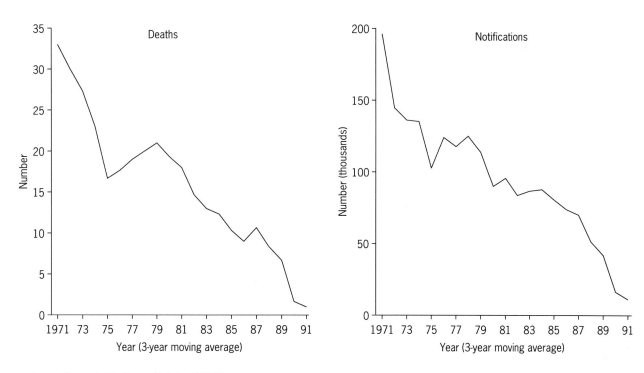

Source: Communicable Disease Statistics 1982-92

Table 6.10 Percentage of children immunised by their second birthday: 1981–1991/92, England

Year	Diphtheria	Tetanus	Polio	Whooping cough	Measles	Mumps/ rubella
1981	83	83	82	46	55	..
1982	84	84	84	53	58	..
1983	84	84	84	59	60	..
1984	84	84	84	65	63	..
1985	85	85	85	65	68	..
1986	85	85	85	67	71	..
1987/88	87	87	87	73	76	..
1988/89	87	87	87	75	80	7
1989/90	89	89	89	78	84	68
1990/91	92	92	92	84	87	86
1991/92	93	93	93	88	90	90

Source: Department of Health

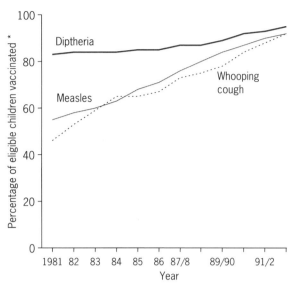

Figure 6.18 Immunisation rates for selected infectious diseases: 1981-92/93 England

* Eligible children vaccinated by end of the second year after birth

Source: Department of Health

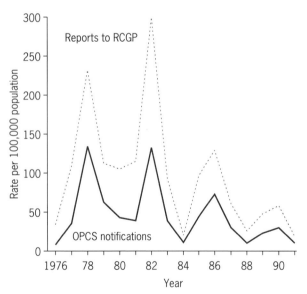

Figure 6.19 Notifications of whooping cough(OPCS) and new episodes of whooping cough reported to Royal College of General Practitioners (RCGP): 1976-91, England and Wales

Source: Communicable Disease Statistics 1976-91

6.4.6 Dental health

The dental health of children has improved greatly over the 1970s and 1980s. The 1993 Survey of Children's Dental Health aimed to estimate the levels of dental disease and other dental problems among school children aged 5–15 in the UK. It is the third survey in a series, the first of which was carried out in 1973 in England and Wales, and the second in 1983, covering the whole

of the UK. Preliminary results show major improvement in levels of caries since 1983. By the age of 15 more than five times as many children were free from caries in 1993 (37 per cent) than in 1983 (7 per cent) (Figure 6.20). The proportion of 15-year-olds with active, untreated decay has fallen from 42 per cent to 30 per cent, and the proportion with fillings is now 52 per cent compared with 85 per cent 10 years ago. Fewer than one in ten 15-year-olds (7 per cent) have had teeth extracted because of decay, compared with almost a quarter (24 per cent) in 1983. Similar patterns of improvement are found in all age groups and across the four constituent countries of UK. Nevertheless, in 1991 children in Northern Ireland still, as in 1983, had significantly higher levels of treated and active caries than the children in England, Wales and Scotland.

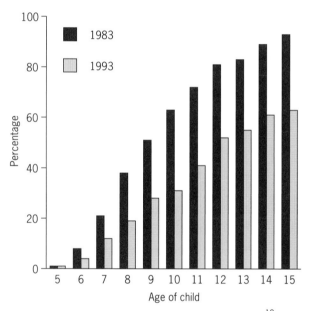

Figure 6.20 Proportion of children with decay experience in the permanent dentition: 1983 and 1993, United Kingdom

Source: Children's Dental Health in the United Kingdom, 1993.[18]

Community Dentists have traditionally treated children with the greatest dental health problems requiring complex treatment. Table 6.11 shows the number of general anaesthetics performed by Community Dentists in 1980 and in 1989/90. The sharp fall in the number of children given a general anaesthetic for dental purposes supports the findings that the dental health of children improved over this period.

Table 6.11 Number of general anaesthetics performed by Community Dentists in 1980 and 1989/90

	1980	1989/90
5–9 year olds	79,786	40,742
10–14 year olds	53,282	17,170

6.4.7 Child abuse and neglect

Unfortunately there is a minority of children who suffer at the hands of those who are supposed to care for them. Table 6.12 shows the number of children on local authorities' child protection registers in England as a result of abuse (neglect, physical, sexual, emotional and grave concern). National data have been compiled from these registers since 1989. The number of children on the register increased from 41,200 in March 1989 to 45,300 in 1991. Of all children under 18 years of age, 4 in 1000 are included on the register at any one time. Children under five years of age are most likely to be included. Over one third of children are included in the register because of 'grave concern' where abuse or neglect is suspected.

6.5 International comparisons

Table 6.13 provides a comparison of infant and childhood mortality between different countries. These comparisons are for 1971, 1981 and 1991, or the most recent year where available.

Since 1971 there have been similar decreases in the stillbirth and infant mortality rates in Scotland and Northern Ireland to those seen in England and Wales. The numbers in Northern Ireland are smaller and the mortality rates fluctuate more, but since 1984 these rates have been close to those in England and Wales and those in Scotland.

The decreasing trends in infant mortality in England and Wales over the past two decades have been paralleled by all the European Union countries. Table 6.14 shows a comparison over time for the countries belonging to the European Union. In 1991, the infant mortality rate for the 12 constituent countries of the European Union combined had fallen to 34 per cent of its 1971 level (Figure 6.21).

Table 6.13 shows infant and childhood mortality rates in selected countries of the world. Comparisons are difficult because of differences in registration and definition of causes of death. For example, some countries include nationals dying abroad, others include all residents

Table 6.12 Children on Child Protection Registers: 1989-91, England*

| | | Number/Rate per 1000 | | |
		1989	1990	1991
Numbers:	On the register	41,200	43,600	45,300
	Registrations	23,000	26,900	28,300
	De-registrations	21,800	24,200	26,700
Rates (per 1,000 population aged under 18 years)	On the register	3.8	4.0	4.2
	Registrations	2.1	2.5	2.6
	De-registrations	2.0	2.2	2.5
On the register Sex	Male	19,700	21,100	22,200
	Female	21,400	22,500	23,100
Age (years)	Under 1	2,700	2,700	2,800
	1–4	13,600	14,200	14,600
	5–9	13,200	14,000	14,500
	10–15	10,100	11,000	11,700
	16 and over	1,600	1,600	1,700
Category of abuse†	Neglect	6,600	7,100	6,800
	Physical	11,400	11,700	10,600
	Sexual	6,600	6,700	6,000
	Emotional	2,000	2,200	2,600
	Grave concern	16,300	17,900	21,100
Registrations Sex	Male	10,900	12,800	13,700
	Female	12,100	14,100	14,600
Age (years)	Under 1	3,000	3,400	4,000
	1–4	7,500	8,800	8,400
	5–9	6,300	7,500	8,000
	10–15	5,500	6,500	7,000
	16 and over	700	700	800
Category of abuse†	Neglect	2,900	3,700	3,300
	Physical	6,200	7,100	6,700
	Sexual	4,100	4,200	3,900
	Emotional	1,000	1,200	1,300
	Grave concern	9,200	11,800	14,100

* Includes estimates for some local authorities. Figures may not add to totals because of rounding.

† Children may be registered under more than one of the categories shown; the sum of the categories therefore exceeds the total number of children on the register.

Source: *Health and Personal Social Services Statistics for England, 1993*[19]

Table 6.13 Infant and child mortality by sex and age: international comparisons, 1991

Year	Country	Rates per 100,000 live births		Rates per 100,000 population			
		Under 1 year		Ages 1–4		Ages 5–14	
		Boys	Girls	Boys	Girls	Boys	Girls
1991	England and Wales	828	643	40	33	21	15
1991	Scotland	869	534	44	43	20	17
1991	N.Ireland	827	645	43	38	21	17
EU countries							
1990	Belgium	1,030	408	50	37	24	20
1991	Denmark	805	640	48	30	25	15
1991	France	833	614	42	36	23	17
1990	West Germany	790	600	43	35	20	15
1991	Greece	941	863	29	20	19	12
1991	Eire	855	658	38	31	24	15
1990	Italy	890	707	31	27	22	14
1991	Luxembourg	900	823	51	21	18	14
1991	Netherlands	770	524	47	34	18	17
1991	Portugal	1,220	935	87	65	51	31
1990	Spain	827	688	49	40	29	20
1991	UK	831	634	40	34	22	16
Other European							
1991	Bulgaria	1,911	1,461	102	89	49	30
1991	Czechoslovakia	1,254	1,030	54	41	31	19
1991	Finland	652	516	28	28	20	15
1990	GDR	836	625	61	46	38	28
1991	Iceland	553	550	44	24	5	10
1990	Israel	1,062	920	48	51	17	19
1991	Norway	690	580	39	39	17	16
1991	Poland	1,684	1,301	59	47	33	23
1991	Sweden	661	567	25	26	13	10
1991	Switzerland	711	530	37	42	28	15
1991	USSR	2,072	1,533	114	87	73	37
1990	Yugoslavia	2,052	1,792	70	62	34	24
Americas							
1990	Argentina	2,741	2,193	116	98	40	28
1991	Canada	693	581	39	28	23	17
1991	Puerto Rico	1,447	1,154	46	38	28	17
1990	USA	1,026	813	52	41	29	19
Africa							
1987	Egypt	4,651	4,359	642	729	155	126
Middle East							
1988	Bahrain	2,242	2,464	66	24	41	22
Other							
1991	Australia	785	610	37	31	21	15
1991	Japan	464	421	46	36	19	13
1986	Sri Lanka	2,553	2,114	178	179	76	68
1991	Singapore	593	492	37	34	23	23
1991	Hong Kong	677	651	28	31	18	18
1991	Trinidad	1,260	944	54	54	36	39
1990	Uruguay	2,262	1,791	84	73	35	28

Source: *World Health Statistics Annual 1991*[20]

including foreign nationals. There are also differences in the ability of some countries to record deaths in remote areas.

In 1991, the Netherlands had the lowest infant mortality rate of the European Community (6.8 per 1,000 live births); Portugal had the highest (12.2 per 1,000 live births).

Recently some of the lowest recorded infant mortality rates have been in Japan (4.6 and 4.2 per 1,000 live births for males and females respectively in 1991), and Iceland (5.5 for both sexes in 1991). Australia, Canada and the USA had rates similar to those of the UK. Poland had higher rates (17.9 for males, 14.0 for females in 1990), as did China (19.0 and 16.8 in 1989). The rates in Egypt were very much higher (46.5 and 43.6 in 1987).

Figure 6.21 Infant mortality: 1971, 1981 and 1991, European Union countries

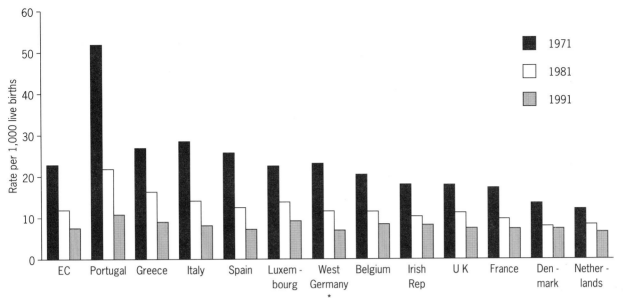

* 1991: Germany (West and East combined)

Source: Eurostat: Demographic Statistics 1988-94.

Table 6.14 Infant and childhood mortality (rates per 100,000 live births/population): 1971, 1981 and 1991, European Union countries

(a) 1971		Under 1 year		Ages 1–4		Ages 5–14	
		Boys	Girls	Boys	Girls	Boys	Girls
Belgium	Number	1,696	1,186	298	213	382	231
	Rate	2,331.2	1,724.5	102.4	76.8	47.8	30.2
Denmark	Number	602	417	126	76	204	119
	Rate	1,545.4	1,145.5	78.9	50.3	52.0	31.8
France	Number	7,195	5,277	1,451	1,191	1,888	1,211
	Rate	1,597.3	1,232.3	85.2	73.0	46.2	30.8
West Germany	Number	10,500	7,641	2,023	1,503	2,714	1,688
	Rate	2,622.2	2,020.9	106.2	83.0	55.0	36.0
Greece	Number	2,098	1,699	284	239	313	194
	Rate	2,877.2	2,490.9	94.1	81.4	43.1	28.3
Eire	Number	703	511	116	86	142	68
	Rate	2,023.0	1,557.9	90.8	70.8	45.2	22.6
Italy	Number	14,700	11,130	1,789	1,461	2,206	1,300
	Rate	3,155.6	2,527.5	98.0	83.6	49.8	30.6
Luxembourg	Number	54	37	11	9	17	10
	Rate	2,302.8	1,763.6	115.8	98.9	64.2	39.4
Netherlands	Number	1,623	1,134	476	316	565	340
	Rate	1,391.5	1,025.9	97.8	68.0	46.3	29.2
Portugal	Number	5,353	4,055	1,085	918	800	508
	Rate	5,503.2	4,418.6	312.7	279.6	93.7	62.4
Spain	Number	7,885	5,747	1,355	1,053	1,557	1,013
	Rate	2,338.0	1,802.4	102.6	84.6	49.1	33.3
UK	Number	9,426	6,798	1,439	1,129	1,889	1,138
	Rate	2,035.4	1,556.7	167.8	147.3	41.1	26.0

Table 6.14 - *continued*

		Under 1 year		Ages 1–4		Ages 5–14	
		Boys	Girls	Boys	Girls	Boys	Girls
(b) 1981							
Belgium*	Number	856	562	150	138	105	78
	Rate	1,360.0	930.0	60.0	60.0	30.0	20.0
Denmark	Number	238	181	64	47	114	84
	Rate	877.7	696.9	51.0	39.2	30.2	23.3
France	Number	4,623	3,200	966	735	1,381	923
	Rate	1,118.1	816.3	63.6	50.9	34.9	24.4
West Germany	Number	4,175	3,082	731	630	1,333	872
	Rate	1,302.1	1,014.1	60.8	55.1	33.2	22.8
Greece	Number	1,309	985	170	117	238	156
	Rate	1,792.1	1,450.5	57.4	42.3	31.5	22.1
Eire	Number	418	328	102	68	132	72
	Rate	1,126.1	930.9	71.2	49.9	37.2	21.4
Italy	Number	5,000	3,786	695	554	1,449	834
	Rate	1,564.8	1,252.5	47.5	40.0	32.3	19.6
Luxembourg (1980)	Number	20	40	3	5	6	13
	Rate	960.6	1,150.0	36.6	63.3	24.1	54.6
Netherlands	Number	854	629	219	180	326	208
	Rate	936.6	719.7	60.4	52.0	28.8	19.2
Portugal	Number	1,840	1,477	416	285	508	346
	Rate	2,348.0	2,002.4	126.0	90.4	58.1	41.1
Spain	Number	3,876	2,768	898	642	1,193	757
	Rate	1,409.0	1,706.3	71.3	54.0	35.0	23.8
UK	Number	4,759	3,402	771	599	1,183	776
	Rate	1,271.4	958.9	55.1	45.2	28.4	19.6
(c) 1991							
Belgium (1989)	Number	625	406	95	77	140	109
	Rate	1008.9	688.6	39.5	33.7	22.6	18.4
Denmark	Number	266	201	58	34	72	42
	Rate	804.6	640.0	47.6	29.5	24.7	15.0
France	Number	3,242	2,269	656	524	856	588
	Rate	832.9	613.5	42.4	35.5	22.9	16.5
West Germany	Number	3,279	2,432	832	619	931	666
	Rate	769.5	602.1	44.8	35.1	21.3	16.0
Greece	Number	496	431	62	40	135	78
	Rate	941.4	863.2	28.5	19.5	19.3	11.9
Eire	Number	232	168	43	33	81	49
	Rate	854.7	657.6	38.3	31.1	23.5	14.9
Italy (1990)	Number	2,663	1,991	356	291	747	466
	Rate	889.8	707.3	30.6	26.5	21.8	14.4
Luxembourg	Number	23	20	5	2	4	3
	Rate	899.5	823.4	50.5	21.1	17.9	14.2
Netherlands	Number	782	509	181	124	162	149
	Rate	769.8	524.3	46.8	33.5	17.6	17.0
Portugal	Number	731	528	208	147	376	218
	Rate	1,220.0	934.6	86.6	65.0	50.5	30.9
Spain (1990)	Number	1,716	1,334	426	326	832	540
	Rate	827.0	687.9	48.8	40.0	28.9	20.0
UK	Number	3,377	2,448	636	512	799	544
	Rate	831.0	634.0	40.1	34.0	21.7	15.6

* Annuaire Statistique de la belgique: tomme 110.

Source: *World Health Statistics Annuals 1971-93*

6.6 Conclusion

While mortality rates in children have shown a definite decline over this period, trends in morbidity are less clear. This is partly because there is less information routinely collected on morbidity than on mortality and because its ascertainment is more complex. Much of the information we do have is about health-care service use rather than the health of the child population. At least in part the information reflects the availability of services rather than the underlying prevalence or incidence of disease or disability.

The information that is available, however, tells a changing story. Different parents interviewed over the period perceived largely similar levels of morbidity in their children, according to the General Household Survey (GHS).[6] There has been an increase in the hospital admission rate for children during the 1970s and 1980s, although the average length of stay has been reduced.

There is evidence that the prevalence of some chronic disabling conditions, such as cerebral palsy, has increased as their case fatality falls and expectation of life of affected individuals increases. On the other hand the availability and high uptake of immunisation against an increasing number of acute infections, such as measles and mumps, has resulted in a fall in the numbers of their notifications.

As the pattern of childhood mortality and morbidity has changed during the 1970s and 1980s, so has the health care provided to children and their families. More time is now spent on child surveillance in primary care, whilst at the same time specialist hospital services for acutely ill children are being developed to ensure that seriously ill children get the best care possible at the most appropriate time. There is also an emphasis on the primary prevention of disease and disability.

Over the next twenty years we will undoubtedly see further changes in the patterns of childhood mortality and morbidity. Infectious diseases, such as measles and whooping cough, are likely to become even less common. Advances in medicine will bring hope of treatment and cure for some diseases which cannot now be successfully treated, thus reducing morbidity and mortality. Mortality rates will probably continue to fall, although they are presently at low levels so the scope for reduction must be limited. Yet the geographical variations in mortality implies that there is such a scope.

The major emerging problems are those due to genetic disorders or other chronic and disabling conditions, where falls in mortality are likely to be associated with increases in morbidity, unless affected pregnancies are terminated or the initial cause can be identified and prevented.

References

1. OPCS. *Occupational Mortality: Childhood Supplement 1979–80, 82–83.* Series DS No 8. HMSO (London 1988).
2. OPCS. *Mortality Statistics - Perinatal and Infant: social and biological factors.* Series DH3, HMSO (various).
3. Botting B and Cooper J. Mother's occupation. Part II. *Population Trends* **74**, HMSO (1993).
4. Botting B and Macfarlane A J. Geographic variation in infant mortality in relation to birthweight. In Britton M (ed.). *Mortality and Geography: A Review in the mid–1980s, England and Wales.* Series DS No 9. HMSO (1990).
5. Alberman E D, Botting B, Blatchley N and Twidell A. A new hierarchical classification of causes of infant deaths in England and Wales. *Archives Disease in Childhood*, **70**, 1994, 403-409.
6. OPCS. *General Household Survey.* HMSO (London annual publication).
7. OPCS. *Morbidity Statistics from General Practice 1991/92* (MSGP4). MB5 Series no. 5, HMSO (1994).
8. Department of Health and Social Security and OPCS. *Hospital In–Patient Enquiry 1985.* HMSO (London 1987).
9. Bone M and Meltzer H. *The Prevalence of Disability Among Children.* OPCS. HMSO (London 1986).
10. Botting B J, Macdonald Davies I M and Macfarlane A J. Recent trends in the incidence of multiple births and associated mortality. *Archives of Disease in Childhood.* **62**, 1987, 941–950.
11. Botting B J, Macfarlane A J, Price F V (eds). *Three, Four and More: a Study of Triplet and Higher Order Births.* HMSO (London 1990).
12. Powell T G, Pharoah P O D, Cooke R W. Survival and mortality in a geographically defined population of low birthweight infants. *Lancet,* **i**, 539–543.
13. Pharoah *et al* . Birthweight specific trends in cerebral palsy. *Archives. Disease Children*, **65**, 1990, 602–606.
14. Hagberg B, Hagberg G and Olow I. Gains and hazards of intensive neonatal care – and analysis from Swedish cerebral palsy epidemiology, *Developmental Medicine and Child Neurology*, **24**, 13-19.
15. Petterson B, Nelson K B, Watson L, Stanley F. Twins, triplets and cerebral palsy in births in Western Australia in the 1980s. *British Medical Journal*, **307**, 1993,12, 39–43.
16. Department of Health. How to reduce the risk of cot deaths. Department of Health (London 1991). (Press Release: H91/S14).
17. OPCS. *Congenital Malformation Statistics: Notifications 1991.* Series MB3 No 7. HMSO (London 1993).
18. O'Brien M. Children's dental health in the United Kingdom 1993. OPCS. HMSO (London 1994).
19. *Health and Personal Social Services Statistics for England*, 1993. p.67. HMSO (1993).
20. World Health Organisation. *World Health Statistics Annual 1991.* WHO (Geneva 1992).

7 The health of infants and children among ethnic minorities

Veena Soni Raleigh and R Balarajan

Key points

- 3 million people of ethnic minority origin reside in England and Wales, constituting almost 6 per cent of the total population.

- In 1991 one million children aged under 16 in Great Britain were considered by their parents to belong to an ethnic minority group.

- Infants of mothers born in Pakistan, the Caribbean and Africa other than those from East Africa, show excess mortality throughout infancy. In infants of mothers born in India, Bangladesh and East Africa, higher mortality in the first few weeks of life is followed by lower mortality in the postneonatal period.

- In England and Wales during 1989–91 the perinatal mortality rate for infants of mothers born in Pakistan was almost double the rate of the UK-born mothers.

- A higher proportion of deaths to infants of Asian-born mothers is attributed to congenital anomalies, compared with infants of UK-born-mothers.

- Infants of Asian and African-born mothers have much lower rates of sudden infant death syndrome than infants of UK-born mothers.

- Some inherited genetic diseases, such as sickle cell anaemia, occur mainly among ethnic minority populations.

- Iron deficiency anaemia and vitamin D deficiency is more common among children from ethnic minority groups.

- Asian children have a higher incidence rate of tuberculosis.

There are an estimated 3 million people of ethnic minority origin residing in England and Wales, constituting almost 6 per cent of the total population.[1] The health of these minority groups, especially of the children, should have attracted sufficient interest to have generated data both routinely and through *ad hoc* research. On the contrary, there is a paucity of information on this subject. This is largely because information on ethnic origin has not previously been recorded in health information systems and population-based statistics. In this chapter an attempt has been made to provide, despite these limitations, an overview on the subject. We examine ethnic differences in the levels and causes of infant and childhood morbidity and mortality and in the uptake of health care.

This chapter focuses on people originating from the New Commonwealth, which includes the countries of India, Pakistan, Bangladesh (these are sometimes aggregated and analysed as the Indian subcontinent), the East African Commonwealth, the rest of the African Commonwealth

and the Caribbean Commonwealth. Other ethnic groups are not included in this review because their numbers are relatively smaller and there has been little research about their health.

The health of ethnic minority children is important for several reasons. Epidemiological research has shown that patterns of disease vary between ethnic groups, and it is important that the individual health needs of different ethnic groups are adequately addressed. The differences between regional and religious subgroups of Asians and Africans are in some instances even greater than those between the ethnic groups and the indigenous population.

7.1 Methodological issues

Mortality has hitherto been used as one of the main yardsticks for measuring ethnic differences in health.[2,3] Information on ethnic origin is not recorded at death registration or (until 1991) in the census. Country of birth has, however, been collected at death registration and (for the parents) at birth registration. Therefore, hitherto, country of birth has been used as a proxy for ethnic origin in analyses of mortality differentials between groups.

The 1991 Census, however, collected information about both country of birth and ethnic group,[4] and this gives some idea of the reliability of using country of birth as a proxy for ethnic origin. The Indian-born and African-born include sizeable numbers of white expatriates, although these are predominantly among older age groups. East Africans are predominantly of Asian origin; about 70 per cent of those born in East Africa gave their ethnic origin as Indian or Pakistani in responding to the 1991 Census question.

People of different ethnic origins born in the UK are classified as UK-born. Since the UK-born constitute an increasing proportion of the ethnic minority populations resident in Britain, country of birth is becoming an increasingly inadequate proxy for examining ethnic differences in health. These issues are examined in greater detail elsewhere.[6]

Despite these limitations, country of birth has so far served as a reasonably adequate measure of ethnic differentials in health among infants (based on the mother's country of birth) and among adults (based on the country of birth of the deceased). This is because the numbers of first generation, foreign-born mothers/adults in this country (though diminishing) are sizeable enough to provide the basis for sound epidemiological analysis. The analysis for infants is made possible by linking information from the child's birth registration to that from its death registration. Unfortunately this linkage previously stopped at age 1, so it was not possible to analyse deaths at older ages in childhood by their mother's country of birth, only by their own country of birth. Country of birth for children is the least satisfactory as a measure of ethnic differences in mortality, because of

the small numbers of children resident in this country but born overseas. Another limitation of examining childhood mortality by country of birth is that the analysis may not be representative of the majority of ethnic minority children who are born and brought up in this country.

7.2 Population size

For the first time in British history we now have data (from the 1991 Census) on the size and composition of the country's ethnic minority populations. Most of the ethnic groups discussed in this chapter moved to Britain in recent decades as young adults. Therefore the age structure of these populations is younger than that of the indigenous population, and they have higher proportions of children (Figure 7.1). Conversely, ethnic minority populations have relatively low proportions of elderly people.

About 10 per cent of the child population (ages 0–14 years) of England and Wales is non-white. The ethnic composition of this population is shown in Figure 7.2, and the numbers of children in different ethnic groups are given in Table 7.1. Indian, Pakistani and Bangladeshi children comprise over half (53 per cent) of the non-white children, and black children comprise about one quarter (27 per cent).

There are approximately 50,000 births annually in England and Wales to mothers born in the New Commonwealth, constituting 7 per cent of all births (Table 7.2).[5] An additional (estimated) 10,000 births occur each year to UK-born mothers of West Indian, African or Asian origin.[6] Hence approximately 8 per cent of births each year are to mothers in these ethnic groups. Pakistanis and Bangladeshis have higher (although falling) fertility rates than other groups (Table 7.2)[5] and hence proportionately greater numbers of children. The numbers of births to ethnic minority mothers will grow in the future as present generations of children and teenagers reach childbearing ages.

Figure 7.1 Age composition by ethnic group: 1991, England and Wales

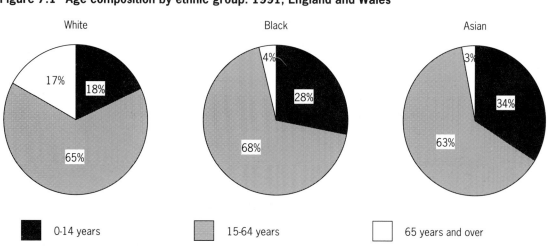

Source: 1991 Census: Ethnic group and country of birth, Great Britain. Vol 2, HMSO (1993).

Figure 7.2 Ethnic composition of the population aged 0-14: 1991, England and Wales

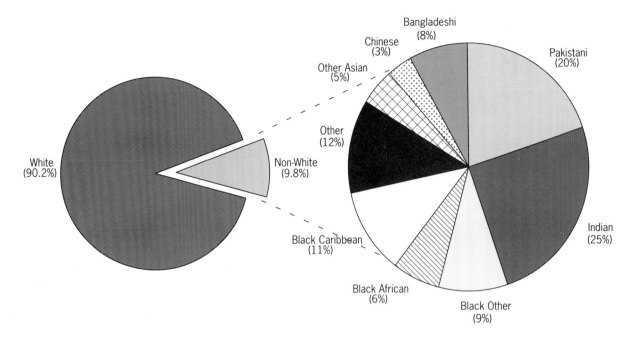

Source: 1991 Census: Ethnic Group and Country of Birth, Great Britain, Vol. 2, HMSO (1993).

Table 7.1 Ethnic composition of children aged 0 to 14 years in England and Wales

Ethnic group	Numbers	Percentage
Total	9,426,387	100.0
White	8,500,412	90.2
Black Caribbean	103,569	1.1
Black African	58,842	0.6
Black Other	85,414	0.9
Indian	231,608	2.5
Pakistani	185,334	2.0
Bangladeshi	72,228	0.8
Chinese	31,621	0.3
Other Asian	44,556	0.5
Other	112,803	1.2

Source: *1991 Census: Ethnic Group and Country of Birth. Great Britain*
Vol 2. HMSO (1993)

Table 7.2 Live births and total period fertility rates by mother's country of birth: 1981, 1986 and 1991, England and Wales

Mother's country of birth	Live births			Total period fertility rates		
	1981	1986	1991	1981	1986	1991
India	12,402	10,650	8,070	3.1	2.9	2.1
Pakistan	13,349	13,559	12,638	6.5*	5.6*	4.6*
Bangladesh	3,079	4,717	5,544			
East Africa	6,800	7,142	6,445	2.1	2.0	1.8
Rest of Africa	3,329	3,700	5,366	3.4	2.8	4.2
Caribbean	6,247	4,674	3,459	2.0	1.8	1.5
New Commonwealth	53,165	52,705	49,297	2.9	2.9	2.5**
England and Wales	634,492	661,018	699,217	1.7	1.7	1.8

* Pakistan and Bangladesh combined.

Source: *Birth Statistics 1991*[5]

7.3 Mortality

7.3.1 Perinatal mortality

Perinatal mortality (stillbirths plus deaths in the first week of life) is generally higher among infants of mothers born in the New Commonwealth countries than in infants of UK-born mothers (Figure 7.3). In England and Wales during 1989–91 the rate for infants of mothers born in Pakistan was almost double the rate of the UK-born group and higher than the rates for Bangladeshi- and Indian-born mothers. This excess was apparent at all maternal ages and parities (within marriage) (Figure 7.4). A similar excess was seen in all social classes (Figure 7.5).

Figure 7.3 Perinatal mortality by mother's country of birth: 1989-91 combined, England and Wales

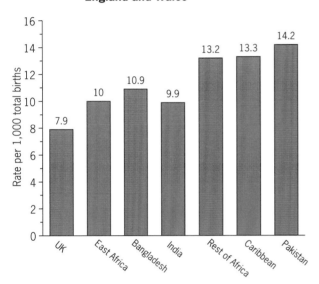

Source: Mortality Statistics - perinatal and infant: social and biological factors, 1989-91

Perinatal mortality was significantly higher also in infants of mothers born in the Caribbean, and in those originating from Africa other than East Africa, with these groups showing an almost 70 per cent excess over infants of UK-born mothers. Levels were not quite so high in infants of Indian and East African mothers, nonetheless they experienced perinatal mortality rates about 25 per cent higher than infants of UK-born mothers. Infants of Bangladeshi-born mothers were also at higher risk, with an excess of 38 per cent.

Perinatal mortality is closely associated with birthweight. In 1991 low birthweight infants (those weighing less than 2,500 grams at birth) constituted 7 per cent of all deliveries in England and Wales, but accounted for 59 per cent of perinatal deaths. Low birthweight is a partial explanation for the higher perinatal mortality of ethnic minority babies. Mothers born outside the UK generally have higher proportions of low birthweight babies than indigenous mothers (Figure 7.6); this is partly due to their genetic predisposition. The proportion of low birthweight babies in 1991 ranged from 9 per cent in Caribbean-born mothers to 12 per cent and 13 per cent respectively for mothers born in India and East Africa. Infants of mothers born in the Caribbean, Pakistan and non-Eastern Africa have higher perinatal mortality than infants of Indian and East African-born mothers, even though the latter groups have higher proportions of low birthweight babies.

There has been a decline in perinatal mortality among all ethnic groups since the mid-1970s, reflecting the trend in UK-born mothers (Figure 7.7). Differentials between the UK group on the one hand and the Indian, East African and Bangladeshi groups on the other have generally narrowed over the decade to 1985, but not thereafter.[7] However, the persistence of a significant excess of perinatal mortality in infants of Pakistani and Caribbean-born mothers over infants of UK-born mothers is worrying.

Figure 7.4 Perinatal mortality by (a) mother's age and (b) parity for mothers born in the UK and the Indian subcontinent: 1989-91 combined, England and Wales

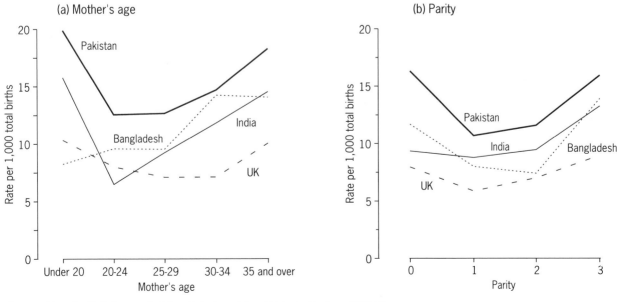

Source: Mortality Statistics - perinatal and infant: social and biological factors, 1989-91

Figure 7.5 Perinatal mortality by social class and mother's country of birth: 1989-91 combined, England and Wales

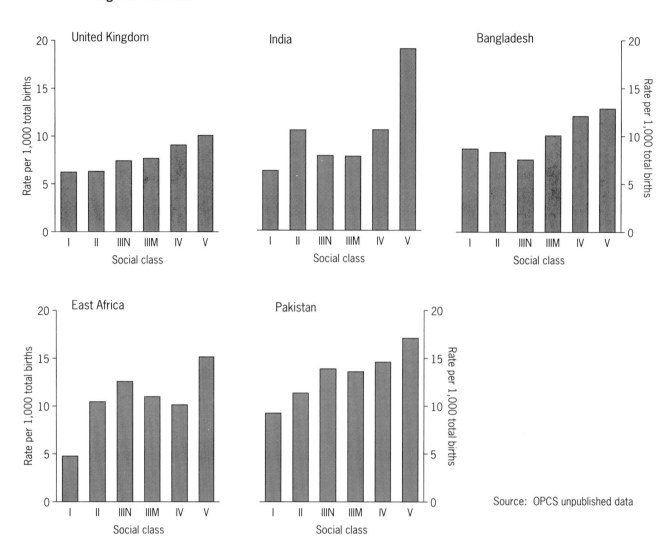

Source: OPCS unpublished data

Figure 7.6
Percentage birthweight distribution (total births) by mother's country of birth: 1991, England and Wales

- ■ Under 2,500 g
- □ 2,500-2,999 g
- ▨ 3,000-3,499 g
- ▦ 3,500 g and over

Source: Mortality Statistics - perinatal and infant: social factors 1975-91.

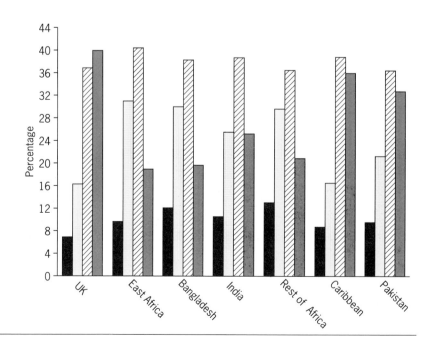

Figure 7.7
Trends in perinatal mortality by mother's country of birth: 1976-90, England and Wales

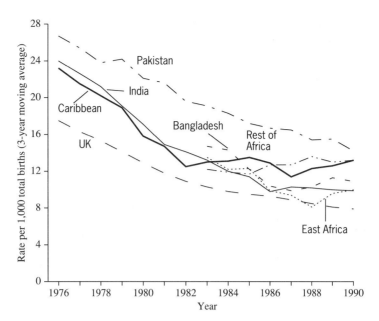

Source: Mortality Statistics - perinatal and infant: social factors 1975-91.

7.3.2 Neonatal mortality

Neonatal mortality was also higher for infants of mothers born outside the UK (Figure 7.8) showing highest rates for mothers born in Pakistan and Africa other than East Africa.

7.3.3 Postneonatal mortality

Postneonatal mortality in England and Wales in 1989–91 was again highest in infants of mothers born in Pakistan (Figure 7.9), followed by those originating in the Caribbean Commonwealth. Infants of mothers born in the UK and non-Eastern Africa had similar rates. Infants of mothers born in India, Bangladesh, and East

Africa had lower postneonatal mortality than infants of UK-born mothers, contrasting with the patterns reported for perinatal and neonatal mortality which was consistently higher in ethnic minority groups. Some explanation for these differences is given in the next section when examining the causes of death at different ages in infancy.

7.3.4 Causes of infant death

Congenital anomalies are a major cause of death among babies, contributing to about one-fifth of all infant deaths and stillbirths in England and Wales.[8] The term 'congenital anomalies' is considered here to include genetic disease and syndromes, not necessarily with

Figure 7.8 Neonatal mortality by mother's country of birth: 1989-91 combined, England and Wales

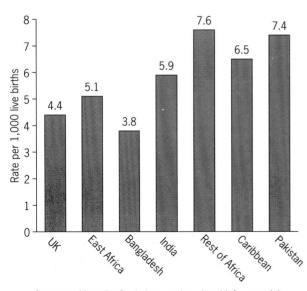

Source: Mortality Statistics - perinatal and infant: social and biological factors, 1989-91.

Figure 7.9 Postneonatal mortality by mother's country of birth: 1989-91 combined, England and Wales

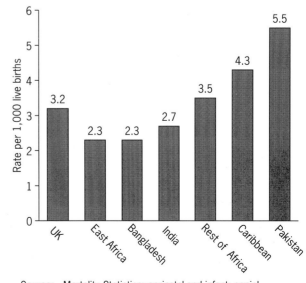

Source: Mortality Statistics: perinatal and infant: social and biological factors, 1989-91

malformations. More detail on causes of death is given in Chapter 6. An analysis of England and Wales data for 1981–5 showed that the proportion of deaths attributed to congenital anomalies was higher for infants of Asian-born mothers, being highest (33 per cent) in infants of Pakistani mothers.[8] Mortality rates from congenital anomalies differ markedly between ethnic groups, with all groups of mothers of Asian origin (including East Africans) showing an excess (Figure 7.10). Age- and social class-adjusted mortality from congenital anomalies was highest in infants of Pakistani-born mothers, being 2.4 times greater than the level in infants of UK-born mothers, and covered virtually all systems (Figure 7.11). Differences in mortality from congenital anomalies accounted for about half of the excess perinatal and postneonatal deaths among Pakistani infants during this period. Mortality from congenital anomalies is low in infants of Afro-Caribbean origin (Figure 7.10).

Several *ad hoc* studies have also reported higher mortality from congenital anomalies in Asian infants in Britain, and particularly in Pakistani infants.[9–12] The aetiology of congenital anomalies is complex and not fully understood. Many factors, including social class, maternal age, parity and nutrition, are associated with incidence. The higher incidence of anomalies in Asian babies in this country is attributed to several possible causes, including differences in immunity to teratogenic viruses, diet and the uptake of screening and therapeutic abortion. The heavy load of mortality from congenital anomalies in Pakistani infants is generally attributed to the greater frequency of consanguineous marriages in this community, and to childbearing at older maternal ages.[9–12]

In 1991, 41 per cent of infant deaths in England and Wales occurred in the postneonatal period. Sudden infant death syndrome (SIDS) accounts for about 40 per cent of all postneonatal deaths. Although the aetiology of this condition is not fully understood, the numbers of such

Figure 7.10 Infant deaths and stillbirths from congenital anomalies by mother's country of birth: 1981-85 combined, England and Wales

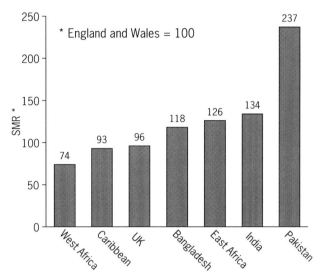

Source: Balarajan R, Soni Raleigh V and Botting B.

deaths fell sharply between 1990 and 1992. As shown in Chapters 6 and 9, SIDS remains a major cause of infant death in England and Wales claiming 1,208 lives in 1990, 1,008 in 1991 and falling to 531 in 1992.

Infants of Asian- and African-born mothers have much lower rates of SIDS than infants of UK-born mothers (Figure 7.12).[13] This is true also of infants of Pakistani mothers, even though they generally experience much higher mortality from other causes. The lower postneonatal mortality of infants with Indian, Bangladeshi and East African mothers, compared with infants of UK-born mothers, results from this lower rate of SIDS. The lower incidence of SIDS among Asian infants in this country has also been demonstrated in more recent studies.[14]

Figure 7.11 Infant deaths and stillbirths from congenital anomalies in infants of mothers born in Pakistan: 1981-85 combined, England and Wales

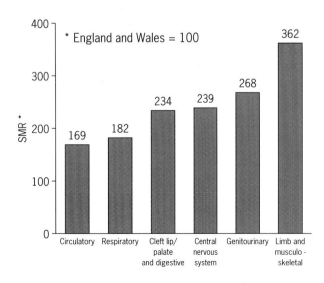

Source: Balarajan R, Soni Raleigh V and Botting B. [8]

Figure 7.12 Sudden infant deaths by mother's country of birth: 1982-85 combined, England and Wales

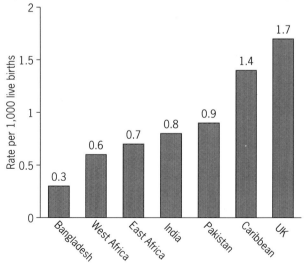

Source: Balarajan R, Soni Raleigh V and Botting B. [8]

The reasons underlying a lower incidence of SIDS in Asian babies are not clear. Asian women belong disproportionately to Social Classes IV and V and have higher proportions of low birthweight babies, variables associated with an increased risk of SIDS.[15] In contrast, they have fewer births outside marriage and few Asian women smoke, variables associated with a lower risk of SIDS. Attention has focused recently on the hypothesis that the supine sleeping position is protective against SIDS,[16] a practice now recommended by the Department of Health to mothers of young infants. Asian babies are generally put to sleep in the supine position,[17] thus supporting this hypothesis.

7.3.5 Summary of infant deaths
In summary, infants of mothers born in Pakistan, the Caribbean and Africa other than those from East Africa, show excess mortality throughout infancy. The excess is greatest among Pakistani infants and adjustments for biological (maternal age and parity) and social factors reduce but do not eliminate the excess mortality nor the higher congenital anomaly rates. In infants of mothers born in India, Bangladesh and East Africa higher mortality in the first few weeks of life is followed by lower mortality in the postneonatal period.

The reasons underlying these ethnic differences in infant mortality are multifactorial. The higher mortality rates reflect the influence of economic factors such as unemployment and socio-economic deprivation, and social factors such as marriage and childbearing patterns, and attitudes to antenatal screening. There are also nutritional differences, which contribute to the higher incidence of high-risk low birthweight babies among ethnic minority mothers. The timing, uptake and quality of health care are also critical factors determining pregnancy outcome and infant health, and these have also been shown to vary between ethnic groups.[18,19]

7.3.6 Childhood mortality
Analysis of childhood mortality by the child's country of birth is subject to the limitations discussed in section 7.1, primarily the small numbers of events. This is particularly true for deaths of children born in the Caribbean Commonwealth, whose numbers are too low for comment.

Standardised mortality ratios (SMRs) for ages 1–4 and 5–14 years for the period 1979–83, years centring on the 1981 Census, show elevated mortality in most ethnic groups examined (Table 7.3). At ages 1–4 the excess was statistically significant among children born in Bangladesh (SMR 197, 95% confidence intervals (CI) 102–344) and for children born in the countries of the Indian subcontinent combined, (SMR 152, 95% CI 107–210). The excess was apparent also in children born in Africa, with an overall SMR for the African Commonwealth of 192 (95% CI 107–316). All ethnic groups other than East Africans experienced higher mortality in older children aged 5–14 years. The excess reached formal statistical significance among children born in the Indian subcontinent (SMR 128, 95% CI 100–161).

Since these results relate to children resident in this country but born overseas, and hence to relatively recent migrants, they probably reflect the influence of the countries of origin. These results may, therefore, not be representative of the experience of the majority of ethnic minority children in this country, who are born and brought up here.

7.3.7 Causes of childhood mortality
The leading causes of childhood mortality in England and Wales during the years 1979–83, the period for which comparable data are available for ethnic minorities, are shown in Figure 7.13. The loss of life at ages 1–4 years was greatest from injury and poisoning followed by congenital anomalies, diseases of the respiratory system and cancers. Analysis by cause is constrained by the small numbers of deaths among foreign-born ethnic minority children. Broadly speaking, the distributions by cause of death among children born in the Indian subcontinent and the African Commonwealth were similar to the patterns seen for the country as a whole.

In England and Wales over the period 1979–83 the loss of life for children aged 5–14 years, was again greatest from injury and poisoning (37 per cent), with motor vehicle accidents (most of them involving child pedestrians) contributing to one fifth of all deaths at these ages (Figure 7.13). Another one fifth of deaths at ages 5–14 years resulted from cancer. Children born in the Indian subcontinent reflected similar patterns of mortality.

Table 7.3 Standardised mortality ratios (SMR) by country of birth: 1979–83 combined, England and Wales

Country of birth	Ages 1–4 years		Ages 5–14 years	
	SMR*	95% CI	SMR*	95% CI
England and Wales	100 (5,764)		100 (8,485)	
Indian subcontinent	152 (37)**	107–210	128 (72)**	100–161
India	74 (3)	15–216	127 (20)	78–196
Pakistan	155 (21)	96–237	135 (38)	96–185
Bangladesh	197 (12)**	102–344	112 (12)	58–196
African Commonwealth	192 (15)**	107–317	110 (41)	79–149
East African Commonwealth	166 (6)	61–361	98 (28)	65–142
Rest of African Commonwealth	214 (9)	98–406	147 (13)	78–251
Caribbean Commonwealth	55 (1)	1–306	138 (8)	59–272

* England and Wales = 100, numbers of deaths in parentheses.
** Statistically significant.

Figure 7.13 Causes of childhood mortality: 1979-83 combined, England and Wales

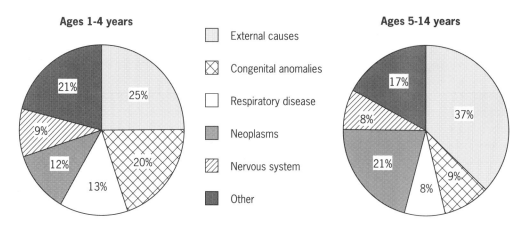

Source: Mortality Statistics - cause, 1979-83

African-born children had proportionately fewer deaths from external causes and a higher contribution from cancer and diseases of the nervous system, although the numbers of deaths were low and these comments should be interpreted with caution.

7.4 Morbidity

7.4.1 Congenital anomalies
As discussed earlier in this chapter, mortality associated with congenital anomalies is greater in Asian infants than in the indigenous population. Little is known about ethnic differences in survival rates for similarly affected infants, or about the quality of life for surviving ethnic minority babies born with congenital anomalies. If congenital anomaly mortality reflects birth prevalence and survival rates are similar in ethnic groups, the numbers of disabled children in some communities may be quite substantial. The level of disability and handicap in ethnic minority children, the health care they receive and how their families cope with such disability, are important issues which deserve investigation.

7.4.2 Rubella
Many Asian women in the UK have not been immunised against rubella, having come to this country as young adults and missed school immunisation. Thus they are at greater risk of contracting rubella in pregnancy and giving birth to an affected child. Antenatal serological data from selected public health laboratories in the country show that susceptibility to rubella is nearly 3-fold higher in Asian than in non–Asian women and is associated with a 2.3-fold excess of congenital rubella among babies born to Asian women.[20,21] It is also reported that Asian women are less likely than non–Asian women to seek diagnostic investigation for possible rubella in pregnancy.[20]

7.4.3 Inherited disorders
Some inherited genetic diseases occur with greater frequency among ethnic minority populations. Sickle cell anaemia occurs mainly among people of Afro–Caribbean descent. The trait of the disease may be found in as many as 1 in 10 Afro–Caribbean babies,[22,23] although the illness will occur only if both parents are carriers. The Sickle Cell Society estimates that about 1 in 300–400 babies of Afro–Caribbean descent is born with the disease.

Another inherited disorder, thalassaemia minor, occurs with greater than expected frequency in people of Asian origin. The incidence of thalassaemia minor, the carrying trait without ill effects, is about 1 in 10–20 Indians and Pakistanis, and 1 in 1,000 British.[23-25] For a child to be born with thalassaemia major, both parents must have the beta thalassaemia trait. Although a programme of detection, counselling and abortion of affected fetuses has proved acceptable to some Asian groups, among whom the thalassaemia major birth rate has fallen by 20 per cent, the programme appears to be less acceptable to the Pakistani population.[26] Most of the births of children with thalassaemia major in the UK are to Indian and Pakistani families.[24,27]

7.4.4 Nutritional disorders
Some of the commonest nutritional problems seen in Asian children are vitamin D deficiency and iron deficiency anaemia. The groups particularly affected by vitamin D deficiency are pregnant women, newborn babies, children and adolescents. Vitamin D deficiency during pregnancy or lactation can result in complications in the fetus or newborn infant. One study reported a pronounced vitamin D deficiency in 22 per cent of Asian adults, while none of the Caucasian controls had such low concentrations.[28] Osteomalacia is commonly reported in Asian women[29] with an enhanced risk of neonatal or congenital rickets in their newborn infants.[30] Studies in Tower Hamlets in the 1980s and in Edinburgh showed that most Asian children and adolescents studied were vitamin D-deficient.[31,32] Such deficiency in girls during the adolescent growth period can result in pelvic deformities and subsequent difficulties in childbearing.

Iron deficiency anaemia is common among Asian women and children in Britain. In one study up to three quarters of Asian women showed features of iron deficiency and one third were anaemic.[33] Iron deficiency is also more common in Asian than in Caucasian children.[34]

7.4.5 Respiratory disease

A high incidence of tuberculosis in Asian adults in Britain has been consistently reported, but it is disturbing that Asian children also have an excess. A report from the Medical Research Council based on a national survey of notifications in 1978–9 reported high levels of tuberculosis in children of Asian origin, including those born in Britain. The rates for British-born children (per 100,000 children under 15) were 72 in Indians and 95 in Pakistanis and Bangladeshis, compared with 3.6 in Caucasians.[35] In a survey of all notifications of tuberculosis in England and Wales in the first half of 1983, incidence was reported at 6.9 per 100,000 for the Caucasian population, 178 for Indians and 169 for Pakistanis and Bangladeshis.[36] The environment of inner cities, with overcrowded poor quality housing, is reported to have contributed to the spread of the disease in populations of Asian origin.[22,37–39]

As will be discussed in Chapter 9, studies suggest that environmental factors in early life have a significant influence on the prevalence of asthma in childhood.[39,40] The prevalence of asthma is reported to be greater in Asian and Afro–Caribbean children born in England than in those born overseas.[40,41] Prevalence is highest in Afro–Caribbean children born in England, being higher than in Caucasian or Asian children born in England and higher than in Afro–Caribbean children born abroad.[40] Although prevalence is estimated to be lower in Asian than in non–Asian children, Asian childrens' higher hospital admission rates for acute asthma could be related to difficulties of communication or compliance with the treatment.[42]

7.4.6 Accidents

As discussed in Chapters 6 and 8, accidents cause considerable injury among children and are the leading causes of death after the first year of life. Information about accidents among ethnic minority children is limited. Some studies report higher rates of accidental injury, especially burns, among Asian and Afro-Caribbean children, attributed mainly to overcrowded homes and low socioeconomic status.[43,44] A West London study showed no significant ethnic differences in home accidents among children, reporting that social class, overcrowding and housing tenure were more significant determinants of accidents and the severity of injuries.[45] Little is known about ethnic patterns of accidental injury outside the home, or among older children.

7.5 Uptake of health care

Information on the uptake of health care among ethnic minorities is sparse. Surprisingly little is known about the accessibility of services, their acceptability, the levels of uptake, the outcome and the reasons for seeking health care. These issues require investigation, since the epidemiological data show pronounced variations in disease patterns between ethnic groups. It is important therefore to establish how adequately the varying health needs of ethnic minorities are currently being met.

The timing and quality of antenatal care has a significant bearing on pregnancy outcome and infant survival and health. Findings about the uptake of antenatal care among pregnant ethnic minority women are mixed. The Leicestershire Perinatal Mortality Study showed a marked improvement over the years in the timing of initial antenatal care in Asian women, so that by the 1980s patterns were very similar to non–Asian women.[18] On the other hand, studies showed late and poor antenatal attendance among Bangladeshi women in East London in the 1980s[46] and Pakistani women in Birmingham and Bradford.[9,47] Few studies have examined the quality of antenatal and obstetric care; the Leicestershire studies show that this is an important determinant of perinatal outcome[18] and that ethnic minority mothers may be at a disadvantage.[19]

Data on immunisation uptake among ethnic minorities are limited. Studies in Bradford and Glasgow show that uptake levels (DPT, measles and polio) in Asian children are higher than in non–Asian children.[48,49]

Although some studies have examined ethnic differences in general practitioner (GP) consultation rates, few have studied children in particular. One study, based on national survey data, investigated ethnic differences in GP consultation rates by age. It noted that consultation rates at ages 0–15 years did not differ significantly between Indian, West Indian and Caucasian children, although levels for Pakistani boys were much higher than for Caucasian boys (Table 7.4).[50]

Another study of a group general practice in the London borough of Brent noted that on average West Indians consulted less often than British patients and that Asian men consulted more often.[51] Asians had higher consultation rates for upper respiratory tract infections and consultations for asthma were raised among both Asians and West Indians. Although the study did not present data for children separately, it noted that West Indian children had significantly higher consultations for eczema and fewer for otitis media.

Research on the uptake of hospital–based care among ethnic minorities has been limited and restricted largely to the examination of differences in case–mix. A study of hospital admissions in Leicestershire noted that Asians were much more likely to be diagnosed as having infectious and parasitic diseases (tuberculosis in particular); endocrine, nutritional and metabolic diseases; blood disorders; heart disease; respiratory disease; diseases of the eye and perinatal morbidity.[52] A more detailed examination showed that, for Asian children aged 5–14 years, the risk of being diagnosed with leukaemia or asthma was greater than in non-Asian children.

A recent study examined hospital in-patient admissions and out-patient attendance in Britain by ethnic origin, investigating children aged 0–15 years separately from adults. The study noted that admissions among Indian, Pakistani and West Indian children did not differ significantly from the rates in Caucasian children and out-patient attendance was lower (Table 7.4).[53] It cannot

Table 7.4 Odds ratios for GP consultations, in-patient admissions, and out-patient attendance, adjusted for age and socioeconomic group,* by ethnic origin for children aged 0–15 years

Ethnic origin	GP consultations 1983–85		In-patient admissions 1983–87		Out-patient attendance 1983–87	
	Boys	Girls	Boys	Girls	Boys	Girls
White	1	1	1	1	1	1
Indian (95% CI)	0.91 (0.60–1.40)	0.94 (0.60–1.47)	0.88 (0.57–1.34)	0.69 (0.40–1.18)	0.50 (0.32–0.80)	0.29 (0.15–0.56)
Pakistani (95% CI)	1.44 (0.88–2.34)	0.78 (0.43–1.41)	0.98 (0.55–1.74)	1.09 (0.61–1.93)	0.54 (0.28–1.03)	0.39 (0.18–0.83)
West Indian (95% CI)	1.00 (0.55–1.81)	0.97 (0.53–1.77)	1.04 (0.57–1.90)	0.73 (0.34–1.58)	0.67 (0.36–1.24)	0.47 (0.22–1.01)

* Socioeconomic group of head of household.

Sources: Balarajan R et al *Ethnic differences in general practitioner consultations*[50]
Balarajan R et al *Hospital care among ethnic minorities in Britain*[53]

be readily explained why the higher morbidity and mortality in ethnic minority infants and children from certain conditions is not reflected in higher hospital admission rates. The possibility of under-utilisation is plausible. Accidents and emergencies account for about a quarter of all out-patient visits in England.[54] Low out-patient attendance in ethnic minority children could reflect lower spontaneous utilisation of out-patient (including casualty) services.

In summary, the limited evidence to date suggests that levels of health service utilisation are not high in ethnic minority children (except for GP consultations in Pakistani boys), although the case-mix varies from that of Caucasian children.

7.6 Conclusions

In 1981 an editorial in the *British Medical Journal* lamented the lack of epidemiological research among Britain's ethnic minorities and argued for more such research including longitudinal studies.[55] Over a decade later the criticism still applies. Much of the research thus far has concentrated on conditions such as rickets, osteomalacia, tuberculosis and heart disease, but little is known about the use and quality of primary care services. Also, little is known about some important aspects of the health of ethnic minority children, such as child abuse, accidental injury and levels of disability and handicap. The inclusion in the 1991 Census of a question on ethnic origin and the incorporation of such information in routine health information systems, should help to bridge many of these information gaps.

Such information as is available suggests that morbidity and mortality is higher in ethnic minority children than in others. The excess spans most stages of infancy and childhood. The causes underlying the poorer health of these children are multifactorial, covering economic, social, environmental and genetic influences. Most of the ethnic minority populations are in low-paid employment and reside in inner city areas, with overcrowded poor quality housing and restricted access

to outdoor facilities. While the underlying social and economic disadvantages faced by ethnic minorities need to be resolved in the longer term, the provision of appropriate preventative and primary care services should be a priority for the NHS now.

References

1. OPCS. *1991 Census: Outline statistics for England and Wales from the County Monitors*. National Monitor CEN91 CM58. OPCS. (1992).
2. Marmot M G, Adelstein A M and Bulusu L. Immigrant mortality in England and Wales 1970-78. Causes of death by country of birth. *Studies on Medical and Population Subjects,* no. 47. OPCS. HMSO (1984).
3. Britton M. *Mortality and Geography: a Review in the mid-1980s, England and Wales.* OPCS Series DS no. 9. HMSO (1990).
4. Balarajan R and Soni Raleigh V. The ethnic populations of England and Wales: the 1991 Census. *Health Trends* 1992; 24: 113–116.
5. OPCS. *Birth Statistics 1991, England & Wales.* OPCS Series FM1 no.20, HMSO (1994).
6. Shaw C. Components of growth in the ethnic minority population. *Population Trends,* **52**, 1988, 26–30.
7. Balarajan R and Botting B. Perinatal mortality in England and Wales: variations by mother's country of birth (1982–85). *Health Trends,* **21**, 1989, 79–84.
8. Balarajan R, Soni Raleigh V and Botting B. Mortality from congenital malformations in England and Wales: variations by mother's country of birth. *Archives Diseases Children,* **64**, 1989, 1457–62.
9. Bundey S, Alam H, Kaur A *et al.* Why do UK-born Pakistani babies have high perinatal and neonatal mortality rates? *Paediatric and Perinatal Epidemiology,* **5**, 1991, 101–14.
10. Chitty L S and Winter R M. Perinatal mortality in different ethnic groups. *Archives Diseases Children,* **64**, 1989, 1036–41.
11. Young I D. Hereditary disorders. In McAvoy B R, Donaldson L J (eds). *Health Care for Asians.* Oxford General Practice Series 18, Oxford University Press (1990).
12. Little J and Nicoll A. The epidemiology and service

implications of congenital and constitutional anomalies in ethnic minorities in the United Kingdom. *Paediatric and Perinatal Epidemiology*, **2**, 1988, 161–84.

13. Balarajan R, Soni Raleigh V and Botting B. Sudden infant death syndrome and postneonatal mortality in immigrants in England and Wales. *British Medical Journal*, **298**, 1989, 716–20.

14. Kyle D, Sunderland R, Stonehouse M, *et al.* Ethnic differences in incidence of sudden infant death syndrome in Birmingham. *Archives Diseases Children*, **65**, 1990, 830–3.

15. Golding J, Limerick S and Macfarlane A. *Sudden Infant Death: Patterns, Puzzles and Problems*. Open Books Publishing (Shepton Mallet 1985).

16. Editorial. Prone, hot and dead. *Lancet*, (Nov 3), 1990, 1104.

17. Farooqui S, Perry I J and Beevers D G. Ethnic differences in sleeping position and in risk of cot death (letter). *Lancet*, **338**, 1991, 1455.

18. Clarke M, Clayton D G, Mason E S and MacVicar J. Asian mothers' risk factors for perinatal death – the same or different? A 10-year review of Leicestershire perinatal deaths. *British Medical Journal*, **297**, 1988, 384–7.

19. Clarke M and Clayton DG. Quality of obstetric care provided for Asian immigrants in Leicestershire. *British Medical Journal*, **286**, 1983, 621–3.

20. Miller E, Nicoll A, Rousseau S A *et al.* Congenital rubella in babies of South Asian women in England and Wales: an excess and its causes. *British Medical Journal*, **294**, 1987, 737–9.

21. Miller E, Waight P, Rousseau S A *et al.* Congenital rubella in the Asian community in Britain. *British Medical Journal*, **301**, 1990, 1391.

22. Donovan J L. Ethnicity and health: a research review. *Social Science Medicine*, **19**, 1984, 663–70.

23. Department of Health. Report of the working party of the Standing Medical Advisory Committee on Sickle Cell, Thalassaemia and other Haemoglobinopathies. HMSO (1993).

24. United Kingdom Thalassaemia Society. Factsheet Stamp Out Thalassaemia.

25. Varawalla N Y, Old J M, Sarkar R *et al.* The spectrum of beta thalassaemia mutations on the Indian subcontinent: the basis for prenatal diagnosis. *British Journal Haematology*, **78**, 1991, 242–7.

26. Modell B, Petrou M, Ward R H T *et al.* Effect of fetal diagnostic testing on birth–rate of thalassaemia major in Britain. *Lancet*, (December 15), 1984, 1383–6.

27. Black J. Paediatrics. In McAvoy B R, Donaldson L J (eds). *Health Care for Asians*. Oxford General Practice Series 18, Oxford University Press (1990).

28. Shaunak S, Colston K, Ang L *et al.* Vitamin D deficiency in adult British Hindu Asians: a family disorder. *British Medical Journal*, **291**, 1985, 1166–8.

29. Dandona P, Okonofua A and Clements R V. Osteomalacia presenting as pathological fractures during pregnancy in Asian women of high socio-economic class. *British Medical Journal*, **290**, 1985, 837–8.

30. Ford J A, Davidson D C, McIntosh W B *et al.* Neonatal rickets in Asian immigrant population. *British Medical Journal*, **3**, 1973, 211–12.

31. Harris R J, Armstrong D, Ali R, Loynes A. Nutritional survey of Bangladeshi children aged under 5 years in the London borough of Tower Hamlets. *Archives Diseases Children*, **58**, 1983, 428–32.

32. O'Hare A E, Uttley W S, Belton N R *et al.* Persisting vitamin D deficiency in the Asian adolescent. *Archives Diseases Children*, **59**, 1984, 766–70.

33. Britt R P, Hollis Y, Keil J E *et al.* Anaemia in Asians in London. *Postgrad Medical Journal*, **59**, 1983, 645–7.

34. Ehrhardt P. Iron deficiency in young Bradford children from different ethnic groups. *British Medical Journal*, **292**, 1986, 90–3.

35. Medical Research Council Tuberculosis and Chest Diseases Unit. Tuberculosis in children in a national survey of notifications in England and Wales, 1978–79. *Archives Diseases Children*, **57**, 1982, 734–41.

36. Medical Research Council Tuberculosis and Chest Diseases Unit. National survey of notifications of tuberculosis in England and Wales in 1983. *British Medical Journal*, **291**, 1985, 658–61.

37. Froggatt K. Tuberculosis: spatial and demographic incidence in Bradford. *Journal Epidemiology Community Health*, **39**, 1985, 20–6.

38. Ahmad W I U, Kernohan E E M and Baker M R. Health of British Asians; a research review. *Community Medicine*, **11**, 1989, 49–56.

39. Honeybourne D. Ethnic differences in respiratory diseases. *Postgraduate Medical Journal*, **63**, 1987, 937–42.

40. Morrison-Smith J. The prevalence of asthma and wheezing in children. *British Journal Diseases Chest*, **70**, 1976, 73–7.

41. Morrison-Smith J and Cooper S M. Asthma and atopic disease in immigrants from Asia and the West Indies. *Postgraduate Medical Journal*, **57**, 1981, 774–6.

42. Ayres J G. Acute asthma in Asian patients: hospital admissions and duration of stay in a district with a high immigrant population. *British Journal Diseases Chest*, **80**, 1986, 242–8.

43. Vipulendran V, Lawrence J C and Sunderland R. Ethnic differences in incidence of severe burns and scalds to children in Birmingham. *British Medical Journal*, **298**, 1989, 1493–4.

44. Learmonth A. Factors in child burn and scald accidents in Bradford 1969–73. *Journal Epidemiology Community Health*, **33**, 1979, 270–3.

45. Alwash R and McCarthy M. Accidents in the home among children under 5: ethnic differences or social disadvantage? *British Medical Journal*, **296**, 1988, 1450–3.

46. Watson E. Health of infants and use of health services by mothers of different ethnic groups in East London. *Community Medicine*, **6**, 1984, 127–35.

47. Lumb K M, Congdon P J and Lealman G T. A comparative review of Asian and British-born maternity patients in Bradford, 1974–8. *Journal Epidemiology Community Health*, **35**, 1981, 106–9.

48. Baker M R, Bandaranayake R and Schweiger M S.

Differences in rate of uptake of immunisation among ethnic groups. *British Medical Journal*, **288**, 1984, 1075–8.

49. Bhopal R S and Samim A K. Immunisation uptake of Glasgow Asian children. *Community Medicine*, **10**, 1988, 215–20.

50. Balarajan R, Yuen P and Soni Raleigh V. Ethnic differences in general practitioner consultations. *British Medical Journal*, **299**, 1989, 958–60.

51. Gillam S J, Jarman B, White P and Law R. Ethnic differences in consultation rates in urban general practice. *British Medical Journal*, **299**, 1989, 953–7.

52. Donaldson L J and Taylor J B. Patterns of Asian and non-Asian morbidity in hospitals. *British Medical Journal*, **286**, 1983, 949–51.

53. Balarajan R, Soni Raleigh V and Yuen P. Hospital care among ethnic minorities in Britain. *Health Trends,* **23**, 1991, 90–3.

54. Department of Health. NHS hospital activity statistics for England, 1979–88/89. *Statistical Bulletin* 2/1/90. Department of Health (London 1990).

55. Editorial. Ethnic factors in disease. *British Medical Journal*, **282**, 1981, 1496–7.

8 Accidents

Stephen Jarvis, Elizabeth Towner and Sean Walsh

Key points

- Accidents are the commonest cause of hospital admission in children aged 5–16 in the UK.

- Accidents cause nearly one half of all deaths at ages 1–19.

- In 1991 boys accounted for 60–65 per cent of all accident deaths at ages 1–19.

- In the UK mortality rates for pedestrian road traffic accidents among children are the second highest in Europe.

- Fires are the major cause of accidental deaths at home.

8.1 The scale of the problem

Unintentional injuries or 'accidents', are the commonest cause of death and hospital admission in children aged 5–16 years in the UK, a fact demonstrated in Chapter 6.

The direct costs to the NHS of accidental injury in childhood are estimated at over £200 million per annum.[1] Injuries result in many other costs beyond those to the NHS. Indeed recent research suggests that the value to the public of the prevention of child *road* casualties alone could be as much as £500 million per annum.[2]

There have been reductions in the child accident mortality rates in England and Wales over the last 20 years. There are major international differences in accident mortality rates. It is not known, however, whether these result from differences in treatment, improvements in preventive measures or other intervening effects. Meanwhile, hospital admission rates for child accidents continue to rise. We do not know whether this reflects a true increase in injury frequency.

Although accidents in childhood appear to have obvious 'causes', it has proved extraordinarily difficult to identify and change the important risk factors.

The interpretation of available causal data is not straightforward. For instance, although most road crossing injuries occur at road junctions, it is actually more dangerous for children to cross straight roads (see section 8.5.1(f)). To arrive at accurate causal information, a detailed account of children's behaviour is needed. Unfortunately there have been few attempts to measure the degree of exposure to known risk factors for accidental injury.

An additional dimension in the 'causal chain' for children is their biological immaturity. There is evidence to suggest that children under the age of 10 may be developmentally incapable of some of the perceptual judgements necessary for road crossing.[3,4] The net result of these uncertainties and of our poor information on the true frequency of injury is that only a small fraction of child accident prevention activity is known to be effective. Indeed some of the interventions could be dangerous. For a child growing up in this country at the end of the twentieth century, the possibility of a serious unintentional injury has become the single greatest threat to health.

8.2 Trends in mortality rates

8.2.1 Age

Accidental injury has remained the leading cause of death for children aged 1–15 years since the 1950s, as shown in Chapter 6. Although there have been reductions in the accident mortality rates for all age groups, these reductions are not as great as for the other major causes of death in childhood (for example, cancers and infections).

The greatest apparent decline in accident mortality has been for infants (children aged under 1 year) but this is likely to be an artefact due to the reclassification, between the eighth and ninth revisions of the International Classification of Diseases (ICD), of 'aspiration and suffocation' deaths into Sudden Infant Death Syndrome.[5]

If mortality trends over time for all types of accidental injury amongst the age groups (a) 1–4 years, (b) 5–9 years and (c) 10–14 years (Figure 8.1) are examined, the striking feature is that all three rates have converged to 80–100 per million population for boys and 40–60 per million girls. This is despite the diverse range of causes and types of injury in the different age bands. This convergence is due to a halving of injury mortality rates amongst 1–9 year olds in the last 20 years, whilst those at 10–14 years have declined less rapidly, especially for

Figure 8.1   Childhood mortality due to accidents and violence by age and sex: 1968-91

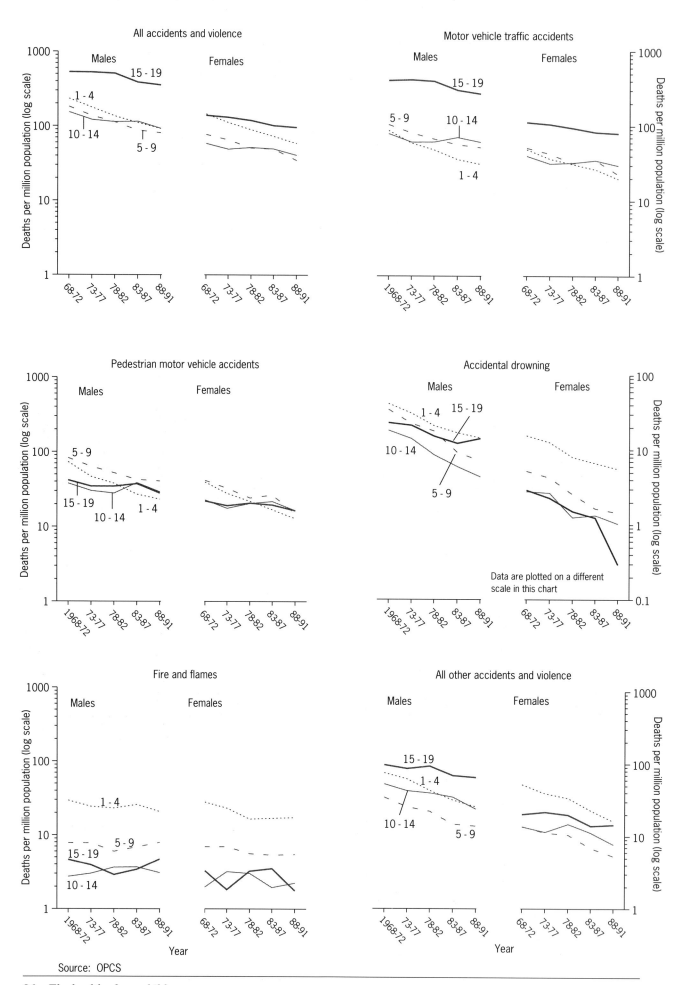

Source: OPCS

pedestrian road traffic accidents (RTA) deaths. Older children tend to have rather higher RTA death rates, especially as cyclists, while younger children predominate amongst drownings and fire deaths. For the next oldest age band (15–19 years), the very high rates of road traffic fatalities, though gradually falling, continue to give great cause for concern.

8.2.2 Gender
Throughout the child accident research literature, the increased risk to boys is apparent with their higher rates of unintentional injury.[6] This remains true for mortality and has stayed constant over time.

Boys account for 60–65 per cent of all accident deaths. The gender differences are less pronounced for certain causes of injury such as poisonings, burns and foreign bodies, while for cycling and drowning fatalities boys outnumber girls by more than three to one.

8.2.3 Social class
Another well established association is the increase in mortality rates amongst children from the disadvantaged socio-economic groupings.[7]

Figure 8.2 shows the Standardised Mortality Ratios (SMRs) by social class for the time period 1970–2 for all injuries; motor vehicle accidents; pedestrian accidents; drowning and for deaths from fires/flames.

It is clear that children from Social Class V have the highest SMRs for all types of injuries. This gradient is particularly striking for certain causes, such as deaths from fires or flames where the ratio of Social Class I to V is 1:9.

Figure 8.2 SMRs for accidents and violence by social class: 1970-71

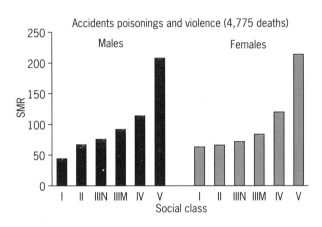

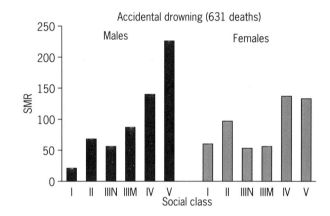

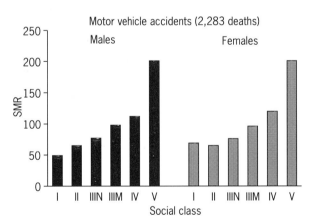

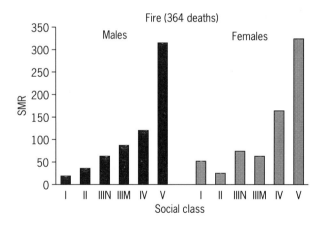

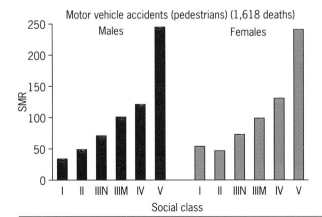

Source: Occupational Mortality: decennial supplement 1970-2

Although the subsequent decennial supplement (1979–80 and 1982–3 data) did not report directly comparable figures, analysis for boys and girls combined shows that these gradients in mortality persisted unchanged.

8.2.4 Ethnicity

Information about accidents among ethnic minority children is limited, as discussed in Chapter 7. The few studies of home[8] and road traffic accidents[9] which have examined the effect of ethnicity not only are confined predominantly to non-fatal injuries, but also suggest that the association of injury risks with ethnicity is heavily confounded by the very powerful influence of social class.

8.2.5 Geographic differences within England and Wales

It is possible to examine the child accident death rates within England and Wales by Regional Health Authority. In Table 8.1 it is seen that there are striking variations between regions, with the more northerly regions having the highest rates.[10] These differences suggest that there is potential for further reduction in the rates to at least the level in the region with the lowest rates.

Table 8.1 Childhood accident death rates (per 100,000 population) by regional health authorities in England and Wales: 1975–91

	1975–79	1980–84	1985–88	1989–91
England and Wales	12.1	10.4	8.3	7.3
England	11.8	10.3	8.3	7.2
Wales	12.6	11.0	8.2	8.1
Northern	12.3	11.9	8.6	9.5
Yorkshire	12.8	12.2	9.6	6.9
Trent	13.0	10.2	8.5	6.2
East Anglia	11.0	9.6	7.5	6.1
NW Thames	11.3	9.1	7.7	6.5
NE Thames	11.7	9.9	7.7	7.7
SE Thames	12.3	10.3	8.3	6.8
SW Thames	11.1	9.0	6.5	6.5
Wessex	11.0	8.7	6.0	7.1
Oxford	11.1	9.9	8.1	5.9
South Western	8.9	7.1	7.4	5.4
West Midlands	12.4	11.6	8.7	7.9
Mersey	11.0	11.0	8.7	7.7
North Western	15.6	11.7	10.6	9.8

For ages 0-14 (1975-84), 1-14 (1985-91).

Source: OPCS unpublished data

8.2.6 International differences

Figure 8.3 examines mortality rates for all injuries (intentional and unintentional) for several European and non–European countries. While the UK fares well against countries such as the USA and Australia it still has not reached the low rates achieved in some northern European countries.[11]

When mortality rates for pedestrian road traffic accidents are examined separately, however, a different picture emerges. The UK rates became second highest in Europe (Figure 8.4).[12]

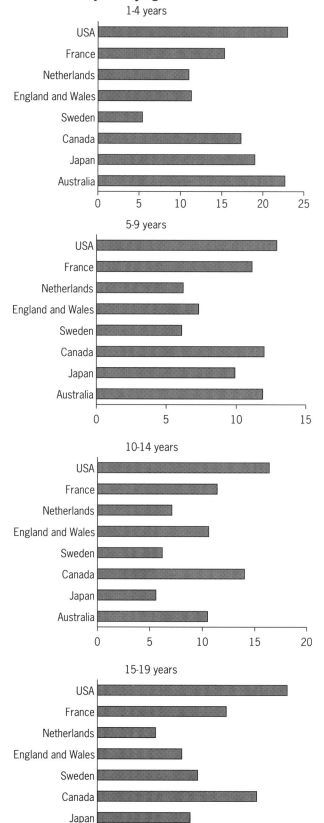

Figure 8.3 International child death rates from injuries by age: 1985

Source: American Journal of Diseases of Children. Vol 144.[11]

Figure 8.4 International child pedestrian death rates: 1991

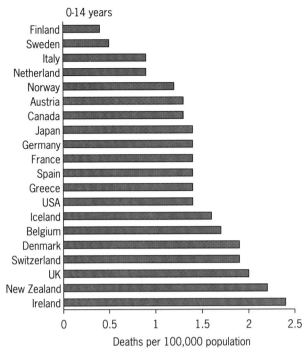

* Source: International road traffic and accident database (OECD). Based on 1989 population figures

8.2.7 Type of injury

The data already presented in this chapter indicate the importance of child accidents as a cause of death, the gradual reduction of these rates and the scope for further reduction implied by local and international variations in rates. If this potential for child injury mortality reduction is to be realised, however, then some disaggregation of the common types of accidental deaths is required. Table 8.2 shows the annual numbers of deaths in 1971–91 in England and Wales for the most common ICD E Code 'causes' of accident mortality. These data are further subdivided by age-group and sex, together with their appropriate denominators.

8.2.8 Limitations of mortality data

Although mortality statistics are an obvious source of data about child accidental injury, they have a number of limitations:

- As described later in this chapter, subclassification of injuries by ICD E codes does not necessarily represent the true 'cause' of injury.
- The alternative ICD subclassification by nature of injury (e.g. fractures, sprains, etc.) is largely unrelated to aetiology.
- Mortality data are susceptible to changes in classification of cause of death (as was seen particularly for Sudden Infant Death Syndrome).
- Reduction in mortality rates may occur either as a result of improved medical care for injured victims or secondary to true reductions in injury events.[13]

- Child deaths are, in statistical terms, 'rare events' and their numbers too few to allow for evaluation of preventive initiatives within small localities.
- Although coroners' inquest files hold a large amount of information on each individual accident, the data compiled for mortality statistics do not include these details.[14]

8.3 The injury 'iceberg'

Deaths only form the tip of the iceberg concerning all injuries occurring to children over time (Figure 8.5). The shape of this iceberg is influenced by the cause or type of injury. Thus, the broad-based iceberg is more likely to be true for injuries related to blunt trauma, for instance falls and road traffic accidents. For asphyxial injury from submersion or mechanical suffocation, however, the iceberg would narrow to a more rectangular shape (i.e. most incidents lead to death or complete recovery).

Figure 8.5 Iceberg of all injuries occurring to children over time

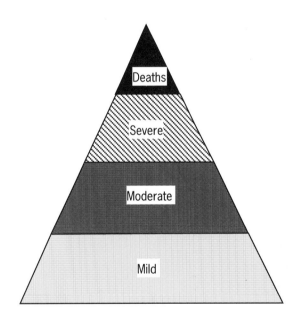

8.4 Non–fatal injuries

Modern accident research has focused on the much larger number of non-fatal accidents and on the differing methods for ascertaining reliable population-based injury rates.

Available sources of data include hospital admissions (e.g. Hospital In-patient Enquiry, Hospital Episode Statistics), hospital accident and emergency (A&E) department attendances (Home Accident Surveillance System) and general practitioner consultations (National Morbidity Studies in General Practice).[15]

Although such Health Service data may be relatively simple to use, there are fundamental epidemiological

Table 8.2 Accident deaths (numbers) by cause, age and sex: 1971–91, England and Wales

Cause	Age and sex		1971	1972	1973	1974	1975	1976	1977	1978	1979	1980	1981
All accidents and late effects (E800–E949)	1–4	M	393	333	307	259	269	237	196	188	155	185	146
		F	212	224	186	178	151	124	119	136	103	90	95
	5–9	M	383	388	344	285	270	255	233	251	242	177	173
		F	160	165	146	150	107	123	103	104	89	80	75
	10–14	M	313	282	251	245	288	236	226	236	245	207	242
		F	123	96	102	108	80	95	93	108	91	97	98
	15–19	M	918	920	893	939	931	1,036	1,046	1,119	1,043	1,076	1,040
		F	244	258	252	230	220	227	223	277	215	234	215
Injury undetermined (E980–E989)	1–4	M	6	4	11	4	5	5	6	1	11	6	14
		F	6	2	4	6	7	6	5	2	10	6	10
	5–9	M	8	0	11	6	9	3	1	2	6	4	9
		F	1	3	1	1	3	2	0	3	0	2	6
	10–14	M	3	6	6	8	9	5	14	11	12	10	19
		F	0	1	0	7	1	4	2	5	8	2	8
	15–19	M	22	18	28	41	45	34	38	38	40	45	96
		F	11	13	10	12	17	22	21	26	24	22	44
Transport accidents (E800–E848)	1–4	M	164	122	122	84	99	88	73	78	57	77	31
		F	80	73	65	63	45	46	48	55	43	31	28
	5–9	M	229	247	220	183	157	142	153	171	149	111	81
		F	108	128	110	105	75	77	64	77	64	53	32
	10–14	M	184	171	144	135	159	131	130	166	152	122	118
		F	94	78	74	84	58	62	68	81	67	74	44
	15–19	M	741	737	726	777	756	857	891	969	894	916	681
		F	195	217	218	197	172	193	181	230	172	207	151
Motor vehicle traffic accidents (E810–E819)	1–4	M	155	114	114	79	84	82	67	72	57	75	31
		F	77	70	64	59	41	44	41	52	42	28	24
	5–9	M	215	229	213	175	149	138	146	164	143	108	77
		F	105	121	105	100	71	73	64	75	62	48	31
	10–14	M	165	157	133	122	140	116	119	157	137	113	105
		F	89	70	68	79	53	49	60	75	60	68	42
	15–19	M	705	713	686	732	715	834	853	935	864	883	662
		F	187	212	211	188	164	189	174	223	168	197	146
Collision with other vehicle (E812)	1–4	M	13	11	18	10	7	7	4	6	7	12	5
		F	9	8	10	11	5	4	3	12	8	5	2
	5–9	M	18	12	11	11	6	4	8	9	8	9	3
		F	8	10	8	9	7	9	9	8	8	8	5
	10–14	M	18	9	11	7	13	10	5	16	6	4	8
		F	14	13	14	15	9	8	10	13	4	7	6
	15–19	M	361	356	332	370	337	408	395	470	422	416	273
		F	80	74	72	64	57	63	68	89	69	73	52
Pedal cyclist injured in collision (E813.6)	1–4	M	8	2	3	0	4	1	0	2	0	2	2
		F	2	1	2	2	0	1	0	0	1	1	0
	5–9	M	30	28	17	19	19	24	12	13	13	14	5
		F	3	9	6	8	2	1	4	5	3	1	0
	10–14	M	65	52	34	44	41	54	43	54	62	49	36
		F	16	7	7	12	2	8	4	9	13	11	7
	15–19	M	21	21	25	12	19	20	28	28	32	30	27
		F	1	3	5	2	6	6	4	6	8	5	3
Collision with pedestrian (E814)	1–4	M	126	95	86	63	59	67	59	61	46	57	19
		F	57	54	46	43	31	35	34	37	31	20	15
	5–9	M	161	186	174	137	114	105	116	134	118	84	53
		F	89	95	84	75	54	53	48	60	50	36	19
	10–14	M	67	85	78	61	76	40	56	77	57	56	41
		F	46	42	40	35	35	28	34	47	42	42	21
	15–19	M	67	96	65	72	47	63	71	75	77	71	58
		F	38	48	35	32	26	41	34	54	36	44	30
Accidental poisoning by drugs, medicaments & biologicals (E850–E858)	1–4	M	10	7	4	9	6	7	5	3	2	2	5
		F	6	8	8	4	8	5	4	8	2	4	2
	5–9	M	0	1	0	1	0	2	0	0	0	0	0
		F	0	1	0	1	1	1	1	0	0	0	1
	10–14	M	1	0	1	2	1	1	0	0	1	0	0
		F	4	2	1	3	1	1	1	3	0	0	3
	15–19	M	9	11	9	12	12	11	16	17	9	8	15
		F	7	7	7	6	19	8	11	16	16	13	7

1982	1983	1984	1985	1986	1987	1988	1989	1990	1991		Age and sex	Cause
149	136	151	156	130	142	117	145	132	112	M	1–4	All accidents and late
91	102	80	84	98	84	91	78	79	58	F		effects
138	171	168	127	110	96	144	150	127	110	M	5–9	(E800–E949)
68	72	73	63	77	73	49	55	53	59	F		
220	226	219	242	150	164	160	157	117	137	M	10–14	
102	94	96	87	69	61	52	66	73	47	F		
1,007	926	847	723	754	716	610	672	672	606	M	15–19	
236	223	202	192	200	169	142	185	152	176	F		
8	13	13	7	5	9	13	11	14	12	M	1–4	Injury undetermined
7	6	9	9	5	8	10	6	3	16	F		(E980–E989)
6	3	1	5	3	1	5	4	8	3	M	5–9	
3	3	4	6	1	3	4	4	3	3	F		
12	4	7	13	6	13	12	5	14	5	M	10–14	
3	2	1	3	4	5	2	5	5	7	F		
55	59	53	63	81	77	89	83	74	81	M	15–19	
26	22	19	31	39	34	35	40	26	33	F		
61	56	57	41	43	52	35	54	49	44	M	1–4	Transport accidents
36	41	28	32	38	33	36	24	26	26	F		(E800–E848)
92	125	109	91	67	60	98	99	82	73	M	5–9	
49	46	57	48	62	48	38	31	37	43	F		
129	144	134	166	106	124	120	114	85	89	M	10–14	
73	76	69	62	57	51	40	53	55	37	F		
820	739	690	602	613	604	497	537	542	471	M	15–19	
209	185	164	157	168	153	122	165	125	142	F		
58	52	52	38	42	49	34	51	44	42	M	1–4	Motor vehicle traffic
34	38	28	30	35	32	34	22	22	25	F		accidents
90	122	103	87	65	58	93	96	79	73	M	5–9	(E810–E819)
47	45	57	48	60	47	37	29	33	41	F		
111	131	126	152	96	110	110	106	78	84	M	10–14	
68	67	62	54	56	49	38	50	51	35	F		
784	692	655	577	591	582	470	516	513	453	M	15–19	
200	177	162	154	162	150	118	163	122	140	F		
7	2	11	5	7	8	6	7	5	3	M	1–4	Collision with other
8	6	5	6	10	8	8	7	4	7	F		vehicle
10	6	6	8	7	7	6	5	8	4	M	5–9	(E812)
6	2	7	4	14	7	6	9	7	7	F		
10	6	8	17	2	13	12	12	7	12	M	10–14	
10	10	5	6	11	7	10	15	6	3	F		
392	317	309	269	273	276	215	236	232	203	M	15–19	
81	60	61	55	66	48	53	74	49	47	F		
0	2	2	0	2	3	1	3	1	1	M	1–4	Pedal cyclist injured in
2	0	0	2	0	1	0	0	0	0	F		collision
9	20	16	10	3	6	10	10	8	5	M	5–9	(E813.6)
3	3	4	2	2	5	2	2	0	5	F		
37	41	50	46	24	38	44	33	25	30	M	10–14	
8	6	9	7	7	8	3	4	5	5	F		
38	33	39	28	27	29	29	24	32	24	M	15–19	
10	8	5	6	6	6	2	2	2	5	F		
47	46	36	31	30	32	25	35	35	33	M	1–4	Collision with
23	26	21	19	19	19	25	13	14	15	F		pedestrian
64	90	76	65	53	43	75	78	59	55	M	5–9	(E814)
34	38	43	38	42	32	26	17	22	28	F		
52	78	63	80	63	51	50	53	37	40	M	10–14	
45	40	40	36	30	33	19	27	29	21	F		
78	86	84	58	85	70	51	65	42	44	M	15–19	
41	40	39	39	33	39	25	32	24	31	F		
6	2	4	1	1	0	2	4	0	1	M	1–4	Accidental poisoning by
1	1	3	2	3	2	0	0	0	1	F		drugs, medicaments &
1	0	0	0	1	0	0	1	1	1	M	5–9	biologicals
0	1	0	0	0	0	0	1	0	0	F		(E850–E858)
1	3	0	1	0	0	1	0	0	1	M	10–14	
3	1	1	3	1	1	2	2	2	3	F		
18	17	10	6	9	11	8	10	10	24	M	15–19	
6	12	9	6	13	5	5	11	10	14	F		

Table 8.2 - *continued*

Cause	Age and sex		1971	1972	1973	1974	1975	1976	1977	1978	1979	1980	1981
Accidental poisoning by	1–4	M	3	4	4	4	1	1	2	2	2	1	1
other solid & liquid		F	3	0	2	0	2	0	0	1	2	2	1
substances, gases &	5–9	M	1	0	0	1	0	3	0	0	2	1	2
vapours		F	0	0	0	1	0	2	2	0	1	1	3
(E860–E869)	10–14	M	0	1	0	0	2	1	0	2	4	3	5
		F	0	0	0	0	0	0	0	0	5	3	6
	15–19	M	4	6	1	4	2	0	4	3	19	21	18
		F	1	1	0	3	0	0	2	0	1	5	2
Accidental falls	1–4	M	28	23	27	19	13	23	7	10	12	10	17
(E880–E888)		F	20	11	9	15	16	7	9	11	5	6	14
	5–9	M	21	21	19	15	14	18	14	11	8	9	18
		F	7	6	5	5	3	7	3	2	5	4	14
	10–14	M	37	19	16	23	19	21	12	10	11	18	22
		F	2	5	5	2	4	4	4	4	4	6	16
	15–19	M	35	25	28	29	25	33	19	20	18	31	77
		F	7	4	3	5	2	6	3	4	6	0	15
Accidents caused by fire	1–4	M	42	45	41	42	40	28	23	33	26	29	32
& flames		F	39	46	38	40	25	30	24	19	17	22	21
(E890–E899)	5–9	M	13	21	14	16	15	17	17	10	10	13	11
		F	14	14	13	15	6	17	16	10	10	12	7
	10–14	M	7	2	7	3	10	4	7	6	13	9	3
		F	7	3	6	5	6	6	8	5	7	5	6
	15–19	M	2	10	11	10	5	7	3	8	5	4	5
		F	8	6	5	2	1	5	3	5	12	3	7
Other accidents and late	1–4	M	143	129	102	97	106	86	83	60	56	63	59
effects		F	62	82	62	53	54	35	31	40	33	24	29
(E900–E929)	5–9	M	116	96	90	68	83	71	48	59	71	43	60
		F	30	16	17	22	20	17	14	14	9	9	18
	10–14	M	76	82	82	77	85	75	74	50	64	54	93
		F	14	6	15	13	11	19	9	13	8	9	23
	15–19	M	115	116	112	97	121	113	106	95	97	95	242
		F	20	13	17	13	19	14	17	15	7	5	32
Accidental drowning	1–4	M	81	70	51	42	48	36	45	26	27	26	21
and submersion		F	20	31	23	24	16	13	10	16	9	8	6
(E910)	5–9	M	79	61	63	40	60	39	27	39	44	24	27
		F	15	6	10	4	7	13	7	6	3	5	6
	10–14	M	27	31	39	28	24	26	29	16	14	18	23
		F	6	2	8	3	8	7	0	2	2	2	3
	15–19	M	42	28	51	20	58	45	22	25	27	25	41
		F	5	4	5	2	5	5	3	4	2	3	4
Inhalation of food &	1–4	M	24	18	20	12	22	22	15	12	8	15	12
other objects causing		F	15	12	18	10	12	2	7	8	9	7	5
obstruction of respiratory	5–9	M	5	7	4	2	2	3	4	2	2	1	1
tract or suffocation		F	1	6	2	3	3	0	1	0	3	0	1
(E911–E912)	10–14	M	4	9	1	3	2	7	8	1	7	0	5
		F	2	1	2	1	1	1	3	3	1	1	4
	15–19	M	9	16	4	9	9	14	9	12	7	8	7
		F	4	2	5	5	5	1	9	5	1	1	2
Suffocation	1–4	M	16	13	9	16	11	5	8	5	7	11	6
(E913)		F	10	17	9	5	15	7	5	10	8	2	5
	5–9	M	10	7	7	2	6	3	5	1	10	1	2
		F	1	1	0	3	3	1	1	1	0	0	0
	10–14	M	12	13	17	14	28	24	11	14	19	22	27
		F	1	1	0	2	0	1	1	1	1	2	2
	15–19	M	14	20	11	12	15	10	21	17	19	17	30
		F	1	0	2	1	2	1	0	1	0	0	0
Populations	1–4	M	1,626.1	1,600.5	1,565.0	1,509.5	1,444.5	1,357.6	1,280.8	1,217.4	1,184.9	1,188.9	1,217.6
(in thousands)		F	1,543.7	1,519.1	1,485.5	1,428.9	1,365.8	1,284.0	1,211.3	1,153.8	1,124.1	1,127.6	1,153.9
	5–9	M	2,079.0	2,097.3	2,092.8	2,065.6	2,022.1	2,000.3	1,951.3	1,895.6	1,818.3	1,740.0	1,642.0
		F	1,976.7	1,989.7	1,985.2	1,962.6	1,920.0	1,895.1	1,849.5	1,795.2	1,717.7	1,646.3	1,554.3
	10–14	M	1,877.6	1,925.5	1,975.0	2,029.2	2,072.9	2,090.5	2,102.9	2,091.8	2,065.4	2,022.3	1,996.6
		F	1,771.8	1,826.6	1,877.8	1,926.2	1,965.7	1,980.8	1,987.7	1,979.0	1,957.2	1,918.7	1,892.1
	15–19	M	1,711.2	1,731.9	1,753.1	1,779.5	1,829.5	1,881.5	1,929.5	1,979.8	2,040.8	2,091.0	2,114.4
		F	1,632.6	1,646.7	1,669.5	1,697.5	1,745.6	1,799.6	1,852.9	1,902.6	1,952.9	1,996.3	2,015.4

Sources: *Registrar General's Statistical Review 1971-3*
   Mortality Statistics: cause 1974-91
   OPCS *Population Estimates 1974-91*

1982	1983	1984	1985	1986	1987	1988	1989	1990	1991	Age and sex		Cause
1	0	1	2	1	2	0	0	0	0	M	1–4	Accidental poisoning by
0	0	1	0	0	1	0	1	0	0	F		other solid & liquid
0	0	1	1	0	1	0	0	0	0	M	5–9	substances, gases &
3	1	2	0	0	0	0	0	1	0	F		vapours
5	2	12	5	2	0	0	3	1	1	M	10–14	(E860–E869)
3	0	2	4	3	0	0	0	1	2	F		
16	22	30	18	10	10	12	6	14	7	M	15–19	
2	5	2	6	7	0	2	2	3	2	F		
9	18	16	12	7	8	5	4	5	6	M	1–4	Accidental falls
10	7	4	5	8	4	6	4	8	2	F		(E880–E888)
3	3	12	8	2	3	6	6	8	7	M	5–9	
2	2	1	1	2	6	2	1	0	2	F		
13	12	17	8	9	10	8	6	3	8	M	10–14	
2	2	2	3	1	1	2	4	3	1	F		
27	25	24	18	19	17	23	29	20	16	M	15–19	
2	4	4	0	3	1	2	1	5	5	F		
20	23	29	44	35	36	30	34	29	21	M	1–4	Accidents caused by fire
16	27	18	21	26	12	28	23	24	15	F		& flames
8	8	13	8	14	10	16	13	12	11	M	5–9	(E890–E899)
7	13	9	2	6	9	8	10	7	9	F		
6	9	8	11	1	3	3	4	6	6	M	10–14	
6	4	6	1	3	2	3	4	4	2	F		
8	7	6	6	7	9	8	12	6	8	M	15–19	
5	8	5	12	4	5	8	1	1	2	F		
52	37	44	55	42	42	45	48	49	40	M	1–4	Other accidents and late
28	25	25	23	23	32	20	25	21	14	F		effects
32	35	33	19	25	22	24	31	24	18	M	5–9	(E900–E929)
7	8	4	11	6	9	1	12	6	4	F		
64	55	48	49	31	27	28	29	20	32	M	10–14	
13	10	15	14	4	6	5	3	8	2	F		
116	115	87	73	96	63	61	78	78	80	M	15–19	
11	7	18	11	5	5	3	5	6	9	F		
28	18	23	31	21	17	22	21	22	15	M	1–4	Accidental drowning
7	9	7	7	8	10	7	8	10	4	F		and submersion
21	20	13	10	17	11	10	22	6	9	M	5–9	(E910)
1	4	0	2	4	2	1	4	2	2	F		
16	18	10	13	8	3	3	16	6	2	M	10–14	
3	0	5	5	0	1	1	2	2	1	F		
41	44	27	12	25	18	21	34	33	15	M	15–19	
2	3	5	2	0	2	0	1	0	1	F		
10	6	5	7	6	3	3	12	8	12	M	1–4	Inhalation of food & other
6	8	7	3	3	7	4	4	5	3	F		other objects causing
2	2	3	2	0	0	3	1	3	1	M	5–9	obstruction of respiratory
3	1	1	4	1	1	0	2	2	1	F		tract or suffocation
4	6	4	2	2	5	4	3	1	1	M	10–14	(E911–E912)
3	3	0	7	0	2	0	0	1	0	F		
6	5	14	15	11	4	3	5	8	3	M	15–19	
4	1	4	2	3	2	1	2	4	3	F		
5	4	6	4	6	9	7	5	9	5	M	1–4	Suffocation
3	5	5	1	4	3	3	5	4	1	F		(E913)
3	3	1	4	1	2	2	2	5	2	M	5–9	
0	1	1	0	0	0	0	0	0	0	F		
22	14	19	17	10	9	11	5	5	11	M	10–14	
2	0	0	1	1	1	1	0	0	0	F		
23	28	12	10	14	10	10	11	10	16	M	15–19	
1	1	0	4	0	0	0	1	0	0	F		
1,253.5	1,280.9	1,287.5	1,283.0	1,297.0	1,314.6	1,334.3	1,367.5	1,382.4	1,400.9	M	1–4	Populations
1,189.6	1,215.5	1,222.6	1,218.4	1,230.8	1,247.1	1,266.8	1,297.7	1,311.4	1,327.5	F		(in thousands)
1,558.5	1,503.0	1,500.4	1,522.7	1,555.0	1,592.8	1,625.5	1,632.0	1,641.1	1,657.0	M	5–9	
1,474.0	1,421.2	1,417.5	1,438.7	1,470.1	1,506.5	1,538.0	1,545.3	1,553.2	1,565.6	F		
1,946.5	1,890.6	1,813.8	1,742.5	1,655.8	1,577.4	1,524.7	1,522.2	1,543.4	1,573.6	M	10–14	
1,844.5	1,787.9	1,712.7	1,645.6	1,562.3	1,487.7	1,438.4	1,434.7	1,454.8	1,484.7	F		
2,136.3	2,127.5	2,084.7	2,041.3	2,010.7	1,966.1	1,912.1	1,836.6	1,768.4	1,685.0	M	15–19	
2,020.7	2,008.9	1,976.3	1,934.6	1,906.0	1,861.3	1,805.7	1,733.7	1,666.1	1,586.5	F		

problems in interpreting the unrefined statistics. First none of these data sources are adequately coded by cause of injury. Even in the most recent Hospital Episode Statistics nearly 40 per cent of injury admissions are not 'E' coded. Second whether a child uses the Health Service or is admitted to hospital is not directly related to the severity of the injury *per se*, but probably has much to do with extraneous factors, including the distance from their home to the hospital, bed supply or social class of the family. Thus differences in the rates of A&E Department attendances or hospitalisations by place or time do not necessarily reflect differences in the true underlying population rates of childhood accidental injury.

For example, it is known that A&E attendances have continuously risen since the 1960s. Meanwhile, hospital admissions for child accidents rose sharply to the mid–1970s (Figure 8.6), then declined and have subsequently continued their slow rise. It is not clear how to interpret such findings in the light of the falling mortality rates. The unanswered question, therefore, is 'what has happened to injury rates in the child population?'.

Figure 8.6   Hospital discharge rates for injury and poisoning by age and sex: 1968-91, England and Wales

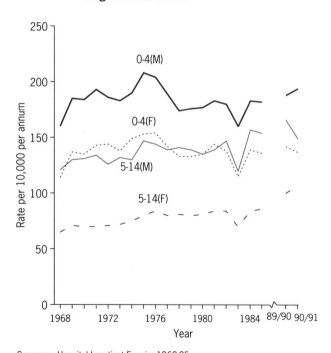

Sources: Hospital In-patient Enquiry 1968-85
Hospital Episodes Survey 1989-90,1990-91

Other morbidity data, available from non-Health Service sources, include police data on RTAs, the General Household Survey, and National Childhood Cohort Studies. Even within these sources, however, the problems of ascertainment and case definition of accident morbidity remain (see also section 8.5.1(e)).

Later in this chapter a study from Newcastle upon Tyne is described. This study uses objective severity scaling to overcome some of these dilemmas.

8.5 Causes of unintentional injuries to children

It is questioned whether existing data collection systems in the UK really help our understanding of the causes of childhood accidental injury. Additional types of data might help to identify causal associations which could be used in the design of appropriate counter-measures.

Effective preventive strategies are the result of advances in the conceptualisation of injuries as a 'disease' rather than as random events.[16] Injuries are not 'accidental' but occur predictably when an interaction of host, agent and environment occurs.[17] The complexity of these interactions means that a simple categorisation of cause will not always provide the full picture: knowledge of how factors interact with each other to produce or avoid injury events is needed.[18]

8.5.1 Existing data concerning causes of unintentional injuries to children

(a) Classification of injuries by E codes
The International Classification of Diseases (ICD) is an internationally accepted listing of disease used in hospital admissions and deaths. The World Health Organisation has developed external causes of injury (E) codes to use with the ICD codes.

E codes provide useful information about how the injury occurred. Within the category coded 'accidental falls' (E880–E888) we are able to distinguish between a fall on or from stairs (E880), a fall from a ladder (E881) and a fall from a building or other structure (E882). There are, however, limitations in the descriptions of the circumstances and conditions. The 'accidental falls' (E880–888) category does not code all injuries resulting from falls. Some excluded injuries are 'falls in or from a burning building' (E890.8, E891.8) and 'falls on edged, pointed and sharp objects' (E920). Furthermore, E codes only address the immediate agent of the injury. A more logical code would have several codes for the circumstances surrounding the injury.[19]

E codes can meet some objectives for public health surveillance but, to obtain more detailed cause-of-injury data or information about the source of injury problems, other surveillance tools are needed.

(b) Home accident surveillance system/leisure accident surveillance (HASS/LASS)
The Department of Trade and Industry collects data about non-fatal injuries from home accidents through its HASS/LASS system. The system collects its data based on the attendances at the accident departments in a sample of hospitals: the 1992 HASS data were collected from 18 hospitals and the 1992 LASS data from 13 hospitals.[20] One of the principal objectives of the HASS/LASS system is 'to monitor the accident problem so that new hazards may be identified and the trend in known hazards investigated'.

Data are included on the individual (age, gender), on the accident type (poisonings, falls), on the injury type (scalds, suffocation), on the location (building, inside stairs), the activity (eating/drinking, gardening) and the product involved (pram, baby bath). More information on the circumstances of the injury is available from this surveillance system than from 'E' codes and much use has been made of this in improving product safety.

The leisure accident survey (LASS) for instance, gives an analysis of the activities related to injuries amongst 5–14 year olds in 1992. There were over 3,000 injuries associated with football, 900 whilst ice/roller skating, 260 during horse-riding and over 2,000 injuries whilst cycling, reported from the sample A&E departments.

Such injury event data, even when supplemented by good information on the host, agent, and environment interaction, however, will still only partly reveal the true causes of injury. To progress further, the numerator data must be linked with some measure of the exposed population (i.e. appropriate denominator data) so that injury risk for different activities can be calculated. For instance, documenting the number of children injured in horse riding or cycling accidents will not reveal whether horse riding is more hazardous than cycling. To interpret these associations, information is also needed on how much time children spend riding horses and cycles.

(c) The Department of Transport RTA Surveillance System

The Department of Transport publishes statistics on road accidents occurring on the public highway and reported to the police.[21] Figure 8.7 shows the trend in childhood RTAs for deaths and non-fatal injuries between 1976 and 1990. Again over the period, deaths declined whilst non-fatal accidents rose slightly. This is in line with Health Service data, but could be due to a true rise in the frequency of RTAs or better ascertainment of less serious injuries. In the annual reports on road accidents[21] a more systematic attempt is made to describe injury severity and to link the events to relevant exposure data (for example, the National Travel Survey). The DoT system is used extensively to specify 'accident blackspots' and to examine the safety of differing road types (for example motorway, etc.). Children killed and seriously injured in road traffic accidents, however, are mostly pedestrians (65 per cent) or cyclists (17 per cent) and fit poorly into this motor vehicle-orientated model of injury prevention. In addition, the data are known to be incomplete for some types of casualty (for example, cyclists) while the description of the severity of injury used in this system is very crude.

(d) The Home Office fire statistics

The Home Office compiles a fire statistics database from reports submitted by local fire brigades on fires attended as an emergency.[22] Fire brigades are called to between 8 and 12 per cent of household fires.

The type of information collected includes both fatal and non-fatal casualties by age and sex, the location of fires (for example, buildings, road vehicles), causes of fires (for example, accidental fires in dwellings), and source of ignition (for example, smokers' materials). Fires and casualties in dwellings discovered by smoke alarms are also reported. In general these fires data are even less complete and well related to exposure data (for example, the prevalence of smoke alarms) than the RTA data described above.

(e) Factors associated with high injury rates

If predictive factors for childhood accidental injury could be identified, then preventive measures could be targeted

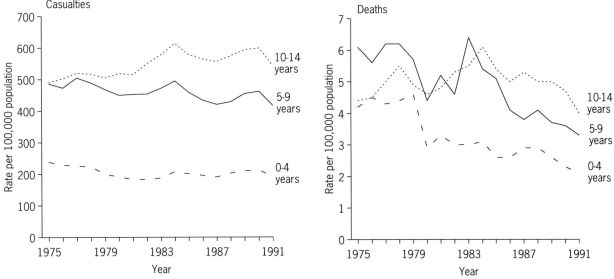

Figure 8.7 Deaths and injuries resulting from road traffic accidents by age and outcome: 1975-91, Great Britain

Source: Road Accidents, Great Britain various years. Department of Transport.

more effectively by using the appropriate exposure data. In attempting to determine aetiology, many associations of possible predictive factors have been postulated. Association, however, is not synonymous with 'cause': association studies can produce results of insufficient specificity to indicate appropriate courses of action.[23]

In the last thirty years there has been an increase in the published literature on studies examining factors associated with high injury rates. These include characteristics of the parent, such as poor maternal physical and mental health,[24,25] and parental age.[26] Other studies have stressed family characteristics such as family size and birth order,[27] single parent families and step families[26] and parental unemployment.[27] The characteristics of the child emerge in some studies as being strongly associated with high injury rates: these primarily include aggression, although the evidence is controversial.[28–31]

A distinction needs to be made between the retrospective and prospective studies that have examined these causal associations. In the retrospective studies[24,28–31] children or their parents have been asked about the presence or absence of risk factors after the accident has taken place. This approach is limited by biases arising from the distorted recall or reporting of, for example, the child's behaviour.[32] Even prospective cohort studies may produce conflicting evidence on causal associations.

For instance, studies of the association between the social and behavioural characteristics of the 1970 British births cohort and their mothers' reports of accidental injury suggested that aggressive and overactive behaviours were independently associated with accidents.[26,29] The authors concluded that the identification of high-risk groups can be used to direct education and to provide safer physical environments to families in which there are children with high-risk behaviours.

A study of more than 16,000 children from the 1958 National Child Development Study cohort, however, found a lack of powerful or consistent predictive characteristics of children or their families in the risk of having a traffic injury[32] and this was confirmed in a large New Zealand cohort study.[33]

A further weakness of association studies is that the apparent association may itself be an artefact of the case definition of accidental injury.

Reliance on attendance at an A&E department or admission to hospital for the case definition of an injury event introduces biases, as does the recording of a diary of injuries. An analysis of the 1970 British births cohort demonstrated that different methods of defining accidents can lead to very different conclusions: for children for whom accidents had been recorded in a diary the conclusion would be that the situation where a young mother living in an average urban neighbourhood would predispose children to accidents.[34] When cases were confined to those admitted to hospital, accidents were strongly related to family type and characteristics of the neighbourhood were no longer important. It was concluded that certain essential tools, such as an injury severity rating applicable to children, are needed before significant progress can be made in identifying the social and environmental factors which predispose children to accidental injury. Nevertheless, there may still be room to develop better case definitions from existing questions in these cohort studies. For instance, in the 1958 National Child Development Study cohort follow-up study, parental reports of 'fractures' of long bones or 'flesh wounds requiring ten or more stitches' describe events which are unlikely to be forgotten and which embody a severity threshold.

(f) Studies documenting hazard exposure
It is exposure to hazardous situations which causes many injuries. Surprisingly little data are available, however, on the prevalence of such hazards or of children's contacts with them.

Researchers in Nottingham attempted to obtain measures of children's exposure to risk as pedestrians by a variety of different interview and observation methods.[35] 'Raw' accidental injury statistics were found to be misleading since a large number of accidents may occur in a low-risk situation provided a sufficiently large number of people are exposed to the risk. Most child pedestrian accidents occur at road junctions, suggesting that it might be more dangerous to cross the road at a junction than elsewhere. When exposure to risk is taken into account, by observation of children crossing roads, the probability of a child having an accident is found to be highest on a straight road crossing rather than at a junction.[36] These early results have now been confirmed and extended in a fascinating and comprehensive study of pedestrian activity and its relationship to risk of road traffic accidents.[37] Such exposure-specific risks and their prevalence may also change over time. For instance, there is evidence that our roads are becoming increasingly dangerous for cyclists.[38] During 1952–87 the mortality risk per mile for cyclists doubled, whilst the average annual mileage travelled by bicycle fell by 80 per cent. A similar increase in exposure-specific risk for pedestrians is proposed to explain the marked reduction over the last twenty years in children's use of the pedestrian environment.[39]

Accurate measures of injury-risk exposure can thus illuminate 'event' data and suggest possible counter-measures.

(g) Studies documenting the effect of hazard removal
The deliberate creation of a non-exposed cohort differs fundamentally from the natural cohort achieved in observational studies. An experimental approach would seek to assign a protective intervention in a randomised manner to establish its effect and the true causal attribute of the risk factor.

Only one adequately controlled trial can be found where child injury reduction has been demonstrated.[40] Even this study was unable to produce a more satisfactory case definition for injury than 'medical attendance'. The majority of preventive effect demonstrations in respect of child accidents are in reality uncontrolled 'before and after' studies.[41] Some of these studies can be very convincing, such as the dramatic decline in hospital admissions of children aged 0–4 years with analgesic/antipyretic poisoning following the introduction of child resistant containers[42] and the decline in fatal window falls amongst children in New York following the use of window bars on high buildings.[43] On the other hand, the expected fall in child passenger fatalities in association with rear seat restraint use has not been demonstrated in the UK; and the sudden decline in cycling injuries in Australia associated with cycle helmet legislation may have as much to do with a reduction in the number of cyclists as with the effect on their safety while riding.[44]

The salutary conclusions of one such study of teenage drivers was that teaching 'safe' driving can have dangerous consequences.[45] Notwithstanding these reservations, in the United States of America it has been calculated that the introduction of 12 preventive strategies with 'known' effects could reduce children's accidental injury deaths by 29 per cent.[46] A similar exercise has not been conducted in the UK.

8.5.2 Causes and counter-measures: are they related?

The sequence leading to an injury usually involves a complex interaction of a large number of events. The major failing of the ICD 'E' code is that it attempts to describe this complex situation by the use of a single code. As has been mentioned earlier, the Department of Trade and Industry's HASS/LASS system provides more detailed cause-of-injury data. It does not, however, take into account the exposure to risk of communities. This information may have to be collected by sample surveys involving questionnaires or direct observation of population groups to establish the injury risk for different activities.

The acid test of causality is whether the experimental introduction or removal of the causal factor produces an increase or decrease in the injury rates. By this standard, virtually all prevention and control activities are inadequately evaluated.[11] The use of a more pragmatic approach still yields very few examples in the literature of evaluated prevention strategies.[41] Even simple road safety training for children must be challenged if research evidence on biologically determined perceptual and behavioural immaturity is to be taken seriously.[3,4]

In the face of such uncertainty concerning the 'causes' of unintentional injury it is clear that injury prevention will not make progress until the interventions are subject to some form of controlled trial. The essential precursor to such studies is the proper definition of injury frequency as a measure of outcome. In childhood, death is fortunately too rare for this purpose (for example, in an average District Health Authority there will only be some four child-injury deaths per year). Death is, in any case, partly a product of treatment. The evaluation and monitoring of injury-prevention initiatives must therefore be based on an accurate and continuing population-based registration of non-fatal injury events.

8.6 The Newcastle studies

8.6.1 Event data

To improve the usefulness and interpretation of Health Service data on childhood accidents, a study was conducted within one UK city. The first part of the project was retrospective, examining child deaths (1980–6) and a systematic sample of hospital admissions due to accidental injury in Newcastle upon Tyne in 1986.[47] The frequency of events was recorded together with an objective assessment of the severity of injury in each case, using internationally recognised severity scaling systems.

A prospective study in 1990 examined all paediatric deaths, hospital admissions and a one in five sample of A & E Department attendances.[48] The method of severity assessment was identical to that of the 1986 retrospective study.

Table 8.3 shows the admission rates for Newcastle children at different levels of severity for the years 1986 and 1990. There was a 47 per cent rise in admissions during that time period. This was not matched, however, for the more serious injuries. Clearly this rise in hospitalisation is a consequence of increased numbers of milder cases being admitted to hospital. The trends in moderately severe injuries, which are less susceptible to bias in ascertainment and thus more likely to reflect true underlying population injury rates, do not support the conclusion that the rise in admissions represent a rise in population injury rates. Indeed the more likely explanation is increased availability of paediatric beds brought about by shorter lengths of stay in hospital for paediatric patients.

Table 8.3 Child accidental injury in Newcastle upon Tyne: admission rates per 10,000 population 1986 and 1990

	1986	1990
All admissions + trauma	117	166
Moderate (ISS 4 or more)	71	75
Severe (ISS 9 or more)	33	40

Source: Walsh SS et al. The annual incidence of unintentional injury amongst 54,000 children[48]

Table 8.4 compares figures for accidental injury mortality, admission and A&E attendance between this study and two other international population-based child-accident studies from Gothenburg in Sweden[49] and Massachusetts, USA.[50] The three studies have similar mortality rates but the UK has the highest admission and A&E attendance rates.

Table 8.4 International comparisons of child accidental injury

	Death	Admissions	Attendances
	Rates per 10,000		
USA (Massachusetts) 1979–1982	1.7	77	2,160
Sweden (Gothenburg) 1976	1.5	113	1,439
Britain (Newcastle) 1990	1.1	166	2,149

Sources: Walsh SS et al. The annual incidence of unintentional injury amongst 54,000 children[48]
Nathorst Westfelt J. Environmental factors in childhood accidents, a prospective study in Gothenburg, Sweden[49]
Gallaher SS et al. The incidence of injuries among 87,000 Massachusetts children and adolescents: results of 1980-81 statewide childhood injury prevention program surveillance system[50]

It is difficult to say from these data whether the UK has true higher rates of child accident morbidity, or whether they merely reflect differences in the Health Service utilisation. Fortunately the Swedish study used a similar method of objective severity scaling to that in the Newcastle study, and thus it is possible to compare the rates of severe injury. These UK rates are only slightly higher than those from the Swedish study.

If the argument is accepted that the severe injuries are far more likely to be accurately ascertained and to represent true population frequency figures, unbiased by Health Service utilisation, the statistics imply that the actual rates of accidental injury are probably similar across these two European cities (and that differences in morbidity figures are biased and contaminated by differences of access to A&E Departments and hospital admission).

Examining the data in a more 'local' setting, the home address postcode of injured children allows mapping of the distribution of accidents across the city of Newcastle upon Tyne. Rates of injury are calculated for each of the 26 census wards and quartile maps are produced to demonstrate in a pictorial fashion the areas of the city with highest rates of injury. Figure 8.8 shows one such map for A&E attendances, whilst Figure 8.9 demonstrates the distribution of severe injuries.

There are striking differences in the distribution of injuries of different levels of severity. Areas with high attendance at A&E are not necessarily coincident with those areas with high rates of severe injury. Again, one explanation must be the difference in A&E utilisation within different census wards of the City. Understanding and appreciating this phenomenon is important if prevention measures are to be targeted at those parts of this and other cities with 'true' high rates of accidental injury.

The examples highlighted from the Newcastle study serve to demonstrate how improvements in the case definition of accidental injury by the appropriate classification of severity may produce more reliable and more accurate population-based frequency statistics and correlates. To assist accident prevention programmes it is important to provide an enhanced case definition which will:

(a) identify the true underlying frequency distribution of accidental injury within a community;
(b) evaluate prevention by demonstrating changes in injury frequency independent of external factors (e.g. changes in admission policy, changes in bed supply);
(c) allow prevention programmes to target the more serious accidents/injuries;
(d) demonstrate whether prevention programmes might result in less severe injuries, even if they are unable to reduce the total frequency figures – such an effective prevention might otherwise be missed.

The accurate collection of event data can thus help to define the problem of accidental injury at a local level. In order to illuminate the causal problem, however, some measure of exposure to risk is also required.

8.6.2 Risk data
As every child carries some degree of risk, population surveys can produce risk profiles for very small populations such as a school or a general practice. This information can be used to inform preventive policies and monitor trends over time.

Risk data has the potential to supplement event data and provide the basis for local preventive action. One such example of an injury prevention initiative was The Wolfson Foundation Study of Accidental Injury in Childhood. This study targeted two groups of children in Newcastle upon Tyne: preschool children and 11–14 year old schoolchildren.

The baseline surveys of injury risk in this study used questionnaires completed by the parents of preschool children and by the 11–14-year-old schoolchildren.[51] The questionnaires were designed to measure the child's exposure to injury risk – thus for the younger child, questions on the home environment and where the child played outside predominated. For the older child the questionnaires concentrated on the road environment, on journeys to and from school and how the child spent leisure time. Detailed feedback was provided for each of the intervention health centres and schools. This compared the injury risk profile for the individual centre with the city-wide picture.

Figure 8.10 shows the use of safety equipment (fireguards, safety gates and smoke detectors) by parents of 3-year-old children in the area served by one health centre. The squares on the map show where homes with no safety equipment were located and from the map it can be seen that these cluster in particular localities. This local information can be used by health visitors, local parent groups and other planners in the implementation of a home safety equipment loan scheme in a particular neighbourhood.

Figure 8.8 All accidents and emergency attendances: 1990, Newcastle upon Tyne

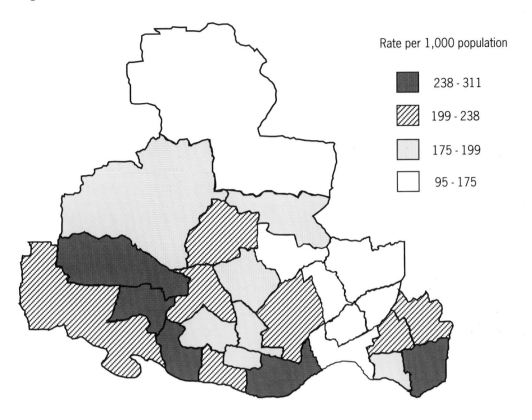

Rate per 1,000 population

238 - 311

199 - 238

175 - 199

95 - 175

Source: Walsh SS et al. The annual incidence of unintentional injury amongst 54,000 children. [48]

Figure 8.9 Hospital admissions for severe childhood accidents: 1990, Newcastle upon Tyne

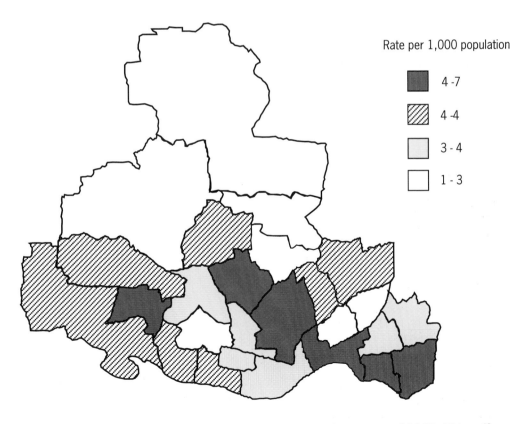

Rate per 1,000 population

4 - 7

4 - 4

3 - 4

1 - 3

Source: Walsh SS et al. The annual incidence of unintentional injury amongst 54,000 children. [48]

Figure 8.10 Use of safety equipment by parents of 3-year-old children, Newcastle upon Tyne

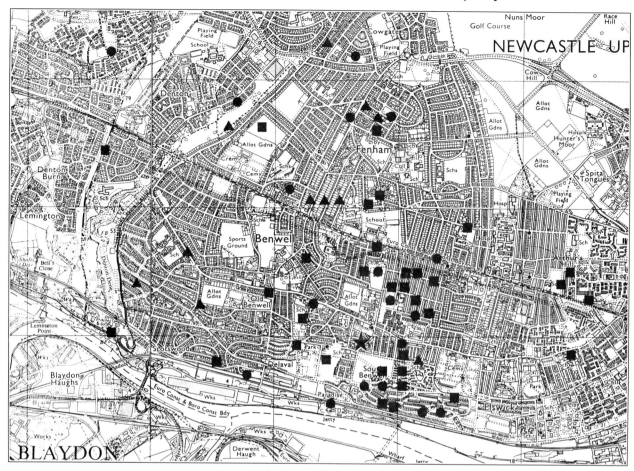

Safety gate, fireguard, smoke alarm:

■ None   ● 1 or 2   ▲ All 3   ★ Health Centre

Risk data can be a useful adjunct to event data in local injury prevention. It can be used to identify priorities and target resources for injury prevention. Local profiles of injury risk can help to inform preventive action. In addition, risk data can be used as a monitoring tool and as an intermediate outcome measure to use in the evaluation of interventions.

8.7 Conclusion

Unintentional injury in childhood is a major problem which has probably changed very little in frequency in the last twenty years. Most of the current data we have about the causes of these injuries is almost impossible to apply in preventive campaigns. Very few of our present interventions, intended to prevent these injuries, are actually known to work. A fresh approach is needed and this should encompass:

- the collection of accurate injury frequency data in the population by the use of case definitions based on severity measurement;
- the measurement of injury risk exposure across whole populations to enhance event data, to inform locality planning and to act as an intermediate measure of preventive outcome;
- the demonstration that preventive campaigns actually lower the rate of unintentional injuries amongst our children.

References

1 Child Accident Prevention Trust. *The NHS and social costs of children's accidents: a pilot study.* CAPT (London 1992).
2 Jones–Lee M, Loomes G, O'Reilly D and Philips P. The value of preventing non–fatal road injuries: findings of a willingness to pay national survey. *TRL Contractor Report* 330. Department of Transport (1993).
3 Sandels ST. *Children in Traffic.* Elek Books (London 1975).
4 Thomson JA. *The Facts about Child Pedestrian Accidents.* Cassell Educational (London 1991).
5 Jackson RH. *Children, the Environment and Accidents.* Pitman Medical (London 1977).
6 Rivara F, Bergman A and Logerfo J. Epidemiology of childhood injuries ii: sex differences in injury rates. *American Journal of Diseases of Children.* **136**, 1982, 502–6.
7 Adelstein A M and White G C. Causes of children's death analysed by social class. In: *Child Health: A Collection of Studies on Medical and Population Subjects* 31. HMSO (London 1976).
8 Alwash R and McCarthy M. Accidents in the home among children under 5: ethnic differences or social disadvantage? *British Medical Journal,* **296**, 1988, 1450–3.

9   Lawson S and Edwards P. The involvement of ethnic minorities in road accidents. Data from three studies of young pedestrian casualties. *Traffic Engineering and Control*, (January) 1991. 12–19.

10 Avery J G, Vaudin J N, Fletcher J L and Watson J M. Geographical and social variations in mortality due to childhood accidents in England and Wales 1975–1984. *Public Health*, **104**, 1990, 171–82.

11 Division of Injury Control. Childhood injuries in the United States. *American Journal of Diseases of Children*, **144**, 1990, 627–46.

12 Transport Road Research Laboratory. *Children Should be Seen and Not Hurt*. Report prepared for Texaco Ltd (London 1990).

13 Becker D and Gudman S. *Text book of Head Injury*. Saunders (London 1989).

14 Levene S. Accident deaths in childhood: an in depth examination of coroner's records. *American Journal of Diseases of Children*, **66**, 1991, 1239–41.

15 Benson A. The collection and disemination of Accident Data. Faculty of Public Health Medicine. Child Accident Prevention Trust (London 1993).

16 Gordon J E. The epidemiology of accidents. *American Journal Public Health*, **39**, 1949, 504–15.

17 Haddon W. Advances in the epidemiology as a basis for public policy. *Public Health Reports*, **95**, 1980, 411–21.

18 Waller J A. Accident prevention: the role of research. In: Manciaux M and Romer C J. *Accidents in Childhood and Adolescence*. World Health Organisation (Geneva, 1991).

19 Langley J. The international classification of diseases: codes for describing injuries and circumstances surrounding injuries: a critical comment and suggestions for improvement. *Accident Analysis and Prevention*, **14**, 1982, 195–7.

20 Consumer Safety Unit . *Home and Leisure Accident Research, 1992*. Data Sixteenth Annual Report of the Home Accident Surveillance System. Department of Trade and Industry (London, 1994).

21 Department of Transport. *Road Accidents Great Britain 1991*. HMSO (London 1992).

22 Home Office. *Statistical Bulletin: Summary Fire Statistics UK 1991* (London 1992).

23 Rothman K J. *Modern Epidemiology*. Little, Brown (Boston/Toronto, 1986).

24 Sibert R, Stress in families of children who have ingested poisons. *British Medical Journal, 3*, 1975, 87–9.

25 Brown G W and Davidson S. Social class, psychotic disorder of mothers and accidents to children. *Lancet, 1*, 1978, 378–80.

26 Wadsworth J, Burnell I, Taylor B and Butler N. Family type and accidents in preschool children. *Journal Epidemiology Community Health, 37*, 1983, 100–4.

27 Bijur P, Golding J, Haslum M and Kurzon M. Behavioural predictors of injury in school-age children. *American Journal of Diseases of Children*, **142**, 1988, 1307–12.

28 Mayer R J, Roelofs H A, Bluestone J and Redmond S. Accidental injury to the pre-school child. *Journal of Paediatrics*, **63**, 1963, 95–105.

29 Bijur P E, Stewart-Brown S and Butler N. Child behaviour and accidental injury in 11,966 preschool children. *American Journal of Diseases of Children*, **140**, 1986, 487–92.

30 Sibert J R and Newcombe R G. Accidental ingestion of poisons and child personality. *Postgraduate Medicine Journal*, **53**, 1977, 254–6.

31 Sobel R and Margalis J A. Repetitive poisoning in children: a psychological study *Paediatrics, 35*, 1965, 641–51.

32 Pless I B, Peckham C S and Power C. Predicting traffic injuries in childhood: a cohort analysis. *Journal of Pediatrics*, **115**, 1989, 932–8.

33 Langley J, Silva P and Williams S. A study of the relationship of 90 background developmental, behavioural and medical factors to childhood accidents. *Australian Paediatrics*, **16**, 1980, 244–7.

34 Stewart-Brown S, Peters T J, Golding J and Bijur P. Case definition in childhood accident studies: a vital factor in determining results. *International Journal Epidemiology*, **15**, 1986, 352–9.

35 Routledge D A, Repetto-Wright R and Howarth C I L. A comparison of interviews and observation to obtain measures of children's exposure to risk as pedestrians. *Ergonomics, 17*, 1974, 623–35

36 Howarth C I and Repetto-Wright R. The measurement of risk and the attribution of responsibility for child pedestrian accidents. *Safety Education, 144*, 1978, 10–13.

37 Ward H *et al. Pedestrian Activity and Accident Risk*. AA Foundation for Road Safety Research 1994.

38 The Public Health Alliance. *Health on the Move: Policies for Health Promoting Transport*. The policy statement of the Transport and Health Study Group. PHA (Birmingham 1991).

39 Hillman M, Adams J and Whitelegg J. *One False Move ... A Study of Children's Independent Mobility*. London Policy Studies Institute (1990).

40 Guyer B, Gallagher S S *et al.* Prevention of childhood injuries: evaluation of the statewide childhood injury prevention program (SCIPP). *American Journal Public Health*, **79**, 1989, 1521–7

41 Towner E M L, Dowswell T and Jarvis S N. *Reducing childhood accidents*: *The Effectiveness of Health Promotion Interventions. A Literature Review*. HEA (London 1993).

42 Jackson R H *et al.* Changing patterns of poisoning in children. *British Medical Journal*, **287**, 1983, 1468.

43 Spiegel C N and Lindaman F. Children can't fly: a program to prevent childhood morbidity and mortality from window falls. *American Journal Public Health*, **67 (12)**, 1977, 1143–7.

44 Whitelegg J and Davis R. Cycle helmets (letter). *British Medical Journal*, **305**, 1992, 504.

45 Robertson L S and Zador P L. Driver education and fatal crash involvement of teenaged drivers. *American Journal of Public Health*, **68**, 1978, 959.

46 Rivara F P. Traumatic deaths of children in the United States: currently available prevention strategies. *Paediatrics, 75*, 1985, 456–62.

47 Walsh S S and Jarvis S N. Measuring the frequency of 'severe' accidental injury in childhood. *Journal of Epidemiology Community Health*, **46**, 1992, 26–32.

48 Walsh S S, Jarvis S N, Towner E M L and Aynsley Green A. *The annual incidence of unintentional injury amongst 54,000 children. Submitted for publication.*

49 Nathorst Westfelt J. Environmental factors in childhood accidents a prospective study in Gothenburg, Sweden. *Acta Paediatrica Scandinavica* (Supplement), **291**, 1982, 75.

50 Gallagher S S, Finison K, Guyer B and Goodenough S. The incidence of injuries among 87,000 Massachusetts children and adolescents: results of the 1980–81 statewide childhood injury prevention program surveillance system. *American Journal Public Health*, **74**, 1984, 1340–7.

51 Towner E M L, Jarvis S N, Walsh S S and Aynsley Green A. Measuring exposure to injury risk in 11–14-yr-old schoolchildren. *British Medical Journal*, **308**, 1994, 449–53.

9 Respiratory disease and Sudden Infant Death Syndrome

Ross Anderson, John Britton, Aneez Esmail, Jen Hollowell and David Strachan

Key points

- For all ages of childhood, respiratory disease accounts for about one third of general practitioner episodes, one fifth of hospital admissions and one twentieth of deaths.

- Most of the hospital admissions for upper respiratory conditions in children aged 5–14 are elective, for surgery on tonsils and adenoids.

- Asthma is the most important cause of emergency admission to hospital.

- Hospital admissions for childhood asthma have increased 13-fold since the early 1960s.

- Consultation rates for hay fever and/or allergic rhinitis increased from 4 per 1,000 in 1955/6 to 28 per 1,000 in 1981/2.

- Between 1986 and 1992 deaths from Sudden Infant Death Syndrome have fallen by over 66 per cent, the greatest fall accompanying public campaigns directed at increasing awareness about risk factors such as prone sleeping position.

- The risk of developing hay fever falls with increasing number of siblings.

- Median age of death for cystic fibrosis sufferers has increased from around six months in 1959 to 17 years in 1986.

9.1 Trends and patterns of respiratory disease

9.1.1 The burden of respiratory disease

The respiratory tract encompasses the upper airways (nose and sinuses) where the incoming air is warmed and filtered; the larynx, trachea and bronchi which conduct the air into the lung and the alveoli where gas transfer takes place. It is constantly exposed to the threat of airborne hazards which include microbes (such as bacteria and viruses), biological material (such as allergens), chemical gases (such as ozone, nitrogen dioxide and sulphur dioxide) and small respirable particles (such as smoke, dust and acid aerosols). It is therefore not surprising that the airways are an important site of disease and that the distribution of respiratory disease is influenced by both the immediate and wider environment in which people live.

Lower respiratory infections, principally pneumonia, remain a major cause of mortality in developing countries. While now less important as a cause of mortality in developed countries, this may reflect a lower case fatality due to better living standards and medical care rather than a lower incidence *per se*. In all parts of the world both upper and lower respiratory disease remain major causes of morbidity.

In developed countries such as the UK, the relative importance of allergic conditions such as allergic rhinitis and asthma has steadily increased. This has probably been due to epidemiological factors (i.e. changes in the cause of disease) but may also reflect greater awareness of these disorders and a relative decline in severe infective conditions.

For all ages of childhood, respiratory disease accounts for about one third of general practitioner episodes, one fifth of hospital admissions and one twentieth of deaths (Figure 9.1).[1-3]

There are indications that respiratory disease in childhood is associated with problems in later life[4-6] and that lung function is an important predictor of mortality.[7] While the causal nature of these relationships has yet to be established, it does raise concern about childhood experience beyond the immediate illness.

Figure 9.1 Contribution of respiratory diseases to GP consultations, admissions and deaths, England and Wales

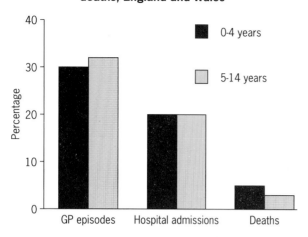

Source: Morbidity Statistics from General Practice 1981/82;[1] Hospital In-patient Enquiry 1985;[2] Mortality Statistics: cause 1989.[3]

The relative contribution of respiratory conditions to mortality during childhood is shown in Figure 9.2. In early life, lower respiratory infections predominate but during the school years the main causes of death are asthma and cystic fibrosis. Sudden Infant Death Syndrome (SIDS) which mostly occurs in the first year of life, is not included in Figure 9.2 because it is not, in classification terms, a respiratory disease. It is likely, however, that in recent years there has been a transfer on death certificates from lower respiratory infections to SIDS. For this reason, a later section of this chapter is devoted to SIDS.

Hospital admissions show a different picture (Figure 9.3). As for mortality, lower respiratory infections are relatively more common in younger than in older children but the admission pattern is dominated by upper respiratory conditions and asthma. Most of the admissions for upper respiratory conditions in children aged 5–14 are elective, for surgery on tonsils and adenoids. Asthma is the most important cause of emergency admission to hospital.

Figure 9.2 Respiratory mortality in childhood: relative importance of main conditions: 1989, England and Wales

☐ Other respiratory disease

■ Upper respiratory tract condition

▨ Cystic fibrosis

▨ Asthma

☐ Lower respiratory tract infection

Source: Mortality Statistics: cause 1989[3]

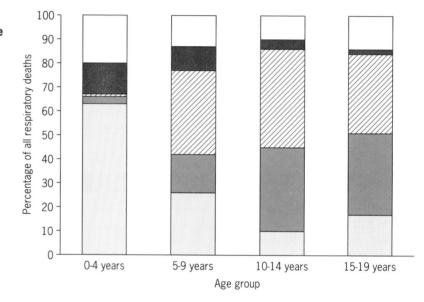

Figure 9.3 Respiratory admissions in childhood: relative importance of main conditions: 1985, England

☐ Other respiratory condition

▨ Upper respiratory tract condition

☐ Asthma

■ Lower respiratory tract infection

Source: Hospital Inpatient Enquiry 1985[2]

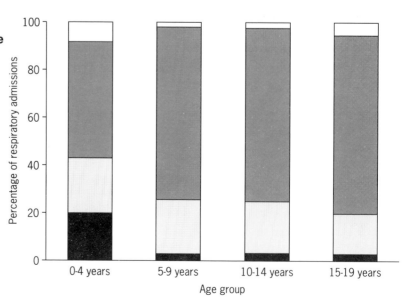

General practice consultations follow the same pattern as hospital admissions, but with an even greater emphasis on upper respiratory conditions (Figure 9.4). Allergic rhinitis also contributes to GP consultations.

Figure 9.4 GP consultations for respiratory disease: relative importance of main conditions: 1981/2, England and Wales

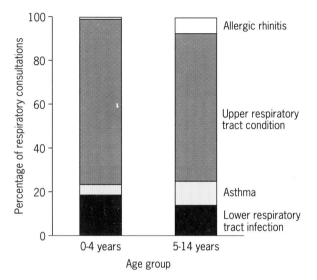

Source: Morbidity Statistics from General Practice 1981/2[1]

9.1.2 Recent trends in respiratory disease

Total mortality from respiratory diseases has fallen progressively since the 1960s, though the pattern of fall differs between the age–groups (Figures 9.5–9.7). In the first year of life there were marked fluctuations in mortality during the 1960s, but thereafter, there has been a marked decline to one tenth of the former level (Figure 9.5). There is a consistent male excess. In the 1–4 age group, there was also some fluctuation during the 1960s but the decline has been progressive over the whole period

(Figure 9.6). The trend for the 5–14 age group is more like that of those aged under one, with fluctuations in the 1960s followed by a fall from the late 1960s.

More insight into the reasons for these patterns can be obtained from inspecting trends in the main diagnoses (Figures 9.8–9.10). Asthma mortality is negligible for children aged under one year. The late 1960s peak is largely explained by an increase in bronchitis, which might have been due to a change relating to the coding of bronchiolitis between successive revisions of the ICD, although there is no corresponding fall in pneumonia deaths. Most significant is the rise in deaths from SIDS following the introduction of this category in 1968 when use of the eighth revision of the ICD began. If these death rates are added to those from respiratory disease, the trend over the period is a reduction in rates of only about one third. In the 1–4 age group, asthma deaths are relatively uncommon and changed little over the period, whereas there was a steady decline in pneumonia and bronchitis deaths. The fluctuating rates for the 5–14 age group, in all respiratory disease in the 1960s, was due to a rise and fall in asthma deaths. Otherwise, pneumonia deaths tended to fall steadily.

The reasons for the longstanding decline in respiratory mortality in children are unclear. It predated the antibiotic era by some 50 years, but more recently improvements in antibacterial therapy and intensive care may have reduced case fatality. There is limited evidence, discussed below, which suggests that the incidence of pneumonia may be declining, but the extent to which this accounts for the decline in mortality is unclear. Many of the factors which may be relevant to trends in disease incidence (changes in family composition, improved childhood nutrition and control of environmental pollution) may also have influenced the severity of illness, and hence case fatality.

Figure 9.5
Mortality for respiratory diseases among children aged under 1 year by sex: 1958-91, England and Wales

Source: OPCS

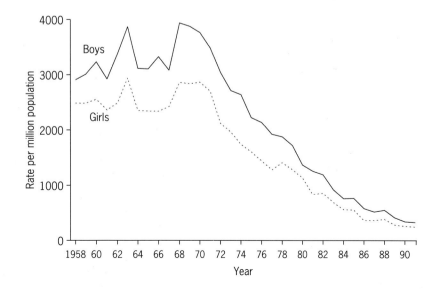

Figure 9.6
**Mortality for respiratory diseases
among 1-4 year old children by sex:
1958-90, England and Wales**

Source: OPCS

Figure 9.7
**Mortality for respiratory diseases
among 5-14 year old children by sex:
1958-91, England and Wales**

Source: OPCS

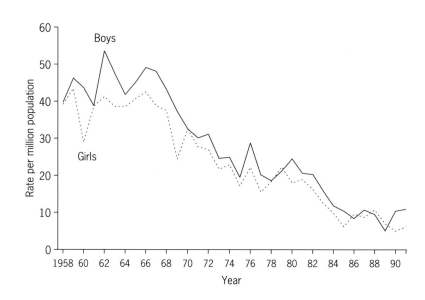

Figure 9.8
**Mortality for respiratory diseases
among children aged under 1 year
by type of disease: 1958-91,
England and Wales**

—— Total

– – Bronchitis

········· Pneumonia

–·–· SIDS

—— SIDS+Total

Source: OPCS

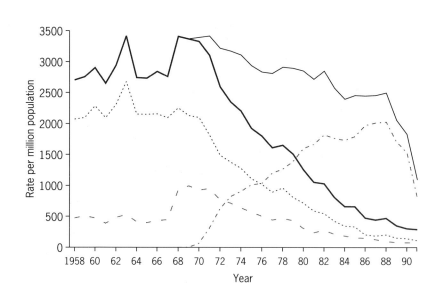

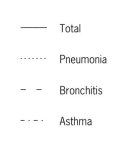

Figure 9.9
Mortality for respiratory diseases among children aged 1-4 years by type of disease: 1958-91, England and Wales

——— Total

········· Pneumonia

– – Bronchitis

–·–·– Asthma

Source: OPCS

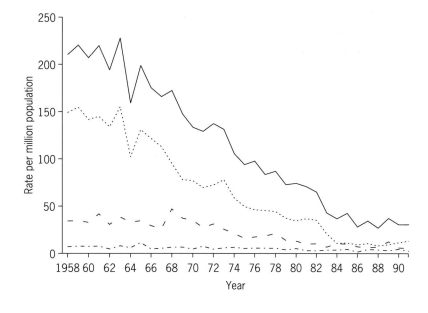

Figure 9.10
Mortality for respiratory diseases among children aged 5-14 years by type of disease: 1958-91, England and Wales

——— Total

········· Pneumonia

– – Bronchitis

–·–·– Asthma

Source: OPCS

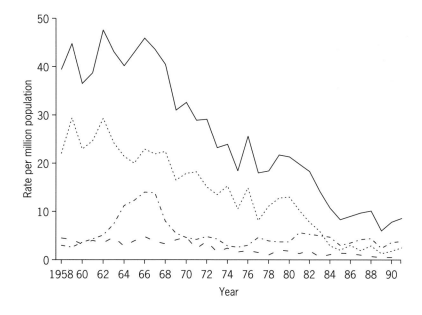

Hospital admissions have shown remarkable trends since the early 1960s (Figures 9.11 and 9.12). In the 0–4 year age group, pneumonia admissions have gone down while acute bronchitis admissions have increased. These two diagnoses show reciprocal shifts in 1968 as acute bronchiolitis is moved from the pneumonia category to the acute bronchitis category in the eighth revision of the ICD, but this does not explain the longer term trend. The most obvious trend is in asthma which has risen 13-fold. It is apparent from Figure 9.11 that this rise cannot be explained by diagnostic transfer, since no other condition, such as wheezy bronchitis and acute bronchitis, showed a corresponding fall. In the 5–14 age group, there was a seven–fold increase in asthma, while all the other lower respiratory diagnoses remained at a relatively low level and tended to fall further.

Trends in children consulting their GP per 1,000 for various respiratory diagnoses in 1955/6, 1970/1 and 1981/2 are shown in Table 9.1. There has been a marked increase in rates for hay fever/allergic rhinitis and asthma,

a moderate rise in acute upper respiratory infections and a fall in rates for pneumonia and hypertrophy of the tonsils and adenoids.

9.1.3 Geographical variations in respiratory disease
Mortality and hospital admissions due to all respiratory disease as a group (ICD 460–519) vary across regional health authorities (RHAs) by a factor of about two.[2,3] Later sections in this chapter will present geographical data for pneumonia and asthma.

9.1.4 Social and ethnic influences
The relationship between social class and mortality from respiratory disease in 1979–80, 1981–82 is shown in Figure 9.13. Taking the 1–15 year age group as a whole, there is a two–fold gradient upwards from Social Classes I and II to Social Classes IV and V but this seems to be explained largely by the social class effect in the 1–4 year age group. Data from general practice indicates that social class is not an important correlate of consultation for respiratory disease (Table 9.2).

Figure 9.11
Hospital admissions for lower respiratory conditions among 1-4 year old children: 1962-85, England and Wales

.... Asthma

- - - - Acute bronchitis

– – Pneumonia

——— Bronchitis unqualified

Source: Hospital Inpatient
Enquiry 1962-85

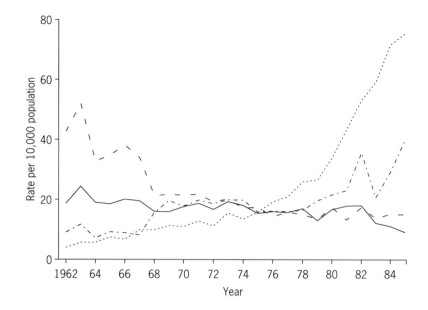

Figure 9.12
Hospital admissions for lower respiratory conditions among 5-14 year old children: 1962-85, England and Wales

.... Asthma

- - - - Acute bronchitis

– – Pneumonia

——— Bronchitis unqualified

Source: Hospital Inpatient
Enquiry 1962-85

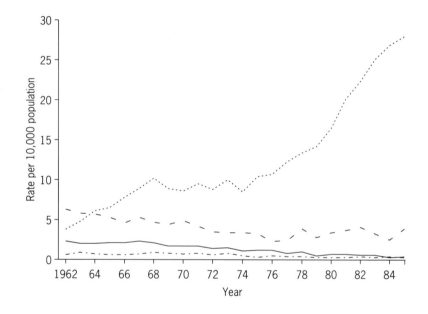

Table 9.1 Trends in childrens, consulting rates per 1,000 for various respiratory diagnoses in three national morbidity surveys at ages 0–14 years

Diagnoses	1955/56	1970/71	1981/82
Acute URTI* (non-febrile)	**	133	197
(febrile)	**	78	92
Acute pharyngitis/tonsillitis	123	152	106
Hypertrophy of tonsils etc.	20	5	3
Chronic pharyngitis/catarrh	16	28	36
Acute laryngitis/tracheitis	14	23	19
Acute bronchitis	70	85	76
Pneumonia	7	3	3
Asthma	9	15	28
Hay-fever/allergic rhinitis	4	14	28

* Upper respiratory tract infection.
** Categories combined in 1955–6 survey.

Sources: *Morbidity Statistics from General Practice 1955/6, 1970/1*[11]
and 1981/2[1]

Table 9.2 Children consulting, per 1,000 in 1981/82 at ages 0–15 years, by parental social class and diagnosis

Diagnosis	Parental social class			
	I/II	IIIN	IIIM	IV/V
Acute URTI*	217	250	265	259
Acute tonsillitis	83	93	103	90
Chronic pharyngitis	36	40	30	22
Cough	52	68	73	63
Laryngitis/tracheitis	16	14	16	13
Acute bronch(iol)itis	64	69	77	73
Asthma	27	30	29	30
Allergic rhinitis	32	31	27	28
Person-years at risk	9,152	2,931	9,907	4,877

* Upper respiratory tract infection.

Source: *Morbidity Statistics from General Practice 1981/2, Socioeconomic Analysis*[75]

Figure 9.13 Mortality for diseases of lower respiratory system among children aged 1-15 years: SMRS by age, sex, social class and cause of death: 1979-80 and 1982-83 combined, England and Wales

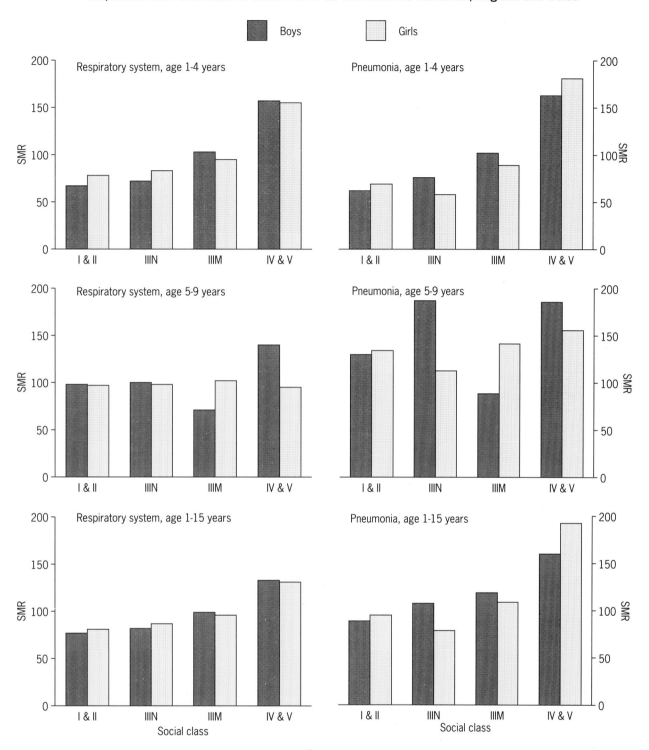

Source: Occupational Mortality: childhood supplement 1979-80, 1982-83[13]

The relationship between ethnic factors and respiratory conditions has been discussed in Chapter 7. Figure 9.14 shows infant mortality rates from diseases of the respiratory system by mother's country of birth. This shows an almost two–fold variation in mortality, with that of babies of Caribbean- and Pakistani-born mothers being higher and that of Indian and East African origin being lower than the UK average.

9.1.5 Scope of remainder of chapter
The main lower respiratory problems are lower respiratory

infections, asthma and cystic fibrosis. The succeeding sections of this chapter will deal with each of these in more detail. Upper respiratory infections are an important cause of morbidity but will not be discussed further. A section will be devoted to allergic rhinitis, the epidemiology of which is linked with that of asthma. Lastly, in view of the importance of SIDS and the strong possibility that diagnostic transfer with pneumonia may have occurred in the past, a concluding section will be devoted to this condition.

Figure 9.14 Infant mortality by main causes of death and mother's country of birth: 1982-85 combined, England and Wales

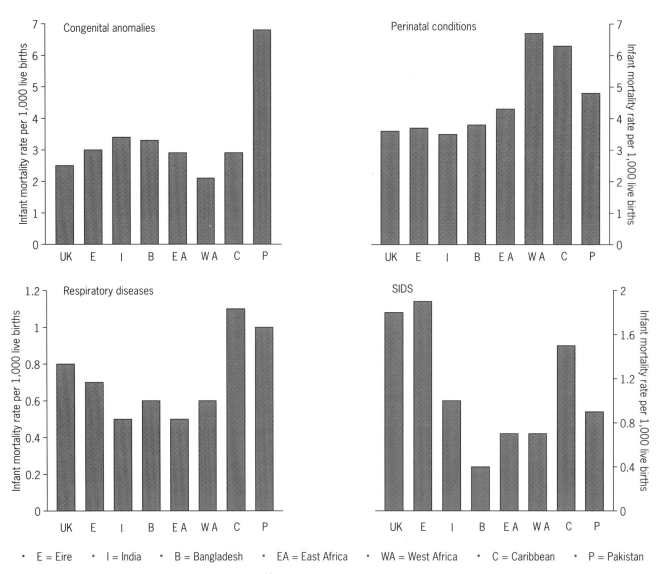

· E = Eire · I = India · B = Bangladesh · EA = East Africa · WA = West Africa · C = Caribbean · P = Pakistan

Source: Mortality and Geography: a review in the mid-1980s[14]

9.2 Lower respiratory infections (pneumonia and bronchitis)

9.2.1 Definitions and diagnoses

A number of terms are used to describe acute lower respiratory tract infections in children. These include 'bronchitis', 'bronchiolitis' and 'pneumonia', which are frequently used as convenient diagnostic labels, with little evidence that the anatomical site of infection implied by the label is, in fact, involved.

Acute bronchitis (ICD9 466.0) and unspecified bronchitis (ICD9 490) are usually combined in estimating the incidence of acute bronchitis. These tend to follow upper respiratory infections and may present clinically with cough, wheeze or both together with varying degrees of fever. In the past, however, many children with cough and wheeze in the presence of upper respiratory ('cold') symptoms were labelled as 'wheezy bronchitis'. This complicates the interpretation of both routine statistics and survey data relating to bronchitis. Although many

children have a cough, few have persistent cough with phlegm production, which are the symptoms used to diagnose chronic bronchitis (ICD9 491) in adults.

Bronchiolitis (ICD9 466.1) is a diagnosis usually applied to the more severe acute lower respiratory illnesses. In the first year of life without radiographic evidence of pulmonary consolidation, such episodes are often related to respiratory syncytial virus infection. Bronchiolitis is rarely diagnosed in children over 12 months of age. It was combined with acute bronchitis (466) in ICD8 and the distinction remains controversial, as there is rarely pathological evidence to implicate the smaller, rather than the larger airways. In the seventh and earlier ICD revisions, bronchiolitis was classified under pneumonia.

The symptom of stridor (noise on inspiration) is characteristic of laryngotracheobronchitis ('croup'). This common and relatively benign illness, which is related to epidemics of parainfluenza virus, does not appear as a separate entity in published statistics.

Pneumonia (ICD9 480–486) is a diagnosis which is strictly applicable only when there is radiological or pathological evidence of pulmonary consolidation, but it is much more widely applied as a label for severe lower respiratory illness, particularly by parents. The epidemiological features of pneumonia may therefore most closely represent the pattern of clinically severe lower respiratory infection in the community.

The majority of lower respiratory infections among infants and young children in the developed world have a viral basis,[15] although bacterial infections cause most of the pneumonias in children above four years of age.[16] It is clear from the epidemiology of these conditions, however, that host and environmental factors also play important roles in determining the incidence and severity of the illness resulting from infection.

9.2.2 Time trends

Mortality attributable to bronchitis and pneumonia has been declining in young children since the turn of the century in England and Wales. As shown earlier in Figures 9.8–9.10, this trend has continued more recently in all age groups. The rate of decline in respiratory mortality among infants accelerated around 1970 (Figure 9.8). As discussed in section 9.1.2 this acceleration coincided with the introduction and increasingly wider usage of the term 'sudden infant death' and it is very likely that many of these sudden deaths were previously attributed to bronchitis or pneumonia (see section 9.6).

Diagnostic transfer is of greater concern in rates of hospital admission for acute bronchitis and pneumonia, because asthma admissions have increased markedly and are now much more common than admissions labelled as bronchitis or pneumonia. As discussed earlier and shown in Figure 9.11, during the 1980s admission rates for acute bronchitis among the 0–4-year-olds increased in parallel with the rise in asthma admissions. This may reflect the use of 'acute bronchitis' or 'bronchiolitis' as

labels for wheezing illness in young children.

GPs see the majority of children with acute lower respiratory infections that result in contact with the health services. Comparison of the three national morbidity surveys suggests that the incidence of episodes labelled as pneumonia may have declined, but consultation rates for acute bronchitis, laryngitis and tracheitis were similar in 1955–6 and 1981–2 (Table 9.1). These changes contrast with the rising proportions of children consulting for asthma and hay fever.

Survey data from two national birth cohorts also suggest that the incidence of pneumonia in childhood may have declined. In the 1970 cohort, followed up at age 5 years, 1.6 per cent of the sample of 13,135 had suffered one or more episodes of pneumonia.[17] The equivalent cumulative incidence of pneumonia by age 5 in the 1958 cohort was 3.5 per cent of a sample of 13,980 children.[18] This was similar to the figure obtained in a survey of 4,700 Kent schoolchildren surveyed in the mid–1960s.[19] Unfortunately, no comparison between the cohorts can be made for bronchitis, since the form of the relevant questions was different and more recent survey data are not available, reflecting the declining epidemiological interest in these conditions.

9.2.3 Geographical and social class variations

Due to the small number of deaths and the Hospital In-Patient Enquiry (HIPE) sample being based on a 10 per cent sample of admissions, it has been necessary to combine a number of years and age groups to obtain a sufficiently large number of events to calculate rates at a regional level. Death from bronchitis and pneumonia in infancy and childhood is more common in the north and west of Britain and in urban areas, particularly Greater London. This is reflected in Table 9.3 which shows high mortality rates for pneumonia in the Thames RHAs and Northern, North Western and Yorkshire RHAs during 1979–85. Despite similar numbers of cases in the

Table 9.3 Rates of hospital admission (per 10,000) and mortality (per million) for pneumonia (ICD 480–486) by hospital region of England and Wales for children aged 0–14 years, 1979–85 combined

RHA	Hospital admissions			Mortality		
	Number	Rate	% of E&W rate	Number	Rate	% of E&W rate
Northern	251	5.71	84	206	46.9	104
Yorkshire	387	7.51	111	252	48.9	108
Trent	390	5.97	88	161	24.6	54
East Anglia	197	7.29	107	82	30.4	67
NW Thames	309	6.74	99	249	54.3	120
NE Thames	393	7.77	114	327	64.6	143
SE Thames	346	7.32	108	313	66.2	146
SW Thames	249	6.55	96	244	64.2	141
Wessex	187	5.00	74	197	52.6	116
Oxford	227	6.48	95	84	24.0	53
South Western	321	7.87	116	117	28.7	63
W Midland	486	6.40	94	299	39.4	87
Mersey	237	6.67	98	144	40.5	89
North Western	462	7.98	117	316	54.6	121
Wales*	261	6.57	97	142	35.7	79
England and Wales	4,703	6.80	100	3,133	45.3	100

* Number of admissions in Wales 1982–5 reduced to 10 per cent of published figures for comparability with remaining data which was derived from HIPE.

Source: *Hospital In-patient Enquiry 1979-85*

numerator, hospital admission rates for pneumonia (calculated from HIPE 10 per cent sample data for 1979–85) show much less regional variation than do death rates. These figures need to be interpreted with caution because they exclude acute bronchitis and bronchiolitis (ICD9 466). Nevertheless, no striking south–east to north–west trend is apparent for hospital admissions for pneumonia. Survey data from the national birth cohorts[17,18] show little regional variation in the incidence of pneumonia in early childhood. This suggests that the geographical patterns shown in mortality statistics may be a reflection of case fatality.

Mortality rates for childhood pneumonia also display a marked social class trend (Figure 9.13). At ages 1–4, children with fathers in Social Class IV or V are three times more likely to die of respiratory conditions than children from families in Social Classes I or II.[13] This variation is greater than the social class trend in incidence as estimated from survey data (see below), which raises the possibility of increased case fatality among children of lower social status. Hospital admission data are not analysed by parental social class and too few children consult with pneumonia for a meaningful social class analysis of the recent national morbidity survey data. There is little evidence of marked social class variation, however, in consultations for bronchitis or bronchiolitis in childhood during 1981–82 (Table 9.2).

In the 1970 cohort at age 5 years, there was marked regional variation in the cumulative incidence of bronchitis, in contrast to pneumonia. High bronchitis incidence was reported in north and west England, and Wales, with low rates in Scotland and East Anglia.[17] Strong social class trends also emerged for parental recall of bronchitis.[17] These social and geographical variations remained significant after adjustment for other correlates of bronchitis, of which maternal smoking was the most important risk factor.

9.2.4 Risk factors for lower respiratory infections in childhood

Recent trends in lower respiratory infections should be interpreted in the light of their known epidemiological associations. In this respect, analyses of illnesses labelled as pneumonia are probably most informative. A similar analysis for bronchitis is less helpful because of the greater uncertainty as to the purely infective nature of such episodes, given their possible relationship to asthma.

Table 9.4 presents previously unpublished data from the national 1958 cohort comparing the incidence of pneumonia at various ages allowing for up to seven selected social and environmental factors.[18] Although these results relate to children brought up in the 1960s, the findings are consistent with findings from the more recent 1970 cohort.[17] The 1958 cohort data have the advantage that the age at the first attack of pneumonia was available for analysis.

Table 9.4 Risk factors for pneumonia from birth to age 7 in the 1958 birth cohort

Risk factors	Percentage of children first developing pneumonia aged:				
	Under 1 year	1 year	2–4 years	5–7 years	0–7 years
Number of older siblings (at age 7)					
0	0.9	0.5	1.0	0.9	3.4
1	1.4	0.7	1.3	1.0	4.3
2	2.1	0.8	1.7	1.2	5.7
3	3.0	1.3	1.6	1.0	6.8
4+	2.5	1.3	1.9	0.7	6.5
Father's social class (at age 7)					
I	1.6	0.3	1.4	2.0	5.3
II	0.8	0.6	1.4	1.0	3.7
IIIN	1.0	0.4	1.5	0.9	3.7
IIIM	1.5	0.8	1.3	0.9	4.5
IV	1.8	0.7	1.1	0.9	4.5
V	3.0	0.9	1.5	0.7	6.1
Unclassified	2.3	1.0	1.5	0.8	5.7
Mother's smoking during pregnancy					
None	1.2	0.5	1.2	1.0	3.9
<10/day	1.9	1.3	1.6	0.7	5.5
10+/day	2.2	0.9	1.3	1.3	5.7
Variable	2.7	0.6	1.6	1.1	6.0
Housing tenure at age 7					
Owned	1.1	0.5	1.2	1.1	3.8
Rented	1.8	0.9	1.4	0.9	5.0
Household amenities shared at age 7					
None	1.4	0.6	1.3	1.0	4.3
Any	2.1	1.1	1.3	0.8	5.3
Breast feeding					
Never	2.0	0.8	1.6	1.3	5.8
<1 month	1.4	0.8	1.3	0.5	4.2
>1 month	1.2	0.6	1.1	0.8	3.7

Source: Strachan DP. *The Childhood Origins of Adult Bronchitis in a British Cohort born in 1958*[18]

Pneumonia in the first two years of life was more common among children from poorer families, as reflected by father's social class, housing tenure or shared use of household amenities. The incidence of early pneumonia was also greater among those with large numbers of older siblings and children of mothers who smoked. These factors were not related to the incidence of pneumonia after 2 years of age. Indeed, there was some evidence of a reversal of the social class trend for episodes of later onset. Breast-feeding was the only factor which had a protective effect and which was consistently related to pneumonia incidence for all ages up to 7. The incidence was similar in males and females at all ages.

Living conditions generally have improved throughout this century and family sizes have declined in postwar years. In the light of the epidemiological data, each of these trends would be expected to reduce incidence. On the other hand, wider uptake of cigarette smoking and artificial infant feeding by mothers in the 1960s and 1970s would be expected to increase the incidence of lower respiratory illnesses (see also Chapter 5). The rise of these adverse factors suggests that there is still room for further reductions in the incidence of lower respiratory infections in early childhood.

9.2.5 Long-term consequences of bronchitis and pneumonia in childhood

The association between chest illnesses such as bronchitis and pneumonia in childhood and respiratory morbidity in adult life has been established from several cohort studies.[20] This raises the possibility that early episodes of chest illness may damage the lung and predispose to later development of impaired ventilatory function.[19] An alternative explanation could be that some individuals are susceptible to chest illnesses of all types from an early age and this susceptibility is manifest in early childhood as symptomatic respiratory illness and in adulthood as chronic cough, wheeze or impaired lung function. One form of chronic susceptibility which has been suggested is a wheezing tendency.[6]

There is certainly a close association between illnesses labelled as pneumonia and those labelled as asthma or wheezy bronchitis in childhood: in the 1958 cohort, over half of the children with a history of pneumonia by age 7 developed asthma or wheezy bronchitis by 23 years of age, compared to one quarter of the remainder of the cohort. This association could arise from confusion between pneumonia and asthma or wheezy bronchitis; confounding by social and environmental correlates; or a causal relationship between pneumonia and wheezing illness. A causal link could operate in either direction: severe episodes of pneumonia might predispose to asthma; or children with an asthmatic tendency may be more susceptible to clinically severe pneumonia.

Confusion between pneumonia and wheezing illness is unlikely, since the risk factors for the two conditions are dissimilar.[21] Confounding has also been excluded.[18] The direction of the causal relationship, however, remains unclear. With recent reports of associations between birthweight, respiratory illnesses in infancy and lung function in later adult life,[22] this debate is likely to continue.

9.3 Asthma

9.3.1 The burden of asthma

Asthma is an abnormal response of the airways to a wide range of environmental factors which results in episodes of obstruction to airflow manifested by wheezy shortness of breath. Asthma is the most important chronic disease in childhood being both common and at times very severe. Over a prior 12-month period about 15 per cent of children will report episodes of wheezing suggestive of asthma and about a quarter of these will have restricted activities due to the condition.[24] Asthma is a common cause of admission to hospital and general practitioner consultation. Anti–asthmatic drugs are the most common prescribed drugs in childhood. There is concern that the prevalence of asthma may be increasing. Fatalities occur but are extremely rare.

The National Child Development Study has contributed important and unique information about the incidence and prognosis of asthma.[24] It shows that by the age of 20, about 30 per cent of children have had asthma (or wheezing illness) at some time during childhood. Of children wheezing at age 7, about 20 per cent are still wheezing at age 23; the proportion rises to 50 per cent if there is more severe asthma at age 7. There is a small but measurable effect of childhood asthma on employment prospects in early adult life.[25]

9.3.2 Mortality

Death from asthma is rare but relatively important in relation to other respiratory causes of death in later childhood (Figure 9.2).

Trends since the 1960s show several interesting features (Figures 9.8–9.10). The most prominent was an epidemic of deaths from asthma in older children which occurred in the late 1960s. Deaths in this age group increased by about four-fold and to an even greater degree in young adults.[26] Similar epidemics occurred in several countries and circumstantial evidence pointed to an association with the introduction of a new and powerful inhaler therapy. The subsequent decline in mortality was associated with withdrawal of the drug. This incident served to emphasise the importance of routine monitoring systems and to remind doctors and patients that treatments may have unforeseen effects. A subsequent epidemic occurred in New Zealand and this too may have been due to iatrogenic factors. It is therefore reassuring that mortality levels are currently flat though it should be noted that current mortality levels are similar to those existing in the late 1950s. Interpretation of the trends needs to balance the opposing effects on mortality of a possible increase in prevalence and the more extensive use of modern therapy. We do not, in essence, know what the underlying trends in mortality are.

The geographical pattern of mortality shown in Table 9.5 shows significant heterogeneity in asthma, with a more than three–fold variation across RHAs from 5.9 per million in North West Thames to 1.6 per million in North Western. Interpretation needs to be cautious because of small numbers, even after combining several years' data. The pattern corresponds to some extent with the pattern of prevalence of childhood asthma described by the 1958 (NCDS) and 1970 (CHES) National cohort studies with higher levels in the south and in Wales.[12,27]

An early analysis of social class and asthma mortality found no association.[28] More recent data have insufficient numbers for analysis. This lack of an association with social class, however, is also observed in most prevalence studies.

9.3.3 Hospital admissions

Trends in hospital admissions for asthma and lower respiratory conditions are shown in Figures 9.11 and 9.12. From 1962 to 1985 (the last year of HIPE data), there was an increase of 1,300 per cent for asthma in the 0–4 age group and of 600 per cent in the 5–14 age group. In recent years the annual increase has been 20 per cent and 12 per cent for these two age groups

Table 9.5 Rates of hospital admission (per 10,000) and mortality (per million) for asthma (ICD 493) by hospital region of England and Wales for children aged 0–14 years: 1979–85 combined

RHA	Hospital admissions			Mortality		
	Number	Rate per 10,000	% of E&W rate	Number	Rate per million	% of E&W rate
North	1,007	22.9	74	19	4.33	109
Yorkshire	1,433	27.8	89	19	3.69	93
Trent	1,971	30.2	97	27	4.13	104
East Anglia	624	23.1	74	15	5.55	139
NW Thames	1,758	38.3	123	27	5.89	148
NE Thames	2,005	39.6	127	26	5.14	129
SE Thames	1,539	32.5	105	13	2.75	69
SW Thames	1,396	36.7	118	17	4.47	112
Wessex	916	24.5	79	9	2.40	60
Oxford	1,152	32.9	106	10	2.85	71
South West	980	24.0	77	17	4.17	105
W Midlands	1,926	25.4	82	37	4.87	122
Mersey	1,107	31.1	100	13	3.66	92
North West	2,501	43.2	139	9	1.56	39
Wales*	1,202	30.2	97	18	4.53	114
England and Wales	21,517	31.1	100	276	3.99	100

* Number of admissions in Wales 1982–5 reduced to 10 per cent of published figures for comparability with remaining data which was derived from HIPE.

Source: *Hospital In-Patient Enquiry 1979-85*

respectively. Similar increases have occurred in most other developed countries. It is clear from the figures that the trend cannot be explained by diagnostic transfer from other respiratory diagnoses or by changes in the ICD classification. Readmission is a feature of asthma but *ad hoc* studies[29] and examination of linked data from the Scottish In-Patient Statistics system indicate that the upward trend is due to an increase in the number of individuals admitted rather than to an increase in readmissions (unpublished data). The reasons for the increase are likely to lie both in changes in the epidemiology of asthma and in its medical care.

It is important to recognise that rates of hospital admission for asthma are of an order of magnitude smaller than that of the prevalence of asthma itself. Therefore a small shift in the way in which hospital referral is viewed by families of asthmatic children and their doctors, could have a much larger proportional effect on asthma admissions. A trend towards self– and GP–referral to hospital has been observed, indicating that there is probably an increased preference of families and their doctors to seek admission for acute asthma.[29,30] This trend has probably been fuelled by publicity about increasing asthma deaths in children (although from Figures 9.9 and 9.10 this is not actually the case), and mounting interest in the diagnosis and medical care of asthma. Another factor in favour of hospitalisation is a relative decline in the demand for hospitalisation for other paediatric conditions.[31] Against this is the evidence that there has not been an increase in readmissions, neither has there been a fall in the spectrum of severity on admission;[29] this suggests that increased morbidity may also be important and this theory has some support from prevalence surveys (see below).

9.3.4 General practitioner consultations
Data from the National GP Morbidity Surveys also show evidence of an upward trend (Table 9.1).[32] It should be noted that the levels of consultation are considerably lower than prevalence estimates; thus the increase could be explained by a change in consulting behaviour. In addition, there is considerable room for diagnostic transfer from other lower respiratory conditions such as bronchitis.

9.3.5 Trends in prevalence
One question is whether the trends in admissions and GP utilisation represent an increase in the prevalence of asthma. A major difficulty in examining this question is that not all asthma is diagnosed as such and an increase in diagnosed asthma could be due to a shift in diagnostic fashion. Indeed it has been found by two repeat surveys that the proportion of wheezy children diagnosed as asthma has doubled from about 30 per cent to over 60 per cent over the last 15 years.[30,33] For this reason it is preferable to compare the prevalence of wheezing (the symptom of asthma) rather than rely on diagnosis.

Analysis of all large published studies from the UK shows that there is some evidence of an increase in the 12-month period prevalence of asthma[23] (Figure 9.15). These studies vary considerably in their methods especially in aspects which relate to the sensitivity and specificity of the questionnaires used. For this reason, there is particular interest in those surveys which have been repeated over time using the same methods. The National Study of Health and Growth has reported that there was an increase over time in the prevalence of wheezing, especially the persistent type.[34] This is consistent with a repeat study from Wales which found that between 1973 and 1988 there had been an increase in prevalence associated with a shift upwards in the spectrum of severity of bronchial hyperresponsiveness, a marker of asthma.[33] The position has, however, been confused by a more recent study among London schoolchildren which found little evidence of an increase in prevalence but marked changes in medical care and diagnosis over the period 1978–91.[30]

Figure 9.15 Percentage prevalence of wheeze and of a diagnosis of asthma

Wheeze

Asthma

Source: Anderson HR, Paediatric
Respiratory Medicine. [23]

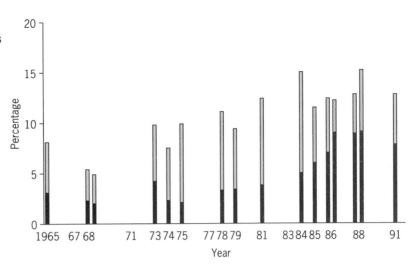

9.3.6 Geographical, social and ethnic effects on prevalence and incidence

In children asthma may be more prevalent in the south of Britain and in Wales than in the north.[12] Using the NCDS 1958 cohort data, an analysis of interregional migration indicated that prevalence relates to the current region of residence rather than to the region of birth, thus pointing towards current exposures to causal agents rather than to those occurring in the perinatal period.[12] The same is probably true for immigrants from overseas, among whom migration in early life is associated with a level of prevalence experienced by native-born residents.[35]

From Table 9.5 it can be seen that in 1979–85 there was no correlation between mortality from asthma by RHA and hospital admission rates. For example, North Western had the lowest mortality and highest admission rates while East Anglian had the equal lowest admission rate and second highest mortality. Two national cohort studies have found that the prevalence of asthma varies by less than a factor of two throughout Great Britain.[12] These variations in mortality and admissions are likely to reflect differences in severity and medical care.

Most studies of infants and children up to about 7 years report an association between social class and the incidence of wheezing illness, possibly reflecting greater exposure to infections and tobacco smoke in the manual classes.[21,36] After about the age of 5 the effect of social factors tends to fade.[21] There is little relationship between social class and the use of hospitals or general practitioners, generally corresponding to the findings of prevalence and cohort studies. In the past there was probably a class effect on labelling[37,38,39] though this has not been observed in recent studies. Asthma in childhood has a measurable though small effect on employment prospects and on social status.[25]

Three epidemiological studies have examined the question of ethnicity and asthma in children. Two found no relationship with ethnicity,[40,41] while the other found a higher prevalence of wheezing in Whites and Afro-Caribbeans.[42] It is reported in Chapter 7 that, despite the lower prevalence of asthma in Asian children, they have higher hospital admission rates for acute asthma. The authors suggest that this could be related to difficulties of communication or compliance with the treatment.

9.3.7 What is the cause of asthma and why might it be increasing?

Three types of factors are important in the aetiology of asthma: heredity; factors influencing the onset of the asthmatic trait or tendency (induction of asthma); and factors responsible for the precipitation of attacks (inciting of asthma). It is clear that environmental rather than genetic factors largely explain the variation in asthma prevalence throughout the world, but the way in which they do so is unknown. It is understandable that the apparent upward trend in asthma has been attributed to changes in environment and lifestyle but there is little evidence to suggest what the responsible agent or agents might be. One of the major difficulties confronting epidemiologists is that the prevalence of asthma is fairly evenly distributed throughout the country and across various lifestyles and ethnicities. This suggests that the environmental factors may be ones to which all the population is exposed. Current interest is focused on macro-environmental factors (air pollution), domestic environment (tobacco smoke, cooking fumes, house dust mites, pets) and lifestyle factors (dietary salt, child's smoking) and intrauterine factors (smoking in pregnancy, intrauterine growth). Lastly it should be mentioned that there is now concern that certain types of therapy may increase rather than decrease morbidity.[43]

9.4 Hay fever

Seasonal allergic rhinitis, colloquially known as hay fever, is of interest for two reasons. First, it is a common condition which causes widespread (albeit relatively minor) morbidity. It is uncertain to what extent this may affect school performance, particularly during the examination season. Secondly, since the triggering allergen (grass pollen) is ubiquitous in season, variations in the occurrence of hay fever may contribute to our knowledge of the distribution and determinants of the underlying tendency to allergic disease (atopy). This in turn is highly relevant to understanding the epidemiology of childhood asthma.

9.4.1 Routine statistics
Death or hospital admission attributed to hay fever is exceedingly rare. Routine statistics are therefore limited to those obtained from general practice. Table 9.1 shows that consultation rates for hay fever and/or allergic rhinitis are comparable to those for asthma and that the proportion of the child population consulting for these complaints increased dramatically from 4 per thousand in 1955–6 to 28 per thousand in 1981–2. Similar increases also occurred in adults.[32] Consultation rates for allergic rhinitis in 1981–2 were similar among children from families of each social class (Table 9.3).

9.4.2 Population surveys
Much of our limited knowledge of the epidemiology of hay fever is derived from population surveys, in which the condition has usually been ascertained simply by enquiry about diagnoses, rather than by a structured symptom questionnaire or by objective measures of allergy such as skin prick tests.

Estimates of the prevalence of hay fever among schoolchildren in different countries vary between 0.5 per cent and 28 per cent,[44] but much of this variation is likely to be due to the diagnostic criteria chosen and the age of the sample studied. Possible changes in the prevalence of hay fever over time may also contribute.[45] In the British national 1958 cohort the proportion with a history of hay fever or allergic rhinitis in the past year was 8.0 per cent at age 11 and 12.0 per cent at age 16. Comparable figures from the later 1970 cohort (at ages 10 and 16) are not yet published, but will be of considerable interest in view of the increase in GP consultations over this period.

In Britain during 1981–2, the proportion of the population (all ages) consulting their GP for hay fever was higher in the south than the north of Britain.[46] A similar north–south gradient was apparent for parental reports of hay fever among 13,135 children from the national 1970 cohort when they were surveyed in 1975.[47] In the national 1958 cohort, hay fever showed a similar geographical pattern at ages 7, 11, 16 and 23, with the highest prevalence in the south-east, intermediate in the south-west and the lowest prevalence in regions north of the Midlands, including Scotland.[12] Little urban–rural variation was apparent.

A very similar regional pattern was found for infant eczema in the 1958 cohort,[12] which suggests that the distribution of hay fever may reflect geographical variation in the prevalence of atopy in general. It remains to be determined, however, whether these regional differences are an artefact of parental reporting, or whether they result from genetic or environmental variation throughout the country.

9.4.3 Risk factors for hay fever or allergic rhinitis in childhood
Table 9.6 summarises the principal social and environmental correlates of hay fever or allergic rhinitis in the 1958 cohort. The results relate to parental reports of these conditions occurring in the year before the child was aged 11 years. Similar patterns apply to prevalence in the year before age 16 (parental report) and in the year before age 23 (self–report).

The most striking correlations were the strong, graded inverse associations between hay fever prevalence and numbers of older and younger children in the family.[48] These were each highly statistically significant and a given number of older children had a significantly stronger effect than the same number of younger children. The effect of number of older children in the household was more influential than was birth order and was independent of maternal age and parity. A similar pattern of decreasing prevalence with increasing numbers of older siblings was found in the national 1970 cohort at age 5.[47]

After adjustment for family size and position in the household, hay fever in the 1958 cohort was more commonly reported by children of professional parents and those brought up in owner-occupied housing with sole use of kitchen, bath and toilet (Table 9.6). No effect of household crowding was apparent after adjustment for the powerful effects of family size.

Maternal age at delivery, birthweight, gestational age and maternal smoking during pregnancy had virtually no

Table 9.6 Risk factors for hay fever or allergic rhinitis at age 11 in the 1958 birth cohort

Risk factors		Percentage of children with hay fever or allergic rhinitis in the past year at age 11*
Number of older siblings at age 11	0	10.0
	1	7.9
	2	5.0
	3	4.0
	4+	2.6
Number of younger siblings at age 11	0	8.9
	1	8.3
	2	7.3
	3	6.5
	4+	5.4
Father's social class at age 11	I	10.8
	II	10.7
	IIIN	9.3
	IIIM	7.3
	IV	6.3
	V	6.4
	Unclassified	5.0
Housing tenure at age 11	Owned	9.0
	Rented	7.1
Household amenities shared at age 11	None	8.4
	Any	6.2
Breast feeding	Never	7.0
	Any	8.5

* Mutually adjusted by multiple logistic regression. All factors shown are statistically significant at the 5 per cent level.

effect on the prevalence of hay fever or allergic rhinitis. As in the 1970 cohort,[47] however, a small but significant excess of hay fever was found among breast-fed babies (Table 9.6).

One explanation which has been advanced to explain many of these associations is that infections acquired by household contact in early childhood may protect against the subsequent development of allergic disease.[48] This could account for the associations of hay fever with small households (particularly few older siblings), richer families, better quality housing and breast-feeding. It might also explain why hay fever, nowadays such a common complaint, was not recognised in the medical literature until the period of the industrial revolution.[49] As yet, however, there have been no epidemiological studies which have directly tested this hypothesis.

Further studies, preferably including objective measures of pollen allergy, are required to confirm that the associations between hay fever and social or environmental factors are not solely due to artefacts of parental reporting. Nevertheless, the intriguing epidemiological patterns of hay fever in the national birth cohorts suggest that this common disease is more complex than a genetically programmed response to a ubiquitous environmental allergen.

9.5 Cystic fibrosis

9.5.1 Definition
Cystic fibrosis is an autosomal recessively inherited disorder which arises from a defect of chloride ion transport in the apical segments of epithelial cell membranes.[50] Cystic fibrosis is characterised biochemically by a high concentration of sodium in sweat and clinically by pancreatic insufficiency and recurrent lung infection. When first described in 1938,[51] cystic fibrosis was almost exclusively a disease of young children, with death resulting either from meconium ileus soon after birth, or from recurrent respiratory infections in infancy or early childhood. Since then, death in childhood has become relatively rare, with most patients now surviving into adult life.[52] Many factors are likely to have contributed to this improvement, although the development of broad spectrum and antipseudomonal antibiotics and of pancreatic enzyme replacement therapy, are likely to have played a major role. The improving outlook for cystic fibrosis represents a major success for medical science, but the consequent increase in the population of patients with cystic fibrosis has substantial implications for the provision of health care resources.

9.5.2 Frequency of cystic fibrosis
Studies from the UK[52] and elsewhere[53–55] suggest that the incidence of cystic fibrosis in Caucasians is approximately 1 in every 2,500 live births. In England and Wales, this currently represents approximately 250 new cases born each year. The incidence of cystic fibrosis in non-Caucasians has not been so clearly defined, but is probably substantially lower than in Caucasians.

9.5.3 Mortality from cystic fibrosis in England and Wales

(a) Availability of data
Deaths from cystic fibrosis were not categorised separately by OPCS until 1968, when the eighth revision of the International Classification of Diseases introduced category 273.0 as an exclusive code for cystic fibrosis and this code continued in the ninth revision as category 277.0. Cystic fibrosis deaths can be identified from seventh revision records, however, in which cystic fibrosis was classified with 'other diseases of the pancreas' in category 587.2 since the bridge coding exercise at the end of the seventh revision reveals a clear age segregation between cystic fibrosis and the remainder of category 587.2 that cystic fibrosis accounts for virtually all deaths below age 50 and few, if any, above that age. Exclusion of deaths at age 50 and above from this category therefore yields reasonable estimates of cystic fibrosis deaths from 1959 to 1967.

(b) Numbers of deaths
With this adjustment to seventh revision data, the annual number of cystic fibrosis deaths has decreased progressively from approximately 180 in 1959/60 to 99 in 1990 (Figure 9.16).

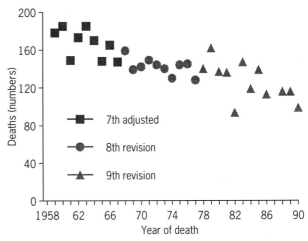

Figure 9.16 Number of deaths in ICD categories for cystic fibrosis: 1959-90, England and Wales

Source: Registrar General's Statistical Reviews 1958-73
Mortality Statistics: cause 1974-90

9.5.4 Factors affecting age at death from cystic fibrosis in England and Wales
Individual mortality records provided by OPCS for the period 1959–1986 have recently been analysed in relation to the time trend in age at death and the effects of sex, social class and region of residence.[56]

(a) Time trend in age at death
Median age at death has increased substantially, from around six months in 1959 to 17 years in 1986 (Figure 9.17). Mortality data published by OPCS since 1986 present age at death in 5-year bands, so small annual changes in median age at death cannot be discerned. The

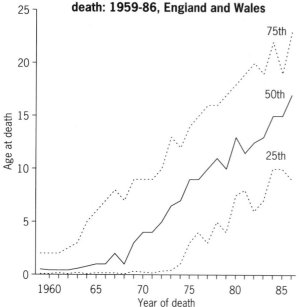

Figure 9.17 Median, 25th and 75th centile ages at death from cystic fibrosis by year of death: 1959-86, England and Wales

Source: Britton JR. Effects of social class, sex and region of residence on age at death from cystic fibrosis. [56]

records show, however, that although median age at death has remained within the 15–19 year band since 1986, the 25th and 75th centiles have continued to improve. Thus the most recent mortality data suggest that the overall trend over the last thirty years towards higher age at death is continuing.

(b) Sex

Until the mid-1970s, when median age at death was around 7 years, there was little difference in age at death between the sexes. Since 1974, however, age at death has been lower in females than in males in all but one

year, typically by about two years (Figure 9.18). The reason for this difference is not understood, though the more rapid decline in lung function described in females during early adolescence[57] and anecdotal evidence that lung function declines more rapidly during pregnancy,[58] suggests that hormonal effects may be important.

(c) Social class

Occupational social class has been coded on most cystic fibrosis death certificates since 1970. The occupation used for coding differs according to age at death. Below age 16, the occupation used is that of the mother, or if she has no paid occupation, that of the father. For deaths at age 16 or above, occupation is coded to that of the index case, or if he or she has no occupation, to that of the spouse.

Occupational social class for deaths at age 16 or above may be unrepresentative of that applying during childhood and adolescence, since recent survey data reveal that adults with cystic fibrosis tend to select non-manual occupations (S Walters, personal communication). Deaths below age 16, however, comprise the majority of those occurring between 1970 and 1986 and since these are coded by the parent's (usually the father's) occupation, they are likely to reflect socioeconomic status during childhood. Age at death is higher in cases from non-manual occupational groups in 13 of these 16 years, by an average of around three years (Figure 9.19), suggesting that higher socioeconomic status confers some survival advantage. This finding is particularly relevant to the appraisal of cystic fibrosis health care facilities, since improved survival amongst patients attending specialist centres within the UK[52] is likely to be confounded to some extent by recruitment of cases from higher socioeconomic classes.[59]

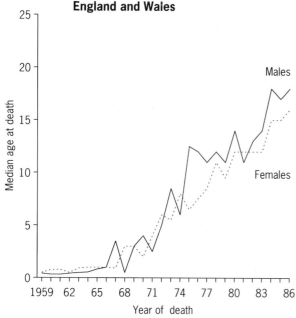

Figure 9.18 Median age at death from cystic fibrosis by year of sex: 1959-86, England and Wales

Source: Britton JR. [56]

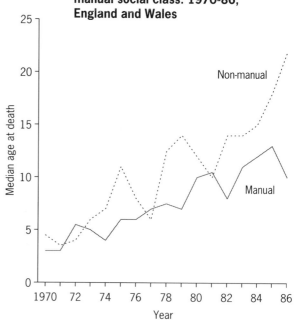

Figure 9.19 Median age at death from cystic fibrosis whether non-manual or manual social class: 1970-86, England and Wales

Source: Britton JR. [56]

(d) Region of residence
Usual region of residence is coded for all mortality records and is available for Regional Health Authority (RHA) since 1974. After adjusting for sex and social class effects, age at death between 1974 and 1986 differed significantly between RHAs, the adjusted odds ratio for death below the median age for the year of death varying by up to three–fold over the extremes of the range. The highest ages at death occurred in Northern RHA and the lowest in Wales (Figure 9.20).

These estimates of regional differences were not weighted by the number of deaths and are therefore biased towards those prevalent during the earlier part of the study period when the majority of deaths occurred. These observations, however, suggest that regional differences in the management of cystic fibrosis and the effects of other potential influences on survival, are worthy of further study.

9.5.5 Use of mortality data for population and survival estimation

It is generally assumed that cystic fibrosis death registrations are complete and that the data may be used to estimate population size and survival trends. An analysis based on this assumption has recently been reported.[60] In this study, median survival was found to have improved substantially in successive cohorts, from under 10 years in those born in 1960, to around 20 years in those born in 1970. On the strength of current trends in the improvement in survival, the life expectancy of children born with cystic fibrosis in 1990 is estimated to be of the order of 40 years.[60]

Amalgamation of numbers surviving within each birth cohort provides estimates that the current total England and Wales cystic fibrosis population is approximately 5,200 individuals,[60] a figure corroborated by independent estimates for the entire UK based on clinical survey data.[50] Approximately one third of this population is aged over 16. The improving survival from cystic fibrosis means that the population is increasing in number by approximately 100 cases per year[60,61] since the proportion of cases who die before reaching age 16 is small, the paediatric cystic fibrosis population is now relatively stable. The majority of the increase in the total population is therefore in the adult group and this trend has obvious relevance to the planning and provision of health-care

Figure 9.20 Ranking of region of residence by independent odds ratios for cystic fibrosis death at above median age for the year of death: 1974-86, regions of England, and Wales

Source: Britton JR.[56]

resources for patients with cystic fibrosis. In both financial and emotional terms, cystic fibrosis is an expensive disease to manage,[62] so an expanding population of patients has major implications for the allocation of resources.

9.5.6 Summary
Survival from cystic fibrosis has increased substantially over the past three decades with the result that most patients alive today will live into adult life and those born today may live well into middle age. Cystic fibrosis therefore accounts for a diminishing proportion of childhood deaths, with the majority of severe morbidity and mortality now occurring in early adult life. Survival from cystic fibrosis is influenced by sex, social class and region of residence. The progressive expansion of the cystic fibrosis population, particularly the adult population, has major implications for resource allocation in the health service.

9.6 Sudden Infant Death Syndrome (SIDS)

9.6.1 Defining SIDS
SIDS was recognised as an entity in the early 1960s and defined in 1969 as 'the sudden unexpected death of any infant or young child which is unexpected by history and in which a thorough post–mortem examination fails to demonstrate an adequate cause of death.'[63] The ICD ascribed the 8th revision code 795 from 1968 to 1978 to describe these deaths, and the 9th revision code 798.0 since 1979. The words 'infant' or 'young child' usually refer to an age range of between 2 weeks and 2 years but the definition was revised in 1989 by the US National Institute of Health to include only infants dying suddenly under 1 year of age.[64] Nevertheless, the diagnosis remains one of exclusion.

The use of the word 'syndrome' is used as an alternative to 'disease'. In medical terminology, a 'disease' is usually due to a single abnormality of which the cause is generally known. There are many well recognised illnesses, however, which have a typical group of symptoms or manifestations but for which the mechanism or cause is not known; these tend to be described as 'syndromes'. SIDS is one of these because it is generally accepted that the sudden unexpected death of an infant in its sleeping place is such a common and characteristic happening that there must be some common factor(s) involved, though this is at present unknown.

'Cot death' is a more colloquial description of SIDS often used by both doctors and the public. Although it is a convenient term for the tragedy, it is not as accurate as the definition of SIDS given above because it only refers to the sleeping place where the infant is found dead. Virtually all SIDS are cot deaths, but not all cot deaths are true SIDS because some babies die in their sleeping place of a known disease.

For any death over 27 days the certifier may provide several causes of death. OPCS assigns the underlying cause of death from this information following the World Health Organisation (WHO) rules for the ICD. Where 'Cot

death', 'SIDS' or some similar term is the only cause given on the certificate, SIDS will be assigned to the underlying cause. Each year there are several cases in England and Wales where the certifier has also given another cause, frequently more precise than SIDS. Thus between 1988 and 1992, 7 per cent of all sudden infant deaths had another cause on the certificate. In these cases the WHO rules usually assign the other cause to the underlying cause. Thus these cases will not be included in an analysis of SIDS based on the underlying cause alone. OPCS present analyses of these more broadly defined sudden infant deaths in an annual Monitor (DH3 93/2). However when comparing SIDS with other causes of death it is necessary to use only those cases where SIDS is the underlying cause.

Since 1986 deaths under 28 days have been certified using a different certificate. The certifier may enter both infant and maternal conditions leading to the death without assigning precedence to any one type of condition. It is therefore no longer possible to derive an underlying cause for deaths under 28 days. Therefore only SIDS occurring in the postneonatal period will be considered here when describing the epidemiology of SIDS using routine data.

9.6.2 Trends
As discussed in Chapter 6, SIDS is numerically the most important cause of death in the postneonatal period. In 1992, in England and Wales, 30 per cent of postneonatal deaths were attributed to SIDS.

Figure 9.21 shows the postneonatal death rate and the SIDS rate per 1,000 live births between 1971 and 1992. It shows the increasing certification of SIDS as a cause of postneonatal death during this period. Between 1969 and 1982 the rise in the mortality rate for sudden infant deaths took place against a fall in the overall postneonatal mortality rate and in particular, as described earlier in this chapter, a dramatic fall in the postneonatal mortality rates attributed to respiratory diseases. The combined postneonatal mortality rate due to respiratory diseases

Figure 9.21 Postneonatal, respiratory and SIDs mortality (rate per 1,000 live births): 1971-92, England and Wales

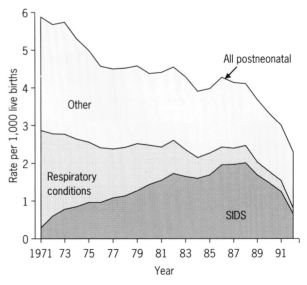

Source: OPCS

and SIDS between 1969 and 1988 remained virtually constant and is likely to reflect a transfer to the SIDS category of many deaths previously assigned to other respiratory conditions.

Mortality attributed to SIDS in the postneonatal period rose to 1.73 per 1,000 live births in 1982. There followed a slight fall to 1.60 in 1984 then a second rise to 1.96 in 1986. Since 1986, it has fallen to 1.25 in 1991. The most dramatic fall, to 0.63 per 1,000 live births, occurred in 1992 following a campaign by the Department of Health ('Back to Sleep' Campaign) and the Foundation for the Study of Infant Deaths to encourage parents to be aware of the risk factors for SIDS. Advice on changing parental behaviour in relation to sleep position, overheating and stopping smoking was reinforced by media and television campaigns. The decline of the SIDS mortality in 1992 cannot be wholly attributed to the effects of these campaign, and several studies are now attempting to explain the reasons for this decline.[65] Figure 9.21 also shows that the fall in SIDS has been responsible for over two thirds of the fall in the overall postneonatal mortality rate between 1986 and 1992.

9.6.3 Risk factors
(a) Age and sex of child
SIDS is much more common among male infants than female. In 1988–92, 62 per cent of SIDS were among male infants who comprise 51 per cent of live births. In the same years, over 86 per cent of SIDS occurred before the age of six months and approximately 60 per cent before the age of four months.

(b) Month of occurrence
There is a clear seasonal pattern of deaths from SIDS with most deaths occurring in the winter months and fewest in the summer months. In the four years 1988–91 for example, there were more than twice as many SIDS in the first quarter as in the third quarter of the year. In 1992, the contrast between these 3-month periods was less marked. The number of SIDS in the first quarter were only 22 per cent higher than those for the third quarter. This indicates that the greatest falls in SIDS in 1992 occurred in winter months. The increase in SIDS in 1986 was partly attributed to the exceptionally cold weather in February of that year.[66]

(c) Twins
The SIDS rate is up to five times higher in twins than in singletons. The high rate in twins is almost certainly because twins are very often premature, often weigh under 2,500 g at birth (low birthweight) and have a higher chance of spending some of their lives in special care units in maternity hospitals. All these factors are thought to be related to an increased risk for sudden infant death.[67,68]

(d) Social class variations
Table 9.7 shows that in the years 1988–91 there were two and a quarter times more deaths from SIDS in infants born to parents in Social Class V compared to Social Class I. The reasons for this are not clear, but excess smoking in Social Class V contributes to this difference.

(e) Maternal smoking
Several studies from seven different countries have found that maternal smoking is associated with twice the risk of SIDS, independent of social factors.[68–74] The risk increases with increasing quantity smoked.

(f) Breast-feeding
A very large case-control study carried out in New Zealand found that babies who were breast-fed had half the risk of dying from SIDS as compared with those who were not breast-fed.[72] This has not been found universally, however, and the role of breast-feeding in preventing SIDS remains controversial.

(g) Prone sleeping position
Several studies both in New Zealand and in the United Kingdom have suggested that babies who are put to sleep in the prone position are at an increased risk of SIDS compared with babies who are put to sleep on their backs or on their sides.[72,74] The evidence for prone sleeping position being an important risk factor has been strengthened by intervention studies which have shown a marked decrease in the SIDS rate when parents have been advised to avoid the prone sleeping position.[65] The prone position is believed to be dangerous because of an increased risk of upper airways obstruction and an increased risk of overheating if babies are well clothed and covered in bed.

9.7 Summary and conclusions

Respiratory disease is a major burden throughout childhood. The main conditions are infections of the upper and lower respiratory tracts, asthma and allergic rhinitis.

Table 9.7 Postneonatal mortality rates (per 100,000 live births) by cause and social class (based on father's occupation) for births inside marriage only: 1988–91 combined, England and Wales

Cause	Social class							
	Total	I	II	IIIN	IIIM	IV	V	Other
All causes	280	228	210	239	263	379	499	510
Respiratory conditions	25	18	17	23	26	32	49	46
Sudden infant deaths	115	97	84	87	110	154	221	215

OPCS unpublished data

Cystic fibrosis is an important cause of respiratory mortality in later childhood and because of improved survival it is increasing as a cause of chronic respiratory disability in later childhood and early adult life. Mortality and hospital admissions due to lower respiratory infections have fallen, probably due to increased host resistance and improved therapy. Some of the fall in respiratory mortality in infants may be due to diagnostic transfer to deaths coded as Sudden Infant Death Syndrome (SIDS).

Since the recognition of 'SIDS' as a category of death in the International Classification of Diseases in 1971, rates increased up until 1986. This may have been partly due to diagnostic transfer from respiratory deaths. SIDS is the largest single cause of infant death in the postneonatal period. Research has identified a number of risk factors, including male sex, twins, season, prone sleeping position and maternal smoking. From 1986 to 1992, there was a dramatic fall of over 66 per cent in SIDS mortality rates, with the greatest relative decrease occurring in conjunction with campaigns to make the public more aware of risk factors. If sustained, this will be a major public health achievement.

Asthma mortality was marked by an epidemic in the 1960s, which was associated in some way with the introduction of a new form of treatment, but otherwise there has been little change in mortality over time. Hospital admissions for asthma have risen steeply probably as a result of changes in both medical care and epidemiological factors affecting incidence and severity. The cause of the latter is unknown, but there is also evidence of an increase in other atopic conditions, namely allergic rhinitis and eczema. Experience over the past three decades can be summarised as showing a fall in serious infections, a rise in allergic disease and an increase in the tendency to use services. Social and geographical variations in mortality, prevalence and utilisation exist but not to any major degree.

References

1 Royal College of General Practitioners/Office of Population Censuses and Surveys/Department of Health and Social Security. *Morbidity Statistics from General Practice: Third National Study 1981–82*. Series MB5 no.1. HMSO (London 1986).

2 Department of Health and Social Security/Office of Population Censuses and Surveys/Welsh Office. *Hospital In-patient Enquiry 1985*. HMSO (London 1988).

3 Office of Population Censuses and Surveys. *Mortality Statistics, Cause, England and Wales 1989, Series DH2 no 16*. HMSO (London 1991).

4 Barker D J P and Osmond C. Childhood respiratory infection and adult chronic bronchitis in England and Wales. *British Medical Journal*, **293**, 1986, 1271–5.

5 Britten N, Davies J M C and Colley J R T. Early respiratory experience and subsequent cough and peak expiratory flow rate in 36-year-old men and women. *British Medical Journal*, **294**, 1987, 1317–20.

6 Strachan D P, Anderson H R, Bland J M and Peckham C. Asthma as a link between chest illness in childhood and chronic cough and phlegm in young adults. *British Medical Journal*, **296**, 1988, 890–3.

7 Ebi-Kryston K, Hawthorn V M, Rose G, Shipley M J *et al*. Breathlessness, chronic bronchitis and reduced pulmonary function as predictors of cardiovascular disease mortality among men in England, Scotland and the United States. *International Journal Epidemiology*, **18**, 1989, 84–8.

8 Office of Population Censuses and Surveys . *Historical Mortality Data for England and Wales*. OPCS (London 1992).

9 Department of Health/Office of Population Censuses and Surveys. *Hospital In-patient Enquiry*. HMSO (London 1962).

10 Logan W P D and Cushion A A. *Morbidity Statistics from General Practice, Vol. 1. General*. Studies on Medical and Population Subjects, No. 14. HMSO (London 1958).

11 Office of Populations Censuses and Surveys. *Morbidity Statistics from General Practice. Second National Survey 1970–71*. HMSO (London 1973).

12 Strachan D P, Golding J and Anderson H R. Regional variations in wheezing illness in British children: effect of migration during early childhood. *Journal Epidemiology Community Health*, **44**, 1990, 231–6.

13 Office of Population Censuses and Surveys. *Occupational Mortality, Childhood Supplement. The Registrar General's Decennial Supplement for England and Wales, 1979–80, 1982–83*. Series DS no.8. HMSO (London 1988).

14 Balarajan R. Raleigh V S. Variation in perinatal, neonatal, postneonatal and infant mortality. In: Britton M (ed). *Mortality and Geography: A Review in the mid-1980s, England and Wales*. OPCS Series DS No 9. HMSO (London 1990).

15 Denny F W. Acute respiratory infections in children: etiology and epidemiology. *Paediatrics in Review*, **9**, 1987, 135–46.

16 Anonymous. Pneumonia in childhood. *Lancet,* 1988, 741–3.

17 Golding J. Bronchitis and pneumonia. In: Butler NR, Golding J (eds). *From Birth to Five. A Study of the Health and Behaviour of Britain's Five-Fear-Olds*. Pergammon (Oxford 1986).

18 Strachan D P. *The Childhood Origins of Adult Bronchitis in a British Cohort born in 1958*. (MSc Thesis). University of London, 1986.

19 Holland W W, Bailey P and Bland J M. Long-term consequences of respiratory disease in infancy. *Journal Epidemiology Community Health*, **32**, 1978, 256–9.

20 Strachan D P. Do chesty children become chesty adults? *Archives Diseases Children*, **65**, 1990, 161–2.

21 Anderson H R, Bland J M, Patel S and Peckham C. The natural history of asthma in childhood. *Journal Epidemiology Community Health*, **40**, 1986, 121–9.

22 Barker D J P, Godfrey K M, Fall C, Osmond C, Winter P D and Shaheen S O. Relation of birth weight and childhood respiratory infection to adult lung function and death from chronic obstructive lung disease. *British Medical Journal*, **303**, 1991, 671–5.

23 Anderson H R. Is asthma really increasing? *Paediatric Respiratory Medicine*, **1**,1993, 6–10.

24 Anderson H R, Pottier A and Strachan D P. The incidence of asthma to age 23. *Thorax,* **47**, 1992, 537–42.

25 Sibbald B, McGuigan S and Anderson H R. Asthma and employment in young adults. *Thorax,* **47**, 1992, 19–24.

26 Inman W H W and Adelstein A M. Rise and fall of asthma mortality in England and Wales in relation to use of pressurised aerosols. *Lancet ,* **2**, 1969, 279–83.

27 Golding J and Butler N. Wheezing and asthma. In: Butler N J, Golding J (eds). *From Birth to Five: a Study of the Health and Behaviour of Britain's five-year-olds.* Pergammon Press (Oxford 1986), pp. 158–70.

28 Office of Population Censuses and Surveys . *Child Health: a Collection of Studies.* Studies on Medical and Population Subjects No. 31. HMSO (London 1976).

29 Anderson H R. Increase in hospital admissions for childhood asthma: trends in referral, severity and readmissions from 1970 to 1985 in a health region of the United Kingdom. *Thorax,* **44**, 1989, 614–9.

30 Strachan D P and Anderson H R. Trends in hospital admission rates for asthma in children. *British Medical Journal,* **304**, 1992, 873–5.

31 Hill A M. Trends in paediatric medical admissions. *British Medical Journal,* **298**, 1989, 1479–83.

32 Fleming D M and Crombie D L. Prevalence of asthma and hay fever in England and Wales. *British Medical Journal,* **294,** 1987, 279–83.

33 Burr M L, Butland B K, King S and Vaughan-Williams E Changes in asthma prevalence: two surveys 15 years apart. *Archives Diseases Children,* **64**, 1989, 1452-46.

34 Burney P G, Chinn S and Rona R J. Has the prevalence of asthma increased in children? Evidence from the national study of health and growth 1973-86. B*ritish Medical Journal,* **300**, 1990, 1306–10.

35 Morrison Smith J. The prevalence of asthma and wheezing in children. *British Journal Diseases Chest,* **70**, 1976, 73–7.

36 Leeder S R, Corkhill R, Irwig L M, Holland W W and Colley J R T. Influence of family factors on the incidence of lower respiratory illness during the first year of life. *British Journal of Social Preventive Medicine,* **30**, 1976, 203–12.

37 Graham P J, Rutter J L, Yule W and Pless I B. Childhood asthma: a psychsomatic disorder? Some epidemiological considerations. *British Journal Preventative Social Medicine,* **21**, 1967, 78–85.

38 Hamman R F, Halil T and Holland W W. Asthma in schoolchildren: demographic associations with peak expiratory flow rates compared with children with bronchitis. *British Journal Preventative Social Medicine,* **29**, 1975, 228–38.

39 Peckham C and Butler N. A national study of asthma in childhood. *Journal Epidemiology Community Health,* **32**, 1978, 79–85.

40 Johnson I D, Bland J M and Anderson H R. Ethnic variation in respiratory morbidity and lung function in childhood. *Thorax,* **42**, 1987, 542–8.

41 Pararajasingam C D, Sittampalam L, Damani P, Pattemore P K and Holgate S T. Comparison of the prevalence of asthma among Asian and European children in Southampton. *Thorax,* **47**, 1992, 529–32.

42 Melia R J W, Chinn S and Rona R J. Respiratory illness and home environment of ethnic groups. *British Medical Journal,* **296**, 1988, 1438–41.

43 Mitchell E A. Is current treatment increasing asthma mortality and morbidity? *Thorax,* **44**, 1989, 81–4.

44 Montgomery Smith J. Epidemiology and natural history of asthma, allergic rhinitis and atopic dermatitis. In: Middleton E, Reed C E, Ellis E F, Adkinson N F and Yunginger J W (eds). *Allergy: Principles and Practice.* C V Mosby (St Louis 1983) pp. 771-803.

45 Aberg N. Asthma and allergic rhinitis in Swedish conscripts. *Clinical Experimental Allergy,* **19**, 1989, 59–63.

46 Fleming D M and Crombie D L. Geographical variations in person consulting rates in general practice in England and Wales, *Health Trends,* **21**, 1989, 51–5.

47 Golding J and Peters T. Hay fever and eczema. In: Butler N R and Golding J (eds). *From Birth to Five. A Study of the Health and Behaviour of Britain's Five-year-olds.* Pergamon, (Oxford 1986) pp. 171–86.

48 Strachan D P. Hay fever, hygiene and household size. *British Medical Journal,* **299**, 1989, 1259–60.

49 Emmanuel M B. Hayfever, a post industrial revolution epidemic: a history of its growth during the 19th century. *Clinical Allergy,* **18**, 1988, 295–304.

50 McPherson M A, Dormer R L, Goodchild M C and Dodge J A. Biochemical basis of cystic fibrosis. *Nature,* **323**, 1986, 400.

51 Anderson D H. Cystic fibrosis of the pancreas and its relation to celiac disease: a clinical and pathological study. *American Journal Diseases Children* **56**, 1938, 344–99.

52 British Paediatric Working Party on Cystic Fibrosis. Cystic fibrosis in the United Kingdom 1977-85: an improving picture. *British Medical Journal,* **297**, 1988, 1599–1602.

53 Wood R E, Boat T F and Doershuk C F. Cystic fibrosis. *American Review Respiratory Diseases,* **113**, 1976, 833–78.

54 Warwick W J. The incidence of cystic fibrosis in Caucasian populations. *Helvetica Paediatrica Acta,* **33**, 1978, 117–25.

55 Allan J L, Robbie M, Phelan P D and Danks D M. The incidence and presentation of cystic fibrosis in Victoria 1955-1978. *Australian Paediatrics Journal,* **16**, 1980, 270–3.

56 Britton J R. Effects of social class, sex and region of residence on age at death from cystic fibrosis. *British Medical Journal,* **298**, 1989, 483–7.

57 Corey M, Levison H and Crozier D. Five to seven-year course of pulmonary function in cystic fibrosis. *American Review Respiratory Diseases,* **114**, 1976, 1085–92.

58 Frydman M I. Epidemiology of cystic fibrosis: a review. *Journal Chronic Diseases*, **32**, 1979, 211–19.

59 Penketh A R L, Wise A, Mearns M B Hodson M E and Batten J C. Cystic fibrosis in adolescents and adults. *Thorax*, **42**, 1987, 526–32.

60 Elborn J S, Shale D J and Britton J R. Cystic fibrosis: current survival and population estimates to the year 2000. *Thorax*, **46**, 1991, 881–5.

61 British Paediatric Association. Working Party on Cystic Fibrosis in the United Kingdom 1977-85: an improving picture. *British Medical Journal,* **297**, 1988, 1599–602.

62 Robson M, Abbott J, Webb K and Walsworth-Bell J. A cost description of an adult cystic fibrosis unit and cost analyses of different categories of patients. *Thorax*, **47**, 1992, 684–9.

63 Discussion of terminology of sudden infant death syndrome. In: *Proceedings of the Second International Conference on Causes of Sudden Infant Death*. University of Washington Press, (Seattle 1970),pp.17–8.

64 Zylke J W. Sudden infant death syndrome: resurgent research offers hope. *Journal American Medical Association*, **262**, 1989, 1565–6.

65 Dwyer T and Ponsonby A-L. Sudden infant death syndrome - insights from epidemiological research. *Journal Epidemiology Community Health*, **46**, 1992, 98–102.

66 Department of Health and Social Security. *Infant Mortality in England. Report by Expert Working Group to the Chief Medical Officer*. HMSO (London 1988).

67 Golding J, Limerick S and Macfarlane A. Sudden Infant Death. *Patterns, Puzzles and Problems*. Open Books Publishing Ltd (Shepton Mallet 1985).

68 Kraus J F, Greenland S and Bulterys M. Risk Factors for sudden infant death syndrome in the US collaborative perinatal project. *International Journal Epidemiology*, **18**, 1989, 113–20.

69 Hoffman H J, Damus K, Hillman L and Krongrad E. Risk factors for SIDS. Results of the National Institute of Child Health and Human Development SIDS Co-operative Epidemiological Study. *Annals New York Academy Sciences*, **533**, 1988, 13–30.

70 McGlashan N D. Sudden infant deaths in Tasmania, 1980-86. A seven year prospective study. *Social Science Medicine*, **29**, 1986, 1015–26.

71 Rinthaka P J and Hirvonen J. The epidemiology of sudden infant death syndrome in Finland in 1969 - 1980. *Forensic Science International*, **30**, 1986, 219–33.

72 Mitchell E A, Scragg R, Stewart A W *et al*. Results from the first year of the New Zealand cot death study. *New Zealand Medical Journal*, **104,** 1991, 71–6.

73 Haglund B and Cnattingius S. Cigarette smoking as a risk factor for sudden infant death syndrome: a population-based study. *American Journal Public Health*, **80**, 1990, 29–32.

74 Fleming P J, Gilbert R, Azaz Y, *et al*. Interaction between bedding and sleeping position in the sudden infant death syndrome: a population based case-control study. *British Medical Journal,* **301**, 1990, 85–9.

75 Office of Population Censuses and Surveys. *Morbidity Statistics from General Practice 1981-2. Third National Survey. Socioeconomic Analysis.* Series MB5 No 2. HMSO (London 1986).

10 Cancer

Gerald Draper

Key points

* In Britain, about 1 child in 600 develops cancer during the first 15 years of life.

* The incidence is slightly higher in males than in females.

* About one third of cases are leukaemias, mostly acute lymphocytic leukaemia, and rather more than a fifth are various types of brain tumours.

* There have been remarkable improvements in survival and consequent reductions in population mortality rates for childhood cancers during the past 25 years. The current 5-year survival rate for all forms of childhood cancer combined is about 70 per cent.

10.1 Incidence of childhood cancer in Britain

10.1.1 Types of childhood cancer

Cancer in childhood is rare, affecting 1 in 10 thousand children each year in Britain and accounting for about one half of 1 per cent of all cancers. The cumulative risk during the first 15 years of life is about 1 in 600 and this is true also for white populations in other Western developed countries.

The distribution of types of cancer occurring in childhood is quite different from that in adults. The common carcinomas of adulthood – lung, breast, stomach or colorectal cancers – hardly ever occur in children, and many childhood cancers are embryonal types that hardly ever occur in adults. The most common types of cancer in children are leukaemia and brain tumours; these also occur in adults but the distribution of histological types is different. In studying childhood cancers it is important to use a classification based on histology rather than, as is usual with adults, on site. The reason for this is that tumours of the same histological type, e.g. rhabdomyosarcoma, occur at a number of different sites and are usually considered as a group, both for treatment purposes and in aetiological studies. On the other hand, for instance, osteosarcoma and Ewing's tumour, which are both tumours of bone, are almost invariably considered separately for both of these purposes. The classification scheme used in this chapter is set out in detail in the volume *International Incidence of Childhood Cancer*[1] and is that recommended by Birch and Marsden[2] with a few minor modifications. It is based on the *International Classification of Diseases for Oncology* (ICD-0).[3] A revised version based on the 10th Revision of the International Classification of Diseases and the associated ICD-0-2 is in course of preparation.

Data on childhood cancer are collected and published by a number of specialised children's tumour registries. There are a number of such registries in various regions of Britain and there is also a National Registry of Childhood Tumours. The information on incidence and survival presented in this chapter is based on data from this national registry.

10.1.2 Incidence rates

Incidence rates using the classification scheme referred to in section 10.1.1 are presented in Tables 10.1 and 10.2. In Table 10.1 rates are presented for all cases of childhood cancer, i.e. cancer diagnosed at ages 0–14 years, registered over the 10–year period 1971–80 in England and Wales, categorised mainly according to the site of occurrence. In Table 10.2 the same data are presented for the main histological categories of childhood cancer. In these tables, because of the rarity of these tumours, rates are presented per million children rather than per 100,000 population as is usual for adults. The age-standardised rates given in the last column of each table are directly standardised rates based on a population with a uniform age-distribution, i.e. they are the rates that would be found in a population with equal numbers of children in each single-year age group if the age-specific rates calculated from these data were to apply to such a population. As explained in section 10.2.5 below, incidence rates for childhood cancer appear to have changed little in the past 20 years, and current rates can therefore be taken to be much the same as, or for some diagnoses slightly higher than, those in Tables 10.1 and 10.2.

The shapes of the age distributions of cancers occurring in children are different from those for cancers occurring in adults. For adult carcinomas there is typically a very sharp rise in incidence with increasing age. This is not true of childhood tumours. Some examples of age

Table 10.1 Childhood cancer incidence by site: age 0–14 years, 1971–80 combined, England and Wales

		Numbers	Annual rates per million	
			crude	age-standardised*
All cases	Male	6,511	114.1	116.0
	Female	4,968	91.9	93.7
	Total	11,479	103.3	105.1
Leukaemias	Male	2,210	38.7	39.7
	Female	1,647	30.5	31.3
	Total	3,857	34.7	35.6
Lymphomas	Male	912	16.0	15.7
	Female	402	7.4	7.3
	Total	1,314	11.8	11.6
Brain and spinal	Male	1,489	26.1	26.2
	Female	1,196	22.1	22.2
	Total	2,685	24.2	24.2
Sympathetic nervous system	Male	379	6.6	7.1
	Female	285	5.3	5.7
	Total	664	6.0	6.4
Retinoblastoma	Male	152	2.7	2.9
	Female	152	2.8	3.1
	Total	304	2.7	3.0
Kidney	Male	343	6.0	6.4
	Female	348	6.4	6.9
	Total	691	6.2	6.6
Liver	Male	46	0.8	0.9
	Female	49	0.9	1.0
	Total	95	0.9	0.9
Bone	Male	317	5.6	5.3
	Female	256	4.7	4.5
	Total	573	5.2	4.9
Soft tissue sarcomas	Male	398	7.0	7.1
	Female	286	5.3	5.4
	Total	684	6.2	6.3
Gonadal and germ cell	Male	124	2.2	2.3
	Female	144	2.7	2.7
	Total	268	2.4	2.5
Epithelial neoplasms	Male	127	2.2	2.1
	Female	191	3.5	3.5
	Total	318	2.9	2.8
Other	Male	14	0.2	0.2
	Female	12	0.2	0.2
	Total	26	0.2	0.2

* See section 10.1.2

Source: Childhood Cancer Research Group

Table 10.2 Childhood cancer incidence for main histological groups: age 0–14 years, 1971–80 combined, England and Wales

Main histological groups		Numbers	Annual rates per million	
			crude	age-standardised*
Acute lymphocytic leukaemia	Male	1,763	30.9	31.8
	Female	1,264	23.4	24.1
	Total	3,027	27.2	28.0
Acute non-lymphocytic leukaemia	Male	345	6.0	6.1
	Female	298	5.5	5.6
	Total	643	5.8	5.8
Hodgkin's disease	Male	359	6.3	6.1
	Female	148	2.7	2.6
	Total	507	4.6	4.4
Non-Hodgkin lymphoma	Male	466	8.2	8.1
	Female	191	3.5	3.5
	Total	657	5.9	5.8
Ependymoma	Male	183	3.2	3.3
	Female	145	2.7	2.8
	Total	328	3.0	3.0
Astrocytoma	Male	513	9.0	9.0
	Female	478	8.8	8.8
	Total	991	8.9	8.9
Medullo-blastoma	Male	341	6.0	6.0
	Female	188	3.5	3.5
	Total	529	4.8	4.8
Neuroblastoma	Male	374	6.6	7.0
	Female	277	5.1	5.5
	Total	651	5.9	6.3
Retinoblastoma	Male	152	2.7	2.9
	Female	152	2.8	3.1
	Total	304	2.7	3.0
Wilms' tumour	Male	333	5.8	6.2
	Female	340	6.3	6.7
	Total	673	6.1	6.5
Hepatoblastoma	Male	35	0.6	0.7
	Female	39	0.7	0.8
	Total	74	0.7	0.7
Osteosarcoma	Male	172	3.0	2.9
	Female	149	2.8	2.6
	Total	321	2.9	2.8
Ewing's sarcoma	Male	122	2.1	2.1
	Female	92	1.7	1.6
	Total	214	1.9	1.9
Rhabdom-yosarcoma	Male	274	4.8	4.9
	Female	174	3.2	3.3
	Total	448	4.0	4.1
Fibrosarcoma	Male	48	0.8	0.8
	Female	48	0.9	0.9
	Total	96	0.9	0.8
Non-gonadal germ cell	Male	37	0.6	0.7
	Female	56	1.0	1.1
	Total	93	0.8	0.9
Gonadal germ cell	Male	84	1.5	1.6
	Female	76	1.4	1.3
	Total	160	1.4	1.5

* See section 10.1.2.

Source: Childhood Cancer Research Group

distributions are given in Figures 10.1–10.6 in which incidence rates are plotted for each year of age in the first 15 years of life. For the characteristic cancers of childhood (acute lymphocytic leukaemia, neuroblastoma, Wilms' tumour, retinoblastoma) there is a peak in incidence early in life. This implies that there is a very early age of initiation for these tumours, probably antenatally in many cases and perhaps preconception. For some other types of childhood cancer there is a rise in incidence throughout childhood that continues to a peak in young adult life; this is shown for Hodgkin's disease in Figure 10.5 and for osteosarcoma in Figure 10.6. (Note: Figures 10.1-10.6 have differing vertical scales.)

10.2 Variations in incidence and possible aetiological factors

10.2.1 The aetiology of childhood cancer

Very little is known about the aetiology of childhood cancer. There is a clear genetic influence in the occurrence of some cases,[4] most notably for retinoblastoma where about 40 per cent of cases are hereditary, the pattern of inheritance being that of a dominant autosomal gene, although the 'retinoblastoma gene' is actually a tumour-suppressor gene, the loss of both copies of this gene leading to the occurrence of the disease. Some other cases of childhood cancer are associated with known genetic diseases, for example neurofibromatosis and Fanconi's anaemia, or occur in recognisable familial patterns, such as the Li–Fraumeni syndrome. There is also evidence of twin concordance and a slightly increased risk among the siblings of affected cases, although these findings could, of course, be attributable to exposure to a common environment, and at least some cases of twin concordance in leukaemia appear to be due to a shared fetal circulation. For the great majority of cases of childhood cancer there is no obvious genetic explanation in the sense of a familial pattern of occurrence or association with genetic disease being observed. There may, however, be genetic determinants that do not manifest in such patterns: the incidence of Ewing's sarcoma, for instance, is strongly related to ethnic group, but there are few reports of familial aggregations of this tumour.

There is less information about environmental factors.[4] Ionising radiation, including antenatal exposure, is implicated in a small proportion of cases. For leukaemia, it has been suggested that preconception exposure of the father may be a causative factor, but this is controversial. The number of cases attributable to artificial sources of radiation (mainly medical exposures) appears, however, always to have been small and should now be smaller as a result of decreasing antenatal exposures; there are at present no reliable estimates of the effects, if any, of natural radiation in inducing childhood cancers. Some studies have suggested that there is a risk from electromagnetic fields, but this must be regarded as unproven. Some chemicals, mainly those used in treating earlier cancers, can cause childhood cancer but, again, the proportion of cases so caused appears to be small. There have been a large number of studies of parental occupational exposures as possible aetiological factors but, because of the large numbers of different types and times of exposures, differences between the types of cancer studied, and the types of study design, these are hard to evaluate and there is no definitely established risk from any parental occupation.

The possible role of viruses in relation to childhood cancer has been considered in a number of ways. First, international variations in incidence may be attributable to differing exposures to viruses; the best documented example of this is the relationship of Burkitt's lymphoma in Africa to Epstein–Barr virus. Second, maternal exposure to viruses during pregnancy has been studied in case-control and cohort studies but no consistent findings have emerged.

There is evidence that the incidence of childhood leukaemia may be related to the level of population mixing, and hence of exposure to infective agents, in a community; it has also been suggested that it may occur as a consequence of mutations occurring during cell proliferation caused by delayed exposure to such agents. It should be emphasised that none of this suggests that leukaemia is an infectious disease.

In sections 10.2.2 and 10.2.3 we consider national and international variations in incidence as possible clues to aetiology.

10.2.2 Regional and social class variations in incidence within Britain

There is some evidence of regional variations in incidence rates for acute lymphocytic leukaemia (ALL), which accounts for 80 per cent of childhood leukaemia in Britain; the reasons for this variation are unknown although they may be related to levels of socioeconomic status. There have been suggestions from a number of studies that childhood leukaemia, or at least ALL, is more common among children of parents of high socioeconomic status or among children living in *areas* of high socioeconomic status. For instance Draper *et al* categorised County Districts and Scottish Districts according to five levels of a 'socioeconomic score' based on car ownership, housing tenure and levels of employment.[5] Incidence rates of ALL were calculated for Districts at each level of this score for three calendar periods and three age groups. The results are shown in Table 10.3. It can be seen that for the first two five-year, age-groups incidence rates were consistently higher in areas of high status. This was not true for the oldest group, but the numbers of cases are smaller and it is of course possible that the aetiology of this group is different.

Childhood leukaemia is unusual among childhood diseases in being associated with high social status. If, as suggested in section 10.2.1, childhood leukaemia may result from delayed exposure to infective agents, this relationship may be a consequence of differences in patterns of exposure to infection in early life, children in more affluent families tending to be more protected from exposure at early ages.

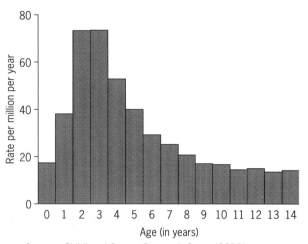

Figure 10.1 Acute lymphocytic leukaemia and unspecified leukaemias: incidence rates for single year age groups: 1971-84, Great Britain

Source: Childhood Cancer Research Group (CCRG)

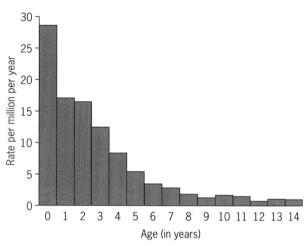

Figure 10.2 Neuroblastoma and ganglioneuroblastoma - incidence rates for single year age groups: 1971-84, Great Britain

Source: CCRG

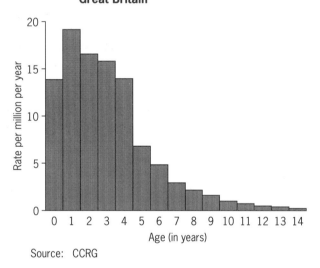

Figure 10.3 Wilms' tumour - incidence rates for single year age groups: 1971-84, Great Britain

Source: CCRG

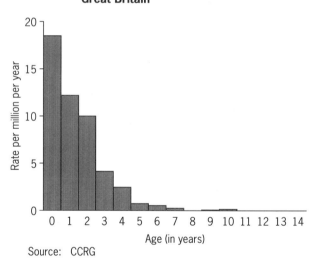

Figure 10.4 Retinoblastoma - incidence rates for single year age groups: 1971-84, Great Britain

Source: CCRG

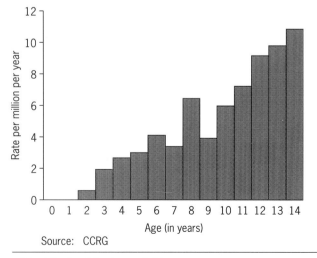

Figure 10.5 Hodgkin's disease - incidence rates for single year age groups: 1971-84, Great Britain

Source: CCRG

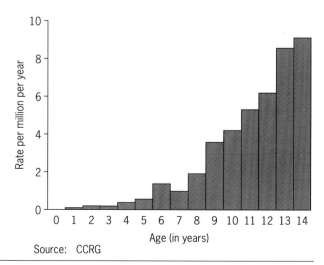

Figure 10.6 Osteosarcoma - incidence rates for single year age groups: 1971-84, Great Britain

Source: CCRG

Table 10.3 Lymphocytic and unspecified leukaemias: 1969–83, Great Britain

Age (years)	Period	Annual incidence rates per million for County Districts of high and low socioeconomic status	
		Socioeconomic score[1]	
		Highest[2]	Lowest[3]
0–4	1969–73	53.0	49.6
	1974–78	62.6	50.5
	1979–83	53.4	48.9
5–9	1969–73	28.7	20.5
	1974–78	31.9	28.5
	1979–83	29.7	22.9
10–14	1969–73	14.0	14.5
	1974–78	12.4	13.7
	1979–83	10.2	14.8

[1] Socioeconomic score is a measure of social status based on housing tenure, car ownership and levels of employment in each County District (District in Scotland).
[2] Incidence rates for the 20 per cent of County Districts having the highest socioeconomic scores.
[3] Incidence rates for the 20 per cent of County Districts having the lowest socioeconomic scores.

Source: Childhood Cancer Research Group

10.2.3 International comparisons

Incidence rates for the various types of childhood cancers are much the same among white populations in other Western developed countries (Western Europe, North America, Australia and New Zealand) as they are in Britain. There are, however, wide international variations if one considers also rates in Asia, Africa and Central and South America. Incidence data from population-based cancer registries are available from a number of such countries or parts of them; for others, information is available from hospital-based registries, and analyses based on the relative numbers of cases in different diagnostic groups can provide information on international variations. Mortality data are less likely to be useful, first because, as explained in section 10.1.1, the site-based International Classification of Diseases is not appropriate for childhood cancers, and secondly because there are likely to be large differences in survival rates which make differences in mortality rates difficult to interpret.

In Table 10.4 we present age-standardised incidence rates for a number of diagnostic groups using data from population-based registries.[1] In this table, as in the original volume, the age-standardised rates are based on a world standard population having the following age-distribution:

Age (years)	Number in standard population
0	2,400
1–4	9,600
5–9	10,000
10–14	9,000

This differs from the method of standardisation used in Tables 10.1 and 10.2, since in making international comparisons it is more appropriate to use a population that reflects an age structure more typical of countries throughout the world.

Perhaps the most notable feature of this table is that the variations in incidence are much smaller than those found in adult tumours. This may indicate the greater importance of environmental factors in the aetiology of adult cancers. However, since the incidence of childhood cancer is so low, and the rarest forms are not even tabulated here, and allowing for problems in ascertaining and diagnosing cases, there could be large differences in incidence that cannot be detected in populations of the size of those studied.

Some of the variations in Table 10.4 will of course be simply chance fluctuations and others will be due to under-ascertainment or misdiagnosis. Nevertheless, in this table, and in the more comprehensive data presented in

Table 10.4 Age-standardised incidence rates for the major types of childhood cancer in selected population-based registries

	Annual incidence per million children aged 0–14 years (directly standardised to world standard population)							
	all cancer	leukaemia	Hodgkin's disease	non-Hodgkin lymphoma	brain & spinal	neuro-blastoma	retino-blastoma	Wilms' tumour
England and Wales	109	38	4	6	24	7	4	7
Federal Republic of Germany	109	43	5	5	13	10	3	8
USA, white	136	44	6	5	25	13	4	9
USA, black	108	25	5	3	22	10	5	11
Australia, Queensland	117	38	5	6	23	10	6	8
Costa Rica	137	59	11	8	14	5	4	5
Puerto Rico	108	40	6	5	16	6	4	7
Brazil, São Paulo	145	34	9	18	21	8	6	7
China, Shanghai	107	41	2	5	20	5	3	1
India, Bombay	71	23	4	5	8	3	5	4
Japan, Osaka	114	38	1	4	24	9	5	4
Nigeria, Ibadan	156	12	97[1]		5	6[2]	8	11[3]
Uganda, Kampala	90	14	28[1]		4	2[2]	7	8[3]

[1] All lymphomas including Burkitt's.
[2] Sympathetic nervous system.
[3] Kidney.

Source: Childhood Cancer Research Group

the volume referred to, there are a number of general patterns that seem to indicate real differences in incidence.

The most notable of these is the variation in the incidence of lymphomas. This is particularly evident for Burkitt's lymphoma which in some countries accounts for a large fraction of all childhood cancer but is extremely rare in British and most other Western populations. There appear to be smaller but real differences in incidence for most of the tumours represented in Table 10.4. Some of these are more striking in data for certain developing countries where, because population data are not available, only relative frequencies rather than population-based absolute frequencies can be calculated. Taking such data also into account, it appears, for instance, that for Hodgkin's disease there are two distinct patterns of age distribution, while for Wilms' tumour the rates for black populations are higher than those for white, and those for some East Asian populations are lower. Retinoblastoma appears to be particularly high in some developing countries, accounting in Bangladesh for one third of all childhood tumours registered. Most of the interest in this tumour concerns the hereditary form, but it appears that the worldwide variations in incidence are attributable to variations in the incidence of the non–hereditary form. One of the most striking features of the incidence of childhood cancer concerns Ewing's sarcoma, a tumour of bone that in Western populations has an incidence roughly comparable with that of osteosarcoma, the other main type of childhood bone tumour (see Table 10.2). Ewing's tumour is almost absent in black populations both in Africa and in the United States, suggesting a very strong genetic component in its aetiology.

10.2.4 Ethnic group differences within Britain
In contrast to adult cancer, few data are available on childhood cancer rates in migrant groups or on comparisons between different ethnic groups living in the same country. A number of papers have been published comparing black and white populations in the

United States, and, for a few countries, data on different ethnic groups are available.[1]

Stiller *et al* analysed the relative frequencies of different types of childhood cancer among white Caucasian, Asian (Indian subcontinent) and West Indian children, treated by members of the UK Children's Cancer Study Group in Britain.[6] Since population data classified by ethnic group were not available, the analysis was based on the relative frequencies of different types of tumour. The three groups had similar patterns of incidence for acute lymphocytic leukaemia, suggesting that the incidence of this disease 'is associated with environmental determinants in the country of residence which are most likely to relate to lifestyle factors'. The pattern of occurrence of Hodgkin's disease among Asian children, however, was similar to that found in the Indian subcontinent; there was an increased incidence of unilateral retinoblastoma in Asians and West Indians which is also found in some series from Asia and Africa; and West Indian children had an excess of Wilms' tumour – a finding which corresponds to the fact that the highest incidence of Wilms' tumour has been reported among black populations both in Africa and in the United States. Thus the occurrence of these three tumours is apparently related more to ethnicity than to geographical location and may reflect genetic factors or environmental exposures specific to the lifestyle of particular ethnic groups. Patterns of infant and childhood mortality for different ethnic groups are discussed in section 7.3.

10.2.5 Time trends
Little information is available on time trends in childhood cancer. A few papers have been published suggesting increases for particular (sometimes rare) diagnostic groups. The most detailed account includes analyses of data from Great Britain over a 30-year period (40 years for leukaemia) and suggests that although a few statistically significant trends are found there is no evidence for any *large* increase or decrease.[7] Figures 10.7 and 10.8 show the results for acute lymphocytic

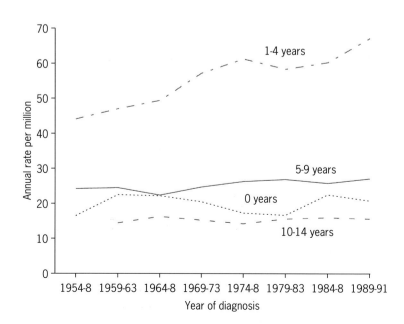

Figure 10.7
Trends in incidence rates for acute lymphocytic leukaemia: 1954-91, Great Britain

Source: Childhood Cancer Research Group

**Figure 10.8
Trends in incidence rates for brain
and spinal tumours: 1962-91,
Great Britain**

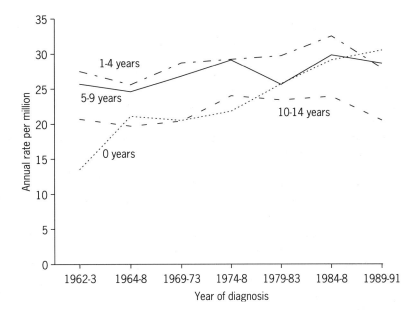

Source: Childhood Cancer Research Group

leukaemia and for brain and spinal tumours. Some of the increases seen in these groups may be due to improvements in ascertainment and diagnosis as compared with the early part of the period covered.

There is no evidence from these or any other published data to suggest that environmental carcinogens have had any substantial impact on national childhood cancer rates, although this cannot, of course, exclude the possibility of changes in incidence in small areas.

10.3 Mortality

As seen in Chapter 6, (section 6.5.4(b)) and Chapter 7 (Figure 7.10) childhood cancer, although rare, is a relatively important cause of mortality after the first year of life. In 1990 out of a total of 2,148 deaths at ages 1–14 years in England and Wales, 364 were ascribed to neoplasms.

Table 10.5 Childhood deaths, all causes: 1971–90, England and Wales

	Numbers			Rates per million per year		
	Males	Females	Total	Males	Females	Total
Ages 0						
1971–75	33,350	24,222	57,572	18,788.7	14,417.9	16,663.4
1976–80	23,113	17,020	40,133	15,176.0	11,778.5	13,521.9
1981–85	18,640	13,715	32,355	11,548.9	8,923.2	10,268.2
1986–90	17,585	12,642	30,227	10,188.3	7,685.1	8,966.8
Age 1–4						
1971–75	5,744	4,488	10,232	741.7	611.1	678.2
1976–80	3,693	2,859	6,552	592.8	484.5	540.1
1981–85	3,155	2,454	5,609	499.3	408.9	455.2
1986–90	2,937	2,384	5,321	439.1	374.5	407.6
Age 5–9						
1971–75	3,977	2,625	6,602	383.9	266.9	326.9
1976–80	3,058	1,958	5,016	325.1	219.9	274.0
1981–85	1,905	1,344	3,249	246.7	184.0	216.2
1986–90	1,712	1,178	2,890	213.1	156.0	185.5
Age 10–14						
1971–75	3,401	1,975	5,376	344.2	210.8	279.3
1976–80	3,007	1,991	4,998	289.9	202.7	247.5
1981–85	2,637	1,663	4,300	280.9	187.1	235.3
1986–90	1,861	1,192	3,053	238.7	161.6	201.2
Age 0–14 *(crude)*						
1971–75	46,472	33,310	79,782	1,561.6	1,180.0	1,375.9
1976–80	32,871	23,828	56,699	1,194.0	913.9	1,057.7
1981–85	26,337	19,176	45,513	1,051.8	808.0	933.1
1986–90	24,095	17,396	41,491	993.8	758.5	879.4
Age 0–14 *(standardised)*						
1971–75				1,693.1	1,283.4	1,493.8
1976–80				1,374.8	1,055.3	1,219.3
1981–85				1,079.0	827.6	956.4
1986–90				946.9	718.1	835.4

Source: Childhood Cancer Research Group

Table 10.6 Childhood deaths, all neoplasms: 1971–90, England and Wales

	Numbers			Rates per million per year		
	Males	Females	Total	Males	Females	Total
Age 0						
1971–75	140	136	276	78.9	81.0	79.9
1976–80	105	100	205	68.9	69.2	69.1
1981–85	92	94	186	57.0	61.2	59.0
1986–90	70	80	150	40.6	48.6	44.5
Age 1–4						
1971–75	671	529	1,200	86.6	72.0	79.5
1976–80	446	337	783	71.6	57.1	64.5
1981–85	369	292	661	58.4	48.7	53.6
1986–90	306	303	609	45.7	47.6	46.7
Age 5–9						
1971–75	798	579	1,377	77.0	58.9	68.2
1976–80	716	425	1,141	76.1	47.7	62.3
1981–85	399	306	705	51.7	41.9	46.9
1986–90	363	286	649	45.2	37.9	41.6
Age 10–14						
1971–75	646	419	1,065	65.4	44.7	55.3
1976–80	554	453	1,007	53.4	46.1	49.9
1981–85	492	346	838	52.4	38.9	45.9
1986–90	318	260	578	40.8	35.3	38.1
Age 0–14 *(crude)*						
1971–75	2,255	1,663	3,918	75.8	58.9	67.6
1976–80	1,821	1,315	3,136	66.1	50.4	58.5
1981–85	1,352	1,038	2,390	54.0	43.7	49.0
1986–90	1,057	929	1,986	43.6	40.5	42.1
Age 0–14 *(standardised)*						
1971–75				75.8	59.1	67.7
1976–80				66.9	51.1	59.2
1981–85				54.1	44.0	49.2
1986–90				43.6	40.3	42.0

Source: Childhood Cancer Research Group

Table 10.7 Childhood deaths, all leukaemias: 1971–90, England and Wales

	Numbers			Rates per million per year		
	Males	Females	Total	Males	Females	Total
Age 0						
1971–75	35	30	65	19.7	17.9	18.8
1976–80	25	15	40	16.4	10.4	13.5
1981–85	19	21	40	11.8	13.7	12.7
1986–90	15	22	37	8.7	13.4	11.0
Age 1–4						
1971–75	260	200	460	33.6	27.2	30.5
1976–80	159	101	260	25.5	17.1	21.4
1981–85	118	91	209	18.7	15.2	17.0
1986–90	101	91	192	15.1	14.3	14.7
Age 5–9						
1971–75	348	275	623	33.6	28.0	30.9
1976–80	332	163	495	35.3	18.3	27.0
1981–85	163	117	280	21.1	16.0	18.6
1986–90	121	91	212	15.1	12.1	13.6
Age 10–14						
1971–75	222	141	363	22.5	15.0	18.9
1976–80	217	161	378	20.9	16.4	18.7
1981–85	195	123	318	20.8	13.8	17.4
1986–90	141	86	227	18.1	11.7	15.0
Age 0–14 *(crude)*						
1971–75	865	646	1,511	29.1	22.9	26.1
1976–80	733	440	1,173	26.6	16.9	21.9
1981–85	495	352	847	19.8	14.8	17.4
1986–90	378	290	668	15.6	12.6	14.2
Age 0–14 *(standardised)*						
1971–75				29.0	22.8	26.0
1976–80				26.6	16.8	21.9
1981–85				19.7	14.9	17.4
1986–90				15.7	12.6	14.2

Source: Childhood Cancer Research Group

In Tables 10.5–10.7 we present data on mortality in the first 15 years of life in England and Wales between 1971 and 1990 for, respectively, all causes, all neoplasms and leukaemia—the most common form of cancer in childhood. There have been remarkable falls in mortality during this period: this change is due to improvements in survival, discussed in section 10.4; as explained in section 10.2.5, there is no evidence for a decrease in incidence. The effect is seen in both sexes and all age groups: between the quinquennia 1971–75 and 1986–90, over the whole age range 0–14 years there was a 49 per cent drop in the number of deaths and a 38 per cent drop in the mortality rate, the difference between these two figures being attributable to the decrease in the population of children. For leukaemia the decrease in mortality is even greater. The fall in death rates, separately for deaths attributed to leukaemia and for all other types of neoplasm, is illustrated in Figure 10.9. During this period there was, of course, also a decrease in mortality from other causes, as shown in Table 10.5. In Table 10.8, deaths from neoplasms are shown as a percentage of all childhood deaths. Within each age group, and for all age groups combined, the proportion of all childhood deaths due to neoplasms has changed remarkably little over the two decades. There are, however, large differences in the proportions for different age groups: in the first year of life cancer is a relatively unimportant cause of mortality, accounting for only 1 death in 200 at this age; at ages 5–9 and 10–14, when deaths are very rare, it is one of the most important causes of mortality, accounting for about 120 deaths per year in England and Wales in 1986–90, i.e. about one fifth of the 600 deaths occurring each year in this 10–year age range.

Reductions in death rates from cancer similar to those shown in Tables 10.6 and 10.7 have been reported from the United States,[8] Italy,[9] Switzerland[10] and Europe generally.[11]

These dramatic improvements are a result of the national and international collaborative studies of the treatment of childhood cancer carried out over the past 25 years.

10.4 Survival rates

The fall in mortality rates described in the previous section is, as explained there, a consequence of improvements in survival rates. Stiller and Bunch carried out a comprehensive analysis of survival rates for the 15-year period 1971–85 covering cases diagnosed in England, Wales and Scotland (Table 10.9).[12] The results for major diagnostic groups are presented in Figures 10.10–10.13. It can be seen from Table 10.9 that the improvements in survival already referred to affected most of the main childhood cancers. Similar results have been reported from clinical trials but it should be emphasised that the results in Table 10.9 relate to all cases registered in England, Wales and Scotland during the period 1971–85 and show the impact of improved treatment on the population as a whole. Population-based survival rates showing similar improvements have been published from the United States Surveillance, Epidemiology and End Results (SEER) programme using data from registries covering 10 per cent of the US population.[13]

Table 10.8 Percentages of childhood deaths due to neoplasms: 1971–90, England and Wales

	Age (in years)				
	0	1–4	5–9	10–14	0–14
1971–75	0.5	11.7	20.9	19.8	4.9
1976–80	0.5	12.0	22.7	20.1	5.5
1981–85	0.6	11.8	21.7	19.5	5.3
1986–90	0.5	11.4	22.5	18.9	4.8

Source: Childhood Cancer Research Group

Figure 10.9
Deaths at ages 0-14 from neoplasms: 1971-90, England and Wales

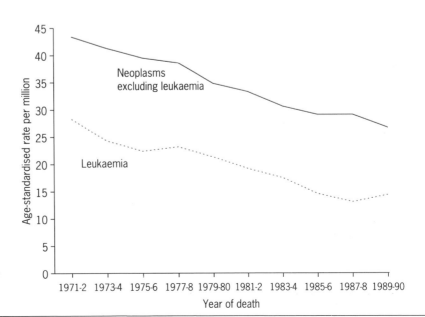

Source: Childhood Cancer Research Group

Table 10.9 Five-year actuarial survival rates for children diagnosed in successive 3-year periods: 1971–85, Great Britain

Diagnostic group	Total registrations	5-year survival rate (%) for years of diagnosis				
		1971–73	1974–76	1977–79	1980–82	1983–85
Acute lymphocytic and other lymphoid leukaemias	4,993	37	47	53	65	70
Acute non-lymphocytic leukaemia	1,052	4	7	18	20	26
Hodgkin's disease	857	76	83	88	90	88
Non-Hodgkin, Burkitt's and unspecified lymphomas	1,128	22	28	39	56	70
Ependymoma	523	38	32	29	37	54
Astrocytoma	1,606	61	54	61	65	72
Medulloblastoma	899	24	30	36	37	42
Neuroblastoma and ganglioneuroblastoma	1,106	15	19	25	37	43
Retinoblastoma	504	87	88	89	86	91
Wilms' tumour	1,088	58	64	76	76	79
Hepatoblastoma	120	8	21	17	30	40
Osteosarcoma	519	17	24	28	34	54
Ewing's sarcoma	373	39	38	34	34	42
Rhabdomyosarcoma, embryonal sarcoma and soft tissue Ewing's tumour	769	26	40	46	48	61
Fibrosarcoma, neurofibrosarcoma and other fibromatous neoplasms	171	69	37	54	71	63
Testicular germ cell neoplasms	144	59	63	69	84	94
Ovarian germ cell and trophoblastic neoplasms	135	43	45	74	85	77

Source: Childhood Cancer Research Group

These improvements in survival were achieved using combinations of surgery, radiotherapy and chemotherapy: modern cytotoxic drugs have had a greater impact on childhood cancer than they have on the generality of adult cancers. There is evidence that this progress has been achieved not only as a result of the availability of modern forms of therapy but also through collaborative clinical trials and the policy of centralisation of treatment for childhood cancers.[14,15] In Britain, over 75 per cent of all cases of childhood cancer are now treated at specialist paediatric oncology centres[16] and many of the remainder will be seen at other types of specialist centre.

The overall 5-year survival rate for all forms of childhood cancer taken together is now about 70 per cent and it seems probable that the great majority of these children will survive into adulthood. Currently in Britain there are well over 10,000 such long-term survivors and we are approaching a situation where about 1 in 1,000 young adults will be survivors from childhood cancer.

There has been considerable concern about the possible long-term effects of childhood cancer, and of its treatment, on the survivors themselves, on the outcome of their pregnancies and on their offspring. One possibility is that there might be a high subsequent mortality among apparent survivors. Substantial numbers of such deaths

do occur, but there is a high continuing survival rate among those who survive 5 years after diagnosis.[17] The possible occurrence of second primary tumours, either because of genetic predisposition or as a consequence of treatment given for the first tumour, is of particular concern. For children treated in Britain in the period 1940–79 the risk appeared to be small; about 4 per cent of children who survived for 3 years developed a further tumour within the next 25 years.[18] The rate is much higher for children with the heritable form of retinoblastoma, although the number of cases of this type is very small. For childhood cancers generally the risk may be increased among those treated with modern multi-agent chemotherapy and it will be necessary to follow up large numbers of children treated with these agents in order to evaluate this risk.

It is well known that some patients will be infertile as a result of their treatment for cancer. Most will, however, be capable of having children, and this raises the question of whether their offspring will themselves have an increased incidence of cancer or of genetic disease. The evidence available at present[19,20] suggests that they do not, but most of these offspring have not been followed up for long periods and the numbers are inadequate to detect small risks affecting particular groups. Again, little information is available on possible genetic risks associated with modern chemotherapy.

Figure 10.10 Five-year survival rates for leukaemias and lymphomas: 1971-85, Great Britain

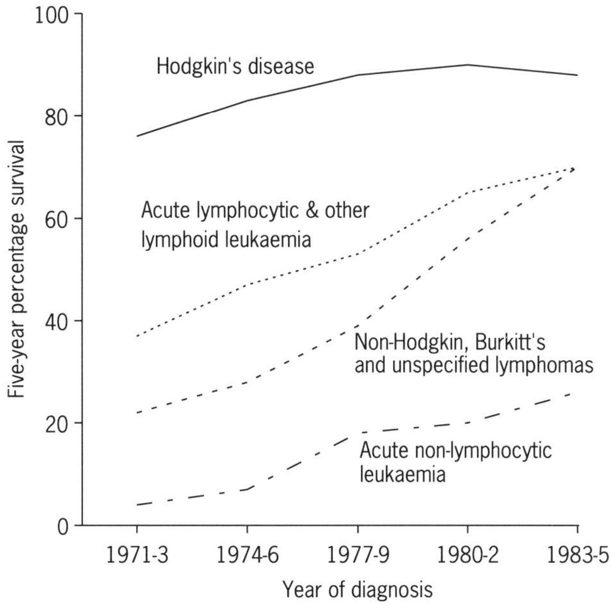

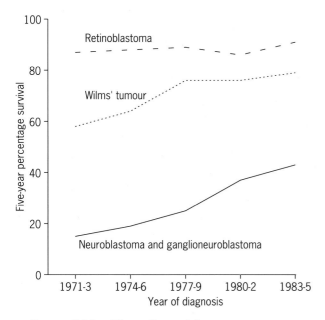

Source: Childhood Cancer Research Group

Figure 10.11 Five-year survival rates for brain tumours: 1971-85, Great Britain

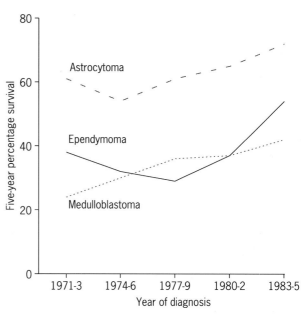

Source: Childhood Cancer Research Group

Figure 10.12 Five-year survival rates for embryonal tumours: 1971-85, Great Britain

Source: Childhood Cancer Research Group

Figure 10.13 Five-year survival rates for sarcomas: 1971-85, Great Britain

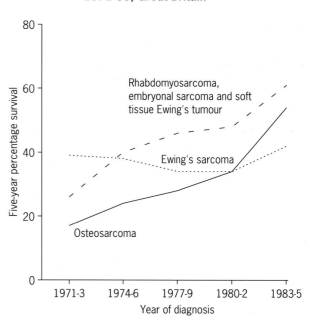

Source: Childhood Cancer Research Group

10.5 Conclusion

Childhood cancer, though rare, is a relatively important cause of mortality after the first year of life. Little is known about its causes: it seems improbable that environmental carcinogens are responsible for any substantial proportion of cases, and any major advance in our understanding of these diseases is likely to be a consequence of developments in molecular biology.

It appears that we can be optimistic about the outlook for childhood cancer survivors and their offspring. There is good reason to believe that the dramatic improvements in survival rates described in this chapter are attributable both to new forms of treatment and to the policy that such treatment is organised from specialised centres, and it seems wise that this policy should be continued. It will be essential to continue monitoring both survival and the long-term effects of therapy, particularly because of the introduction of new forms of chemotherapy.

Acknowledgements

I am deeply indebted to my colleagues at the Childhood Cancer Research Group who did much of the work on which this chapter is based: Mary Kroll for incidence and mortality tables and some of the figures, Tim Vincent for the age distributions and computing generally, Charles Stiller and Kathryn Bunch for the survival analyses and Sue Medhurst for secretarial assistance.

I am grateful to cancer registries in England, Wales and Scotland, OPCS, the Registrar General for Scotland, and to members of the UK Children's Cancer Study Group for providing much of the data on which the National Registry of Childhood Tumours is based and for the use of data from the UKCCSG Annual Report.

The Childhood Cancer Research Group is supported by the Department of Health and the Scottish Home and Health Department.

References

1. Parkin D M, Stiller C A, Draper G J, Bieber C A, Terracini B, Young J L (eds). *International Incidence of Childhood Cancer*. IARC Scientific Publications, No. 87. International Agency for Research on Cancer (Lyon 1988).
2. Birch J M and Marsden H B. A classification scheme for childhood cancer. *International Journal of Cancer*, **40**, 1987, 620–4.
3. World Health Organisation. *International Classification of Diseases for Oncology*. WHO (Geneva 1976).
4. Stiller C A. Malignancies. In Press I B (ed). *The Epidemiology of Childhood Disorders*. Oxford University Press (New York, Oxford 1994). 439–72.
5. Draper G J, Vincent T J, O'Connor C M and Stiller C A. Socioeconomic factors and variations in incidence rates between County Districts. In: Draper G J (ed). *The Geographical Epidemiology of Childhood Leukaemia and Non–Hodgkin Lymphomas in Great Britain 1966–83*. HMSO (London 1991) 37–45.
6. Stiller C A, McKinney P A, Bunch K J, Bailey C C and Lewis I J. Childhood cancer and ethnic group in Britain: a United Kingdom Children's Cancer Study Group (UKCCSG) study. *British Journal of Cancer*, **64**, 1991, 543–8.
7. Draper G J, Kroll M E and Stiller C A. Childhood cancer. In Doll R *et al* (eds). *Cancer Surveys* Vol 19/20: Trends in cancer incidence and mortality. Cold Spring Harbor Laboratory Press (New York 1994) 493–517.
8. Miller R W and McKay F W. Decline in US childhood cancer mortality. *Journal of American Medical Association*, **251**, 1984, 1567–70.
9. La Vecchia C and Decarli A. Decline of childhood cancer mortality in Italy, 1955–1980. *Oncology*, **45**, 1988, 93–7.
10. Levi F and La Vecchia C. Childhood cancer in Switzerland: Mortality from 1951 to 1984. *Oncology*, **45**, 1988, 313–17.
11. Levi F, La Vecchia C, Lucchini F, Negri E and Boyle P. Patterns of childhood cancer incidence and mortality in Europe. *European Journal of Cancer*, **28A**, 1992, 2028–49.
12. Stiller C A and Bunch K J. Trends in survival for childhood cancer in Britain diagnosed 1971–85. *British Journal of Cancer*, **62**, 1990, 806–15.
13. Ries L A G. Cancer in children. In Miller B A *et al* (eds). *Cancer Statistics Review 1973–1989*. National Cancer Institute. NIH Publication Number 92–2789 (Bethesda 1992) XXVII.1 – XXVII.15.
14. Stiller C A. Centralisation of treatment and survival rates for cancer. *Archives of Diseases of Childhood*, **63**, 1988, 23–30.
15. Stiller C A and Draper G J. Treatment centre size, entry to trials and survival in acute lymphoblastic leukaemia. *Archives of Diseases of Childhood*, **64**, 1989, 657–61.
16. United Kingdom Children's Cancer Study Group (UKCCSG). *Scientific Report* (1993).
17. Hawkins M M, Kingston J E and Kinnier Wilson L M. Late deaths after treatment for childhood cancer. *Archives of Diseases of Childhood*, **65**, 1990, 1356–63.
18. Hawkins M M, Draper G J and Kingston J E. Incidence of second primary tumours among childhood cancer survivors. *British Journal of Cancer*, **56**, 1987, 339–47.

19. Draper G J. General overview of studies of multigeneration carcinogenesis in man, particularly in relation to exposure to chemicals. In: Napalkov N P *et al* (eds). *Perinatal and Multigeneration Carcinogenesis*. IARC Scientific Publications, No. 96. International Agency for Research on Cancer (Lyon 1989) 275–88.

20. Hawkins M M. Is there evidence of a therapy–related increase in germ cell mutation among childhood cancer survivors? *Journal of National Cancer Institute*, **83**, 1991, 1643–50.

11 Congenital anomalies

Beverley Botting

Key points

- In England and Wales about 5 per cent of all babies are born with a congenital malformation or other developmental defect.

- The notification rate for central nervous system malformations fell by 52 per cent between 1981 and 1991.

- In 1991 a quarter of all deaths to children aged under 1 year were attributed to congenital malformations.

- Folic acid supplementation has been shown to prevent 72 per cent of neural tube defects in women who were at high risk of having a pregnancy with a neural tube defect.

11.1 Background

About 5 per cent of all babies born in England and Wales are born with a congenital malformation or other developmental defect.[1] Many of these are visible at birth but others only become apparent later. Some malformations are incompatible with life, others can be corrected with surgery and others are compatible with continued life but cannot be corrected with treatment.

Congenital anomalies broadly arise in three ways;
(a) mutagenic, with the fetus inheriting a gene defect or chromosomal anomaly through their affected family or through a new mutation;
(b) at conception, including most non-inherited chromosomal anomalies;
(c) teratogenic, where postconception some agent has non-heritable effects.

The effect of any teratogen will depend on when in the pregnancy it acted, the strength of the dose, and the fetal genetic susceptibility to that teratogen.

Relatively little is known of the cause of most congenital anomalies. Estimates suggest that approximately 14 per cent are due to single mutant genes and major chromosomal abnormalities, about 5 per cent are due to environmental factors (mainly drugs, infections, etc.), a further 20 per cent are due to the combined effects of environmental and genetic factors, but the cause of the remaining 60 per cent or more of malformations remains unknown.[2]

As infant mortality from other causes declines, congenital defects are accounting for an increasing proportion of infant deaths and the search for causal factors becomes more urgent. This chapter examines trends in notification

rates since 1971, the impact of malformations on infant mortality, the effect of increasing prenatal diagnosis and subsequent termination of pregnancy, and summarises some research findings on causal factors.

11.2 National congenital malformation monitoring system

Since 1964 the Office of Population Censuses and Surveys (OPCS) has run a notification system for congenital malformations in England and Wales. This system was initiated following the thalidomide epidemic in order to detect quickly any similar hazard. The primary purpose of this system is to detect changes in the frequency of reporting any particular malformation or group of malformations rather than trying to estimate prevalence at birth. Before 1995 only malformations detected at or within 10 days of birth (live or still birth) were currently included in the system, to ensure rapid reporting and thus fast detection of any increase in reporting levels.

The local health authorities extract from the birth notification forms details of babies born with malformations. This information is commonly supplemented with details obtained from midwives, hospitals, doctors and health visitors.

Although the OPCS scheme is primarily for monitoring changes in the frequency of reporting malformations, it provides the most extensive data on prevalence levels available in England and Wales. The major disadvantage of using these data to measure prevalence arises from deficiencies in its coverage, in that the notification scheme is voluntary and, more importantly, previously covered only those malformations identified up to 10 days after birth. Some conditions, for example cardiovascular malformations, are frequently not identified until some time after birth, whereas other visible, more serious conditions, for example anencephaly, will invariably be identified at birth. The notification system only records malformations identified in live or still births; it does not include pregnancies which are terminated following prenatal diagnosis of a malformation. Statistics about these pregnancies can, however, be derived from the data included on the statutory notification forms of all terminations carried out under the 1967 Abortion Act.

11.3 Comparisons with other sources of malformation information

Since the national congenital malformation notification scheme has been in operation there have been a number of validation exercises, comparing the national data with local registers or registers of those with specific conditions. These have shown incompleteness and false positive notifications for particular malformations[3] and evidence of potential biases in notification.[4] As an example, the rate of Down's syndrome births notified to OPCS is thought to be about 33 per cent incomplete.[5] These constraints on the national data must be allowed for in any analysis.

11.4 Trends in notification rates

Table 11.1 shows the number and rate of notifications of selected malformations between 1971 and 1991. These malformations were selected either because they are reasonably common and/or easily diagnosed or because at some time they have caused concern nationally or internationally because of either an apparent increase in their rate or a cluster having been observed. Comparisons with international data for some of these malformations are made in section 11.12.

Prior to 1990, all malformations, however minor, were notifiable to OPCS. In January 1990 an exclusion list of minor malformations was introduced. This list was based on that used by EUROCAT (a Concerted Action of the European Economic Community for the epidemiological surveillance of congenital anomalies). It excludes from notification conditions such as glandular hypospadias, clicking hip unless confirmed as dislocatable, clubfoot of postural origin, cardiac murmurs, minor anomalies of ear, nose and face, and skin anomalies with a surface of less than 16 cm².

As a result, between 1989 and 1990 the number of congenital malformation notifications received by OPCS fell by 34 per cent from 12,462 to 8,202;[6] 94 per cent of this fall was accounted for by categories in the exclusion list.

Table 11.1 shows that there has been a long-term decrease in central nervous system (CNS) malformations in England and Wales. The notification rate for CNS malformations fell by 76 per cent between 1981 and 1991 (from 19.2 per 10,000 births to 4.6 in 1991). This decrease has not been uniform over all the conditions within the CNS group. Those which are most likely to be detected prenatally by diagnostic ultrasound or alphafetoprotein screening showed the largest decrease. For example, the notification rate for anencephalus, which should be detected during antenatal screening, fell by 92 per cent between 1981 and 1991 (from 4.0 per 10,000 births to 0.3). The notification rate for hydrocephalus (without spina bifida) which is unlikely to be detected by alphafetoprotein screening but might be identified by ultrasound examination, fell by 48 per cent from 2.9 per 10,000 births in 1981 to 1.5 per 10,000 births in 1991.

Whilst most of the other selected malformations have shown reductions in their notification rates over time, none have shown such dramatic falls as those for the CNS malformations. Only the rates for Down's syndrome and diaphragmatic hernia, however, showed little change over time.

11.5 Mortality due to malformations

In the last fifty years deaths due to congenital malformations in infants aged under 1 year have formed an increasing proportion of infant mortality as the number of deaths from infections has declined considerably. In 1991, 29 per cent of the 5,200 infant deaths had a main fetal condition (neonatal deaths) or an underlying cause (postneonatal deaths) of congenital malformation (codes 320–459, 740–759 of the ninth revision of the International Classification of Diseases (ICD9) compared with 20 per cent of the 15,000 infant deaths in 1971 (Figure 11.1) and 12 per cent of the 34,000 infant deaths in 1941.

11.6 Abortion after prenatal diagnosis of abnormality

The detection of fetal abnormalities antenatally can be important as it allows the parents to be informed about the condition and the options for continuing the pregnancy. The parents may choose to continue the pregnancy, rarely involving prenatal treatment. Alternatively, a legal termination of pregnancy may be offered for serious fetal abnormalities which are incompatible with life or which carry a substantial risk of serious mental or physical disability.

In recent years there has been an increasing awareness and advances in techniques for prenatal diagnosis of malformations. This may result in changes in the number of affected fetuses being aborted and thus not being included in the congenital malformation notification system (which only collects data relating to live and still births). The introduction of new antenatal screening

Table 11.1 Congenital malformations: 1971–91, England and Wales

Condition	Year										
	1971	1972	1973	1974	1975	1976	1977	1978	1979	1980	1981
Numbers											
Central nervous system (ICD 740-742,320-359)	3,378	3,129	2,553	2,452	2,227	1,915	1,869	1,757	1,637	1,476	1,229
Anencephaly (ICD 740)	1,116	1,084	849	849	775	644	568	525	455	342	247
Spina bifida (ICD 741)	1,552	1,537	1,267	1,185	1,101	880	881	841	845	756	663
Encephalocele (ICD 742.0)	298	286	184	136	144	135	148	136	81	73	74
Hydrocephaly not with Spina bifida (ICD 742.3)	432	364	336	313	249	267	259	244	227	222	188
Ear malformations (ICD 744.0-744.3)	393	413	393	338	280	352	361	304	317	339	534
Transposition of the great vessels (TGV) (ICD 745.1)	*Not available*								29	24	32
Hypoplastic left heart syndrome (HLHS) (ICD 746.7)	*Not available*								6	10	8
Cleft palate not with cleft lip (ICD 749.0)	321	302	333	274	279	283	277	277	273	291	259
Total cleft lip (ICD 749.1-749.2)	742	695	652	700	583	586	566	558	585	627	605
Esophageal atresia (ICD 750.3)	133	102	121	95	87	107	98	113	104	108	112
Anorectal atresia (ICD 751.2)	186	190	182	199	166	185	147	172	190	179	157
Renal agenesis or dysgenesis (ICD 753.0)	*Not available*								53	62	72
Hypospadias, epispadias (ICD 752.6)	934	1,016	945	912	875	887	907	953	1,079	1,000	1,016
Limb reduction defects (ICD 755.2-755.4)	316	297	286	378	320	294	257	284	264	302	256
Diaphragmatic hernia (ICD 756.6)	*Not available*								75	103	86
Abdominal wall defects (ICD 550-553,756.7)	*Not available*								275	315	305
Down's syndrome (ICD 758.0)	582	560	523	419	454	399	425	444	463	481	475
Rates											
Central nervous system (ICD 740-742,320-359)	42.6	42.6	37.3	37.9	36.6	32.5	32.6	29.2	25.5	22.3	19.3
Anencephaly (ICD 740)	14.1	14.8	12.4	13.1	12.7	10.9	9.9	8.7	7.1	5.2	3.9
Spina bifida (ICD 741)	19.6	20.9	18.5	18.3	18.1	14.9	15.3	14.0	13.1	11.4	10.4
Encephalocele (ICD 742.0)	3.8	3.9	2.7	2.1	2.4	2.3	2.6	2.3	1.3	1.1	1.2
Hydrocephaly not with Spina bifida (ICD 742.3)	5.4	5.0	4.9	4.8	4.1	4.5	4.5	4.1	3.5	3.4	2.9
Ear malformations (ICD 744.0-744.3)	5.0	5.6	5.7	5.2	4.6	6.0	6.3	5.1	4.9	5.1	8.4
Transposition of the great vessels (TGV) (ICD 745.1)	*Not available*								0.5	0.4	0.5
Hypoplastic left heart syndrome (HLHS) (ICD 746.7)	*Not available*								0.1	0.2	0.1
Cleft palate not with cleft lip (ICD 749.0)	4.0	4.1	4.9	4.2	4.6	4.8	4.8	4.6	4.2	4.4	4.1
Total cleft lip (ICD 749.1-749.2)	9.4	9.5	9.5	10.8	9.6	9.9	9.9	9.3	9.1	9.5	9.5
Esophageal atresia (ICD 750.3)	1.7	1.4	1.8	1.5	1.4	1.8	1.7	1.9	1.6	1.6	1.8
Anorectal atresia (ICD 751.2)	2.3	2.6	2.7	3.1	2.7	3.1	2.6	2.9	3.0	2.7	2.5
Renal agenesis or dysgenesis (ICD 753.0)	*Not available*								0.8	0.9	1.1
Hypospadias, epispadias (ICD 752.6)	11.8	13.8	13.8	14.1	14.4	15.0	15.8	15.9	16.8	15.1	15.9
Limb reduction defects (ICD 755.2-755.4)	4.0	4.0	4.2	5.8	5.3	5.0	4.5	4.7	4.1	4.6	4.0
Diaphragmatic hernia (ICD 756.6)	*Not available*								1.2	1.6	1.3
Abdominal wall defects (ICD 550-553,756.7)	*Not available*								4.3	4.8	4.8
Down's syndrome (ICD 758.0)	7.3	7.6	7.6	6.5	7.5	6.8	7.4	7.4	7.2	7.3	7.4

Sources: *Congenital Malformation Statistics: notifications 1971-91*. OPCS unpublished data

1982	1983	1984	1985	1986	1987	1988	1989	1990	1991	Condition
										Numbers
1,016	917	806	728	637	511	509	426	360	324	Central nervous system (ICD 740-742,320-359)
162	114	89	59	52	31	41	34	26	22	Anencephaly (ICD 740)
511	422	378	360	267	209	157	135	120	104	Spina bifida (ICD 741)
62	48	45	39	41	24	30	24	21	23	Encephalocele (ICD 742.0)
177	194	153	133	138	117	137	109	92	102	Hydrocephaly not with Spina bifida (ICD 742.3)
597	605	649	599	661	683	605	631	345	272	Ear malformations (ICD 744.0-744.3)
31	40	36	37	50	34	33	35	30	30	Transposition of the great vessels (TGV) (ICD 745.1)
11	18	20	25	16	18	10	24	12	9	Hypoplastic left heart syndrome (HLHS) (ICD 746.7)
304	286	300	276	275	251	274	275	217	261	Cleft palate not with cleft lip (ICD 749.0)
565	568	579	556	611	588	529	543	542	526	Total cleft lip (ICD 749.1-749.2)
105	105	98	123	94	97	70	77	63	58	Esophageal atresia (ICD 750.3)
179	152	166	171	159	161	138	125	130	126	Anorectal atresia (ICD 751.2)
60	80	68	64	54	83	82	50	44	43	Renal agenesis or dysgenesis (ICD 753.0)
1,056	1,160	1,152	1,072	1,036	1,123	1,102	1,063	869	740	Hypospadias, epispadias (ICD 752.6)
265	297	323	326	276	311	301	247	210	258	Limb reduction defects (ICD 755.2-755.4)
88	81	128	83	111	96	92	89	89	94	Diaphragmatic hernia (ICD 756.6)
279	320	271	254	265	270	292	261	187	173	Abdominal wall defects (ICD 550-553,756.7)
527	497	505	442	445	459	428	487	415	440	Down's syndrome (ICD 758.0)
										Rates
16.1	14.5	12.6	11.0	9.6	7.5	7.3	6.2	5.1	4.6	Central nervous system (ICD 740-742,320-359)
2.6	1.8	1.4	0.9	0.8	0.5	0.6	0.5	0.4	0.3	Anencephaly (ICD 740)
8.1	6.7	5.9	5.5	4.0	3.1	2.3	2.0	1.7	1.5	Spina bifida (ICD 741)
1.0	0.8	0.7	0.6	0.6	0.4	0.4	0.3	0.3	0.3	Encephalocele (ICD 742.0)
2.8	3.1	2.4	2.0	2.1	1.7	2.0	1.6	1.3	1.5	Hydrocephaly not with Spina bifida (ICD 742.3)
9.5	9.6	10.1	9.1	10.0	10.0	8.7	9.1	4.9	3.9	Ear malformations (ICD 744.0-744.3)
0.5	0.6	0.6	0.6	0.8	0.5	0.5	0.5	0.4	0.4	Transposition of the great vessels (TGV) (ICD 745.1)
0.2	0.3	0.3	0.4	0.2	0.3	0.1	0.3	0.2	0.1	Hypoplastic left heart syndrome (HLHS) (ICD 746.7)
4.8	4.5	4.7	4.2	4.1	3.7	3.9	4.0	3.1	3.7	Cleft palate not with cleft lip (ICD 749.0)
9.0	9.0	9.0	8.4	9.2	8.6	7.6	7.9	7.6	7.5	Total cleft lip (ICD 749.1-749.2)
1.7	1.7	1.5	1.9	1.4	1.4	1.0	1.1	0.9	0.8	Esophageal atresia (ICD 750.3)
2.8	2.4	2.6	2.6	2.4	2.4	2.0	1.8	1.8	1.8	Anorectal atresia (ICD 751.2)
1.0	1.3	1.1	1.0	0.8	1.2	1.2	0.7	0.6	0.6	Renal agenesis or dysgenesis (ICD 753.0)
16.8	18.3	18.0	16.2	15.6	16.4	15.8	15.4	12.3	10.5	Hypospadias, epispadias (ICD 752.6)
4.2	4.7	5.0	4.9	4.2	4.5	4.3	3.6	3.0	3.7	Limb reduction defects (ICD 755.2-755.4)
1.4	1.3	2.0	1.3	1.7	1.4	1.3	1.3	1.3	1.3	Diaphragmatic hernia (ICD 756.6)
4.4	5.1	4.2	3.9	4.0	3.9	4.2	3.8	2.6	2.5	Abdominal wall defects (ICD 550-553,756.7)
8.4	7.9	7.9	6.7	6.7	6.7	6.1	7.1	5.9	6.3	Down's syndrome (ICD 758.0)

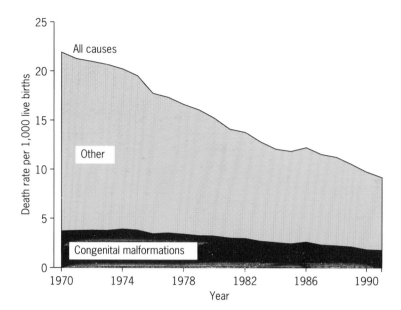

Figure 11.1
Infant mortality due to congenital malformations: 1970-91, England and Wales

Source: OPCS

techniques and changes in the use of these over time will have had an impact on the notification data sent to OPCS. The impact will have differed across England and Wales.

There are regional differences in antenatal screening practice. Some methods of prenatal diagnosis are only available at specialised centres. In some districts all mothers will be offered a serum alphafetoprotein estimation as a screening test for certain neural tube defects or test to detect Down's syndrome. In all districts mothers above a certain age, usually 37 years, are offered an amniocentesis to exclude Down's syndrome. These

differences in diagnostic practice will account, in part, for geographic differences in the rate of terminations for prenatally diagnosed malformations.

Therefore, for completeness, Table 11.2 provides the number of legal abortions carried out in 1979–91 in England and Wales under statutory grounds '4' (now known as grounds E) of the 1967 Abortion Act, a category used for terminations where there is a substantial risk that if the child were born it would suffer from such physical or mental abnormalities as to be seriously disabled. In 1991 there were 1,779 terminations under grounds '4' compared with 2,728 in 1979.

Table 11.2 Medical grounds for legal abortion, numbers: 1979–91, England and Wales .

Condition		Year												
		1979	1980	1981	1982	1983	1984	1985	1986	1987	1988	1989	1990	1991
655	Known or suspected fetal abnormality affecting management of mother	2,728	2,426	2,233	2,178	2,190	2,379	2,131	2,088	1,982	1,812	1,735	1,684	1,779
655.0	Central nervous system malformations in fetus	285	418	441	486	511	546	520	557	531	468	478	452	500
655.1	Chromosomal abnormality in fetus	173	173	262	288	254	283	286	313	288	315	318	277	347
655.2	Hereditary disease in family possibly affecting fetus	89	66	85	82	98	116	105	114	74	78	81	85	83
655.3	Suspecting damage in fetus from viral disease in mother	757	328	218	255	331	301	136	180	140	85	88	58	55
	Rubella (056)	431	153	89	136	182	144	66	90	64	37	3	7	7
	Rubella contact (VO1.4)	144	47	46	44	50	32	8	21	10	8	15	3	9
	Rubella immunisation (VO4.3)	156	101	63	46	72	100	42	31	34	11	18	5	8
655.5	Suspected damage to fetus from drugs	254	298	277	310	289	331	273	221	225	176	180	196	175
655.6	Suspected damage to fetus from radiation	113	128	141	115	112	143	105	77	81	53	37	33	36
655.8	Other known or suspected fetal abnormality, not elsewhere classified	655	603	456	329	271	312	321	277	318	377	346	374	430
	Presence of IUCD (V45.5)	556	518	325	187	148	90	78	51	48	25	36	28	23
655.4, 655.9	Suspected damage to fetus from other diseases in the mother and unspecified fetal	402	412	353	313	324	347	385	349	325	260	207	209	153

Source: *Abortion Statistics 1979-91*

Notified abortion following prenatal diagnosis does not account for most of the reduction in birth prevalence of CNS defects. Figure 11.2 shows the notification rate for CNS defects, together with the rate of legal terminations following antenatal detection of CNS defects, both rates calculated per 10,000 total births plus abortions from 1969 to 1991. A similar decrease in birth prevalence has also been reported in the Republic of Ireland[7] where there are no screening programmes and abortion is only permitted under the case law which existed in England and Wales before the 1967 Abortion Act.

A previous analysis of babies with neural tube defects notified to OPCS and terminations of pregnancy associated with a CNS malformation showed a reduction of 77 per cent in the birth prevalence of neural tube defects notified between 1964-72 and 1985 in England and Wales.[8] Thirty–one per cent of this reduction could be attributed to prenatal detection and selective abortion. In Scotland, between 1974 and 1982, there was a 75 per cent reduction in birth prevalence of CNS malformations, 49 per cent of which was attributable to antenatal detection and selective abortion.[9]

11.7 Geographical variation in notified malformations

Table 11.3 shows the rates for selected malformations by Regional Health Authority and for Wales based on combined data for 1987–91. The smallest geographical variation is for cleft lip with or without cleft palate, a malformation not likely to be detected antenatally and which is usually corrected by surgery. It is also apparent, detected at birth and therefore tends to be well notified. The other malformation groups show more geographical variation. In part this will be due to the different regional antenatal screening policies discussed in section 11.5 and

reporting practices. Differing reporting practices are suspected to account for much of the variation in malformations of the heart and circulatory system. These show wide variation from 4.5 per 10,000 births in North East Thames RHA to 17.1 in Trent RHA. Many of these malformations will become apparent in the days following birth; most will be detected within the 10-day reporting period but possibly not at the time the birth is notified.

A clear geographical pattern is seen for spina bifida, a condition easily recognised and notified at birth. The rates are higher for more northerly regions in England with the highest rates in Northern and North Western RHAs and the lowest in Oxford, East Anglia and the Thames RHAs. The rates for spina bifida for the RHAs in the north of England are similar to those of Scotland, although there are essential differences between the two notification systems. In Scotland information is taken from observations on all babies until discharge home.[10] A study on the geography of spina bifida in England and Wales between 1983 and 1985[11] confirmed earlier findings that differences in the maternal screening policies of health authorities were an important factor in explaining geographical differences in prevalence, although geographical differences were reported before prenatal diagnosis techniques were in widespread use.

11.8 Effect of occupation on anomalies

Recent years have seen an increasing recognition of the potential effect of hazards encountered in the working environment on human reproduction. Studies have investigated a wide range of adverse reproductive outcomes and their association with parental occupational exposure. This section provides a brief review of some of the main findings, together with more detail from two studies undertaken by OPCS.

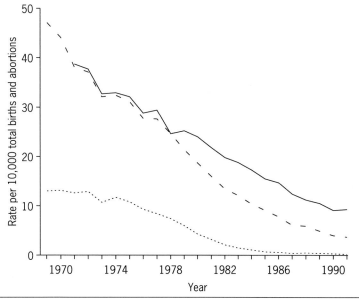

Figure 11.2
Notification rates of anencephalus, other central nervous system malformations, and legal abortions due to central nervous system malformations in fetus: 1969-91, England and Wales

‒ ‒ CNS malformation notifications

········ Anencephalus notifications

_____ Notifications/abortions due to CNS malformations

Source: OPCS

Table 11.3 Congenital malformations: 1987-91 combined, regional health authorities in England and Wales

RHA	Total births	Down's syndrome	Central nervous system	Spina bifida	Cleft lip with/ without cleft palate	Malformation of of heart and circulatory system
Numbers						
Northern	202,413	118	168	84	159	329
Yorkshire	252,135	152	142	42	214	253
Trent	312,555	208	192	58	265	534
East Anglia	131,786	78	79	22	116	75
NW Thames	253,381	196	140	35	194	188
NE Thames	284,377	176	130	32	206	129
SE Thames	257,175	163	120	41	176	234
SW Thames	197,211	179	124	39	158	280
Wessex	189,473	112	117	43	148	101
Oxford	179,536	76	98	29	133	133
South Western	203,845	123	110	47	156	363
West Midlands	369,816	221	242	89	294	328
Mersey	167,141	121	124	42	110	169
North Western	289,540	184	239	79	247	295
Wales	192,519	122	105	43	152	253
Rates *(per 10,000 total births)*						
Northern		5.8	8.3	4.2	7.9	16.3
Yorkshire		6.0	5.6	1.7	8.5	10.0
Trent		6.7	6.1	1.9	8.5	17.1
East Anglia		5.9	6.0	1.7	8.8	5.7
NW Thames		7.7	5.5	1.4	7.7	7.4
NE Thames		6.2	4.6	1.1	7.2	4.5
SE Thames		6.3	4.7	1.6	6.8	9.1
SW Thames		9.1	6.3	2.0	8.0	14.2
Wessex		5.9	6.2	2.3	7.8	5.3
Oxford		4.2	5.5	1.6	7.4	7.4
South Western		6.0	5.4	2.3	7.7	17.8
West Midlands		6.0	6.5	2.4	8.0	8.9
Mersey		7.2	7.4	2.5	6.6	10.1
North Western		6.4	8.3	2.7	8.5	10.2
Wales		6.3	5.5	2.2	7.9	13.1

Source: *Congenital Malformation Statistics: notifications 1987-91*

There is evidence that hazards encountered in certain occupations are linked with an excess risk of malformation to the children of the exposed parents. One persistent finding is that of mothers employed in laboratory work having an increased risk of children with intestinal malformations.[12–14] The agent responsible is as yet unknown but exposure of mothers to volatile solvents appears to be a consistent observation.[15,16] There is tentative evidence that paternal exposure to solvents also may be linked with an increased risk of malformations.[17,18]

There has been some evidence that both maternal and paternal exposure to anaesthetic gases increases the risk of malformations[19,20] but the findings are not consistent.[21,22] Other hypothesised associations include paternal employment in agriculture[23] and electrical substations,[24] and maternal employment as telephone operators, teachers,[25] food production workers,[25] visual display unit operators[26] and general industrial workers.[25,27] In addition a wide range of industrial chemicals have been shown to be potentially capable of causing congenital defects, although few of the very large number of substances in current use have been tested.[28]

Despite reservations about the quality of the data, OPCS undertook an analysis of parental occupation from notifications to the England and Wales Congenital Malformation monitoring programme from 1974 to 1979.[29] This analysis showed a number of occupations with consistent excesses of certain malformations. These included an excess of all malformations for fathers who were coal miners, railway porters, clerks, shop assistants and school teachers, an excess of anencephalus and/or spina bifida for children whose fathers were moulders and coremakers and engineering workers, and an excess of cleft lip for children of policemen. An excess was shown for mothers working as clothing workers and labourers (anencephalus and/or spina bifida), paper and print workers (cleft lip and/or palate) and professional workers (Down's syndrome).

These analyses did not take account of differences in maternal age, and the mother's occupation study was limited in scope. Therefore, a second analysis of England and Wales malformation notifications data for 1980 to 1982 from the OPCS monitoring scheme took these factors into account.[30]

High proportional notification ratios for clefts were found for both publicans and barmaids. These could be related to alcohol intake, which has been associated with adverse reproductive outcome.[31] There is also evidence of a role of maternal smoking in the aetiology of clefts which may be a factor.[32] There was a high ratio for nurses for polydactyly and syndactyly. A similar high proportion for these malformations were seen for counter hands, kitchen porters, packers and bottlers and barmaids.

There was a high ratio for spina bifida in office machine operators which is of interest in view of concern over the possible reproductive hazards of work with visual display units (VDUs).[26] Office machine operators, are however, likely to be exposed to a variety of other machinery (such as photocopiers) which may present their own hazards. There were consistently raised ratios for road transport drivers and related occupations confirming the earlier study results.[29] The excesses noted for anencephaly and for spina bifida in the previous study were also confirmed by these data.

The raised ratios for cleft lip with or without cleft palate observed in the earlier study for policemen[29] were confirmed for 1980–82. It is difficult to envisage an occupational hazard in this association. It is more likely that behavioural factors related to the nature of the work or a confounding factor is connected both with a propensity for clefts in children and selection into the police force.

11.9 Role of diet, drugs and other teratogens in the epidemiology of malformations

Certain congenital malformations are known to be related to the use of drugs during pregnancy. Two of the best known examples were the limb reduction defects caused by thalidomide[33] and the relation of oral clefts to the use of anticonvulsants.[34]

A case-control study in the mid-1980s[35] examined prescription data for the three months before the last menstrual period and for the first trimester of pregnancy. The study population consisted of all infants born with oral cleft and/or major limb reduction defects during the 12 month period from 1 October 1983 and notified to the OPCS congenital malformation surveillance system together with a matched control. For children with limb reduction defects their mothers were prescribed more drugs generally although this did not reach statistical significance. For oral clefts, significantly more drugs were prescribed to study mothers in the three months before the last menstrual period. Anticonvulsant drugs, in particular phenobarbitone and phenytoin, were prescribed significantly more frequently to study mothers during the whole period of the study. These drugs have been repeatedly shown to be teratogens associated with oral cleft, nail and digit reduction defects and cardiac abnormalities.[36–38] Steroid sex hormones, particularly oral contraceptives, were also prescribed significantly more frequently to the study members.

Other published work shows a considerable range of opinion on the possible teratogenic effect of steroid sex hormones. A review of the teratogenic effects of chemicals and drugs revealed that although a number of studies showed an association between steroid sex hormones and various congenital defects, the findings have varied.[39] There is, therefore, doubt about a relationship between oral clefts and oral contraceptives. Any risk is likely to be small and non–specific.

A further study into the epidemiology of facial clefts in Glasgow[40] showed that clefts were more common in the socioeconomically deprived areas of the city. This suggested that either a teratogenic factor may be more prevalent in such areas, or that an essential dietary factor is deficient or that a deprived environment enhances the susceptibility of a population to a specific teratogen. Possible teratogens cited included infection, drugs and diet.

It has long been suspected that diet has a role in the causation of neural tube defects. In 1964 the possibility was raised that folic acid might be involved.[41] In 1980 and 1981 the results of two intervention studies were published in which vitamin supplementation around the time of conception was given to women who had had a previous pregnancy with a neural tube defect.[42,43] Both these studies had methodological problems, so a new trial was launched in July 1983 with the aim of obtaining information on the outcome of at least 2,000 high risk pregnancies unless a sufficiently clear result emerged sooner.

By April 1991, sufficiently conclusive results had emerged to warrant ending the trial. The results showed that folic acid supplementation prevented 72 per cent of neural tube defects in women who were at a high risk of having a pregnancy with a neural tube defect.[44] The results also demonstrated that it was folic acid, rather than any of the other vitamins trialled, that was responsible for the preventive effect.

A recent Chinese case-control study of paternal smoking and birth defects identified a modest relationship between paternal smoking and overall birth defects.[45] Higher risks were identified for anencephalus, spina bifida, pigmentary anomalies of the skin and certain anomalies of the feet. Other published studies have shown that paternal smoking produced an increased risk for birth defects in their children, such as anencephaly and spina bifida[46] and facial abnormalities,[47] but these studies were limited by the small number of cases. Current knowledge suggests that malformations are theoretically possible by the sperm–mediated effects of smoking.[48] For example, smokers have been shown to have increased frequency of abnormal sperm morphology.[49] Alternatively, maternal passive smoking might have an impact on congenital malformations.

11.10 Impact of maternal age on congenital malformations

In developed countries increasing numbers of women are delaying childbearing to an older age. The risk of chromosomal disorders is known to increase with increasing maternal age,[5] but other studies have shown no association between other birth defects of unknown aetiology and maternal age.[50] Table 11.4 presents notification data by mother's age. This table shows that apart from the oldest age group there was little difference in age–specific rates for most conditions. The rates were generally highest for mothers aged 40 and over. Down's syndrome showed the usual pattern of increasing rates with increasing age of mother.

11.11 Ethnic differences in malformation rates

The notification data do not include ethnic origin or the mother's country of birth. The latter characteristic would be needed to calculate rates, since the mother's country of birth (but not ethnic origin) is collected at birth registration. Chapter 7 discusses ethnic differences in prevalence and mortality rates for malformations.

11.12 International comparisons

Statistical summaries from the OPCS congenital malformation monitoring system are reported to the International Clearinghouse for Birth Defects Monitoring Systems (the 'Clearinghouse'). This organisation has a formal relationship as a non–governmental organisation of the World Health Organisation.

Currently 25–30 different monitoring programmes around the world participate in the Clearinghouse. Quarterly data are exchanged on selected malformations plus reports of unusual events, suspected outbreaks of birth defects or suspected teratogens. Its primary goal is to exchange information in a timely manner so that preventive action could be taken, if indicated. Annual Reports are published, and data for 1974–88 for 22 malformations have also been published.[51]

From these data it is possible to compare trends in neural tube defects with the declining rates in England and Wales. There was marked variability in the rates of anencephaly among the programmes. In many, but not all programmes, the rates declined during the period. The South America, Asian and Northern Ireland programmes had slightly elevated rates compared with the majority of the programmes. For spina bifida, clearly declining rates were seen in Northern Ireland, Hungary and New Zealand, while an increasing trend was seen in Mexico. Such geographical and secular variation in rates for neural tube defects also persisted in Europe during 1980–6,[52] independent of the practice of prenatal diagnosis.

Table 11.4 All babies notified (rates per 10,000 total births) by age of mother and condition: 1987–91 combined, England and Wales

ICD number	Condition	Age of mother						
		Total	Under 20	20-24	25-29	30-34	35-39	40 and over
	All babies notified	156.2	167.9	156.8	149.0	149.0	166.6	193.3
320-359, 740-742	Central nervous system malformations	6.1	8.3	6.8	5.3	5.3	6.3	7.5
740	Anencephalus	0.4	0.5	0.5	0.4	0.4	0.3	1.1
741	Spina bifida	2.1	2.5	2.5	1.8	1.8	1.8	1.9
742.3	Hydrocephalus (not with spina bifida)	1.6	2.6	1.8	1.3	1.2	1.8	2.8
360-379, 743	Eye malformations	1.5	1.9	1.7	1.3	1.5	1.5	2.3
744.0-744.3	Ear malformations	6.9	6.3	6.9	7.1	6.3	6.6	7.7
749.1-749.2	Cleft lip	7.8	7.9	7.8	7.2	8.4	7.9	8.1
749.0	Cleft palate(excluding lip)	3.7	3.6	3.4	3.7	3.5	4.0	5.3
750.3	Tracheo-oesophageal fistula, oesophageal atresia and stenosis	1.0	1.2	0.9	1.0	1.1	1.4	1.3
751.2	Rectal and anal atresia and stenosis	2.0	2.2	1.8	2.0	1.7	2.3	2.1
390-459, 745-747	Malformations of heart and circulatory system	10.5	10.2	9.8	10.3	10.3	12.3	13.4
752.6	Hypospadias and epispadias	14.1	16.0	15.1	13.2	12.8	13.8	14.5
755.0	Polydactyly	8.7	9.9	8.9	8.7	8.1	8.2	4.7
755.1	Syndactyly	6.7	6.4	6.3	6.8	6.4	7.1	6.8
754.5-754.7	Deformities of feet	23.6	28.2	24.5	22.9	22.0	21.5	18.1
755.2-755.4	Reduction deformities of limbs	3.8	5.2	4.1	3.3	3.5	3.9	4.0
756.7	Exomphalos, gastroschisis	2.2	6.5	2.7	1.4	1.2	1.3	2.6
758.0	Down's syndrome	6.4	3.7	3.9	4.5	7.6	17.7	37.5

Source: *Congenital Malformation Statistics: notifications 1987-91*

11.13 Conclusions

Although the England and Wales notification data are known to be deficient, it is the largest dataset of birth prevalence of congenital anomalies in England and Wales. Taken together with statistics about legal terminations it will help monitor the impact of policies on folic acid supplementation and other primary prevention strategies. The notification system has just been reviewed by a working group of the Registrar General's Medical Advisory Committee.[53] It is hoped that the data will become more complete and hence be more valuable as the notification system adopts the recommendations from this review.

References

1. Weatherall J A C. A review of some effects of recent medical practices in reducing the number of children born with congenital abnormalities. *Health Trends*, **14**, 1982, 85–8.
2. Kalter H and Warkany J. Congenital malformations: etiologic factors and their role in prevention. *New English Journal Medicine*, **308**, 1983, 424–31, 491–7.
3. Knox E G, Armstrong E H and Lancashire R. The quality of notification of congenital malformations. *Journal of Epidemiology and Community Health*, **38**,1984, 296–305.
4. Swerdlow A J and Melzer D. The value of England and Wales congenital malformation notification scheme data for epidemiology: male genital tract malformations. *Journal of Epidemiology Community Health*, **42**,1988, 8–13.
5. Cuckle H, Nanchahal K and Wald N. Birth prevalence of Down's syndrome in England and Wales. *Prenatal Diagnosis*, **11**, 1991, 29–34.
6. OPCS. *Congenital Malformation Statistics: Notifications 1990*. Series MB3 no 6. HMSO (1992).
7. Kirke P N and Elwood J H. Anencephaly in the United Kingdom and Republic of Ireland. *British Medical Journal*, **289**, 1984, 1621.
8. Cuckle H and Wald N. The impact of screening for open neural tube defects in England and Wales. *Prenatal Diagnosis*, **7**, 1987, 81–99.
9. Carstairs V and Cole S. Spina bifida and anencephaly in Scotland. *British Medical Journal*, **289**, 1984, 1182–4.
10. Scottish Health Services. *Congenital Anomalies: Provisional Data for the 1989 Birth Cohort*. Health Briefing no 91/02/CGEN. Information & Statistics Division. SHS Common Services Agency (1991).
11. Lovett A A and Gatrell A C. The geography of spina bifida in England and Wales. *Transachois Institute British Geographical Society*, **13**, 1988, 288–302.
12. Meirik O *et al*. Major malformations in infants born of women who worked in laboratories while pregnant. *Lancet*, 1979, 91.
13. Ericson A. *et al*. Gastrointestinal atresia and maternal occupation during pregnancy. *Journal Occupational Medicine*, **24**, 1982, 515.
14. Hansson E *et al*. Pregnancy outcome for women working in laboratories in some of the pharmaceutical industries in Sweden. *Scandinavian Journal Work Environmental Health*, **6**, 1980, 131–4.
15. Holmberg P C. Central nervous system defects in children born to mothers exposed to organic solvents during pregnancy. *Lancet,* 1979, 177–9.
16. Holmberg P C *et al*. Oral clefts and organic solvent exposure during pregnancy. *International Archives Occupational Environmental Health*, **50,** 1982, 371–6.
17. Fedrick J. Anencephalus in the Oxford Record Linkage Study. *Developmental Medicine Child Neurology*, **18**, 1976, 643–56.
18. Olsen J. Risk of exposure among laboratory staff and painters. *Danish Medical Bulletin,* **30**, 1983, 24–28.
19. Cohen E N *et al*. Occupational disease among operating room personnel: a national study. *Anaesthesiology*, **41,** 1974, 321–40.
20. Cabett T H *et al*. Birth defects among children of nurse–anaesthetists. *Anaesthesiology*, **41**, 1974, 341–4.
21. Knill-Jones R P *et al*. Anaesthetic practice and pregnancy: a controlled survey of male anaesthetists in the United Kingdom. *Lancet*, 1975, 807–9.
22. Knill-Jones R P *et al*. Anaesthetic practice and pregnancy: a controlled survey of women anaesthetists in the United Kingdom. *Lancet*; 1972, 1326–28.
23. Balarajan R and McDowall M. Congenital malformations and agricultural workers. *Lancet*, 1983, 1112–3.
24. Nordstrom S, Birke E and Gustausson L. Reproductive hazards among workers at high voltage substations. *Bioelectromagnetics*, **4**, 1983, 91–101.
25. Hemminki K *et al*. Congenital malformations by the parental occupation in Finland. *International Archives Occupational Environmental Health*, **46**, 1980, 93–8.
26. Landrigan P J *et al*. Reproductive hazards in the workplace: development of epidemiologic research. *Scandinavian Journal Work Environmental Health*, **9**, 1983, 83–8.
27. Hemminki K *et al*. Congenital malformations and maternal occupation in Finland:multi–variate analysis. *Journal Epidemiology Community Health*, **35**, 1981, 5–10.
28. Barlow S and Sullivan F. *The Reproductive Hazards of Industrial Chemicals*. Academic Press (1982).
29. OPCS. *Congenital malformations and parent's occupation*. OPCS Monitor MB3 82/1. OPCS (1982).
30. McDowall M E. *Occupational Reproductive Epidemiology*. OPCS Studies on Medical and Population Subjects no.50, HMSO (1985).
31. Harlap S. Gender of infants conceived on different days of the menstrual cycle. *New England Journal Medicine*, **300**, 1979, 1445–8.
32. Ericson A *et al*. Cigarette smoking as an aetiologic factor in cleft lip and palate. *American Journal Obstetrics Gynaecology*, **135**, 1979, 348–52.
33. McBride W G. Thalidomide and congenital abnormalities. *Lancet*, 1961, 1358.
34. Meadow S R. The teratogenicity of epilepsy. *Developmental Medicine Child Neurology*, **16**, 1974, 376–81.

35. Hill L, Murphy M, McDowall M and Paul A H. Maternal drug histories and congenital malformations: limb reduction defects and oral clefts. *Journal Epidemiology Community Health*, **42**, 1988, 1–7.

36. Greenberg G, Inman W H W, Weatherall J A C, Adelstein A M and Haskey J C. Maternal drug histories and congenital abnormalities. *British Medical Journal, 2*, 1977, 853–6.

37. Speidel B D and Meadow S R. Maternal epilepsy and abnormalities of the foetus and newborn. *Lancet*, 1972, 839–43.

38. Mastroiacovo P, Bertolini R, Morandini S and Segri G. Maternal epilepsy valproate exposure and birth defects. *Lancet,* 1983, 1499.

39. Schardein J L. *Chemically Induced Birth Defects*. Marcel Dekker (New York/Basel 1985) 260–338.

40. Womersley J and Stone D H. Epidemiology of facial clefts. *Archives Disease Childhood*, **62**, 1987, 717–20.

41. Hibbard BM. The role of folic acid in pregnancy with particular reference to anaemia, abruption and abortion. *Journal Obstetrics Gynaecology British Commonwealth*, **71**, 1964, 529–42.

42. Smithells R W, Shephard S, Schorah C J *et al.* Possible prevention of neural tube defects by periconceptional vitamin supplementation. *Lancet*, 1980, 339–40.

43. Laurence K M, James N, Miller M H, Tennant GB and Campbell H. Double–blind randomised controlled trial of folate treatment before conception to prevent recurrence of neural tube defects. *British Medical Journal*, **282**, 1981, 1509–11.

44. MRC Vitamin Study Research Group. Prevention of neural tube defects: Results of the Medical Research Council Vitamin Study. *Lancet*, **338**, 1991, 131–7.

45. Zhang J, Savitz D A, Schwingl P J and Cai W W. A case control study of paternal smoking and birth defects. *International Journal Epidemiology*, **21**, 1992, 273–8.

46. Hearey C D, Harris J A, Usatin M S *et al.* Investigation of a cluster of anencephaly and spina bifida. *American Journal Epidemiology*, **120**, 1984, 559–64.

47. Mau G and Netter P. Die auswirkungen des vaterlichen zigarettenkonsums auf die perinatale sterblichkeit und die mifsbildungshaufigkeit. *Deutsche Medizinische Wochenschrift*, **99**, 1974, 1113–18.

48. Bridges B A, Clemmesen J and Sugimura T. Cigarette smoking – does it carry a genetic risk? *Mutation Research*, **65,** 1979, 71–81.

49. Weisberg E. Smoking and reproductive health. *Clinical Reproduction Fertility*, **3**, 1985, 175–86.

50. Baird P A, Sadovnick A D and Yee I M L. Maternal age and birth defects: a population study. *Lancet,* **337**, 1991, 527–30.

51. International Clearinghouse for Birth Defects Monitoring Systems. *Congenital Malformations Worldwide*. Elsevier (1991).

52. EUROCAT Working Group. Prevalence of neural tube defects in 20 regions of Europe and the impact of prenatal diagnosis, 1980–1986. *Journal of Epidemiology Community Health*, **45**, 1991, 52–8.

53. Working Group of the Registrar General's Medical Advisory Committee. *A review of the National Congenital Malformation Notification System*. OPCS Occasional Paper no. 43 OPCS (London 1995).

12 Mental health

Barbara Maughan

Key points

- International data suggest that between 14 and 20 per cent of children will be affected by some level of psychiatric disturbance during childhood or adolescence.

- British studies have found that moderate or severe behaviour problems were present in 7 per cent of inner-city 3-year-olds and that rates of mental health problems rise in adolescence.

- Studies suggest a prevalence of anorexia nervosa of around 2 per 1,000 in women and girls, with rates being highest (at about 10 per 1,000) in middle-class school girls.

- Rates of suicide for males aged 15–19 increased by almost 45 per cent between the late 1970s and the late 1980s. Comparable rates for teenage girls fell by 23 per cent over the same period.

12.1 Background

Mental health problems in childhood range from relatively transitory emotional and behavioural difficulties to severe, pervasive developmental disorders such as autism. Epidemiological studies suggest that between 14 and 20 per cent of children will be affected by some level of psychiatric disturbance,[1] with conduct and emotional disorders making up the great majority of those figures. The OPCS surveys of disability in Great Britain,[2] focusing on more severe conditions, found that behavioural difficulties were the most common disabling problems of childhood, affecting 2 per cent of under 16-year-olds. Although many of the more common child psychiatric disorders are self-limiting, follow-up studies show that a significant proportion persist for a number of years, and that some have long-term sequelae. About a third of children with conduct disorders, for example, experience continuing problems in their adult lives,[3] and childhood depression significantly elevates the risk of affective disorder in adulthood.[4] Looking backwards from adulthood, almost all men with severe antisocial problems are likely to have shown behavioural deviance in childhood.[3] From both short- and longer-term perspectives, psychiatric disorders clearly constitute an important area of concern in the child health field.

This volume is primarily concerned with time trends in child health problems. In the mental health arena, our knowledge of such trends is extremely limited; indeed, in many instances we have only recently begun to chart the prevalence of specific disorders in different age groups and their natural histories as children mature. Problems in assessing longer-term trends stem from two main sources: first, that regularly collected statistics do not tap the full extent of psychiatric problems, and second,

that the specially designed studies that can provide more reliable estimates have not yet been repeated.

Relevant official statistics in the mental health field include data on psychiatric service use, consultations with GPs and others on mental health problems, and trends in specific problem areas such as substance abuse, delinquency and suicide. Data on service use are perhaps the most problematic as indicators of prevalence rates or secular trends for one simple but important reason: the great majority of psychiatric problems go untreated. This has long been recognised in relation to adult disorders,[5] and epidemiological studies suggest that it is also true in childhood.[6] Although data on trends in service use are important in their own right, they are as likely to reflect variations in the availability of services, in the policies and practices of referring agencies, and in public willingness to seek help for psychiatric problems, as changes in rates of disorder *per se*.

A second difficulty with official statistics is that when children do receive help for psychiatric problems, it may come from a range of agencies: paediatric, educational, and social services, as well as psychiatric. A comprehensive picture, even of service use, would require comparable information from all these sources. Inevitably, however, many of the professionals who assess and treat behaviourally or emotionally disordered children in these different settings do not use psychiatric diagnostic classification systems in their own practice. Even among paediatricians, recognition of emotional and behavioural problems is probably limited.[7]

For all these reasons, statistics on service use give little indication of the full extent of child psychiatric disorder. As a result, this chapter will focus on two other types of evidence: first, the general picture of the prevalence of disorder derived from specially designed case-finding studies, and second, data on trends in selected specific problem areas.

12.2 Epidemiological and other community studies

A number of major British epidemiological surveys have been conducted since the mid-1960s, some assessing the full range of child psychiatric problems, others focusing on particular mental health and developmental conditions. The first, which in many ways set the pattern for subsequent work in the field, were carried out in the late 1960s on the Isle of Wight.[6,8] These studies focused on middle childhood (ages 10 and 11), and adolescence (ages 14 and 15), and were followed by area comparisons with inner London for the middle-childhood age range.[9-10] Comprehensive data on preschool children have also been collected on inner city samples,[11] while studies of specific conditions have been undertaken in a number of regions. More recently, the OPCS disability survey included national assessments of childhood disability in 1985,[2] and the three national birth cohort studies, together with other local surveys, provide further valuable information.

12.2.1 Levels of mental health problems
These various sources all point to quite high rates of psychiatric disorder in childhood. Combining all types of difficulty, moderate or severe behaviour problems were present in 7 per cent of inner-city 3-year-olds, and more minor difficulties in a further 15 per cent. The middle-childhood studies found rates of approaching 7 per cent on the Isle of Wight, and by adolescence rates had risen a little further, to around 9 per cent, for teacher- or parent-reported problems. If the adolescents' own accounts were included, a further 10 per cent reported marked internal feelings of misery or worthlessness not noted by adults. Broadly similar overall rates of disorder have been reported in epidemiological investigations in the USA, New Zealand and Puerto Rico,[1] though there are wider disparities in estimates of the prevalence of specific conditions.

12.2.2 Types of disorder and developmental trends
The nature of the more common psychiatric problems changes across childhood and adolescence, and differs for boys and girls. Disabling behaviour problems are more common in school age children than among preschoolers,[2] but milder difficulties are common in young children. Restlessness and overactivity, control problems, aggression and anxieties over separation dominate the picture at the preschool stage. Boys are slightly more likely to show problems than girls at this point, in particular in terms of overactivity; preschool girls are more likely to be troubled by fears. In middle childhood, conduct disorders and mixed disorders of conduct and emotions account for the major part of psychiatric morbidity, with boys up to four times more likely to show antisocial behaviour and aggression than

girls. Rates of hyperactivity vary markedly depending on the diagnostic criteria adopted. One recent British study,[12] for example, reported a prevalence of 1.7 per cent for hyperkinetic disorder in 7- and 8-year-old boys, but over twice that rate when DSM-III criteria for Attention Deficit Disorder with Hyperactivity were applied.

Emotional problems affected some 2.5 per cent of 10- and 11-year-olds in the Isle of Wight studies, and showed a slight preponderance in girls. Overt depressive disorders were rare at this age, but by adolescence, depressive phenomena were considerably more common, and beginning to show the clear female preponderance typical of the adult disorder.[13] For boys, antisocial behaviour is much more common in the teens, although the sex ratio for delinquency has changed considerably in recent years. Other disorders, such as anorexia nervosa and bulimia, also become more common during adolescence. Prevalence figures here come from case registers, medical records and some specially designed studies, and vary widely. The incidence of anorexia nervosa peaks in the late teens and early twenties, with girls up to 10 times more likely to be affected than boys. Eating problems meeting full diagnostic criteria for anorexia are rare: most studies suggest a prevalence of around 2 per 1,000 in women and girls, with rates being highest (at about 10 per 1,000) in middle-class school girls.[14]

Severe developmental disorders, such as autism, occur in 3–4 per 10,000 children, and severe learning difficulties (IQ below 50), in about 3 per 1,000. More mild learning difficulties, in the IQ range between 50 and 70, affect some 2.5 per cent of children. Psychoses are rare in pre-pubertal children, but schizophrenia occurs at a rate of 3 per 10,000 in later adolescence. Manic depressive psychoses also begin to become evident at this stage.

12.2.3 Social class and ethnic group differences
Data from the national birth cohort studies and from local epidemiological surveys all suggest that generalised behavioural deviance, especially as rated by teachers, shows clear social class trends. Social class differences in specific disorders vary markedly: conduct problems are probably more common in lower social groups, while depression shows few links with social status, and some eating problems, as noted above, are much more concentrated in the middle classes. Associations with social class thus need to be examined separately for each disorder. In general, however, more specific indicators of family difficulties and disturbance have been regarded as more important risk factors for children's psychological well-being than family social position *per se*.

Information on ethnic group differences is more limited. Evidence from local surveys and clinical studies up to the late 1970s, focusing in particular on children of Afro-Caribbean origin,[15] suggested that Afro-Caribbean children were more likely than whites to show behaviour problems at school (though not necessarily at home), and that patterns of disorder might also vary, with Afro-Caribbean girls in particular showing higher levels of conduct problems than their white counterparts. Studies of Asian children are much more scattered. A recent small-scale clinical study[16] suggested that Asian children were under-represented in referrals to psychiatric clinics, and were more likely to present with somatically-related conditions than with conduct problems. It is unclear how far findings of this kind reflect real differences in the prevalence and type of problems in Asian children, or cultural variations in parents' perception of their children's difficulties. Once again, in this study, there were suggestions of higher rates of difficulty at school than at home.

Finally, brief mention must be made of the reports of much elevated rates of schizophrenia in the Afro-Caribbean population, which have generated extensive debate and concern. These findings apply of course primarily to adults. In one recent prospective study, however, mean incidence rates were quite as high for 16–29-year-olds as in older age groups, and ethnic group differences were if anything more marked in second generation Afro-Caribbean young people.[17] Many different factors – including variations in diagnostic practice – have been advanced to account for these differences, but we are still far from understanding which play the most important part.

12.2.4 Links with other conditions

Children with physical illness, disabilities, and other medical conditions seem especially vulnerable to psychiatric problems. In the Isle of Wight studies, for example, children with asthma had almost twice the rate of psychiatric disorder found in the general population, and those with epilepsy and neurological disorders three or four times expected rates.[6] High levels of psychiatric disturbance have also been found in children attending both primary and secondary medical settings,[7,18] and among those with physical disabilities.[2] As many as 40 per cent of children with severe learning difficulties show severe psychiatric problems,[19] and virtually all children living in children's homes and other communal establishments were rated as having disabling behaviour problems in the OPCS disability survey.[2] At a more general level, behavioural and emotional problems are often associated with educational under-achievement and poor peer relationships, and may affect other aspects of children's functioning. There has been considerable debate, for example, over the role that characteristics such as aggression, impulsivity and hyperactivity play in children's vulnerability to accidents (see Chapter 8 for a discussion of this evidence).

12.2.5 General issues

The literature also highlights a number of other important aspects of mental health problems in childhood. The first is that co-morbidity between psychiatric disorders – the occurrence of two or more disorders in the same child – is found much more often than would be expected by chance.[20] Little is known as yet of what this may imply for aetiology, risk factors or prognosis. Second, estimates of disorder vary depending on whether reports are taken from parents, teachers or children. This suggests that

although many problems are pervasive across situations, some are primarily confined to the home or school, and others – especially worries and depressive affect – would go largely unrecognised without direct reports from children themselves. This point has been especially underlined in recent studies of children involved in disasters. For many years, it had been assumed that children did not suffer the post-traumatic stress disorder commonly found in adult survivors of disasters. Recent studies, involving direct interviews with children, make it clear that a very similar clinical picture is seen in childhood, and that appropriate help is needed for children just as much as for adult survivors of traumatising events.[21] As in adulthood, less severe stressors and life events also seem to play a role in the genesis of some child psychiatric problems.[22] In addition to the family disruptions and difficulties that some children experience, 'normative' events, faced by all children, are especially interesting here. Individual studies suggest, for example, that up to 10 per cent of children may be disturbed by starting school,[23] and that levels of affective problems are raised across the board for adolescents at the time of public examinations.[24]

Longitudinal studies have demonstrated that although many behavioural and emotional problems are relatively transitory,[25] others, even among the more common psychiatric disorders, are quite persistent throughout childhood. In the study which followed inner-city 3-year-olds to the age of 8 years, three quarters of the boys and half the girls with difficulties at the first assessment still showed problems some five years later.[11] In the Isle of Wight studies,[8] just under half the adolescents with disorder had also been previously assessed as disordered at age 10. Child psychiatric problems may also have longer-term effects. In the National Child Development Study, for example, the risk of psychological problems in the late teens and early twenties was over three times higher for girls rated by their teachers as showing deviant behaviour at 16, and was increased almost four-fold for boys.[26] Perhaps equally important, this same study showed that effects were not confined to the psychological domain. Adolescents with deviant behaviour ratings were also more likely to be downwardly socially mobile in their teens and early twenties. These findings underline the picture emerging from longitudinal studies of more specific conditions: not only will a significant proportion of children with mental health problems go on to experience psychiatric disorder in their adult lives, but they are also likely to face problems at work, in social and marital relationships, and in other aspects of adult functioning. The legacy of child psychiatric problems is by no means trivial.

Finally, all studies that have investigated service use have shown that very few children identified by researchers as meeting criteria for psychiatric disorders were in contact with professional help. In the Isle of Wight studies, only 1 in 10 of the 10- and 11-year-olds identified as disordered was under any form of psychiatric care, while a further 10 per cent were seeing a GP or social worker, or attending a special school; 4 out of 5 children with a handicapping psychiatric condition were not receiving help of any kind.[6]

12.3 Trends over time

The findings presented so far in this chapter were all derived from studies of particular age cohorts of children, or from cross-sectional surveys undertaken at particular points in time. The detailed case-finding methods used in these studies are clearly essential to gain reliable estimates of the prevalence of psychiatric disorder. But studies of single age-cohorts cannot, by their very nature, provide information on secular trends. Because of this, we have relatively little UK data on recent trends in rates of the more common childhood problems. The three British birth cohort studies have all included both parent and teacher behaviour questionnaires in their various childhood waves, but direct comparisons of overall rates of disorder in these populations are hampered by variations in measurement and design. It is clear that certain specific behaviours, such as truancy from school, have risen markedly since the 1960s, but more general trends in either conduct or emotional problems are difficult to assess.

International data on secular trends in a range of adolescent problems have recently been brought together by Academic Europaea.[27] This volume highlights the methodological difficulties of establishing a clear picture of changes in underlying rates of disorder when diagnostic criteria, professional and public perceptions of psychiatric problems and the response of health and other agencies are all also changing. It does, however, highlight a series of important trends emerging from international studies that are likely to be paralleled in the UK. In the case of depression, for example, there has almost certainly been some increase in prevalence in recent generations,[28] while for eating disorders, despite suggestions of a rise of epidemic proportions, there are currently too few well-designed studies to allow for any firm conclusions on trends.[29,30]

UK data are available in some specific problem areas, in particular drug and alcohol misuse, suicide and parasuicide, and delinquency. In each case, regularly collected statistics focus on particular problem behaviours or treatment needs, rather than disorders *per se*. Even so, the figures provide valuable pointers to specific aspects of psychiatrically related morbidity.

12.3.1 Drug and alcohol problems

Both US and European data showed increases in drug and alcohol use among young people in the 1970s, followed by a levelling, and in some cases a decline, during the 1980s.[31] Chapter 5 discusses recent trends in alcohol use by children. Figure 12.1 shows the numbers of males and females aged under 20 admitted to mental hospitals and units with a main diagnosis of drug psychosis, drug dependence and non-dependent misuse of drugs (excluding alcohol and tobacco) during the early 1980s. The numbers in these extreme groups are small, but nevertheless suggest a marked rise for both males and females over the period, of over 80 per cent in each case. Rates were twice as high for adolescent boys as girls throughout; admissions for drug abuse appear to have peaked for girls in the early 1980s, but continued to rise for males.

Heavy alcohol consumption is associated with a range of adverse consequences – accidents, poisonings, violence and crime – although it is often difficult to determine the exact part that alcohol played. Recent surveys suggest that alcohol misuse among young people has become established as a chronic problem in the UK, but that both use and misuse have stabilised over the last decade, and that rates of some alcohol-related problems have declined.[32] For young people, the most severe consequences seem to reflect the effects of acute intoxication rather than chronic heavy drinking or alcohol dependence. Very small numbers of young people are recorded as dying from clearly alcohol-related causes, but drinking is implicated in many road traffic accidents. During the 1980s there was a marked decline in the proportions of British riders and drivers killed in road

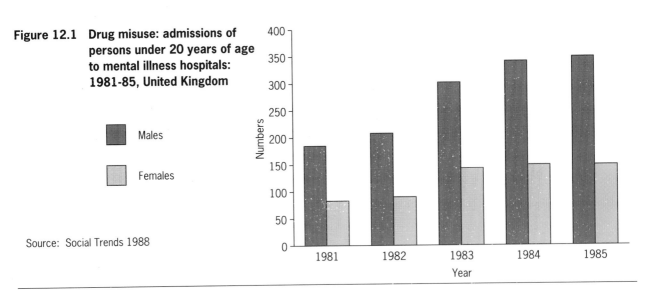

Figure 12.1 **Drug misuse: admissions of persons under 20 years of age to mental illness hospitals: 1981-85, United Kingdom**

Males

Females

Source: Social Trends 1988

traffic accidents who were over the legal blood alcohol limit for drivers. Figure 12.2 shows the figures for 16–19-year-olds. The decline in alcohol-related accidents has been sharpest in this age group, falling by over 50 per cent. There has also been a fall in the numbers of males under 18 cautioned for offences of drunkenness.[33]

12.3.2 Suicide and parasuicide

The true extent of both completed suicide and parasuicide (non-fatal deliberate self-harm) is almost certainly under-represented in official statistics. From the data available, however, both appear rare in children under the age of 12. The rate of recorded suicides rise throughout the teens with each year of age from 14. Although suicide occurs at a lower rate among teenagers than in any adult age group, it nevertheless constitutes one of the most important causes of death in 15–24-year-old males, ranking second only to motor vehicle accidents in England and Wales in 1990. Parasuicide, by contrast, is a largely adolescent and early adult phenomenon and much more common in young women. Hospital admissions for self-poisoning are at their highest for women in the 15–19 year age range, and show a sharp decline with age thereafter. For men, the peak ages are in the twenties, but rates for 15–19 year-olds are also high. Sex ratios contrast strongly with completed suicides: while men are more likely than women to commit suicide at all ages, 70 per cent or more of teenage hospital admissions for self-poisonings are by females.

Recorded suicide rates in England and Wales have shown peaks and troughs over recent decades, but the overall trend has been rising. For 15–19-year-olds, this pattern has been more marked.[34] Teenage suicides rose in both sexes from the 1950s to the mid-1960s, then fell as domestic gas was detoxified. Figure 12.3 shows the rates in more recent years, contrasting trends for 15–19-year-olds with those for all adults of age 20 and above. Rates for men of 20 and above rose by 11 per cent between 1976–80 and 1986–90; for 15–19 year-old males, the comparable increase was of almost 45 per cent. For adult women, rates have declined since the mid-1970s, by 34 per cent between 1976–80 and 1986–90. Rates have also declined somewhat for teenage girls, but show a lower percentage change (23 per cent). The gender gap has become more marked in recent years in all age groups: for 15–19-year-olds, male-female ratios were around 2:1 in the late 1970s, in the order of 3:1 in the early 1980s, and then rose sharply, to over 4:1, in 1990. Among males, increases in hanging, strangulation and suffocation, together with the use of firearms, explosives and poisoning by exhaust fumes, were especially notable between the early 1970s and 1980s.[35]

Many factors are likely to have contributed to these trends. Although there are marked international differences in levels of completed suicide, similar recent increases in adolescent and early adult suicides have been reported in many European countries and in the USA.[36] At the societal level, changes in suicide rates among 15–29-year-olds in 18 European countries have been found to be associated with increases in unemployment, the proportion of women employed, and in divorce, homicide and alcohol use.[37] At the individual level, psychological autopsies suggest high rates of psychiatric disorder in adolescent suicides; 90 per cent or more showed some disorder, with affective disorders, substance misuse and personality disorders among the most important diagnoses.[38] Other risk factors include disturbed family relationships, experience of suicidal behaviour in the

Figure 12.2   **Alcohol-related road deaths: percentage of 16-19 year old drivers and riders killed who were over the legal blood alcohol limit: 1979-92, Great Britain**

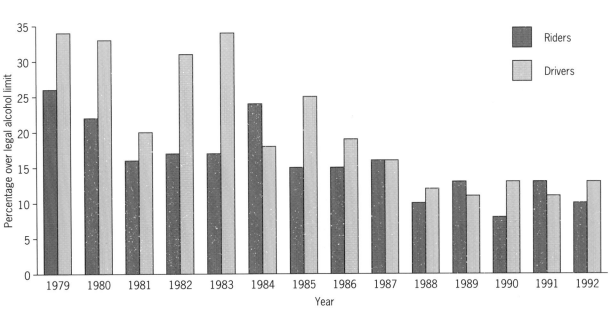

Source: Department of Transport

family or peer group, and access to a means. In that context, the recent increases in male suicides due to hanging, strangulation and suffocation are especially concerning, as all these means are readily available. Although suicide rates in themselves clearly cannot be taken as pointers to changes in underlying rates of disorder, the recent increases for young men in particular suggest increasing pressures on vulnerable individuals. Broader social and economic changes, together perhaps with increases in drug and alcohol misuse, may well be implicated here.

Figures on hospital admissions for parasuicide show different trends. Self-poisoning is one of the commonest reasons for hospital admissions in adolescence. Rates of parasuicide rose markedly in Britain, as in many other European countries, from the early 1950s to the late 1970s, then levelled out for 12–15-year-olds in the first half of the 1980s (to about 10 per 10,000), and showed a slight fall for older teenagers. Comparisons from the special monitoring units in Oxford and Edinburgh[39] suggest declines for both males and females in the 15–19-year age range between 1976–7 and 1983–4. Self-poisoning with barbiturates halved over this period, and poisonings from minor tranquillisers (the most common reason for admission) also decreased. More recent data from the Oxford unit,[40] however, show that rates of self-poisonings in older teenage girls rose steadily over the second half of the 1980s, reaching 88 per 10,000 in 1989. The Oxford data also reflect a dramatic rise in the use of paracetamol. For both sexes, paracetamol was involved in just under a quarter of self-poisonings in 1976–7, but almost half of those recorded in 1988–9.

The social and clinical picture in parasuicides shows a much increased risk in lower social class groups. Formal psychiatric disorder is less usual than in completed suicides, but high levels of disturbance are reported in both the adolescents and their families. Relationship problems are common, especially among girls, and unemployment rates in the Oxford series were considerably higher than the local rates for older teenagers. Drug and alcohol problems were more frequent in males, but alcohol use at the time of the act was common in both sexes. Clinical studies[41] suggest that antisocial and behavioural problems are also frequently present.

12.3.3 Delinquency

Probably the most striking feature of delinquency and criminality is its association with age: the majority of both officially recorded and self-report crimes are committed by teenagers and young adults. National statistics[42] confirm that a quarter of males are likely to be convicted of at least one offence by the age of 20 and that the peak age for most offending is between 15 and 19. For teenage boys in particular, the chances of some minor involvement in delinquency are very high, and will not, in most instances, indicate persistent antisocial tendencies. In practice, between 10 and 20 per cent of delinquents are likely to suffer from psychiatric disorder. In the late 1950s, 14–16-year-old boys were about 10 times more likely to be cautioned or found guilty of an offence than girls. By the end of the 1980s, the gender gap had closed, with the male–female ratio at about 4:1. For both sexes, theft offences dominate the picture in the teens.

Figures 12.4 and 12.5 show the proportions of males and females respectively in various age groups found guilty of, or cautioned for, indictable offences between 1970 and 1992. In all groups aged under 21, rates of known offenders rose, in some cases sharply, up to the mid 1970s. For 14–16-year-old girls in particular, this trend continued into the 1980s, though for males the curves essentially stabilised. From the mid-1980s until 1989 there was a sharp drop in the rates in all groups, but some rises since 1990. More detailed data suggest that the falls for juveniles in the late 1980s were almost entirely accounted for by changes in convictions and cautions for burglary and theft, both of which essentially halved since the mid-1980s, while rates for other categories of offences remained stable.

A number of points need to be borne in mind in interpreting these figures. The first and most obvious is

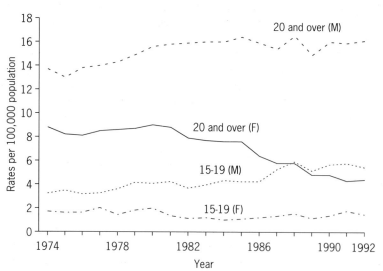

Figure 12.3 Suicide rates by age and sex: 1974-92, England and Wales

Source: Mortality Statistics: cause 1974-92
Population Estimates 1974-92

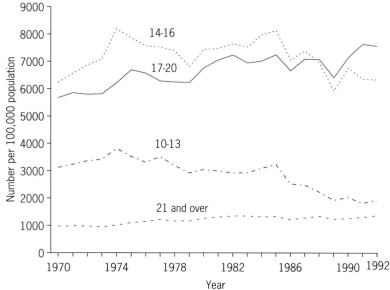

Figure 12.4 Males found guilty of, or cautioned for, indictable offences per 100,000 population by age group: 1970-92, England and Wales

Source; Criminal Statistics 1970-92

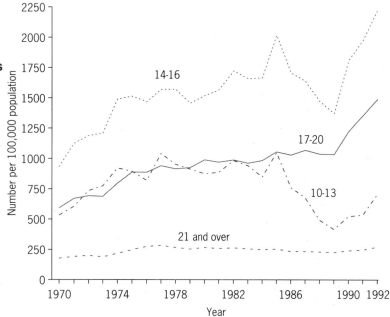

Figure 12.5 Females found guilty of, or cautioned for, indictable offences per 100,000 population by age group: 1970-92, England and Wales

Source; Criminal Statistics 1970-92

that officially recorded crime represents only a fraction of all illegal acts. Self-report studies might well show different trends. Second, changes over time need to be seen against the background of relevant changes in police policy and practice. The sharp rise in recorded juvenile crime in the late 1970s coincided with a major increase in the use of cautions, and possibly also convictions, for incidents that might previously have been dealt with informally. In a similar way the drop in the figures in the late 1980s almost certainly owed a great deal to moves towards increasing use of juvenile diversionary schemes, designed to keep young people out of the criminal justice system by use of informal warnings and other approaches.[43]

Charges of this kind argue for caution in drawing conclusions on trends in underlying rates of juvenile offending; it will be some years yet before we can adequately assess the implications of more recent figures.

12.3.4 Implications of changing social and economic conditions

Finally, alongside these data on specific problem areas, it is important to note the likely implications of recent changes in the social and economic context of childhood (described in Chapter 2) for children's mental health problems. Known risk factors for specific psychiatric disorders vary, and often involve both genetic and biological influences, but adverse social and family circumstances have also been found to be frequent correlates of children's psychiatric problems. Social disadvantage, poor and overcrowded housing conditions, discord and marital breakdown between parents, and illness (especially depression) in mothers, together with disadvantaged schooling, have all emerged as consistent correlates of behavioural and emotional problems in numerous studies. In the London–Isle of Wight comparisons, for example, rates of disorder were almost twice as common in the inner city, largely reflecting higher levels of social and family difficulties in the urban context.[10] Many of the demographic and economic changes of recent decades – especially increases in family poverty, homelessness, and in divorce, family dissolution and reconstitution – seem only too likely to increase the stresses on families that in their turn play a major role in the genesis of child psychiatric disorders. Secular changes in the pattern of family life are exposing children to new challenges at home, and the possibility of periods of unemployment in the teens carries well-known risks of increased psychiatric morbidity[44] and offending.[45] Though we currently lack data documenting the precise effects of these broader social changes on children's mental health, they do not give grounds for optimism.

12.4 Conclusions

Mental health problems are diverse and complex, and this chapter has inevitably been highly selective in its focus. Even this brief account, however, is enough to illustrate the extent of psychiatric morbidity in childhood, and the complexities of attempting to tease out trends in children's mental health problems over time. In many areas, appropriate data to draw firm conclusions are not yet available. Where figures are known, they suggest differing trends in different areas, some encouraging, others giving more cause for concern. At present, our understanding of the causes of children's mental health problems, and how best to treat and ideally prevent them is still very limited. The postwar years have seen major improvements in many aspects of child health. The challenge for the future is to ensure that these are paralleled by similar improvements in the psychological well-being of the next generation of children.

References

1. Brandenberg N A, Friedman R M and Silver S E. The epidemiology of child psychiatric disorder: prevalence findings from recent studies. *Journal American Academy Child Adolescent Psychiatry,* **29**, 1990, 76–83.

2. Bone M and Meltzer H. *The Prevalence of Disability among Children.* OPCS Surveys of Disability in Great Britain, Report 3. HMSO (London 1989).

3. Robins L N. Conduct disorder. *Journal Child Psychology Psychiatry*, **32**, 1991, 193–212.

4. Harrington R, Fudge H, Rutter M, Pickles A and Hill J. Adult outcomes of childhood and adolescent depression. *Archives General Psychiatry*, **47**, 1990, 465–73.

5. Greenley J R and Mechanic D. Social selection in seeking help for psychological problems. *Journal Health Social Behaviour*, **17**, 1976, 249–62.

6. Rutter M, Tizard J and Whitmore K. *Education, Health and Behaviour.* Longmans (London 1970).

7. Garralda M E and Bailey D. Psychiatric disorders in general paediatric referrals. *Archives Disease Childhood*, **64**, 1989, 1727–33.

8. Rutter M, Tizard J, Yule W, Graham P and Whitmore K. Research report: The Isle of Wight studies 1964–1974. *Psychological Medicine*, **6**, 1976, 313–32.

9. Rutter M, Cox A, Tupling C, Berger M and Yule W. Attainment and adjustment in two geographical areas. I. The prevalence of psychiatric disorder. *British Journal Psychiatry,* **126**, 1975a, 493–509.

10. Rutter M, Yule B, Quinton D, Rowlands O, Yule W and Berger M. Attainment and adjustment in two geographical areas. III. Some factors accounting for area differences. *British Journal Psychiatry*, **126**, 1975b, 520–33.

11. Richman N, Stevenson J and Graham P J. *Pre-school to School: a Behavioural Study.* Academic Press (London 1982).

12. Taylor E, Sandberg S, Thorley G and Giles S. *The Epidemiology of Childhood Hyperactivity.* Oxford University Press (1991).

13. Angold A and Rutter M. The effects of age and pubertal status on depression in a large clinical sample. *Development Psychopathology*, **4**, 1992, 5–28.

14. Crisp A H, Palmer R L and Kalucy R S. How common is anorexia nervosa? A prevalence study. *British Journal Psychiatry,* **128**, 1976, 549–54.

15. Taylor M. *Caught between: A Review of Research into the Education of Pupils of West Indian Origin.* NFER-Nelson (Windsor 1981).

16. Jawed S H. A survey of psychiatrically ill Asian children. *British Journal Psychiatry*, **158**, 1991, 268–70.

17. Harrison G, Owens D, Holton A, Nielson D and Boot D. A prospective study of severe mental disorder in Afro-Caribbean patients. *Psychological Medicine*, **18**, 1988, 643–57.

18. Garralda M E and Bailey D. Children with psychiatric disorders in primary care. *Journal Child Psychology Psychiatry*, **27**, 1986, 611–24.

19. Graham P J. Behavioural and intellectual development in childhood epidemiology. *British Medical Journal*, **42**, 1986, 155–62.

20. Caron C and Rutter M. Comorbidity in child psychopathology: concepts, issues and research strategies. *Journal Child Psychology Psychiatry*, **32**, 1991, 1063–80.

21. Yule W. Resilience and vulnerability in child survivors of disasters. In: Tizard B and Varma V (eds). *Vulnerability and Resilience: Festschrift for Ann and Alan Clarke.* Jessica Kingsley (London 1991) pp. 182–98.

22. Goodyer I M. *Life Experiences, Development and Childhood Psychopathology.* Wiley (Chichester 1990).

23. Beardsall L and Dunn J. Adversities in childhood: siblings' experiences, and their relations to self-esteem. *Journal Child Psychology Psychiatry*, **33**, 1991, 349–59.

24. Cairns E, McWhirter L, Barry R and Duffy U. The development of psychological well-being in adolescence. *Journal Child Psychology Psychiatry*, **32**, 1991, 635–43.

25. Ghodsian M, Fogelman K, Lambert L and Tibbenham A. Changes in behaviour ratings of a national sample of children. *British Journal Social Clinical Psychology*, **19**, 1980, 247–56.

26. Power C, Manor O and Fox J. *Health and Class: the Early Years*. Chapman and Hall (London 1991).

27. Rutter M and Smith D. *Psychosocial Disorders in Young People: Time Trends and their Causes*. Wiley. (Chichester 1995)

28. Fombonne E. Depressive disorders: time trends and possible explanatory mechanisms. In: Rutter M and Smith D (eds). *Psychosocial Disorders in Young People: Time Trends and their Causes*. Wiley (Chichester 1995) 544-615.

29. Lask B and Bryant-Waugh R. Early-onset anorexia nervosa and related eating disorders. *Journal Child Psychology Psychiatry*, **33**, 1992, 281–300.

30. Fombonne E. Eating disorders: time trends and possible explanatory mechanisms. In: Rutter M and Smith D (eds). *Psychosocial Disorders in Young People: Time Trends and their Causes*. Wiley (Chichester 1995) 616-85.

31. Silbereisen R, Robins L and Rutter M. Secular trends in substance use: concepts and data on the impact of social change on alcohol and drug abuse. In: Rutter M and Smith D (eds). *Psychosocial Disorders in Young People: Time Trends and their Causes*. Wiley. (Chichester 1995) 490-543.

32. Plant M and Plant M. *Risktakers: Alcohol, Drugs, Sex and Youth*. Routledge (London 1992).

33. Home Office. *Offences of Drunkenness, England and Wales 1989. Statistical Bulletin* 40/90. Home Office (London 1990).

34. Charlton J, Kelly S, Dunnell K, Evans B, Jenkins R and Wallis R. Trends in suicide deaths in England and Wales. *Population Trends*, **69,** 1992, HMSO.

35. McClure G M G. Recent changes in suicide among adolescents in England and Wales. *Journal Adolescence*, **9**, 1986, 135–43.

36. Diekstra R F W. Suicide and suicidal behaviour among adolescents. In: Rutter M and Smith D (eds). *Psychosocial Disorders in Young People: Time Trends and their Causes*. Wiley. (Chichester 1995) 686-761.

37. WHO. *Correlates of Youth Suicide*. Division of Mental Health, World Health Organisation (technical document) (Geneva).

38. Martunnen M J, Aro H M, Henriksson M M and Lonnqvist J K. Mental disorders in adolescent suicide. *Archives General Psychiatry*, **48**, 1991, 834–39.

39. Platt S, Hawton K, Kreitman N, Fagg J and Foster J. Recent clinical and epidemiological trends in parasuicide in Edinburgh and Oxford: a tale of two cities. *Psychological Medicine,* **18**, 1988, 405–18.

40. Hawton K and Fagg J. Deliberate self-poisoning and self-injury in adolescents: a study of characteristics and trends in Oxford, 1976–1989. *British Journal Psychiatry*, **161**, 1992, 816–23.

41. Kerfoot M. Deliberate self-poisoning in childhood and early adolescence. *Journal Child Psychology Psychiatry*, **29**, 1988, 335–43.

42. Home Office Statistical Bulletin. *Criminal and Custodial Careers of Those Born in 1953, 1958 and 1963*. Home Office (London 1989).

43. Barclay G C and Turner D. Recent trends in official statistics for England and Wales on juvenile offending. Paper presented at the *Eighth International Workshop for Juvenile Criminology*, Leeds 1991.

44. Winefield A H, Tiggerman M and Winefield H R. The psychological impact of unemployment and unsatisfactory employment in young men and women: longitudinal and cross-sectional data. *British Journal Psychology*, **82**, 1991, 473–86.

45. Farrington D P, Gallagher B, Morley L, St Leger R J and West D. Unemployment, school leaving and crime. *British Journal Criminology*, **26**, 1986, 335–56.

13 Infectious diseases in childhood

Anna McCormick and Susan Hall

Key points

- Over the last hundred years the contribution of infections to morbidity and mortality among children has declined dramatically.

- Deaths due to diphtheria in England and Wales fell from 2,480 in 1940 (the year when immunisation was introduced) to nil in 1978.

- Since the introduction of the combined measles, mumps and rubella vaccine (MMR) in 1989, the number of measles notifications in England and Wales fell from 26,222 in 1989 to 9,680 in 1991.

- In 1991, 95 per cent of notifications of whooping cough were for children aged under 15 years.

- New infections have emerged in recent years which threaten our children and challenge any complacency which may have arisen.

- AIDS is an example of a new disease to which children are at risk through infection transmitted during pregnancy, delivery or breast feeding by an infected mother.

- To safeguard the future of our children, research into new immunisations and treatments is needed to consolidate our prevention programmes and minimise morbidity resulting from infections.

At the end of the nineteenth century, infectious diseases were a major cause of death among children. For example, the mean annual death rates in England and Wales per 100,000 population aged under 15 years between 1891 and 1895 for scarlet fever, measles and pertussis were 49, 116 and 114 respectively, but in 1992 there were only three childhood deaths due to these diseases.

While the incidence of many infectious diseases among children has declined dramatically over the last hundred years, new infections are emerging, or are becoming apparent through improved diagnostic techniques. Declining numbers of some infections may lead to complacency among health-care planners and parents, with a risk of reducing the preventive efforts required to maintain low incidence. Reduction in the number of cases also leads to inexperience among doctors, most of whom will never have seen a patient with one of the currently rare diseases such as diphtheria. This may diminish awareness of the possible cause of the illness, resulting in delayed diagnosis and inappropriate or inadequate treatment.

Declining mortality rates from infectious diseases among infants and children as a result of the improved treatments now available have resulted in more children surviving but sometimes with continuing handicap subsequent to the initial infection. This has implications for the health care, social services and educational resources required.

13.1 Sources of data

Mortality data are based on the diagnosis stated on the certificate of cause of death by the doctor or coroner, or on information subsequently supplied to the Office of Population Censuses and Surveys (OPCS).[1] The latter information may become available from post mortems or from laboratory results received after the certificate has been signed. It is particularly helpful in maintaining the accuracy of infectious disease data. Cause of death is currently coded using the International Classification of Diseases (ICD) 9th Revision. Many infectious diseases, however, are not included in the ICD chapter headed 'Infectious and parasitic diseases' and careful analysis of the data is required to ensure they are all included. For example, some infections of the respiratory system such as pneumonia and influenza are included in the respiratory chapter, some infections of the nervous systems such as encephalitis are in the nervous system chapter and, if hepatitis is not specified as 'viral' or 'gastroenteritis' as 'infective', they are included in the chapter on diseases of the digestive system. The number of deaths from selected infectious diseases is shown in Table 13.1.

Table 13.1 Deaths by infectious disease and age group: 1992, England and Wales

	Under 1*	1–4	5–9	10–14
Intestinal infectious diseases (ICD 001-009)	8	3	1	0
Tuberculosis (ICD 010-018)	1	3	1	0
Whooping cough (ICD 033)	1	0	0	0
Streptococcal sore throat & scarlatina (ICD 034)	0	0	1	0
Meningococcal infection (ICD 036)	34	38	6	9
Septicaemia (ICD 038)	19	5	2	0
Acute poliomyelitis (ICD 045)	1	0	0	0
Viral encephalitis nos (ICD 049.9)	0	0	2	0
Chickenpox (ICD 052)	0	2	1	0
Measles (ICD 055)	0	1	0	0
Viral hepatitis (ICD 070)	1	2	0	1
Haemophilus meningitis (ICD 320.0)	6	12	1	0
Pneumococcal meningitis (ICD 320.1)	5	0	0	1
Meningitis of unspecified cause (ICD 322)	5	4	3	1
Viral pneumonia (ICD 480)	7	4	0	1
Pneumococcal pneumonia (ICD 481)	1	1	2	0
Other bacterial pneumonia (ICD 482)	6	1	0	0
Bronchopneumonia, organism unspecified (ICD 485)	17	13	1	1
Pneumonia, organism unspecified (ICD 486)	25	2	1	0

* Excludes deaths aged under 28 days.

Source: *Mortality Statistics: cause 1992*

Incidence is estimated by the number of cases reported to several data collection systems, each contributing a different facet to our understanding of the epidemiology of an infectious disease and each suffering from the inadequacies of all data collection systems.[2] For infectious diseases, sources include patients notified under the Public Health (Control of Disease) Act 1984 and the Public Health (Infectious Diseases) Regulations 1988.[3] The notifications reported to OPCS in 1992 are shown in Table 13.2. New episodes of illness presenting in their surgeries each week are reported by a sample of general practitioners to the Royal College of General Practitioners (RCGP) Research Unit in Birmingham.[4] Reports of identifications of organisms such as bacteria, viruses and parasites from laboratories throughout England and Wales are reported to the Public Health Laboratory Service Communicable Disease Surveillance Centre (CDSC). Diagnostic data on discharges from and deaths in hospital, based previously on hospital activity analysis (HAA), are currently based on hospital episode statistics (HES). In 1986, the British Paediatric Association (BPA), the Public Health Laboratory Service (PHLS) and the department of epidemiology at the Institute of Child Health, London started an active reporting system, called the British Paediatric Surveillance Unit (BPSU).[5] This contacts paediatricians monthly and asks them to report details of any case of a limited number of rare infections and infection-related disorders, many of which are not ascertained by other reporting systems.

Table 13.2 Notifications of infectious disease: 1992, England and Wales

	0–4	5–14
Typhoid fever	18	36
Paratyphoid fever	3	10
Food poisoning (all cases)	9,973	6,096
Dysentery	4,393	6,087
Tuberculosis (all types)	161	335
Whooping cough	1,225	915
Acute poliomyelitis	1	0
Scarlet fever	1,865	2,047
Meningitis (all forms)	1,406	287
- meningococcal	549	144
- pneumococcal	113	21
- haemophilus influenzal	441	18
- viral	39	39
Meningococcal septicaemia without meningitis	165	44
Malaria	42	120
Leptospirosis	0	3
Measles	6,253	2,945
Rubella	3,695	1,567
Mumps	875	946
Hepatitis A	424	2,852

Source: *Communicable Disease Statistics 1992*

13.2 Reasons for changing incidence

During the twentieth century the incidence and outcome of infectious diseases among children has been influenced by the way of life in England and Wales, the introduction of immunisation schedules, improved methods of diagnosis and the emergence of modern therapeutic procedures.

Migration from rural to urban areas has created communities living in close proximity, increasing the likelihood of contact and spread of infections. Grouping of children in day nurseries, playgroups, schools and public transport increases the opportunity for developing subclinical natural immunity, but may also provide a 'reservoir' of susceptible children should an infection be introduced into the group.

Increased national travel reduces the chances of epidemics remaining localised and therefore more easily controlled. The escalation of international travel introduces into this country infections now usually only encountered in other climates and environments, such as malaria[6] and cholera, or more rarely, exotic diseases like yellow fever and dengue. It also may introduce typhoid fever, poliomyelitis and diphtheria which have been largely eradicated from this country, but which are still widespread elsewhere. With the speed of air transport, passengers may now arrive in Britain during the incubation period of an infection and disperse to any part of the community before their disease becomes clinically apparent.

General living standards have improved, particularly with improvements in the water supply and drainage systems, and the acquisition of domestic appliances such as refrigerators. Changes in food production and preparation, however, have not been without problems. Battery production of chickens has increased the possibility of widespread salmonella infection of both the birds and their eggs. Imported food stuffs such as cheese and prawns have been responsible for outbreaks of food poisoning. Factory-prepared foods are quickly and widely distributed throughout the country, disseminating contamination throughout the population as exemplified by an outbreak of food poisoning due to contaminated baby milk powder affecting 46 babies[7] and another due to imported chocolate affecting 108 children.[8] More preprepared food ('ready meals'), are being purchased. These foods may have a long shelf-life and are highly processed and subject to contamination, in particular by listeria, a bacterium which can survive and grow at refrigeration temperatures. Inadequate reheating of these foodstuffs or their consumption uncooked can cause listeriosis, a serious infection when acquired by a pregnant woman who may pass it on to her fetus.

Changes in the sexual habits of adults may affect the incidence of infection amongst their offspring acquired before birth or at the time of delivery. This is exemplified by the increasing incidence of human immunodeficiency virus (HIV), genital herpes and *Chlamydia trachomatis* infection among adults, all of which may be transmitted to the fetus or newborn infant. In the USA there has been a dramatic increase in congenital syphilis in recent years, associated with the epidemic of crack cocaine use and the exchange of sex for drugs.

Advances in medical care, particularly the widespread availability of immunisation against common childhood infections, has brought about a decrease in the incidence of these diseases. Antibiotic and immunoglobulin prophylaxis given to contacts of infected people has also contributed to the control of spread in individual outbreaks of, for example, meningococcal meningitis and hepatitis A. Treatment given for some non-infectious conditions such as immunosuppressive therapy for cancer or transplant surgery, however, predisposes the patient to opportunistic infections such as *Pneumocystis carinii,* listeriosis, pneumonia and toxoplasmosis.

The increased use and often misuse of antibiotics since their introduction in the 1940s has generated strains of organisms resistant to antibiotics which are difficult to treat; a current example is the multi-resistant tuberculosis causing major problems in inner cities in the USA.

13.3 Diseases of declining incidence

The major declining childhood infections in England and Wales are those for which immunisation has been available for many years. These are poliomyelitis, tetanus, measles, tuberculosis, diphtheria and pertussis. This protection of the community depends upon a high level of 'herd immunity', so that if a person becomes infected there are a limited number of susceptible contacts exposed, reducing the likelihood of further transmission. In addition, a decline has occurred in the complications of some infection related diseases for which no immunisation is available but for which early antibiotic treatment prevents serious sequelae. The prime example of this is streptococcal infection which may cause scarlet fever, rheumatic fever, chorea and glomerulonephritis, although there are also other contributing factors including changes in the streptococcus itself. Streptococcal infections are discussed more fully in section 13.4.6.

13.3.1 Diphtheria
After mass immunisation was introduced in 1940, notifications and deaths due to diphtheria in England and Wales declined from 46,281 and 2,480 respectively in that year to 964 and 49 in 1950 and to 0 for both in 1978 and 1979. The immunisation rate among children having their second birthday in 1990/91 was 92 per cent. Isolated cases still occur, however, almost all among people thought to have been infected abroad and who have not been adequately immunised. Between 1980 and 1991, 36 cases were notified with one death.

13.3.2 Poliomyelitis
Immunisation with killed vaccine began in England and Wales in 1959 and this was replaced by live attenuated vaccine in 1962. Annual notifications of paralytic poliomyelitis then declined from 4,000 in 1955 to 257 in 1960 and to 9 in 1979 (Figure 13.1). Between 1980 and 1991, 24 cases of paralytic poliomyelitis were notified. As a direct result of immunisation, a high proportion of the few cases now occurring are associated with vaccination, either the child vaccinated or the carer of a recently vaccinated child because, very rarely, the live attenuated vaccine virus can revert to virulence. Between 1978 and 1984, 54 per cent of the 26 cases notified were vaccine-associated. The uptake rate of vaccination among children having their second birthday in 1990/91 was 92 per cent.

13.3.3 Measles
The number of deaths from measles in England and Wales was declining long before mass immunisation was introduced in 1968 (Figure 13.2). From a peak of approximately 1,300 per million total population in the 1880s, there was a sharp decline between 1915 and 1955, and there were 126 deaths between 1980 and 1989. In 1990 and 1991 there was only one death each year, that in 1991 being of an adult. Between 1946 (when measles became notifiable) and 1968 there was little change in the number of cases reported, with biennial epidemics. After 1968, the characteristic biennial pattern disappeared, with a smaller increase in numbers in two out of every three years. Since the introduction of the combined measles, mumps and rubella vaccine (MMR) in 1988, this more recent pattern has largely disappeared with a sharp decline in the number of cases notified, to 26,222 in 1989, 13,302 in 1990 and 9,680 in 1991. The proportion of children having their second birthday in 1990/91 who had been immunised against measles was 87 per cent.

Figure 13.1 Poliomyelitis notifications: 1912-92, England and Wales

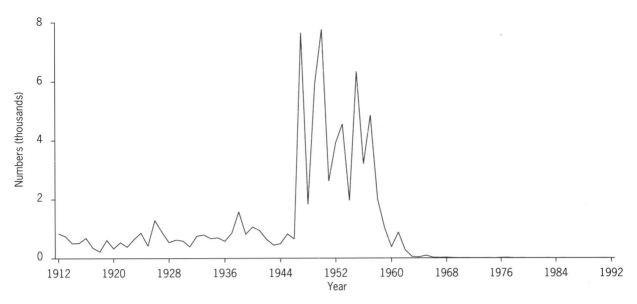

Sources: Registrar General's Statistical Review 1912-73
Communicable Disease Statistics 1974-92

Figure 13.2 Measles quarterly notifications: 1955-92, England and Wales

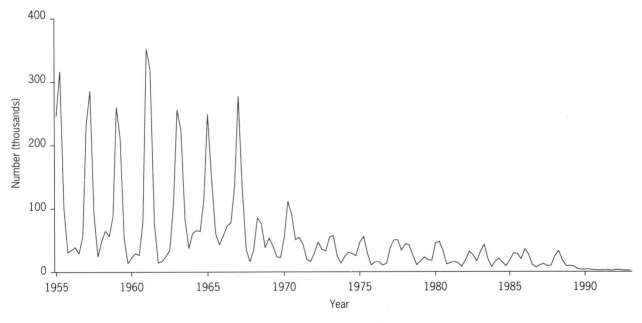

Sources: Registrar General's Quarterly Returns 1955-73
Communicable Disease Statistics 1974-92

13.3.4 Tuberculosis

In developed countries tuberculosis is now primarily an infection occurring in the indigenous elderly and immigrant populations, although there has been a recent upsurge among homeless younger people in the USA and in the UK. Tuberculosis most commonly affects the lungs (respiratory cases), but can also involve other parts of the body such as bones, intestines and kidneys (non respiratory cases). In 1945, notifications among children under 15 years formed 7.5 per cent of all respiratory cases and 52 per cent of all non-respiratory cases (3,000 and 5,000 notifications aged under 15 years respectively). The corresponding figures for 1991 were 6.6 per cent and 12.6 per cent (262 and 187 notifications respectively).

Figure 13.3 Respiratory tuberculosis notifications: 1913-92, England and Wales

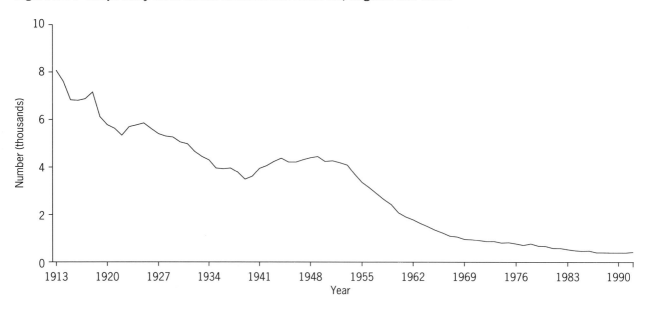

Source: Registrar General's Statistical Review 1913-73
         Communicable Disease Statistics 1974-92

The total number of notifications and of deaths from tuberculosis was already declining steadily for many decades before the introduction of chemotherapy, BCG vaccination and the mass X-ray programmes in the early 1950s. After 1950 this decline in the number of both notifications and deaths accelerated until 1970 although it has occurred at a slower rate since that year (Figure 13.3). The ratio of deaths to notifications, however, decreased from 1 in 3 in 1950 to 1 in 13 in 1991. In 1991 there were 449 notifications and one death from tuberculosis in children aged under 15 years. Evidence from the USA and Africa suggests that there has been an increase in the incidence of tuberculosis among HIV-positive people.[9] Although this is not yet apparent in England and Wales, should it occur it may increase the risk of exposure of children to tuberculosis and an increase in the number infected may be expected.

13.3.5 Pertussis

Trends in the incidence of pertussis over the last 40 years illustrate the effect of changes in immunisation uptake.[10] Between 1940 and 1950, the average annual number of notifications was 103,451. After the introduction of immunisation in the 1950s, this number fell rapidly to an annual average of 9,863 between 1969 and 1974 with immunisation uptake rates in England and Wales of 77–81 per cent for babies born between 1966 and 1972. During the mid-1970s, however, the uptake rate fell sharply to 30 per cent among babies born

in 1976, due to concern about the safety of the vaccine. As a result, peaks in the number of notifications occurred subsequently, with 173,361 notifications in 1977 and 139,487 in 1981 (Figure 13.4). Uptake rates have increased since 1976 to 84 per cent of children having their second birthday in 1990/91. There has been a corresponding reduction in the number of notifications to an average annual number of 10,711 in 1989–91. In 1991, 95 per cent of notifications of whooping cough were for children aged under 15 years.

13.3.6 Streptococcal infections

The reduction in the number of cases of acute rheumatic fever and rheumatic heart disease began before the introduction of antibiotics in the treatment of streptococcal sore throats. There is evidence that this decline was associated with diminished overcrowding and improvement in nutrition. The number of hospital admissions for rheumatic fever among people of all ages declined from 1,606 in 1968 to 380 in 1978 and 18 in 1985. None of those admitted in 1985 was under 15 years of age. The number of streptococcal infections manifesting as scarlet fever fell continuously between the 1930s, when there were an annual average of 105,566 notifications between 1930 and 1939, and 1970 when there were 13,149. Since that year the rate of decrease has slowed, with 5,217 notifications in 1991, 87 per cent of which were for those aged under 15 years (Figure 13.5).

Figure 13.4 Whooping cough notifications - cases and deaths: 1940-92, England and Wales

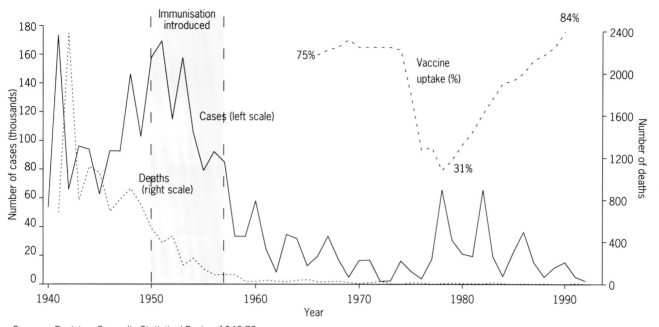

Sources: Registrar General's Statistical Review 1940-73
Communicable Disease Statistics 1974-92

Figure 13.5 Scarlet fever notifications: 1938-92, England and Wales

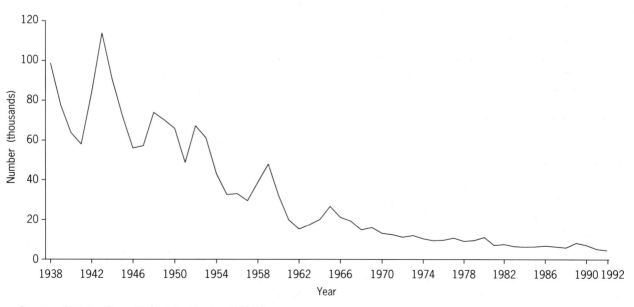

Sources: Registrar General's Statistical Review 1938-73
Communicable Disease Statistics 1974-92

Infectious diseases in childhood   173

13.4 Diseases with varying incidence

13.4.1 Hepatitis

There are a number of forms of infectious hepatitis caused by different viruses. Type A, spread by the faeco-oral route, and type B, spread by transfer of body fluids, are the commonest in this country. Type A is the most frequent cause of viral hepatitis in children.

Increases in the incidence of hepatitis A infections occur over several years with a peak every 10 years, for reasons which are not understood.[11] There was a peak in the number of notifications of 'infective jaundice' in 1982, at least partly caused by contaminated shellfish, when there were 10,605 notifications, and again in 1990 when there were 9,005 notifications of 'viral hepatitis'. The number of laboratory reports of hepatitis B over these periods remained fairly constant, indicating that the increase in notifications of infective jaundice/viral hepatitis was due to hepatitis A infection (Figure 13.6). In recent years, highest notification rates have been among adults and children aged 5–9 years. The proportion of all notifications (40 per cent in 1991) which were for children aged less than 15 years has remained similar during the years of increased incidence.[12]

13.4.2 Meningococcal infection

Meningococcal infection is caused by the bacterium *Neisseria meningitidis* and includes both meningococcal septicaemia and meningitis. It has been notifiable since 1912, but definitions of the condition to be notified have changed from time to time making interpretation of long term trends difficult. Since 1968, notifiers have been asked to specify the causal organism of all notifications of 'acute meningitis', if known. The data suggest a peak of increased incidence of meningococcal disease every 15 years or so lasting for six or seven years.[13] In 1982, the number of notifications of meningococcal meningitis was 401 compared with 1,138 in 1990 and 1,117 in 1991.[12] Since 1983 there was a gradual increase particularly during the winter months of each year, with 68 per cent of the notifications between 1987 and 1991 being for children aged under 15 years, the rate being highest for babies aged less than one year.

There are several different serogroups of *Neisseria meningitidis*. In 1991, group B accounted for 69 per cent of infections in England and Wales, and group C for 28 per cent,[14] while group A is the most common type found outside Europe. Vaccines are effective except in infants, but available only against groups A and C.

13.5 New or increasing infections

13.5.1 Food- and milk-borne infections

The number of notifications of food poisoning for people of all ages declined from a peak of 12,719 in 1955 to 4,539 in 1966. This number has steadily increased, however, to 35,291 in 1991 for all ages, and from 1,533 in 1966 (34 per cent of the total) to 8,783 in 1991 (25 per cent of the total) among those aged under 15 years.[12] This recent increase has been mirrored by the increase in the number of laboratory reports of salmonella from 9,994 in 1976 to 23,325 in 1991. The increase has largely been due to *Salmonella enteritidis*, commonly associated with poultry. Some outbreaks of food poisoning, for example that of *Salmonella napoli*[8] due to contaminated Italian chocolate in 1982 and of *Salmonella ealing*[7] in milk products for infants in 1985, have been entirely or almost entirely confined to children.

Figure 13.6 Viral hepatitis quarterly notifications and laboratory reports: 1975-93, England and Wales

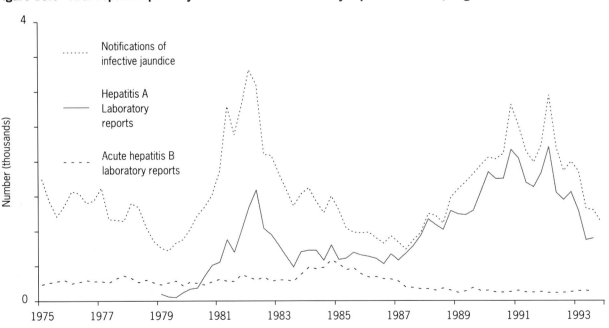

Source: Communicable Disease Surveillance Centre.

There has also been a gradual increase in laboratory reports of campylobacter identifications, from 1,349 in 1977 to 32,636 in 1991. Campylobacter is now the commonest reported cause of bacterial gastroenteritis in England and Wales, and may be foodborne (poultry are often implicated) or acquired from contaminated milk or water.

During the last few years, *Yersinia enterocolitica* has been recognised with increasing frequency as a cause of bacterial gastroenteritis. Laboratory reports of this organism increased from 183 in 1983 to 404 in 1991; 32 per cent of reports in 1991 were for children aged under 15 years. Part of this increase is undoubtedly due to improved laboratory diagnostic techniques and reporting.

Listeria monocytogenes is another cause of food-borne infection which has been recognised during recent years.[15] Outbreaks and sporadic cases in the UK have been associated with the consumption of, for example, pâté, soft cheeses, cream and ready-cooked meals. This infection is extremely rare in healthy children but the infection can be transmitted by an infected mother to her fetus causing death or serious illness such as septicaemia and meningitis in the newborn baby. In 1991, seven of the 30 laboratory reports of listeria associated with meningitis were for infants and children aged under 15 years.

13.5.2 Human parvovirus (B19 infection)

This virus was discovered about twelve years ago to be the cause of a common rash in childhood.[16] It causes 'slapped cheek' syndrome, also known as fifth disease, with a typical appearance of erythema of the face and lacy rash on the trunk and limbs. Outbreaks frequently occur among young schoolchildren. It is usually mild, but can cause severe anaemia in children with blood disorders and those who are immunocompromised. It can also affect the fetus if the virus is acquired in pregnancy. Cases of this infection occur every year but there are epidemics every three to four years.

13.5.3 Haemorrhagic colitis and haemolytic uraemic syndrome (HUS)

In 1977, the association between both acute haemorrhagic colitis (a severe diarrhoeal illness) and HUS (now the commonest cause of acute renal failure in children in this country) and verocytotoxin-producing *Escherichia coli* (mainly *E. coli* 0157) was established in the USA.[17] The number of laboratory reports of *E. coli* 0157 increased from 119 in 1989 to 337 in 1991 in England and Wales. It is not well understood how these infections are acquired, but beef and dairy products as well as water have been implicated in the USA and in some UK incidents.

13.5.4 Lyme disease

This infection, due to *Borrelia burgdorferi*, a spirochaete bacterium, was first recognised in the USA in 1977.[18] It is transmitted by *Ixodes ricinus* ticks found in areas inhabited, in particular, by deer. An average of 18 cases were reported annually between 1987 and 1990 from various parts of England and Wales;[19] 10 per cent of these were under 15 years of age.

13.5.5 Acquired immune deficiency syndrome (AIDS)

Human Immunodeficiency virus (HIV) among children in the UK is acquired mainly from untreated blood products (before 1985), or by transmission before, during or after delivery (through breast milk) from an HIV-positive mother. By the end of January 1994, 146 children under 15 years of age in the UK had developed AIDS and 523 were known to be HIV positive, of whom 223 (43 per cent) was probably infected by mother-to-infant transmission and 297 (57 per cent) by blood or blood products. The majority of infected children lived in the south-east of England or in Scotland.

13.6 Conclusions

While many infectious diseases encountered during childhood have decreased in incidence and in severity over recent decades, others remain or have become of increasing importance. Continued surveillance, investigation and research are required to safeguard future generations. As Tyrrell has said, 'The study of infections is not a matter of past history or routine, but an area of growing knowledge and interest'.[21]

References

1. Ashley J and Devis T. Death certification from the point of view of the epidemiologist. *Population Trends* **67**, 1992,22-8.
2. PHLS Communicable Disease Surveillance Centre. Quarterly communicable disease review July to September 1992. *Journal Public Health Medicine* **15**, 1993, 103-11.
3. McCormick A. The notification of infectious diseases in England and Wales. *Communicable Disease Report*, **3**, 1993, R19-25.
4. Fleming D M, Norbury C A and Crombie D L. *Annual and Seasonal Variations in the Incidence of Common Diseases. Occasional Paper 53*. RCGP (London 1991).
5. Lynn R and Hall S M. The British Paediatric Surveillance Unit: activities and developments in 1990 and 1991. *Communicable Disease Report* **2,** 1992 R145-8.
6. Bradley D J and Warhurst D C. Malaria imported into the United Kingdom during 1991. *Communicable Disease Report* **3**, 1993 R25-8.
7. Rowe B, Begg N T, Hutchinson DN *et al*. Salmonella ealing infections associated with the consumption of infant dried milk. *Lancet*, 1987, 900-3.
8. Gill O N, Sockett P N, Bartlett C L R *et al*. Outbreak of *Salmonella napoli* infection caused by contaminated chocolate bars. *Lancet*, 1983, 574-7.
9. Snider D E Jr and Roper W L. The new Tuberculosis. *New England Journal Medicine* **326**, 1992,703-5.
10. Miller E, Vurdien J E and White J M. The epidemiology of pertussis in England and Wales. *Communicable Disease Report*, **2**, 1992, R152-4.

11. Maguire H, Heptonstall J and Begg N T. The epidemiology and control of hepatitis A. *Communicable Disease Report*, **2**, 1992, R114-17.
12. Office of Population Censuses and Surveys. *Communicable disease statistics 1991. Series MB2 no. 18*. HMSO (London 1993).
13. Abbott J D, Jones D M, Painter M J and Young S E J. The epidemiology of meningococcal infections in England and Wales, 1912–1983. *Journal Infectious Diseases*,11, 1985 241-57.
14. Jones D M and Kaczmarski E B. Meningococcal infections in England and Wales: 1991. *Communicable Disease Report*, **2,** 1992, R61-3.
15. Newton L, Hall S M, Pelerin M and McLauchlin J. Listeriosis surveillance. *Communicable Disease Report,* **2,** 1992, R142-4.
16. Anderson M J, Jones S E, Fisher Hoch S P *et al.* Human parvovirus, the cause of erythema infectiosum (fifth disease)? *Lancet*, 1983, 1378.
17. Karmali M A, Petric M, Lim C *et al.* The association between idiopathic hemolytic uremic syndrome and infection by verotoxin-producing *E. coli*. *Journal Infectious Diseases*, **151,** 1985, 775-82.
18. Steere A C, Malawista S E, Syndham D R *et al.* Lyme arthritis: an epidemic of oligoarticular arthritis in children and adults in three Connecticut communities. *Arthritis Rheumatism,* **20,** 1977, 7-17.
19 Anon. Lyme disease surveillance. *Communicable Disease Report,* **1,** 1991, 39.
20. Tyrrell D A J. The abolition of infection. Hope or illusion? The Rock Carling Fellowship,. Nuffield Provincial Hospitals Trust (London 1982).

Appendices

Appendix 1 Sources of data for monitoring child health

This section provides background information about the main sources of data for monitoring child health. Table 1 shows a full list of centrally available statistics on child health.

Birth registrations

Birth statistics are compiled from information collected at birth registration. Information is collected about sex of child, age of mother, whether within or outside marriage, parity if inside marriage, occupation of parents, place of birth of mother, date of birth, birthweight, place of birth, and usual address.

Births within marriage
Generally speaking a birth within marriage is that of a child born to parents who were lawfully married to one another either a) at the date of the child's birth, or b) when the child was conceived even if they became divorced or the father died before the birth. Only for a birth within marriage will the registrar enter onto the draft entry, confidential particulars relating to the date of the parents' marriage, whether the mother has been married before and the number of the mother's previous live and stillborn children.

Births outside marriage
The father's name and other particulars are recorded if the father is present at the birth registration. In 1992, 76 per cent of births registered outside marriage were registered jointly by both parents.

Parity
Information on previous live born and stillborn children is only available for women registering a birth within marriage.

Social class
Information on the occupation of the father is collected at the registration of a birth within marriage or jointly registered birth outside marriage but this is only coded on a 10 per cent sample of live births. Social class is derived from occupation and employment status. From 1982 to 1990 occupation was coded using the *1980 Classification of Occupations*. Occupation codes were allocated as far as possible to the Registrar General's social class used in the 1981 Census.

Social Class categories are:

I	Professional occupations
II	Managerial and technical
IIIN	Skilled occupations (non-manual)
IIIM	Skilled occupations (manual)
IV	Partly skilled occupations
V	Unskilled occupations

An 'other' category includes Armed Forces, students and those whose occupations are inadequately described.

Since 1986 the mother's occupation has been recorded at birth registration if she wishes. However by 1990 only 48 per cent of live birth records had a mother's occupation recorded.

Country of birth
Information about the country of birth of parents of children born in England and Wales has been recorded at birth registration since 1969. It should be noted that birth place does not necessarily equate to ethnic group.

Birthweight
Birthweight, recorded in grammes, has been provided to Registrars by District Health Authorities since 1975. Between 1983 and 1989 birthweight was recorded for 99.9 per cent of live births.

Death registrations

Infant deaths
Since 1975 infant death records have been linked to their corresponding birth records in order to obtain information about the baby's social and biological background. In addition to the limited amount of information collected at death registration, all the information described in the previous section is available from the birth registration rcord.

Deaths of infants are divided into five age-groups which are not mutually exclusive:

- stillbirths (babies born showing no signs of life after 24 completed weeks of gestation (prior to 1 October 1992 the gestation criterion was 28 completed weeks));
- perinatal deaths (stillbirths and deaths occurring in the first week of life);
- neonatal deaths (occurring in the first four weeks of life);
- postneonatal deaths (occurring from 28 days of life but within one year of birth);
- infant deaths (occurring in the first year of life).

In 1986 new stillbirth and neonatal death certificates were introduced in England and Wales which allow the certifier to include both maternal and fetal conditions which contributed equally to the death. These certificates follow the recommendations of the World Health Organisation (WHO) given in the ninth revision of the International Classification of Diseases. The causes of death are collected separately in the following categories:

(a) main diseases or conditions in fetus or infant;

(b) other diseases or conditions in fetus or infant;

(c) main maternal diseases or conditions affecting fetus or infant;

(d) other maternal diseases or conditions affecting fetus or infant;

(e) other relevant causes.

For deaths at older ages in infancy (and throughout the rest of life) the death certificate includes a detailed listing of causes of death:

1a Cause or condition directly leading to death.
1b Other disease or condition if any leading to (1a).
1c Other disease or condition if any leading to (1b).
2 Other significant conditions contributing to the death but not related to the disease or condition causing it.

Again, coding follows rules laid down by WHO. The general rule is that the condition entered alone on the lowest used line of Part 1 is the underlying cause of death unless it is highly improbable that this condition could have given rise to all the conditions entered above it.

Congenital malformations

The collection and notification of information on congenital malformations in England and Wales began in 1964 following the thalidomide epidemic. The aim was to detect any similar hazard more quickly. The main aim of the scheme is to detect changes in the frequency of reporting particular malformations. The secondary aim is to estimate the prevalence of these malformations.

Information about malformations is passed monthly to OPCS by each DHA using a standard notification form. Before 1995, the scheme included all babies where the malformation was observed or at or within 10 days of birth. The time limit was removed on January 1995. The DHA is informed if any significant rise in any monitored malformation is detected.

The scheme does provide the most extensive data on prevalence data available in England and Wales but there are deficiencies in its coverage: the scheme is voluntary and before 1995 it only covered congenital malformations identified up to 10 days after birth.

Census

In the 1991 Census 25 basic questions were asked. There were four additional questions to those asked in 1981. These related to ethnic group, limiting long-standing illness, term-time address of students and hours worked. The question on limited long-term illness was: 'Does the person have any long-term illness health problem or handicap which limits his/her daily activities or the work he/she can do?'

The 1991 Census was the first for which tables concerning children and young people were brought together in a separate topic report.[1] The analyses include information on age, sex, marital status (for those aged 16 and over) migration, long-term illness, ethnic group, housing characteristics, family type, tenure, economic activity (for those aged over 16), social class (defined by occupation) and qualification level.

OPCS Longitudinal Study

The Longitudinal Study (LS) was set up following the 1971 Census. A sample of about 1 per cent of the population was drawn from their Census records. Since 1971, the members of the LS have been followed, using flagging on the National Health Service Central Register (NHSCR), by linking data from birth and death registrations, from cancer registrations and by linking data from the 1981 and 1991 Censuses.

A birth to a mother included in the LS or the death of an LS member or the spouse of an LS member is noted. The NHSCR provides information on LS members entering or leaving England and Wales.

The LS sample is continually topped up with a sample of births registered in England and Wales and with a sample of migrants entering the NHSCR. Extra members are identified at each census.

The LS is a very rich source of data on patterns of family formation, birth intervals, ethnic populations, parity (within and outside marriage), infant death and stillbirth.

General Household Survey

The General Household Survey (GHS) is a large annual survey which has been conducted by the Social Survey Division of OPCS since 1971. In 1992, interviews were carried out in over 10,000 private households with more than 19,000 people aged 16 and over. Data about children in the household have also been collected.

Since 1971, the GHS has included questions on population and fertility, housing, health, employment and education. Within these areas the survey has tried to balance continuity and flexibility to meet changing policy demands. Ethnic origin has been collected since 1983.

Since 1979, questions on long-standing illness or disability and acute sickness have been included. The current wording is:

> Do you have any long-standing illness, disability or infirmity?

> [If YES] Does this illness or disability limit your activities in any way?

Acute sickness is defined as restriction of the level of normal activity because of injury or illness at any time during the two weeks before interview.

The GHS also includes questions about the utilisation of health services.

Tabulations include prevalence of acute sickness, long-standing illness, all and limiting, by age and sex. There are differences in the wording of this question and the 1991 Census question on long-term illness.

OPCS surveys of disability

The OPCS surveys of disability were commissioned in 1984.[2] Four separate surveys were carried out between 1985 and 1988, covering adults in private households, children in private households, adults in communal establishments and children in communal establishments.

The surveys focused on disability rather than health and health-related problems. Disability is defined as a restriction or lack of ability to perform normal activities, which has resulted from the impairment of a structure or function of the body or mind. The surveys attempted to cover all kinds of disability whatever their origin and used a relatively low threshold of disability to obtain information over a wide range of severity. The surveys distinguished 13 different kinds of disabilities based on categories in the International Classification of Impairments, Disabilities and Handicaps. The surveys also constructed an overall measure of severity which can be used to classify individuals with different numbers and types of disabilities. The children's surveys took account of the normal developmental age for achievement in assessing the severity of the disability.

Prevalence rates were estimated by age, sex, type of disability, severity and region.

Survey of smoking among secondary school children

The first of this series of surveys was carried out in 1982 to provide estimates of the proportion of pupils who smoked and to describe the smoking behaviour of those who did smoke. Similar surveys have been carried out every two years to provide further estimates from which trends in the prevalence of smoking amongst secondary school children can be monitored. In 1992[3] information was obtained from around 9,000 children; about 3,000 living in England, Wales and Scotland respectively. Questions were also asked about drinking behaviour and solvent abuse. An extra survey was carried out in England in 1993 and information was obtained from 3,140 pupils. The surveys were carried out amongst pupils aged 11-15 attending all types of school. A self-completion questionnaire asked about current smoking behaviour, frequency of smoking, purchase of cigarettes and smoking among other household members. A diary recording all cigarettes smoked during the previous seven days was completed and saliva samples taken from all pupils in half the sample schools.

Infant feeding survey

Infant feeding surveys have been carried out in 1975 in England and Wales, in 1980 and 1985 also covering Scotland, and in 1990 covering the whole of the United Kingdom.

In 1990[4] questionnaires were sent out to mothers when the babies were between six and ten weeks old, second stage questionnaires when they were four months old and a third stage questionnaire when the babies were at least nine months old. In total 9,064 births were selected in England, Wales and Scotland; 2,041 births were selected in Northern Ireland. The survey reported on the incidence and duration of breast-feeding, influences on the choice of method of feeding and weaning practices up to the age of nine months.

Children's dental health

The first survey of children's dental health was carried out by OPCS in 1973. Further studies were carried out in 1983 and 1993[5] in collaboration with the dental schools at the Universities of Birmingham and Newcastle; they covered the whole of the United Kingdom. The surveys involved a dental examination of all selected children and the collection of background information from the parents of a sample of the selected children. The criteria for examination was developed by the dental schools. They were designed to collect information that could be compared directly with that collected in the 1973 survey. However, in some areas of dental health, different methods of assessment had been developed since 1973 and these were included. Information was also collected on topics which had not been relevant in 1973.

Examinations were made on almost 21,000 children. Parents of just under 7,000 children in the sample aged 5, 8, 12 and 15 years completed a postal questionnaire covering the child's dental history, the parent's attitudes towards dental health and their children's teeth, current dental practices and the parents' own dental status and social class.

The surveys reported on the condition of children's teeth, comparisons between 1973, 1983 and 1993 in dental decay, treatment and care, and orthodontic assessments. Accidental damage to teeth was also reported.

References

1. OPCS/GRO(S). *1991 Census Children and Young Adults in Great Britain*, HMSO (London 1994).
2. Bone M and Meltzer H. *OPCS Surveys of Disability in Great Britain. Report 3 The prevalence of disability amongst children*. HMSO (London 1989).
3. Thomas M, Holroyd S and Goddard E. *Smoking amongst secondary school children in 1992*. HMSO (London 1993).
4. White A, Freeth S and O'Brien M. *Infant feeding 1990*. HMSO (London 1994).
5. O'Brien M. *Children's dental health in the United Kingdom 1993*, HMSO (London 1994).

Table 1 Centrally available statistics on child health

Indicators	Description of data available	Publication	First available	Frequency
Stillbirths	Numbers and rates by sex, month of occurrence, cause, place of confinement, gestation, birthweight, area	DH3, Mortality – perinatal and infant DH6, Mortality – childhood	1975	Annual
Early neonatal deaths	Numbers by sex, cause, month of occurrence, area			
Perinatal deaths	Rates by sex, cause, month of occurrence and area			
All infant deaths	Numbers and rates by sex, age group, cause, month of occurrence and area			
Stillbirths Perinatal deaths Neonatal deaths Post-neonatal deaths All infant deaths Live births	Linking of information from birth and death registration allows a wide range of tabulations by age of mother, parity, legitimacy, social class, country of birth of mother, month of birth and birthweight	DH3, Mortality – perinatal and infant	1975	Annual
Trends in infant mortality	Deaths, numbers and rates, from selected causes in infants under one year are given for each of the previous 10 years	DH3, Mortality – perinatal and infant	1975	Annual
Birthweight	Since 1975 birthweight provided by health authorities has been added to birth registrations. This process has been virtually complete since 1983. Mortality of infants of different birthweights can be monitored as described above. In addition the birthweight of all livebirths can be tabulated by social class, age of mother, parity, and country of birth	DH3, Mortality – perinatal and infant	1975	Annual
Low birthweight babies	Number, number of deaths by time of death	DH Summary (Form LHS27/1)	1953	Annual to 1987
Childhood deaths at ages: 1, 2, 3, 4, 5–9, 10–14 and all ages under 15	Number of deaths by sex for each cause	DH3, Mortality – perinatal and infant	1975	Annual
Childhood deaths at ages: under 1, 1–4, 5–14	a) Rates per million population from principal causes for boys and girls	DH2, Mortality – cause		Annual
	b) Also for each administrative and health area	DH5 fiche, Mortality – area		Annual
	c) Numbers and rates are published in more detail for deaths due to accidents and violence, e.g. accidents at home, road traffic accidents	DH4, Mortality – accidents and violence		Annual
	d) Detailed analysis of childhood deaths in terms of rates, SMRs and PMRs by parents' social class based on occupation, socioeconomic group and occupation order	DS no. 8 – Occupational Mortality, Childhood Supplement	1959–63	Ten-yearly
Glue sniffing deaths at ages 10, 11, 12, 13, 14	Estimates of deaths related to glue sniffing by sex	Series of reports from St George's Hospital Medical School	1971	Annual
Cancer registration rates for children aged under 1, 1–4, 5–9, 10–14	Numbers and rates by sex and site	MB1 – general mortality	1962	Annual
	More details from the National Registry for Childhood Tumours	Series of publications and regular reports to DH on incidence and survival	1962	Annual
Rare childhood disorders, e.g. AIDS, diabetes, galactosaemia, drowning and near drowning, Reye's syndrome	Notification of specific diseases by paediatricians to the British Paediatric Surveillance Unit – follow-up for clinical and epidemiological study	BPSU annual reports	1986	Annual

Table 1 - *continued*

Indicators	Description of data available	Publication	First available	Frequency
Notifications of malformations identified in live births or stillbirth	Rates per 10,000 births by condition, age of mother	MB3 – Congenital malformations	1964	Annual
Dental health at single years of age 5–15	Proportion of children with active decay, filled teeth, extractions, gum condition, crowding. Based on survey and dental examinations	Children's dental health in the UK 1973, 1983 and 1993	1973	Repeated ad hoc survey
Dental treatments to children aged 0–4, 5–9, 10–14	Numbers provided from the General Dental Service and the Community dental service – covers fillings, extractions, etc.	Dental practice board reports	1948	Annual
Prescriptions dispensed in general practice to children aged 0–15	Numbers from the Prescription Pricing Authority	Statistical Bulletin DH	1977	Annual
Conceptions to girls aged under 14, 14, 15	Numbers and rates of conceptions and proportions ending in births and terminations	Birth statistics	1968	Annual
Live and stillbirths to girls aged 11, 12, 13, 14, 15	Numbers of births	Birth statistics		Annual
Abortions to girls aged under 15, 15	Number of abortions	AB – Abortion statistics	1968	Annual
Children in need of protection	Numbers from local authority registers by age, sex, category of abuse, legal status and whether in care	DH publication	1987-88	Annual
Height, weight for children aged 10-11, 14-15	Mean heights and weights by age and sex	The diets of British schoolchildren, DHSS/OPCS	1983	Ad hoc survey
Height, weight, anthropometry for children aged 5–9	Means and distributions obtained from a large sample of schoolchildren followed up through primary school	St Thomas's survey of height and growth	1979	Annual/ continuous
Birthweight	See above			
Diets of schoolchildren aged 10-11, 14-15	Intakes of main nutrients by height, weight, age, sex, social class based on parents' occupation, family type	The diets of British schoolchildren, DHSS/OPCS	1983	Ad hoc survey
Infant feeding at ages up to nine months	Proportion of babies breast and/or bottle fed at different ages by age of mother, social class based on parents' occupation, education, region	Infant feeding reports 1975, 1980, 1985	1975	Five-yearly surveys
Smoking among children aged 11, 12, 13, 14, 15	Prevalence of different levels of smoking by sex	Smoking among secondary school children in 1982, 1984, 1986, 1988	1982	Two-yearly surveys
		Smoking among secondary school children in England in 1988	1988	Repeated questions
Drinking among children aged 13, 14, 15	Prevalence of different levels of drinking by sex	Adolescent drinking	1984	Ad hoc survey
Vaccination and immunisation for diphtheria, tetanus, polio, whooping cough, measles, mumps and rubella	Uptake rates for completed primary courses in different years of life	DH Summaries (Form SBL607/ KC51)	1950	Annual
Rubella immunisation for schoolgirls aged 10, 11, 12, 13, 14, 15	Uptake and cumulative uptake rate as a percentage of the schoolgirl population	DH Summaries (Form SBL607/ KC51)	1950	Annual
TB tests and BCG vaccinations	Numbers tested, found positive and negative and vaccinated	DH Summaries (Form SBL655/ KC50)	1971	Annual

Source: Dunnell K. Monitoring childrens health. *Population Trends* **60**, 1990, 16-22

List of tables and figures

Tables

table no		page

Chapter 1

1.1 Population of children aged under 20 and life expectancy by sex: 1841-1991, England and Wales — 2

1.2 Mortality rates by age and sex: 1841-1991, England and Wales — 3

1.3 Stillbirth and infant mortality rates: 1931-91, England and Wales — 4

1.4 Percentage survival to 1991 of boys born since 1950, England and Wales — 6

1.5 Percentage survival to 1991 of girls born since 1950, England and Wales — 7

Chapter 4

4.1 Measures of birthweight over time, England and Wales — 29

4.2 Mean birthweight and percentage low birthweight by sociodemographic factors for live births: 1989, England and Wales — 31

4.3 Summary of selected factors associated with birthweight in the 1970 birth cohort — 33

4.4 Mean increase in height from 1972 to 1979 before and after adjusting for social and biological variables — 35

4.5 Mean height and BMI in British 16-24-year-olds — 35

4.6 Average BMI by social class for 16-19-years-olds — 39

Chapter 5

5.1 Activity of 16-24-year olds in the National Fitness Survey: 1990, England — 48

5.2 Participation in sports of 16-19 year olds; 1987 and 1990, Great Britain — 48

5.3 Reported drinking among 13-15 year olds: comparison of 1984 survey of adolescent drinking in England and Wales and 1990 survey of school-children's smoking in England — 53

5.4 Type of drinker among 16-17 and 18-24 year olds by sex: 1987 and 1989 combined, England and Wales — 53

5.5 Contraception use among 16-19-year-old women: 1983-89, Great Britain — 55

5.6 Outcome of conceptions inside and outside marriage by age of women at conception: 1979-91 (selected years), England and Wales — 56

5.7 Fertility rates per 1,000 women aged under 20 for selected countries: 1966-91 (selected years) — 56

5.8 Legal abortion rates for women aged under 20 and all women, for countries for which data or estimates are available — 57

Chapter 6

6.1 Stillbirth and infant mortality rates by sex: 1971-91, England and Wales — 62

6.2 Childhood mortality rates (per 100,000 population) by sex and age: 1971-91, England and Wales — 63

6.3 Mortality of children aged 1-15 years SMRs (all causes) by age, sex and social class : 1979-80, 82-83, England and Wales — 63

6.4 Infant mortality rates by social class (based on father's occupation): 1981 and 1991, England and Wales — 64

6.5 Infant mortality rates by mother's social class (as defined by occupation): 1986-90 combined, England and Wales — 64

6.6 Mortality rates (per 100,000 live births/population) by age: 1989-91 combined, England, and Wales — 65

6.7 Proportional distribution of main causes of death by sex and age: 1981 and 1991, England and Wales — 66

6.8 Percentages of children using health services by sex and age: 1981, 1991, Great Britain — 69

6.9 Children consulting (rates per 10,000 person years at risk) by type of condition: 1991/92, England and Wales — 69

6.10 Percentage of children immunised by their second birthday: 1981-1991/2, England and Wales — 75

6.11 Number of general anaesthetics performed by Community Dentists in 1980 and 1989/90, — 76

6.12 Children on Child Protection Registers:1989-91, England — 77

6.13 Infant and child mortality by sex and age: international comparisons 1991, — 78

6.14 Infant and childhood mortality (rates per 100,00 live births/population): 1971, 1981 and 1991, European Union countries — 79

Chapter 7

7.1 Ethnic composition of children aged 0 to 14 years in England and Wales — 84

7.2 Live births and total period fertility rates by mother's country of birth: 1981, 1986, and 1991, England and Wales — 84

7.3 Standardised mortality ratios (SMR) by country of birth: 1979-83 combined, England and Wales — 89

7.4 Odds ratios for GP consultations, in-patient admissions and out-patient attendance, adjusted for age and socioeconomic group, by ethnic origin for children aged 0-15 years — 92

Chapter 8

8.1 Childhood accident death rates (per 100,000 population) by regional health authorities in England and Wales: 1975-91 — 98

8.2 Accident deaths (numbers) by cause, age and sex: 1971-91, England and Wales — 100

8.3 Childhood accidental injury in Newcastle upon Tyne: admission rates per 10,000 population 1986 and 1990 — 107

8.4 International comparisons of child accidental injury — 108

Chapter 9

9.1 Trends in childrens' consulting rates per 1,000 for various respiratory diagnoses in three national morbidity surveys at ages 0-14 years — 118

9.2 Children consulting, per 1,000 in 1981/82 at ages 0-15 years, by parental social class and diagnosis — 118

9.3 Rates of hospital admission (per 10,000) and mortality (per million) for pneumonia (ICD 480-486) by hospital region of England and Wales for children aged 0-14 years: 1979-85 combined — 121

page

9.4 Risk factors for pneumonia from birth to age 7 in the 1958 birth cohort 122

9.5 Rates of hospital admission (per 10,000) and mortality (per million) for asthma (ICD 493) by hospital region of England and Wales for children aged 0-14 years: 1979-85 combined 124

9.6 Risk factors for hay fever or allergic rhinitis at age 11 in the 1958 birth cohort 126

9.7 Postneonatal mortality rates (per 100,000 live births) by cause and social class (based on father's occupation) for births inside marriage only: 1988-91 combined, England and Wales 131

Chapter 10

10.1 Childhood cancer incidence by site, age 0-14 years: 1971-80 combined, England and Wales 136

10.2 Childhood cancer incidence for main histological groups, age 0-14 years: 1971-80 combined, England and Wales 136

10.3 Lymphocytic and unspecified leukaemias: 1969-83, Great Britain 139

10.4 Age-standardised incidence rates for the major types of childhood cancer in selected population-based registries 139

10.5 Childhood deaths, all causes:1971-90, England and Wales 141

10.6 Childhood deaths all neoplasms: 1971-90, England and Wales 142

10.7 Childhood deaths all leukaemias: 1971-90, England and Wales 142

10.8 Percentages of childhood deaths due to neoplasms: 1971-90, England and Wales 143

10.9 Five-year actuarial survival rates for children diagnosed in successive 3-year periods: 1971-85, Great Britain 144

Chapter 11

11.1 Congenital malformation: 1971-91, England and Wales 150

11.2 Medical grounds for legal abortions, numbers: 1979-91, England and Wales 152

11.3 Congenital malformations: 1987-91 combined, regional health authorities in England and Wales 154

11.4 All babies notified (rates per 10,000 total births) by age of mother and condition: 1987-91 combined, England and Wales 156

13.1 Deaths by infectious disease and age group: 1992, Englan and Wales 169

13.2 Notifications of infectious disease: 1992, England and Wales 169

Figures

Chapter 1

1.1 Population pyramids of population aged under 20 by sex: 1841-91 (selected years), England and Wales 2

1.2 Fertility rates: 1838-1991, England and Wales 3

1.3 Mortality rates for boys by age: 1841-1991, England and Wales 4

1.4 Mortality rates for girls by age: 1841-1991, England and Wales 4

1.5 Stillbirth and infant mortality rates: 1931-91, England and Wales 4

1.6 Percentage survival to 1991 of boys born since 1950, England and Wales 5

1.7 Percentage survival to 1991 of girls born since 1950, England and Wales 5

page

Chapter 2

2.1 Total period fertility rate: 1961-91, England and Wales 9

2.2 Age-specific fertility rates: 1961-91, England and Wales 10

2.3 Marital status of lone mothers: 1971 and 1991, Great Britain 11

2.4 Economic activity rates for women aged under 60: 1951-91, Great Britain 12

2.5 Economic activity of women of working age with youngest child aged under five years: 1973-91, Great Britain 13

2.6 Male and female unemployment: 1959-91, UK unadjusted 15

2.7 Education and labour force market status of young people aged 16: 1974-90, Great Britain 18

Chapter 4

4.1 Infant mortality by birthweight: 1989-91 (combined), England and Wales 29

4.2 Proportion of live births with very low birthweight (<1500 g) and heavier birthweight (<3500 g): 1975-91, England and Wales and Scotland 30

4.3 Median birthweight (g) for singletons, live plus stillbirths, for selected countries: 1970-88 30

4.4 Main factors influencing birthweight: summary of inter-relationships 32

4.5 Factors influencing height: summary of inter-relationships 36

4.6 Factors influencing weight-for-height: summary of inter-relationships 38

Chapter 5

5.1 Breastfeeding at 3 months: 1920-86, England 43

5.2 Proportion of infants put to the breast at birth and proportions of infants being breast fed at 6 weeks by social class of husband: Great Britain 1990 43

5.3 Percentage of schoolchildren aged 11, 13 and 15 who exercised four or more hours a week outside school: 1989-90, selected countries 46

5.4 Frequency of participation in games or activities outside school in Welsh schoolchildren 1986-88 47

5.5 Weekly time (minutes) spent taking exercise:children aged 11-18 by sex and age: Northern Ireland 47

5.6 Regular smoking in children aged 11 - 15 years: 1982-90, England 49

5.7 Cigarette smoking among 16-19 year olds by sex: 1972-90, Great Britain 49

5.8 Cross-national comparison of smoking in school-aged children: 1989-90 50

5.9 Prevalence of cigarette smoking among 16-19 year olds by sex and by socio-economic group of head of household: 1990, Great Britain 51

5.10 Drivers of cars and other motor vehicles: percentage of fatalities in excess of 80 mg/100ml blood alcohol level by age: 1980-90, Great Britain 52

5.11 Volatile substances abuse mortality rates for 15-19 year olds by sex: 1983-91, United Kingdom 54

5.12 Conception rates for teenage women: 1969-91, England and Wales 55

Chapter 6

6.1 Mortality (all causes) of children aged 1-15 years SMRs by age, sex and social class: 1979-80, 1982-3, England and Wales 63

6.2 Infant mortality by social class (for births within marriage): 1981 and 1991, England and Wales 64

6.3 Main causes of childhood mortality by age and sex: 1991, England and Wales 67

6.4 Neonatal deaths by cause classification: 1986-91, England and Wales 68

6.5 Trends in morbidity by age and category: 1981-91, Great Britain 68

page

6.6 Percentage distribution of GP consultations by age and cause: 1991/2, England and Wales 69

6.7 Percentage distribution of admissions to hospital by age and cause: 1985, England and Wales 70

6.8 Prevalence of disability by age and sex: 1985, Great Britain 70

6.9 Estimates of prevalence of disability among children: 1985, Great Britain 70

6.10 Proportion of maternities resulting in a triplet or higher order birth: 1938-91, England and Wales 71

6.11 Birthweight-specific infant mortality rates: 1982-91, England and Wales 71

6.12 Impairment rates in low birthweight survivors: 1979-81 combined, in Mersey, England 72

6.13 Neonatal survivors of under 1,501 grams: 1967-83 (three-year moving average) Mersey, England 72

6.14 Cumulative postneonatal deaths by selected causes: 1963-91, England and Wales 72

6.15 Cancer mortality and incidence by sex: 1971-88, England and Wales 73

6.16 Mortality of children aged 1-15 years from external causes of injury and poisoning (ICD E800-E999): SMRs by social class and sex: 1979-80, 1982-83, England and Wales 74

6.17 Deaths and notifications of measles: 1971-92, England and Wales 75

6.18 Immunisation rates for selected infectious diseases: 1981-92/93, England 76

6.19 Notifications of whooping cough (OPCS) and new episodes of whooping cough reported to Royal College of General Practitioners(RCGP): 1976-91, England and Wales 76

6.20 Proportion of children with decay experience in the permanent dentition: 1983 and 1993, United Kingdom 76

6.21 Infant mortality: 1971, 1981 and 1991, European Union countries 79

Chapter 7

7.1 Age composition by ethnic group: 1991, England and Wales 83

7.2 Ethnic composition of the population aged 0-14: 1991, England and Wales 84

7.3 Perinatal mortality by mother's country of birth: 1989-91 combined, England and Wales 85

7.4 Perinatal mortality by (a) mother's age and (b) parity for mothers born in the UK and the Indian subcontinent: 1989-91 combined, England and Wales 85

7.5 Perinatal mortality by social class and mother's country of birth: 1989-91 combined, England and Wales 86

7.6 Percentage birthweight distribution (total births) by mother's country of birth: 1991, England and Wales 86

7.7 Trends in perinatal mortality by mother's country of birth: 1976-90, England and Wales 87

7.8 Neonatal mortality by mother's country of birth: 1989-91 combined, England and Wales 87

7.9 Postneonatal mortality by mother's country of birth: 1989-91 combined, England and Wales 87

7.10 Infant deaths and stillbirths from congenital anomalies by mother's country of birth: 1981-85 combined, England and Wales 88

7.11 Infant deaths and stillbirths from congenital anomalies in infants of mothers born in Pakistan: 1981-85 combined, England and Wales 88

7.12 Sudden infant deaths by mother's country of birth: 1982-85 combined, England and Wales 88

7.13 Causes of childhood mortality: 1979-83 combined, England and Wales 90

Chapter 8

8.1 Childhood mortality due to accidents and violence by age and sex: 1968-91 96

page

8.2 SMRs for accidents and violence by social class: 1970-71 97

8.3 International child death rates from injuries by age: 1985 98

8.4 International child pedestrian death rates: 1991 99

8.5 Iceberg of all injuries occurring to children over time 99

8.6 Hospital discharge rates for injury and poisoning by age and sex: 1968-91, England and Wales 104

8.7 Deaths and injuries resulting from road traffic accidents by age and outcome: 1975-91, Great Britain 105

8.8 All accidents and emergency attendances: 1990, Newcastle upon Tyne 109

8.9 Hospital admissions for severe childhood accidents: 1990, Newcastle upon Tyne 109

8.10 Use of safety equipment by parents of 3-year -old children, Newcastle upon Tyne 110

Chapter 9

9.1 Contribution of respiratory diseases to GP consultations, admissions and deaths 114

9.2 Respiratory mortality in childhood: relative importance of main conditions 114

9.3 Respiratory admissions in childhood: relative importance of main conditions 114

9.4 GP consultations for respiratory disease: relative importance of main conditions 115

9.5 Mortality for respiratory diseases among children aged under 1 year by sex: 1958-91, England and Wales 115

9.6 Mortality for respiratory diseases among 1-4 year old children by sex: 1958-90, England and Wales 116

9.7 Mortality for respiratory diseases among 5-14 year old children by sex: 1958-91, England and Wales 116

9.8 Mortality for respiratory diseases among children aged under 1 year by type of disease: 1958-91, England and Wales 116

9.9 Mortality for respiratory diseases among children aged 1-4 years by type of disease: 1958-91, England and Wales 117

9.10 Mortality for respiratory diseases among children aged 5-14 years by type of disease: 1958-91, England and Wales 117

9.11 Hospital admissions for lower respiratory conditions among 1-4 year old children: 1962-85, England and Wales 118

9.12 Hospital admissions for lower respiratory conditions among 5-14 year old children: 1962-85, England and Wales 118

9.13 Mortality for diseases of lower respiratory system among children aged 1-15 years 119

9.14 Infant mortality by main causes of death and mother's country of birth: 1982-85 combined, England and Wales 120

9.15 Percentage prevalence of wheeze and of a diagnosis of asthma 125

9.16 Numbers of deaths in ICD categories for cystic fibrosis: 1959-86, England and Wales 127

9.17 Median, 25th and 75th centile ages at death from cystic fibrosis by year of death: 1959-86, England and Wales 128

9.18 Median age at death from cystic fibrosis by year of death and sex: 1959-86, England and Wales 128

9.19 Median age at death from cystic fibrosis whether non-manual or manual social class: 1970-86, England and Wales 128

9.20 Ranking of region of residence by independent odds ratios for death at above median age for the year of death: 1974-86, regions of England, and Wales 129

9.21 Postneonatal, respiratory and SIDs mortality (rate per 1,000 live births): 1971-92, England and Wales 130

Chapter 10

10.1 Acute lymphocytic leukaemia and unspecified leukaemias: incidence rates for single year age groups: 1971-84, Great Britain 138

10.2 Neuroblastoma and ganglioneuroblastoma: incidence rates for single year age groups: 1971-84, Great Britain 138

10.3 Wilms' tumour: incidence rates for single year age groups: 1971-84, Great Britain 138

10.4 Retinoblastoma: incidence rates for single year age groups: 1971-84, Great Britain 138

10.5 Hodgkin's disease: incidence rates for single year age groups: 1971-84, Great Britain 138

10.6 Osteosarcoma: incidence rates for single year age groups: 1971-84, Great Britain 138

10.7 Trends in incidence rates for acute lymphocytic leukaemia: 1954-91, Great Britain 140

10.8 Trends in incidence rates for brain and spinal tumours: 1962-91, Great Britain 141

10.9 Deaths at ages 0-14 from neoplasms: 1971-90, England and Wales 143

10.10 Five-year survival rates for leukaemias and lymphomas: 1971-85, Great Britain 145

10.11 Five-year survival rates for brain tumours: 1971-85, Great Britain 145

10.12 Five-year survival rates for embryonal tumours: 1971-85, Great Britain 145

10.13 Five-year survival rates for sarcomas: 1971-85, Great Britain 145

Chapter 11

11.1 Infant mortality due to congenital malformations: 1970-91, England and Wales 152

11.2 Notification rates of anencephalus, other central nervous system malformations, and legal abortions due to central nervous system malformations in fetus: 1969-91, England and Wales 153

Chapter 12

12.1 Drug misuse: admissions of persons under 20 years of age to mental illness hospitals: 1981-85, United Kingdom 162

12.2 Alcohol-related road deaths: percentage of 16-19 year old drivers and riders killed who were over the legal blood alcohol limit: 1979-92, Great Britain 163

12.3 Suicide rates by age and sex: 1974-92, England and Wales 164

12.4 Males found guilty of, or cautioned for, indictable offences per 100,000 population by age group: 1970-92, England and Wales 165

12.5 Females found guilty of, or cautioned for, indictable offences per 100,000 population by age group: 1970-92, England and Wales 165

Chapter 13

13.1 Poliomyelitis notifications: 1912-92, England and Wales 171

13.2 Measles quarterly notifications: 1955-92, England and Wales 171

13.3 Respiratory tuberculosis notifications: 1913-92, England and Wales 172

13.4 Whooping cough notifications - cases and deaths: 1940-92, England and Wales 173

13.5 Scarlet fever notifications: 1938-92, England and Wales 173

13.6 Viral hepatitis quarterly notifications and laboratory reports: 1975-93, England and Wales 174

Index

Page numbers in *italics* and **bold** refer to illustrations and tables respectively that appear away from the relevant text. Particular age groups of children will be found under *infants; preschool children; primary school children; school children; young adults*, where specific data have been mentioned. Otherwise entries refer to all sets of children. Specific countries are either mentioned or will be found under entries for *ethnic groups or international comparisons.*

abortion
    after prenatal diagnosis of congenital malformations 149-53
    in teenagers 56-57
abuse and neglect 77
accidents 95-112
    alcohol consumption and 52
    causes 104-7
    counter-measures 106-7
    deaths 74, 95-99, **100-3**
        in ethnic groups 89
        infants 65
    in ethnic groups 91
    high injury rates 105-6
    'iceberg' 99
    mental health and 161
    non-fatal 99-104
    scale of problem 95
    see also specific types e.g. poisoning
advertising of tobacco effects 51
African-born *see* ethnic groups
Afro-Caribbean *see* ethnic groups
age data
    accident mortality 95-97
    cancer **136**
    congenital malformations 155-6
    cystic fibrosis 127-8
    disability *70*
    ethnic groups *83*
    health service use *69, 70*
    morbidity and *68*
    mortality 3, *4*, 62-64, 66, *67*, **78**
        infant, in ethnic groups 88
    smoking 51
    sudden infant deaths 131
    suicide *164*
    see also maternal age
AIDS 54, *57*, 175
alcohol consumption 51-53
    factors influencing 53
    international comparisons 53
    mental health and 162-3
    trends over time 52
allergic rhinitis 125-6
    risk factors 126
anaemia in ethnic groups 90
anaesthetic gases, congenital malformations and 154
anaesthetics in dentistry **76**
anencephaly 149, *153*, 156
anorexia nervosa 160
antenatal care uptake by ethnic groups 91
antibiotics for infectious diseases 170
anticonvulsant drugs effects on congenital malformations 155

Asian-born *see* ethnic groups
asthma 123-5
    burden 123
    cause 125
    in ethnic groups 91
    GP consultations 124
    hospital admissions *118*, 121, 123-4
    mental health and 161
    mortality 115, 117, 123
    regional variations 123
    trends in prevalence 124-5
Australia, infant mortality 78

B19 infection 175
Bangladeshi-born *see under* ethnic groups
bed and breakfast accommodation 17
behaviour, health-related 42-60
behavioural difficulties 159, 160
biological variables affecting height and growth 36
births
    to ethnic group mothers 83
    order influencing birthweight 33
    registrations, compulsory 1
        statistics 178
    outside marriage 178
        related to fertility rates 10-11
    within marriage 178
birthweight 28-33
    affecting height and growth 35
    ethnic groups 86
    factors influencing 30-33
    impact on mortality and morbidity 71
    international comparisons 29-30
    statistics 178
    trends over time 28-29
black children population size 83
Boarding School Line 25
Body Mass Index 37
borreliosis 175
bottle-feeding, respiratory diseases 122
boys *see* sex
brain tumours 135, *141*, *145*
breast-feeding
    affecting behaviour 42-44
    respiratory diseases 122, 126
    sudden infant deaths 131
    surveys 180
bronchiolitis 120
bronchitis 120-23
    GP consultations 121
    hospital admissions *118*, 121
    long-term consequences 123
    mortality 121
        in infants *116*, 117
Brook Advisory Centre 25
bulimia 160
Bullying Line 25
Burkitt's lymphoma 140
burns 105
    deaths from *96*, *97*, **102-3**

campylobacter infections 175
Canada
    height and growth of children 34
    infant mortality 78

cancer 73, 135-47
    aetiology 137-41
    classification 135, **136**
    incidence 135-41
    international comparisons 139-40
    mortality 141-43
        in ethnic groups 89
        infants 65
    survival rates 143-4, *145*
    time trends 140-1
    types 135
Caribbean-born *see under* ethnic groups
Census 179
cerebral palsy risk 71
child care in Britain 12-13
Child Protection Registers **77**
childbearing, employment consequences 13-14
Childline 25
Children Act 1989 18, 22
China, infant mortality 78
chip consumption 44
chlamydiasis 170
chromosomal abnormalities 148
Clearinghouse 156
cleft lip/palate 74, 154-5
CNS malformations 74
    abortions for 153
    notifications 149
cohabitation rates related to fertility rates 10-11
confidentiality 25
congenital anomalies 148-58
    abortion following diagnosis 149-53
    ethnic groups 90
    international comparisons 156
    monitoring system 148-9
    morbidity 74
    mortality from 74, 87-88, 89, 149
    notification rate trends 149, **150-1**
    statistics 178
congenital syphilis 170
consent to treatment 24
consumerism 17
contraception 55
contraceptive pill
    effects on congenital malformations 155
    social effects 18
country of birth
    as ethnic origin proxy 83
    of mother *see under* maternal statistics 178
crime 164-5
croup 120
cyclist accidents 105, 106, 107
    deaths **100-1**
cystic fibrosis 127-30
    definition 127
    frequency 127
    mortality 127-30

data sources for child health monitoring 178-82
death *see* mortality
delinquency 164-5
demographic changes 8-20
Denmark
    child care 12
    fertility rates 11
    height and growth of children 37
dental health 76
    surveys 180

Department of Transport RTA Surveillance
     System 105
depression 159, 160
diet
     affecting behaviour 42-45
     affecting birthweight 33
     affecting congenital malformations 155
     affecting height and growth 34
     disorders in ethnic group 90
     infant mortality in ethnic groups and 89
     weight-for-height and 39
dieting 44, 45
diphtheria 76, 170
disability 70-71
     alcohol consumption and 52
     surveys 180
disease
     influence of birthweight on 33
     see also infectious diseases
divorce
     effect on children 14
     fertility rates and 11-12
Divorce Reform Act 1969 11
Down's syndrome 74
     incomplete reporting 149
     maternal age 156
     regional variations in screening 152
driving accidents see road traffic accidents
drowning 96, 97, **102-3**
drug
     misuse, mental health and 162-3
     effect on congenital malformations 155

East African-born see ethnic groups
eating problems 160
economic changes 8-20
eczema 126
education changes 17-18
Egypt, infant mortality 78
embryonal tumours 145
emotional problems 160
employment
     changes 17-18
     experiences, alcohol consumption and 53
     fertility rates and 12
     see also unemployment
Employment Protection Act 1975 13
environmental factors
     asthma and 125
     birthweight and 30
     cancer and 137
     changes for children 17
     congenital malformations and 153
epilepsy, mental health and 161
ethnic groups
     accident mortality 98
     birthweight and **31**, 33
     cancer 140
     congenital malformations 156
     economic activity of women 14
     family composition 11
     fertility rates 9
     health of children 82-94
          methodological issues 82-83
     health services uptake 91-92
     height and growth 35
     mental health 160-1
     morbidity 90-91
     mortality 85-90
     population size 83, 84
     respiratory diseases 117, 119, 120, 125
     weight-for-height 38
European Union
     fertility rates 9, 11
     mortality and morbidity 77, **79-80**
Ewing's sarcoma 137, 140

family
     changes in circumstances of children
          14-17
     disruptions, mental health and 161
     dissolution and reconstitution, fertility
          rates and 11-12
          impact on children 14-17
          labour market participation and 12
     life, mental health and 166
     size, affecting height and growth 34, 35
          impact on child health 10
Family Credit 14
Family Income Support 14
Family Law Reform Act 1969 25
Family Law Reform Act 1987 11
famine influencing birthweight 33
fat intake affecting behaviour 44
fertility rates
     changes 9-12
     impact of 1, 3-7
     in teenagers 55-56
fire see burns
folic acid, congenital malformations and 145
food poisoning 170, 174-5
France, child care 12
fruit and vegetable intake 44-45

ganglioneuroblastoma 138
General Household Survey 179-80
general practitioner
     access by children 23
     consultations 69
          for accidents 74, 99
          by ethnic groups 91
          for respiratory diseases 114, 115, 117,
          118, 121, 124, 126
          for violence 74
generation size related to fertility rates 10
genetic factors
     affecting birthweight 30
     affecting height and growth 36
     in cancer 137
     in congenital anomalies 148
genital herpes 170
gestational age influencing birthweight 32, **33**
girls see sex
Great Britain, physical activity of children 48
haemolytic uraemic syndrome 175
haemorrhagic colitis 175
handicapped children treated as responsible
          people 25
hay fever 125-7
     risk factors 126
hazard
     exposure studies 106
     removal studies 106-7
health
     care resources for children 21-27
          access 23
          assessment 24-25
          experience 23-24
          mental disorders 159
          at school 23
          uptake by ethnic groups 91-92
          use 69
     education from school 22
     -related behaviour 42-60
          social norms 22
height of adults 34
     as attribute in Britain 36
height and growth of children 34-37
     factors influencing 35-36
     international comparisons 35
     trends over time 34-35
height of mother influencing birthweight 32, **33**

hepatitis 174
hereditary diseases, mortality and morbidity 74
HIV 54, 170, 175
Hodgkin's disease 138, 140
Home accident surveillance system/leisure acci-
          dent surveillance 104-5
Home Office fire statistics 105
home ownership 16
homelessness 16-17, 19
hormonal therapy for height increase 36
hospital
     admissions 69, 70
          for accidents 74, 99, 106, 107, 109
          for respiratory diseases 114, 117, 118,
          121, 122, 123-4
          for violence 74
     experiences 24
     out-patient services, uptake by ethnic
          groups 91-92
          uptake by children 25
     services uptake by ethnic groups 91
house prices
     fertility rates and 9
     income and 16
household amenities 16
housing 16
Housing Support 19
human parvovirus 175
hydrocephaly 149
hyperactivity 160

illness, long-standing 65
immunisations 74-75, 76, 170
     uptake in ethnic groups 91
immunoglobulin prophylaxis for infectious
          diseases 170
income gaps 15-16
Income Support 15, 18-19
Indian-born see under ethnic groups
infant feeding surveys 180
infant mortality **4**, 61-62, 130
     accidents 95
     causes 87-89
          classification 68
     congenital malformations 149, 152
     ethnic groups 87
     international comparisons **78, 79**
     related to birthweight 28, 71
     respiratory diseases 115, 116
     statistics 178-9
infectious diseases 168-76
     classification 168
     incidence changes 169-70
          declining 170-3
          new or increasing 174-5
          varying 174
     mortality and morbidity 74-75
     notifications **169**
     sources of data 168
infertility from cancer 144
inherited disorders in ethnic groups 90
injury see accidents
International Classification of Diseases E
          codes 104
International Clearinghouse for Birth Defects
          Monitoring 156
international comparisons
     abortion rates 56-57
     accident mortality 98, 99
     alcohol consumption 53
     birthweight 29-30
     cancer 139-40
     congenital anomalies 156
     height and growth 35
     mortality and morbidity 77-80
     physical activity 46, 48
     smoking 49-50

suicide and parasuicide 163-4
weight-for-height 37-38
ionising radiation, cancer and 137
iron intake 44
iron-deficiency in ethnic groups 90

Japan
birthweights 29
infant mortality 78

laboratory work, congenital malformations and 154
labour market participation see employment; unemployment
laryngitis, GP consultations 121
laryngotracheobronchitis 120
learning difficulties 160
leukaemia 135, **139**
acute lymphocytic 137, *138*, 140
causes 137
mortality **142**, 143
survival *145*
life expectancy 1
by sex 2
life-style
factors causing asthma 125
mental health and 166
role in behaviour 57
limb reduction defects 155
listeriosis 170, 175
living conditions 16
infectious diseases and 170
lone parents
duration of state 12
fertility rates and 11-12
income 12
poverty 14
remarriage 12
low birthweight impact on mortality and morbidity 71
Lyme disease 175
lymphomas 140
survival *145*

manufacturing industries recession 14
marital status, birthweight and **31**
maternal age
birthweight and **31**
congenital malformations and 155-6
at first birth, related to fertility rates 10
maternal country of birth 83
birthweight and **31**, *86-87*
congenital anomalies and *120*
deaths from *88*
live births and total period fertility rates and 85
neonatal mortality and *87*
perinatal conditions and *120*
mortality from *85-86*
postneonatal mortality and *87*
respiratory diseases and 119, *120*
sudden infant death syndrome and *88, 120*
maternal height influencing birthweight 32, 33
maternal occupation, congenital malformations and 154
maternal smoking
congenital malformations and 155
height and growth of children and 35
sudden infant deaths and 131
maternal social class, infant mortality **64**
maternity rights legislation 13
measles 74, 75, 76, 168, 170, *171*
men, weight-for-height 37-38
meningococcal infection 75, 174
mental health 159-67
co-morbidity between psychiatric disorders 161
epidemiological and community studies 160-2

trends over time 162-6
types of disorders 160
migration, infectious diseases and 169
milk consumption 44
milk-borne infections 174-5
MMR vaccine 74, 170
moral status of children as people 24
morbidity
ethnic groups 90-91
trends 65, *68*, 69-71
mortality
in adults, influence of birthweight on 33
alcohol-related road traffic accidents in young adults *163*
cancer 141-3
causes 65, 66, 67
congenital malformations 147, *152*
cystic fibrosis 127-30
ethnic groups 85-90
infectious diseases 168, **169**
rates by age and sex 1, 3, *4*
changes impact 1, 3-7
infants 4, 7
registration statistics 178-9
related to birthweight 28
respiratory diseases *114*, 115, *116*-17 123
trends and patterns 61-81
volatile substance abuse 53-54
multiple births
birthweight and 31
impact on mortality and morbidity 71
mumps 74-75, 170

negotiation of children's part in treatment decision-making 24-25
Neisseria meningitis infection 174
neonatal mortality see infant mortality *4*
Netherlands, infant mortality 78
neural tube defects 153, 156
neuroblastoma *138*
neurological disorders, mental health and 161
New Commonwealth see ethnic groups
Newcastle upon Tyne accidental injury study 107-10, *111*
Northern Ireland
mortality and morbidity 77
physical activity of children 45, *47*
Norway
birthweights 29
height and growth of children 34
nursery places 13
nutrition see diet

obesity 37, 44
occupational effect on congenital malformations 153-5
OPCS
Longitudinal Study 179
surveys of disability 70-1,180
oral contraceptives see contraceptive pill
osteomalacia in ethnic groups 90
osteosarcoma *138*
out-patient clinics see under hospital
overweight in children 37

Pakistani-born see under ethnic groups
parasuicide 163-4
parental body size influencing weight-for-height of children 38
parental height affecting children's growth 35
parental perception of children's health 65
parental role in health care for children 21-27
parity
hay fever and 126
perinatal mortality and 85
statistics 178
within marriage, birthweight and **31**

paternal smoking, congenital malformations and 155
pedestrian accidents 105, 106
mortality *96, 97, 100-1*
peer group pressure in smoking habits 51
perinatal mortality, ethnic groups 85
pertussis *75, 76*, 168, 172, 173
physical activity 45-48
physical development of children 28-41
physical illness linked to mental health 161
pneumonia 120-23
hospital admissions *118*, 121,122
long-term consequences 123
mortality 121
in infants *116*, 117
poisoning
accidents 104
mortality *74, 97, 100-1*
in ethnic groups 89
in infant 65
see also food poisoning; self-poisoning
Poland, infant mortality 78
poliomyelitis 170, *171*
polydactyly 155
population size
changes of children 1, *2*
ethnic groups 83, *84*
Portugal, infant mortality 78
post-traumatic stress disorder 161
postneonatal mortality **4**, *130*
congenital malformations 149
ethnic groups 87
poverty effect on children 14-17
pregnancy in teenagers 54, 55-56
prenatal diagnosis of congenital malformations 149-53
preschool children
diet 44
mental health 160
mortality rates **4**
respiratory diseases *116*
population size changes 1
preschool health services 23
primary school children height and growth 34
psychiatric disorders see mental health
psychoses 160

regional variations
accident mortality 98
cancer incidence 137
congenital malformations 152, 153
cystic fibrosis 129
infant mortality 64-65
respiratory diseases 117,121-2, 123, 125, 126,
unemployment 14
respiratory disease 72-73, 113-30
in ethnic groups 91
deaths from 89
long-term consequences 123
risk factors 122
trends and patterns 113-19
retinoblastoma 137, *138*, 140, 144
rheumatic fever 172
rheumatic heart disease 172
rickets in ethnic groups 90
rights of children 18, 22
road traffic accidents 105
alcohol consumption and 52, *163*
deaths *96, 97, 100-1, 105*
rubella 74-75, 170
ethnic groups 90

salmonella infection 170, 174
sarcomas *145*
scarlet fever 168, *173*
schizophrenia 160, 161

school children
    diet 44
    height and growth 34
    mental health 160
    mortality from respiratory diseases *116*
    smoking surveys 180
school health
    education 22
    services 23
school nurses 23
Scotland
    alcohol consumption of children 53
    sexual activity in teenagers 54
    physical activity of children 45
seasonal allergic rhinitis 125-6
seasonal pattern in sudden infant deaths 131
secondary school children height and growth 34
self-poisoning 163, 165
Severe Hardship payments 19
sex data
    accident mortality 97
    alcohol intake **53**
    cancer mortality *73*
    cystic fibrosis 128
    delinquency 164, *165*
    disability *70*
    health service use **69**
    mental health 160
    mortality 1, 3, **4**, *62-64, 66, 67*, **78**
    respiratory diseases 119
        deaths *116*
    skinfolds 37
    sudden infant deaths 131
    suicide and parasuicide 163, *164*
    survival percentage **6**, *7*
    volatile substance abuse, mortality and *54*
sexual behaviour 18, 54-57
    infectious diseases and 170
sickle cell anaemia in ethnic groups 90
skinfolds 37
sleeping position, sudden infant deaths and 131
smoking habits 23, 48-51, 57
    birthweight and 32, 33
    congenital malformations and 155
    factors associated with 51
    height and growth and 35
    international comparisons 50
    respiratory diseases and 122
    sudden infant deaths and 131
    surveys 180
    trends over time 49-50
social class
    accidents and violence 74
        mortality 97-98
    birthweight 30, **31**
    breast-feeding *43*
    cancer incidence 137
    cystic fibrosis 128
    diet 44
    fertility rates 11-12

height and growth 34
infant mortality 62-64
    in ethnic groups 88, 89
mental health 160, 161
perinatal mortality *86*
physical activity 48
respiratory diseases 117,*118,* 122, 125
statistics 178
sudden infant deaths 131
suicide 164
unemployment 14
weight-for-height 39
social climate changes 17-19
social context of children's knowledge 22-23
social norms of health behaviour 22
social policy changes towards children 18-19
sociodemographic factors influencing
        birthweight **31**
socioeconomic conditions
    birthweight and 33
    congenital malformations and 155
    hay fever and 126
    height and growth and 35
    mental health and 165-6
    obesity and 39
spina bifida 153, 155, 156
spinal tumours *141*
state benefits 14, 15
statistical sources 178-82
steroid sex hormone effects on congenital
        malformations 155
stillbirths
    birthweights *30*
    ethnic groups 85
    registrations 1
    statistics **4**, *6*, 61, 65, 178-9
streptococcal infections 170
sudden infant death syndrome (SIDS) 72-73, 95,
        114, 115, *116,* 130-32
    definition 130
    ethnic groups 88
    risk factors 131-2
    trends 130-1
suicide 163-4
Supplementary Benefit 15
survival rates since 1950 **6**, 7
Sweden
    birthweights 29
    child care 12
    fertility rates 9, 11
    height and growth of children 34, 37
syndactyly 155
syphilis, congenital 170

teenagers see young adults
teratogens 148, 155
thalassaemia minor in ethnic groups 90
tobacco price and availability effects 51
total period fertility rates 9
tracheitis, GP consultations 121
travel, infectious diseases and 169

tuberculosis 171-2
    in ethnic groups 91
twins
    cancer 137
    sudden infant deaths 131

UK-born ethnic groups 83
    perinatal mortality *85*
unemployment
    benefit, young adults 18
    effect on poverty 14-15
    suicide and 163
USA
    birthweights 29, 33
    height and growth of children 34, 37

vaccinations see immunisations
very low birthweight 29, *30*
violence causing deaths 74, 96
viral hepatitis 174
viruses, cancer and 137
visibility of children 22
vitamin D deficiency in ethnic groups 90
vitamin supplements to prevent congenital mal-
        formations 155
volatile substance (VS) abuse 53-54

waiting times dissatisfaction 24
Wales
    alcohol consumption of children 53
    physical activity of children 45, 47
weight-for-height in children 37-39
    factors influencing 38-39
    international comparisons 37-38
    trends over time 37
West Indian-born *see* ethnic groups
wheeze prevalence *125*
whooping cough *see* pertussis
Wilms' tumour *138*, 140
Wolfson Foundation Study of Accidental Injury
        in Childhood 108
women
    changing role 9
    weight-for-height 38
World War I
    effects on fertility rates 1
    effects on mortality rates 3
World War II
    effects on mortality rates 3, 7
    increase in fertility rates following 1

Yersinia enterocolitica infection 175
young adults
    alcohol-related road deaths *163*
    height and growth **35**, 37
    physical activity 45, 47-48
    sexual behaviour 54-57
    smoking habits 49
Youth Opportunities 17
Youth Training Scheme 18